D1486443

The Protocol of the Gods

The Protocol
of the Gods

*A Study of the Kasuga Cult
in Japanese History*

ALLAN G. GRAPARD

University of California Press

BERKELEY   LOS ANGELES   OXFORD

University of California Press
Berkeley and Los Angeles, California

University of California Press, Ltd.
Oxford, England

Library of Congress Cataloging-in-Publication Data

Grapard, Allan G.
    The protocol of the gods : a study of the Kasuga cult in
Japanese history / Allan G. Grapard.
        p.   cm.
    Includes bibliographical references and index.
    ISBN 0-520-07097-6 (alk. paper)
    1. Kasuga Taisha (Nara-shi, Japan)—History.   2. Kōfukuji
(Nara-shi, Japan)—History.   3. Shinto—Relations—
Buddhism.   4. Buddhism—Relations—Shinto.   I. Title.
BL2225.N32K423   1992   299'.561'0952184—dc20.   92-16300
                                                        CIP

Printed in the United States of America
9 8 7 6 5 4 3 2 1

The paper used in this publication meets the minimum requirements of
American National Standard for Information Sciences—Permanence of
Paper for Printed Library Materials, ANSI Z39.48-1984. ♾

For Carolyn

Contents

Maps, Figures, Diagrams, and Tables

Tables

Acknowledgments

This study was initiated in 1978 and was funded through a postdoctoral fellowship granted by the Social Science Research Council, which enabled me to do fieldwork in Japan in 1981–82. I hereby wish to express my appreciation to the council for its support, in particular to the members of the council's Taskforce on Medieval Japanese Studies, who recognized the need for this type of study and encouraged me to apply for funding: professors Karen Brazell, Cameron Hurst III, John Rosenfield, Barbara Ruch, and Paul Varley. Writing was completed under the auspices of the East-West Center in Honolulu, Hawaii, in 1985. The East-West Center's president at the time, Victor Li, tirelessly encouraged me and generously granted me time to pursue my effort, and so much is a result of his support that words are unable to express my gratitude.

In Japan I received much advice and inspiration from Kuroda Toshio, Professor Emeritus at Osaka University, who over the years has supported my views and constantly prodded me to continue my work when I wished to abandon it. Murayama Shūichi, Professor Emeritus at Tezukayama University, has also generously given of his time and knowledge over the years, and I thank him for his encouragements. Professor Ueda Masaaki, of Kyoto University, granted me an interview and helped me focus my research on the early stages of the Kasuga cult. My mentor at Kyoto University since 1968, Professor Sakakura Atsuyoshi (emeritus) has supported me through difficult personal times and has kindly introduced me to various scholars over the years; I wish to recognize him especially here, for he has had an influence over me he may not be aware of, or be willing to admit, because of his extraordinary distinction and modesty. Kasan-no-in Chikatada, head-priest of the Kasuga Shrine, and Ōhigashi Nobukazu, head of the Cultural Affairs Office of the Kasuga Shrine, have supported my research throughout my stay, made rare documents available to me, answered my queries with thoughtful lucidity, and allowed me to witness the entire ritual cycle of the Kasuga Shrine. I hereby wish to thank them and to underscore my appreciation for their generous and perceptive stance. Should this study help anyone understand a little better the complex world of Japanese classical religious institutions, I will take this as an honor that is deserved by all people mentioned above.

Professor Neil McMullin, of Toronto University, has kindly copyedited the original lengthy manuscript, which had to be cut by one third. That work took several months, for he had to correct my poor treatment of the English language. How could I thank him properly?

The process between submission of this study to the University of California Press and its publication has been lengthy and convoluted, but I wish to express my sincere appreciation to Betsey Scheiner, editor at the press, who, ever since she joined this project, engaged in all possible efforts to see this book to press in a timely manner, and to Marilyn Wilderson, who did a superb job during the final copyediting steps.

All maps and figures were generated on computers granted to me by Apple Corporation, which I wish to recognize here as a staunch supporter of computing in the humanities. All translations are mine unless otherwise stated; and finally, all mistakes are mine alone.

My wife, Carolyn, has been of invaluable support through it all, and I dedicate this book to her in loving gratitude.

A Note on Japanese Names and Terms

The Japanese custom of giving surnames first, followed by given names, has been observed throughout this study.

There are several ways of referring to Shinto shrines (which I call "shrines" in this study), depending on their historical status or rank. Thus, one speaks of Matsuyama-*sha* (the Matsuyama Shrine), Yoshida *jinja* (the Yoshida Shrine), Kasuga *taisha* (the Kasuga Shrine), or Ise *jingū* (the Ise Shrine). The term *yashiro* (shrine) also exists but always stands alone: it is never preceded by a proper name.

There are also several ways of referring to Buddhist temples (always called "temples" in this study), depending on the way in which the proper name of the temple is pronounced. Japanese compounds can be pronounced according to Sino-Japanese convention, or according to Japanese convention; if the proper name of a Buddhist temple is customarily pronounced the Sino-Japanese way (*on-yomi*) in Japan, usually that name is followed by the term *ji*, as in Kōfukuji, "Temple to Promote Posthumous Felicity" (there are exceptions to this general rule, particularly in Kyushu). Even though it is redundant to refer to Kōfukuji as "the Kōfukuji Temple," I have chosen to do so because "the Kōfuku Temple" sounds somewhat contrived in relation to common Japanese ways. If the proper name of a Buddhist temple is pronounced the Japanese way (*kun-yomi*), usually that name is followed by the term *tera* or *-dera*, as in Yoshino-*dera*, "the Yoshino Temple"; in that case, it seems far more contrived to refer to the temple as "the Yoshino-dera Temple," and I have therefore dropped the term *-dera*.

I always translate the term *jisha* (shrine-temple) as "shrine-temple multiplex," for reasons explained in the study. One sometimes, though rarely, finds the Japanese term *shaji* to refer to the same phenomenon.

There are several difficulties involved in referring to the names of Shinto and Buddhist divine entities. I have attempted to remain consistent in the following manner: when a Shinto entity is introduced, it is referred to as "the *kami* so-and-so" and thereafter only through its name, even though the proper rendition of *kami* names is complex, depending upon the entity's status in mythology. Problems are more obvious in the case of Buddhist entities that are referred to by their Sanskrit or Japanese names, and here academic works offer no common rule. I therefore give names in Sanskrit (as in, "the bodhisattva Avalokiteśvara") and in Japanese (the same bodhisattva is referred to as "Kannon *bosatsu*"). It is not uncommon, however, to refer to that figure of the Buddhist pantheon as "the bodhisattva Kannon," a phrase in which the Sanskrit term *bodhisattva* is used because it has entered the English language, and in which the term *Kannon* is used because it is such a popular entity in Japan and is best referred to in this way. One will never see, however, phrases such as "Kannon Bodhisattva" or "Avalokiteśvara *bosatsu*," although one will find the phrase "Kannon, the Bodhisattva of Compassion." Finally, the Japanese term *shimbutsu* is rendered as "*kami* and buddhas or bodhisattvas."

Introduction

The Kasuga Shrine (*Kasuga taisha*) is the main ancestral and tutelary shrine of the Fujiwara house, which was the leading aristocratic lineage in Japan during the Heian period (794–1185), and as such it is one of the most important Shinto shrines in Japanese history. It is located in the city of Nara at the foot of Mount Mikasa, which has been its symbol for centuries, and next to the Kōfukuji, a Buddhist temple with which it has been closely associated ever since its establishment in the eighth century. Even though the Kasuga Shrine and the Kōfukuji are separate institutions today, for most of their history they formed what will be called in this study a shrine-temple multiplex, i.e., a unified Shinto-Buddhist cultic center.[1]

What came to be known as the Kasuga belief system (*Kasuga shinkō*) is a combinative cult, which means that the elements of Shinto and Buddhist creeds and practices that compose it were conceived of as forming a single cohesive system. In the shrine component of the Kasuga-Kōfukuji multiplex, that cult is dedicated to the "ancestral and tutelary *kami*" (*ujigami*) of the Fujiwara house, and in the temple component, to the spirits of deceased Fujiwara leaders.[2] It is impossible to understand this cult until one appreciates the nature and history of the systematic relations that evolved between the shrines and temples that are the core of the Japanese tradition. The purpose of this study is to reconstruct the essential features of those relations in the case of the Kasuga cult from its inception up to 1868, when by order of the Meiji government (1868–1912) the *kami* of the shrines were dissociated from the buddhas and bodhisattvas of the temples with which they had been identified over the centuries. These dissociations imposed on the shrines and the temples a new, thoroughly artificial, and theretofore unknown segregation. Before that government action, the Kasuga-Kōfukuji multiplex and its belief system were ex-

1

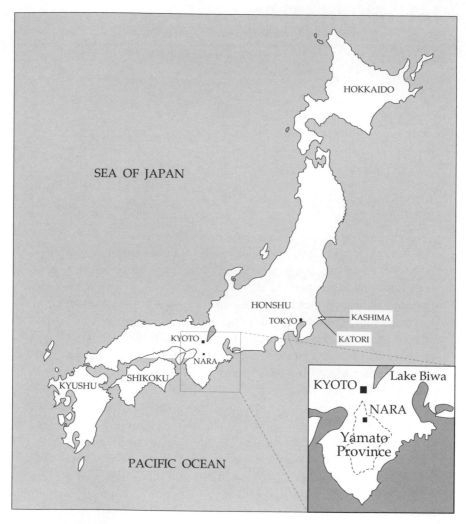

Map 1.   Japan and Yamato Province.

tremely important aspects of the classical and medieval ideology of the
Japanese state. Furthermore, the multiplex gave birth to the city of Nara
and governed the province of Yamato, all the while developing a unique
culture.

   Although Nara is touted as the cradle of Japanese culture, there is little
material in foreign languages on its shrines and temples, their rituals and
art, and their history and belief systems. The reasons for this scarcity have

to do with the way in which Western scholarship on Japan has evolved, and they bear directly on the issues raised in this study.

THE STUDY OF JAPANESE CULTIC CENTERS

Most modern studies of Japanese religious history are characterized by disciplinary categories invented by certain Western cultural systems. The concepts used in those studies, however familiar they may appear to us, are dangerous in that they prevent us from acquiring an adequate understanding of Japanese society.[3] It is commonly asserted, for instance, that there are several religions in Japan: Shinto, Buddhism, popular religion, and more recently, the new religions. Accordingly, scholars and students specialize either in Shinto or in Buddhism; often (there are sound exceptions) they emphasize the elite and scriptural traditions to the detriment of the popular traditions, and they also fail to analyze the interactions between the various currents that compose the Japanese religious tradition. As a result of such attitudes and practices, Shinto has been treated as though it were a single and universally shared body of ideas, practices, and institutions in premodern Japan. Moreover, although scholars have studied the sects of Buddhism, analyzed the teachings of their founders, provided exegesis of their major scriptures, and researched the lives of their great masters, there is no comprehensive study of any of those sects. Thanks to the studies undertaken so far much has been revealed about Japan, but it is becoming increasingly clear that if we continue on the same trajectory our understanding of Japanese religiosity and history will be limited and flawed.

Most Western-language studies of Japanese Buddhism present expositions of the various sects by way of accounts of the teachings of their founders in India, China, or Japan. Unfortunately, scholars have produced virtually no studies of the history of those sects in Japan and no studies of their institutions (which is considered to be institutional, not religious, history). The interactions among these sects or between them and other liturgical and ritual systems have not been studied, such as the still poorly understood Confucian tradition and the mélange of magical-religious practices that were derived from shamanism and Taoism and to which the name of Shinto has been affixed. A few modern studies deal with "medieval syncretism," but they generally treat that phenomenon as odd and fleeting, hardly worth serious investigation. Recent work in other fields, especially art and literature, provides abundant proof that the categories drawn from Western cultures are painfully inadequate and that new hypotheses need to be formed, tested, and discussed.

The present study is based on the three following hypotheses:

First, Japanese religiosity is grounded in specific sites at which beliefs and practices were combined and transmitted exclusively within specific lineages before they were opened to the general public.

Second, Japanese religiosity is neither Shinto nor Buddhist nor sectarian but is essentially combinative. The few exceptions appear to prove the rule.

Third, those combinative systems, which evolved in specific sites, were indissolubly linked, in their genesis as in their evolution, to social and economic structures and practices as well as to concepts of legitimacy and power, all of which were interrelated and embodied in rituals and institutions marking those sites.

These three propositions need to be developed and refined.

Grounded in Specific Sites

The Japanese term that was adopted in the Meiji period to indicate the Western concept of religion is *shūkyō*, a compound word meaning, etymologically, "lineage [*shū*] teachings [*kyō*]." Two points must be made with regard to that term. First, although the term *shū* is usually translated "sect" (as in *Shingon-shū*, meaning "Shingon sect"; *Rinzai-shū*, meaning "Rinzai sect," and the like), it is much more appropriate to preserve its literal meaning of "lineage," because in Japanese temples, attention was always paid to master-disciple relationships and to transmissions within lineages, and in the shrines there were sacerdotal lineages that specialized in the transmission of specific notions and in the performance of specific rituals. This tendency prevails even in modern Japan, especially in the so-called new religions. The Japanese have rarely been sectarian in the European sense of the word, although the term is definitely appropriate for today's situation—either in religion or academia. Second, the term *kyō* does denote a teaching, but because the Japanese have always favored ritual practice over doctrinal inquiry, the term *kyō* might better be translated as "orthopraxis." Because the word *religion* calls to mind culture-specific notions that are common to the West but are not necessarily found in Japan, that word will not be used in this study; rather, I will speak of the Japanese tradition, even though it is clear that that term is also problematic.

If the term *shūkyō* was coined in the Meiji period to render a Western concept, how, we might ask, did the premodern Japanese refer among themselves to what we would call their religions? They used terms such as *Shingon-shū* or *Rinzai-shū* extremely rarely, for they much preferred to use place names, such as *Nanto* (the Southern Capital: Nara), *Hokugaku* (the Northern Mountain: Mount Hiei), *Tō-Eizan* (Mount Hiei of the East:

the Kan'eiji of Edo), *Nangaku* (the Southern Mountain: Mount Kōya), and a host of other place names such as Kumano, Ise, Usa, Tōnomine, Hakusan, Fujisan, Honganji, Daisen, and Kasuga. Otherwise the Japanese referred directly to sublineages of transmission by using the terms *ha* or *ryū*, which mean "currents," "rivers," or "streams"; and *ke*, meaning "house." In many cases in the classical literature the term *ha* is preceded by the name of the cultic center at which that *ha* originated, and the term *ryū* is generally preceded by the name of its founder, although that is not true for the various Zen lineages. The term *ke* has been used to indicate a specific sacerdotal lineage, as in *shake* ("shrine-house"),[4] but it has also been used with the meaning of "specialist," as in *Kike* ("Chroniclers"), which is a group of lineages at Mount Hiei that specialized in the transmission of teachings and practices related to Shinto-Buddhist combinations.[5] The main focus, then, was on lineages of transmission at specific sites, and it is appropriate to conform to the Japanese practice when interpreting the Japanese tradition.

It is true that from the early medieval period (from the thirteenth century onward) the Japanese used terms like *Ise Shintō*, meaning "the Shinto of Ise" (a place name), which is also known as *Watarai Shintō*, meaning "the Shinto of Watarai" (a sacerdotal lineage); and they have also used terms like *Miwa Shintō*, meaning "the Shinto of Miwa" (both a place and a lineage name). These terms refer to combinative and locale-specific systems of associations between particular *kami* and particular buddhas and/or bodhisattvas. The phenomena designated by those terms have elements in common, but it would be wrong to call that common element "Shinto," as will become clear in the course of this study.

The word *Shinto* is in quotation marks for two reasons. First, it denominates in fact several systems that were the outcome of complex combinations of elements derived from other ritual lineages, including Buddhist lineages, in particular sites of cult. Second, those systems have little in common with what has been called *Shinto* since the end of the nineteenth century, when the Japanese government forced on all sites of cult a systematic dissociation of the *kami* from the buddhas and bodhi- sattvas with which they had been associated for about a thousand years and built a new system that it also called *Shinto*. In other words, the term *Shinto*, as it is presently used, is a recent concoction: it denotes a system that bears little resemblance to whatever existed before 1868. In fact, Shinto might well be termed a "new religion."

The word *bukkyō*, which means "teachings of buddhas," refers today to a conglomerate of opinions, practices, and institutions bearing little resemblance to what existed before the Meiji period. The fundamental characteristics of tradition before 1868 were an insistence on lineage, both in the sense of filiation in sacerdotal lineages and in the sense of transmission between master and disciple, and a grounding of ritual and ideas in specific sites of cult ruled by those lineages. Most temples were associated with specific shrines, and the world of meaning they exhibited was combinatory. Any interpretation of Japanese tradition that fails to take those elements into consideration can only be partially correct for it will be structurally flawed.

The overwhelming tendency of the Japanese to relate to space in specific ways must also be taken into account. That issue has to do first, with the intensely cultural notion of territory and second, with specific sites or physical landscapes that symbolized various territories and became themselves objects of worship. Space, however, is also made by people; as we will see, not only were certain spatial configurations the products of social systems, but they also reinforced those systems and sometimes called them into question. Little was more important in ritual and architecture, as well as in social relations, than spatial arrangement, and entire cultural systems were linked to land and to the cult of special places. In other words, an anthropology of space will shed light on what is generally called religious behavior, though the term *symbolic behavior* would be more appropriate.

Second, we must take into account Japanese conceptions of time: divinities were worshiped in certain places at certain times and according to different conceptions thereof. The experience of space is not separable from the experience of time in the act of perception, *a fortiori* in the ritual act, not to mention in social or political acts. And third, we must also take into account the ways in which people related to those conceptions of space and time through the medium of ritual. Various categories of the organization and management of space and territory corresponded to specific conceptions of time, be it in terms of the consciousness of history or of the role of myth in the structuring of sociocosmic realities. Conceptions and practices of time and space were further related to specific forms and philosophies of action manifested in, or altered by, ritual as well as political and economic behavior.

The first approach, then, will be geographical, or what might be termed *geosophic*. The second approach will be to take concepts of time into consideration, whether at the level of ritual or at the level of conceptions of history. The third approach will entail a consideration of lineage, both sacerdotal and at the level of the Fujiwara house. Space, time, and lineage came together in specific socioeconomic forms of relation to territory, in either a geopolitical sphere of influence or a land domain, and these interrelated conceptions manifested themselves at the level of ritual modes, institutional structure, and social organization.

The evidence that this is indeed how the Japanese world was organized is constantly before our eyes: the centers of cult, from Hiko-san in Kyushu to Osore-zan at the northernmost tip of Honshu, are what have formed the real infrastructure of the matters that should be studied from an inter-disciplinary perspective under the name of religious history. It is not, as is often claimed, that Buddhism spread and in the process took on a local coloration, but rather that local units accepted aspects of Buddhism in a structurally significant manner. We find in these sites—from the most complex cultic center to the most simple place of worship—common elements in their organization of sacred space, in ritual and sacerdotal lineages, in combinations, and in their social and economic aspects. Local differences, though important, do not hide the patterns along which the tradition was fundamentally organized. Thus, even though there were remarkable distinctions between, for example, the universe of meaning of the Dewa Mountains and that of the Kunisaki Mountains, those cultic centers were identical at the structural level, and a historical analysis of them yields an understanding of the Japanese tradition that is fundamentally different from traditional, text-oriented studies. It is through such analyses that there can best be discerned the combinative aspects of the tradition, the processes of popularization, the changes of land possession patterns in relation to social forms, the evolution of religious art, the contents and history of practice and ritual, and the function of institutions. None of those were ever separate entities.

Neither Shinto, nor Buddhist, but Combinative

Although it was in the medieval period that various combinations between *kami* and buddhas/bodhisattvas reached their apex, it was not the only period in which such phenomena occurred. Today Kōfukuji monks, seated next to Shinto priests, still chant Buddhist scriptures in front of the Kasuga shrines, as they have done for more than one thousand years.

In 1868 the Japanese government ordered that all *kami* be separated from the buddhas/bodhisattvas with which they had been associated in all sites of cult. This revolution occurred against an ideological backdrop that was formed during the Muromachi period (1333–1573) and evolved throughout the Edo period (1600–1868). New ritual systems were created a mere one hundred years ago by ideologues who claimed they were returning to the forms of a classical Golden Age in which the essence of

Japan was manifested in ritual and other forms of behavior. As parts of this study will demonstrate, however, that claim was spurious. And yet, not only do many Japanese behave today as if the claim were true, but many modern students of Japanese culture appear to remain under the influence of ideologues of the Meiji period, for they treat Japanese "religions" according to the artificial categories that those ideologues established. Indeed, many think of Buddhism and Shinto as entirely separate entities, both in the past and in present-day Japan; they are researched separately, written about separately, and their history is taught separately.

Some scholars attempt to show that there was such a thing as "pure" Buddhism in the Japanese tradition. There was no such entity, however, in premodern Japan: a study, for example, of Shingon esotericism that does not take into account non-Buddhist forms of ritual and doctrine in India, Taoist accretions in China, and the indigenous accretions in the Japanese context is doomed to fail. Vice versa, any study of Shinto that fails to include Chinese, Korean, and Buddhist elements and associations is fundamentally inadequate.

 Those associations occurred at the institutional, ritual, doctrinal, and philosophical levels everywhere throughout Japanese history and formed the backbone not only of what has been called religion but also of Japanese culture in general: associations are a fundamental element of the Japanese tradition. It is imperative that artificial separations between supposedly independent systems of meaning not be applied to the past, and that ways and means of expressing the changing composition of combinative systems of belief be developed. Most Buddhist temples were built next to Shinto shrines and usually by the same lineages, although different ritual lineages were ordered to take care of them. Some temples were the headquarters of Buddhist lineages (the Kōfukuji, for example, was the center of the Hossō lineage), but the monks who studied in those temples were not sectarian, for they studied and practiced other lineages besides their own. As a consequence, one finds in the temples elements of several lineages, both doctrinal and ritual, and elements from neighboring shrines with which the temples interacted over the centuries. How, then, can we continue to speak of sects? There is no reason to be more royalist than the king.

The main tendency in such centers of cult was to treat comprehensively various elements of native and foreign ritual systems and gradually to combine them with increasing rigor. An exception is found in the early Pure Land lineages, which state, "You need not worship the *kami* of

Heaven and Earth in order to be saved" (*jingi fuhai*), a statement that caused untold complications in the twelfth century.[6] Despite that attitude, combinative tendencies resurfaced extremely quickly in the Pure Land tradition and soon pervaded it, as is the case in Ippen's Ji lineage. The same can be said, with qualifications, about the Nichiren lineage. Both the Pure Land and Nichiren lineages tended to be exclusivistic, but in the overall picture of the development of what Kuroda Toshio aptly calls *kenmitsu taisei* (the "conglomerate of exoteric and esoteric" lineages), they are anomalies.[7]

Even the lineages of Zen did not escape the combinative genius of the medieval age, for its various lineages and branches were tremendously influenced by aesthetics (in which one can recognize indigenous elements), by doctrines issued from esoteric circles, and by rituals belonging originally to anything but Zen. Various Sōtō branches of Zen readily blended with local cults, large ones such as Hakusan or smaller ones such as Toyokawa Inari.[8] The same can be said of particular cases within the Rinzai tradition, such as the Fuke-shū and its *shakuhachi*-playing *komusō*,[9] or of people such as Takuan Sōhō, Suzuki Shōzan, and Hakuin Ekaku, for whom the worship of *kami* posed little or no problem.[10]

It is not the claim of this study that Japanese religiosity is a kind of puree or that everything under the sun is combinative, but given that an analysis of specific sites of cult and specific lineages shows that combinations were a central part of their being, combinations must be taken seriously. The interactive structures of those combinations in each major site are yet to be studied; however, on the basis of what has been accomplished so far it is clear that the distinctions established in Meiji simply do not hold as categories for understanding the past. Japanese religious history needs to be rewritten.

The associations between the *kami* of the shrines and the buddhas/ bodhisattvas of the temples were not arbitrary but obeyed what might be called rules of combination. Such rules have to do with linguistic rules of association in that those cultic centers were universes of meaning that expressed opinions concerning the existential situation. Standing at the crossroads of time, space, and ritual, the centers were also centers of communication between distinct cultural systems issuing from India, China, Korea, and Japan. The ways in which those systems communicated were to a considerable extent linguistically structured.

Because the organization of the cultic centers reveals much about the minds of the people who created and lived in them or under their influence, and because they were located in physical landscapes that people saw as ideas embodied in nature, they might be called mindscapes. The world of combinations is an essential part of their structure.

Embodied in Institutions

A focus on space, time, and lineage leads naturally to a consideration of some aspects of the social structure in the periods under scrutiny, which, in turn, invites an analysis of economic practices and of the relations—if any—that those might have with ritual and other institutions. Both ritual and its main aspect in Japan, protocol, together with notions of legitimacy, have to do with territory and economic order.

Classical Japanese conceptions of legitimacy and power were also essentially combinative. The governmental institutions of the Heian period (794–1185), for example, were intimately related to rites performed in Japan's major shrines and temples: these were not separate entities but parts of a single whole. An investigation of those concepts involves an examination of the role played by land gifts at the time of grand rites.

The intricate interrelations of land, ritual, and power tend to obscure our understanding of some central aspects of the Kasuga belief system. Together they formed the brocade of existence for the aristocrats and the rough material of existence for the peasants under the spiritual and economic rule of Kasuga. The sun and the moon born from Izanagi's head became gold and silver for the Fujiwara, while peasants worked under the Fujiwara yoke until they moved to liberate themselves from it.

The Kasuga cult was originally a Fujiwara house (uji) cult, which means that only members of the Fujiwara house could participate in it. This restriction became even more pronounced when the cult came to be sponsored by the imperial lineage, many of whose members issued from the Fujiwara house. Not only did the shrines and temples of Kasuga express views of the world held by the most powerful lineages of Japan during the Heian period, but the cult that evolved in them during the following Kamakura (1185–1333) and Muromachi (1333–1573) periods maintained those views against historical events. Indeed, ritual performances served to reinforce a specific ideology and specific socioeconomic practices. Many of those rites were grounded in a mythology whose underlying conceptions of power they served to uphold. Thus, as the Kasuga cult evolved during the Heian period, and as the shrines and temples were granted immense land holdings, the cultic center gave birth to the sacred city of Nara. That is to say, Nara developed as a city that catered to the needs of the monasteries and shrines that governed the province of Yamato, and not as a remnant of Heijō-kyō, the capital in the eighth century. It was ritually organized, ritually built, and ritually governed and lived in, and it was a ritual structure that allowed the province to be such a unified entity for so long. As Nara classical views and practices continued to be held well beyond the eighth century, however, and in its effort to maintain these specific views and practices, the sacred city went against what some have called the dialectics of history.

Toward the end of the Heian period a new shrine, Wakamiya, was built on the grounds of Kasuga. Its festive rite, the *On-matsuri*, has been performed with great pomp for more than eight hundred years—and still is today. The Wakamiya Shrine was structurally different from the main Kasuga Shrine, and so was its cult. Although the Kasuga cult celebrated at the main shrine had been exclusively reserved to the Fujiwara house, the Wakamiya cult was a Shinto-Buddhist belief system open to outsiders, ritually governed by monks and priests of the shrines and temples, and organized by the inhabitants of Yamato Province, which was ruled by the cultic center. That development witnesses to the popularization of the Kasuga cult that began during the medieval period. At the time of the festive rite of the Wakamiya Shrine, the services of a number of groups composed of people of low status that specialized in the performance of theater, dances, and songs were called upon by the multiplex. Four such groups were the four major troupes of Nō players, the *Yamato-za*, which did not belong to the multiplex but were sponsored by it, and thus, the multiplex was instrumental in the creation of a specific culture. Much of the world of Nō drama is intimately connected with Nara's combinatory culture. Social structure, economic practices, legitimacy, ritual, art, architecture, and combinations were fundamentally related components of the cultic center and of the Japanese tradition in the province of Yamato. They formed what might be called a cultural system.

A MORPHOLOGY OF CULTURAL SYSTEMS

If the words *Shinto, Buddhism, sect,* and *religion* are inadequate because they compartmentalize a reality that is not cut up in the manner implied by those words, then we have to use other terms for that reality or coin new ones. Those terms may be useful for expressing the modern situation, but they fail to be adequate for communicating an understanding of the past.

Part of the problem with modern interpretations of Japanese religions is rooted in an old fixation with texts, a sort of bibliolatry. A good example is provided by philosophical literature: the Chinese tradition used the term *Three Teachings* to indicate Confucianism, Taoism, and Buddhism, especially in the context of writings composed over the centuries to compare the relative values and claims of those teachings.[11] The Japanese tradition also developed a comparative literature, though different from the Chinese in both style and content because of differences in the cultural contexts. Initiated by Kōbō Daishi (Kūkai, 774–835) in his *Sangō-shiiki,* it saw increased vigor during the medieval period and lasted up to the twentieth century.[12] Most notable about that literature is the fact that the texts written before the medieval period to compare the Three Teachings do not include "Shinto" in that comparison. There seems to have been no clear consciousness on the part of the Japanese of the classical period that there was a specific entity called *Shinto.* This does not mean, however, that there was nothing at all, for there was the practice of *jingi sūhai,* "worship of the *kami* of Heaven and Earth," a matter inextricably linked to politics, court life, and shrine-temple multiplexes. That practice was not a text in the traditional sense of the term, however, and it was not to be compared to the other traditions as one text compared to others. It most certainly was a discourse, one so pervasive and so powerful that other texts were mediated by it. For example, no matter how interesting and profound some Buddhist scriptures might have been on their own, they were seen in Heian Japan only within the parameters of the protection of the state (*chingo-kokka*), which was predetermined by the modes of worship of the *kami* of Heaven and Earth.

Things changed during the medieval period: as Kuroda Toshio points out, the term *Shinto* is medieval.[13] In its medieval usage, however, Shinto denoted more than the practice of worship; it denoted both a "way" that had been developed ritually, doctrinally, and institutionally in combination with other systems, as well as a number of texts that came to be analyzed in the light of other traditions. The Japanese were not comparativists at the time but rather what might be called "combinativists."

From the medieval period on, the word *Shinto* appears in many texts and in some even replaces Taoism, from which it had freely borrowed in the past and continued to do so.[14] One might write a history of those texts from the late Nara period up to the twentieth century, and the history of ideas that such a work might reveal would differ in some important respects from the history of ideas disclosed by the study of practices and institutions. Another approach to the "Shinto" problem would be to examine rituals and practices in order to determine whether they are Shinto, Buddhist, Taoist, or Confucianist, and more important, to determine what kind of discourse they partly hide and partly reveal. Here again traditional categories do not exactly fit the reality. Very little has been done either in the West or in Japan on the topic of ritual: obsessed with ideas and denominations, we have overlooked practices. If we look carefully at the various belief systems that evolved in Japan, it becomes clear that questions of terminology and practice must be asked.

An analysis of Japanese ritual and belief systems yields several of their characteristics: first, they were locale-specific; second, these systems were combinatory; and third, they were related to shrines and temples, institutions of power, and therefore to political, social, and economic order. That is why it is appropriate to use the term *cultural system* to refer to these complex entities and to the ways in which they interrelated.

Indeed, we are confronted with systems that are both ideological and institutional and whose various elements enter into combination to control this or that aspect of a given society in a given geographical area at a given time. The term *combination* is used because in a combination the elements that are combined do not disappear; rather, the new reality is the result of mixtures of elements that can still be identified. A comparison to contemporary science may be useful: colored balls and quasi tetrahedrons are arranged in loops to show the relations between atoms in a molecular model of benzene, or in double helixes in a model of genes. The same type of model could be used to show the combinations of Shinto-Buddhist-Taoist-Confucian elements in the Japanese tradition, the structure of each belief system at a given time, and the changes that come about in the belief systems because of internal or external factors. The dynamics of change in the structure of the belief systems is a difficult problem that requires more research before it is solved; but, in any case, these combinations form the real structure of the mindscapes through which the cultural systems of Japan found expression. The Japanese tradition before Meiji was always combinatory. In that tradition, reality was neither Shinto nor Buddhist but exhibited an interrelational structure for which an appropriate morphology must be created, perhaps on the basis of the opposition between marked and unmarked elements as found in the linguistics of Roman Jakobson. The present study does not propose this morphology; it will have achieved its purpose if it simply demonstrates the need for one.

ORGANIZATION OF THE BOOK

The chapters of this study are organized to identify the most important elements of the belief and ritual system of Kasuga and to explain how those elements entered into combination to form a cultural system.

The first chapter discusses the locale of the Kasuga Shrine and the origins and structure of that shrine and of the Kōfukuji (hereafter referred to as the Kasuga-Kōfukuji multiplex), in order to show that that multiplex was a ceremonial center that embodied concepts of the state and social organization during the Nara period.

The second chapter investigates the associations between the divinities of the shrines and the temples and suggests that the organization of the multiplex during the Heian period gave birth to Nara as a sacred city.

In the third chapter the connections among the ritual, economic, and institutional aspects of the Kasuga cultural system are examined.

The fourth chapter discusses the historical processes by which the combinations between indigenous and imported concepts and practices led from originally simple practices of sacred space to grandiose visions of Kasuga as a metaphysical landscape related to the evolution of the concept of Japan as a sacred land.

The fifth chapter explores what happened to the system in the Edo and Meiji periods.

1 The Creation of the Ceremonial Center

The Kasuga Shrine, created in the eighth century, is in the city of Nara, which is located at the western foot of the Kasuga range of hills that extend from north to south on the eastern border of Nara prefecture (see map 2). Leaving the main railway station, a modern visitor emerges in front of a statue of the monk Gyōki (also referred to as *Gyōgi-bosatsu*, 668–749), passes immediately through a covered market street that borders the Kōfukuji, and then turns left toward Sarusawa Pond. A flight of stone steps leads to the entrance to the Kōfukuji, a gap where there used to be a large wooden gate. To the left stands the Nan'endō, "Southern Round Hall," which is in fact an octagonal structure that houses a statue of one of the manifestations of Kannon, the Bodhisattva of Compassion. Directly to its north stands the Hokuendō, "Northern Round Hall," another octagonal building housing an image of Miroku, the Buddha of the Future. Directly in front of the visitor is the Chūkondō, "Central Golden Hall," which is always closed to the public, and behind it stands the Kōdō, "Lecture Hall." To the right are the oldest parts of the temple, the Tōkondō, "Eastern Golden Hall," which is filled with various images, and to its right, a five-storied pagoda. To the north of the Eastern Hall, on the site that used to be occupied by the refectory, is a museum in which a few of the statues that were made at the beginning of the thirteenth century, the heyday of the monastery, can be seen.

Moving eastward toward the range of hills, the visitor passes the Ōyuya, the bathhouse of the monastic community, and crosses a road to pass through the first *torii* of the Kasuga Shrine. From that vantage point the Kasuga range is more impressive than it was from afar, and a hill at its foot stands out because of its elegant rounded form. That is Mount Mikasa, the shrine's sacred hill, which has been celebrated by poets over the centuries

15

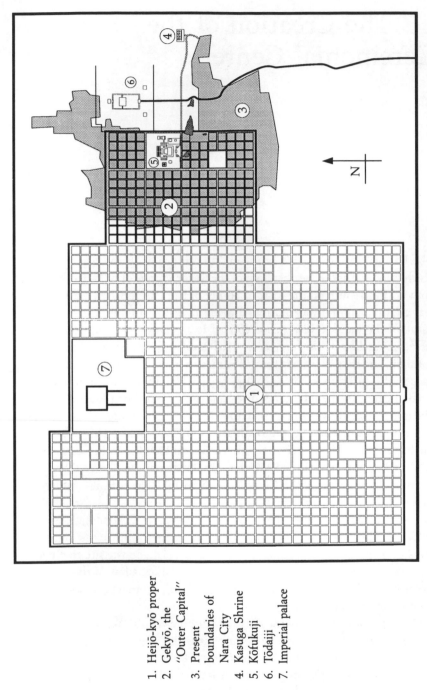

Map 2. Heijō-kyō (Nara) at the End of the Eighth Century. Computer-assisted rendering based on Aiga Tetsuo, ed., *Kōfukuji*, vol. 5 of *Meihō Nihon no bijutsu* (Tokyo: Shōgakkan, 1981), 35, figure no. 2.

1. Heijō-kyō proper
2. Gekyō, the "Outer Capital"
3. Present boundaries of Nara City
4. Kasuga Shrine
5. Kōfukuji
6. Tōdaiji
7. Imperial palace

since the time of the *Manyōshū* and is now preserved by law because of its rare trees and butterflies. The main shrine of Kasuga sits at the foot of Mount Mikasa (see map 3). The path that leads east from the first *torii* across the Tobihino Plain is covered with sand and pebbles and flanked by a small stream and pine, cryptomeria, and camphor trees. Among the trees roam the sacred deer of Kasuga, the theriomorphic emblem of the cult and the shrine. In the fall the male deer are rounded up and their antlers are ceremoniously cut to prevent them from accidentally injuring visitors. On the Tobihino Plain, wisteria, the natural emblem of the Fujiwara house (the word *Fujiwara* means "wisteria plain"), abounds, its creepers hugging almost every tree. Several resting places are set here and there under wisteria bowers. At the northern limit of that plain begin the grounds of the Tōdaiji; between the trees one can glimpse its huge southern gate and the massive building behind it.

Twenty yards beyond the first *torii*, to the right, is a pine tree surrounded by a fence; among the branches of that tree, we are told, the *kami* of Kasuga manifested themselves in dance, and the tree, held to be sacred for centuries, has been painted on the backdrops of all Nō stages.

Continuing on, the visitor passes a few small shrines and reaches the second *torii* of Kasuga, which is flanked by *Koma-inu* (theriomorphic protectors of shrines) and stone lanterns, and near which is a basin where visitors are to purify their mouths and hands. To the right is the Carriage Hall, where the ox-drawn carriages of aristocrats and prelates used to be kept during ritual performances and pilgrimages, and to the left is a small shrine where imperial messengers were purified before entering the compounds of the main shrines. The path continues, bordered by hundreds of stone lanterns dedicated to the power of the *kami* of Kasuga.

Finally, at the foot of Mount Mikasa, a visitor reaches the main sanctuary, which is surrounded by a Chinese-style wooden corridor that has a thatched roof and is painted in cinnabar, cut in four places for gates. Passing through the Southern Gate, which used to be reserved for the leaders of the Fujiwara house, one enters the front yard of the sanctuary and approaches the Hall of Offerings. Through the hall can be seen the inner courtyard, which is covered with white pebbles and is where dances are performed at the time of ritual. There are two sacred trees in that courtyard: an apple tree to the southeast and a cryptomeria to the northwest. To the right side of the Hall of Dances, which is set on the western side of the sanctuary next to a wisteria bower, a flight of stairs leads to the second Inner Corridor, which is closed to the public. Behind that corridor can be seen the tops of the roofs of the four main shrines of Kasuga, which are set next to each other on an east-west axis facing south.

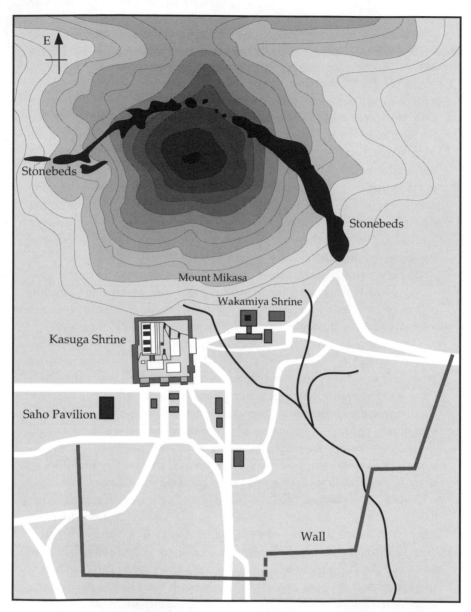

E

Stonebeds

Stonebeds

Mount Mikasa

Wakamiya Shrine

Kasuga Shrine

Saho Pavilion

Wall

Map 3.   The Kasuga Shrine in the Heian Period. Computer-assisted rendering of Kasuga Kenshōkai, ed., *Kasuga taisha Nara-chō chikuchi ikō hakkutsu chōsa hōkoku* (Nara: Kasuga Kenshōkai, 1977), plate no. 2.

Going back through the main Southern Gate and passing around a sacred stone set in front of it, a visitor then proceeds south toward the fifth shrine of Kasuga, the Wakamiya, built in 1135. A path leading to the top of Mount Mikasa starts there; marked by a small *torii*, it is closed to visitors and used by priests only at the time of ritual. The Wakamiya Shrine, which is flanked by smaller shrines and various buildings, stands in front of a pavilion where *kagura* dances are performed. Continuing southward beyond the Wakamiya Shrine, a visitor reaches the paths, which are bordered with stone statues and engravings, that lead into the Kasuga range through the Valley of Hell.

Such is the general layout of the Kasuga-Kōfukuji multiplex as it exists today, some twelve hundred years after its creation. It is but a pale reflection of its past grandeur: before 1868 there was a much larger number of temples and pavilions, the sight of which would have moved visitors to acknowledge the formidable power that the Kasuga-Kōfukuji multiplex once wielded as a cultic center, as the governor of Yamato Province since the year 1135, and as the largest landholder in Japan before 1570. Today, that grandeur and power can be intuited only at the time of the rituals that mark the passing of the seasons: the Kasuga Grand Rite performed in March and the *On-matsuri*, the main rite of the Wakamiya Shrine, in December. Only by careful observation will the visitor recognize that the Kōfukuji is closely associated with the Kasuga shrines, as in January, for example, when the monks chant Buddhist scriptures in front of these shrines.

THE CEREMONIAL CENTER

In their book *From Court to Capital*, Paul Wheatley and Thomas See suggest correctly that the ancient royal palaces of Japan were ceremonial centers, but they offer neither descriptions of the ceremonies that took place there, nor anything at all concerning shrines and the worship of the *kami* of Heaven and Earth.[1] Had Wheatley and See investigated the relations that existed between ceremonial centers, ceremonies, and the social construct of the people who participated in them, they would have seen that beyond the visibility of new foreign structures there survived important autochthonous elements, especially ones related to the ceremonies of accession to the throne and to the various "clans" (*uji*) and their shrines. The closest they come to asking such questions is when they suggest that the appearance of an Outer Capital (*gekyō*) in Nara was an oddity and that it might have had something to do with the erection of the Kōfukuji, but they do not mention the presence of the Kasuga Shrine next to the Kōfukuji.

Nonetheless, the Kasuga-Kōfukuji multiplex was a ceremonial center precisely in the sense intended by those authors. The present chapter will examine this topic and consider the nature of the relations between the social, political, and liturgical realities that the Fujiwara house came to represent in its early evolution. This requires an examination of the emergence of Buddhist institutions in Yamato as a house-related phenomenon (the *ujidera*), and the creation and organization of the shrines of Kasuga and the temples of the Kōfukuji. Finally, by analyzing the rites performed in those sites of cult, it will be shown that the shrines and temples played complementary roles that served as a basis for ulterior systems of combination.

THE *UJIDERA* PHENOMENON

The Japanese tradition has it that Buddhism was introduced to Japan in 538 or 585 C.E., but by the word *introduced* is meant that Buddhism came to be recognized at the level of the state at that time. In fact, Buddhism had been known in Japan long before the middle of the sixth century, at least by immigrants (*kikajin*) who had come in large numbers from China and Korea, and was certainly known in Kyushu long before it was brought to the attention of the emerging court of Yamato.[2] Most historians, however, have associated Buddhism with the court of Yamato, and the western parts of Japan have never been studied in detail. In fact, the court would have had to introduce Buddhism into state documents only after it had become obvious that Buddhism represented a cultural system that could not be ignored by a state then in the process of formation under continental influence, and only after an acceptable reaction to Buddhism had surfaced in society.

The court, and Yamato society in general, were undergoing major structural changes during the sixth century, at the same time the international situation demanded special attention on the part of the rulers. The clans supporting the major Yamato lineage were vying for power and, as Wheatley and See put it, discrepancies had occurred between rank at the court and actual political position.[3] The best example of such discrepancies is provided by the Soga *uji*: although that *uji* managed the redistributive sector of the economy and therefore wielded immense power, it was ranked well below other groups that had been part of the high nobility for a longer time. Accordingly, the Soga began to claim an ancestral *kami* of extreme antiquity (according to the official mythology then in the making), but this did not bring them to the rank they hoped would accompany such a mythical and ritual grounding of legitimacy. They were in close association with several groups of immigrants and were, for economic reasons, interested in international affairs and politics: their dealings with Korea put them in contact with the continent and its culture. Their position on the international scene was probably the reason why they were charged by the court with the adoption of Buddhism, which they then used to enhance their status and legitimize the elevation of their position in early Yamato society.

There is little doubt that is the real reason why the Soga were met with extreme prejudice and opposition on the part of the Mononobe and Nakatomi lineages, who supported a vision of the state grounded in other (non-Buddhist) principles. The Soga fought with and removed that opposition, at least for some time, and created institutions highly symbolic of their victory, the first and foremost of which is a building of what might be Yamato's oldest Buddhist institution, the Asuka-dera (Gangōji).

This temple, built in 596, stood in the southern part of Yamato Basin as a new symbol of political power. To state that the temple was a "new" symbol of power does not imply that it was totally foreign: although the temple appeared, at least on the surface, to be an entirely new phenomenon, its structure followed patterns of thought, organization, and practice that existed from the past. Archaeological excavations at the site of that temple have revealed that a chamber under the pagoda contained, as one would expect, Buddhist relics but also a set of armor, weapons, a bell that was part of the trappings of horses, and three curved stones (*magatama*). These implements are not simply objects representing battles fought by the Soga to establish Buddhism or to establish themselves through the acceptance of Buddhism. In light of the fact that weapons are commonly found at sites of cult, it is likely that the temple was treated like a shrine and that the implements enshrined there were emblems of the Soga clan, perhaps even symbols of their ancestral *kami*. If such was the case, then the Asuka-dera was, from the beginning, a house-temple (*ujidera*), and Buddhism, from its inception onwards, was associated with ancestor worship. If this supposition is correct, then the Asuka-dera was an institution that reflected the spiritual and political components of the Soga *uji* in a pattern similar to the relation between those components in the imperial lineage and inherent in the original structure of ancestor worship and legitimation processes in ancient Japan, even though a tendency to differentiate political from liturgical functions was becoming manifest at the court level.

Some documented evidence suggests that after the death of Shōtoku Taishi in 622 the Soga wanted to establish a "Buddhist" state to replace the kind of state being developed by the imperial lineage and its satellite clans such as the Mononobe, the Urabe, the Nakatomi, and others. The Soga began to behave in such a manner that it was felt that they might try to usurp the throne. This prompted Imperial Prince Naka no Ōe and his advisor, Nakatomi no Kamatari, to assassinate the leader of the Soga *uji* in 643, and to bring Japan into a new era with the promulgation of the Taika Reform in 645 and the institution of legal codes based on those of China. The reform in question "formalized socio-political changes taking place in seventh-century Japan in terms of T'ang legal codes" and led to a complete centralization of government.[4] Prince Naka no Ōe ascended the throne under the name of Tenji in 662.[5] When his close aide, Kamatari, who had become the equivalent of great minister of state, died in 669, Tenji conferred on him the title-name (*kabane*) Fujiwara. The *Shoku-Nihongi* records the following imperial order of 698: "The *kabane* Fujiwara *ason* granted to Kamatari shall be kept by his son Fuhito. Since Omimaro and others [of the Nakatomi lineage] are dedicated to liturgical matters, they shall revert to the use of the name Nakatomi."[6] This decree officially created the Fujiwara house and ensured that there would thenceforth be a clear demarcation between the Fujiwara and the Nakatomi, a demarcation that corresponds to a distinction between the political and liturgical functions of government. In the government structure, political duties would be assumed by the Fujiwara house, liturgical duties would be performed by the Nakatomi sacerdotal lineage, and the two aspects would be merged in the figure of the emperor. This distinction is important, for it reveals that the competition between the Fujiwara and the Nakatomi was not just an *uji* matter but was one of a broad sociopolitical nature. The new organization of the state provided that an Office of the *Kami* of Heaven and Earth (*jingikan*) be created above the Department of State (*dajōkan*), a complete departure from the Chinese model. It was probably the Asuka-Kiyomihara code, which was put into effect in 689, that created this office. Although on paper the *jingikan* stood above the *dajōkan*, it did not do so in fact: the ranks of its officers were much lower than those who served in the Department of State. Judging from the definition of the *jingikan*, the duties of its members consisted mainly of fixing the ceremonies and rites of the court, some of which had existed before the promulgation of the codes. The term *jingi-haku*, which designates the head of the office, did not appear before 701, when it replaced *jingikan chōjō*.

The Office of the *Kami* of Heaven and Earth came to be directed by members of the Nakatomi sacerdotal lineage.[7] Consequently, the Nakatomi, while retaining some nominal prestige, were in fact put under the Fujiwara house. It would be wrong to see in this arrangement solely the result of a political competition between the old Nakatomi and the new Fujiwara: the arrangement reflected a further separation between the political and liturgical functions of government. This question is of utmost importance because the concept of legitimacy in Japan contains a close relation between political and liturgical functions. By the establishment of the two offices a tension was created between those two aspects of government, and it was exacerbated every time a crisis at the national or international level appeared. This problem of the relations between political and liturgical duties pervaded Japanese history from that time onward and is at the core of the evolution of the Kasuga-Kōfukuji multiplex.

As Wheatley and See have noted, the earliest extant explicit reference to an *uji* dates back to the middle of the sixth century; in many ways the *uji* of classical Japan were created by the development of the Yamato court. Kondō Yoshirō regards the *kofun* (funeral tumuli) as "representing a lineage relationship which finally came to signify political legitimation."[8] The use of funeral tumuli was abandoned around the time of the Taika Reform of 645. It is most likely the case that political power in the seventh and eighth centuries was accompanied by ritual ways to legitimize that power, and that if in ancient times the funeral tumuli played that legitimating role, in later periods Buddhist temples—together with shrines dedicated to ancestral and tutelary *kami*—played a similar role. Shrines and temples were established for various reasons, some of which were religious, no doubt, but some of which were social and political, for the appearance of these shrines and temples coincided exactly with the appearance of new social groups and with the formulation of a mythology that implied a mirror relation between the social structure and the pantheon of ancestral *kami*. The creation of the Kasuga Shrine and the Kōfukuji coincided with the appearance of the Fujiwara house; their structures were related at all levels.

Kamatari belonged to the Nakatomi sacerdotal lineage, though it is not known whether he issued from the main line or from a peripheral branch that had settled on the eastern seaboard of Japan in Hitachi Province around Kashima and Katori, which is located just a few miles west of Kashima. Since this is a question of some importance, it should be examined in detail.

The Japanese tradition never forgot that the first member of the Fujiwara house was a Nakatomi: it claims that he worshiped the ancestral *kami* of that lineage, Ame-no-koyane-no-mikoto, and his consort Himegami, and that he was born in Yamato. A later tradition recorded in the *Ōkagami*, however, states that he was born in Hitachi and that he worshiped the *kami* Takemikazuchi-no-mikoto and Futsunushi-no-mikoto, which were enshrined in Kashima and Katori and are the first two of the four *kami* enshrined at Kasuga.[9] Modern Japanese historians are sharply divided on this issue. The apparently older tradition states that Kamatari was born near the foot of Mount Ama-no-kagu-yama, in what the Nakatomi naturally claim was the main branch of the court ritualists. If that were the case, then Kamatari would have worshiped the ancestral *kami* of that branch. That is, *if* Kamatari was in such a position in the lineage as to worship those *kami*, and *if* there was worship of that type at the time.[10]

The other Ōkagami position is that Kamatari was born in Kashima and that he was adopted by the main branch of the Nakatomi family in Yamato. This position is defended by Tamura Enchō, who claims that "one cannot lie about one's ancestral *kami*."[11] Tamura argues that Kamatari worshiped the Kashima *kami* and that he was instrumental in creating the state orthodoxy to which, much later, the name *Shinto* was given. There is, however, absolutely no confirmation of the claim that Kamatari was born in Kashima. Had that been the case, it is safe to assume that the officials of the province of Hitachi—who included members of the Nakatomi and Urabe lineages—would not have failed to mention in the *Fudoki* that one of Japan's leading political figures was born in their domain or in their lineage. The problem of the ancestral character of the *kami* of Kashima with respect to Kamatari can be solved without much doubt: namely, they are ancestral to anyone but him. It is doubtful that Kamatari was born in Kashima, and although it is not known whether Kamatari chose to own land in that part of Japan, the *Fudoki*'s account according to which Kamatari was granted land in Hitachi Province after the Taika Reform is most likely correct. It is likely that the author of the *Fudoki* linked Kamatari with Hitachi Province on the basis of the presence in Hitachi of important members of the Nakatomi lineage who worshiped the *kami* of Kashima, whatever those may have been at the time.

Most likely it was Kamatari's land holdings in Hitachi that allowed his descendants in the Fujiwara house to borrow and rename the Kashima *kami* in order to take them as their tutelary *kami*. It is most improbable that Kamatari would have worshiped the *kami* of Kashima during his lifetime. The only ancestral *kami* of the Fujiwara house are the ancestral *kami* of the Nakatomi sacerdotal lineage, Ame-no-koyane-no-mikoto and his consort Himegami, as they were claimed to be some time during the Nara period (710–773). The *kami* of Kashima are tutelary, not ancestral, deities. The borrowing of these *kami* by the Fujiwara served to show the demarcation between the Nakatomi and Fujiwara lineages, which was a matter of politics, protocol, and social hierarchy, and which will be discussed under the heading "Enigmatic Identities." Therefore, the appearance of the Kashima and Katori *kami* in Yamato was a late phenomenon—it occurred well after Kamatari's death and possibly as late as the Heian period (794–1185)—that was associated with the creation of the Fujiwara house and was astutely chosen as a way of suggesting a vast geopolitical sphere of influence on the part of the new house.

In order to consolidate the new state that had emerged through the inception of the T'ang legal codes, a new capital was built on the Chinese model: that is, Heijō-kyō (Nara), which opened its doors in 710. It was outside of that capital and on its eastern edge, at the foot of the Kasuga range of hills, that the Kasuga Shrine and the Kōfukuji were built. Kamatari himself was given a separate cult in the southern part of the Yamato Basin.[12]

THE CREATION OF THE KASUGA SHRINE

The oldest document concerning the Kasuga Shrine is a map that was discovered a few years ago in the Shōsō-in. This map, which is dated 756, shows the compound of the Tōdaiji as well as Heijō-kyō's eastern range of hills, and a square drawn near the western foot of Mount Mikasa bears the inscription "sacred ground" (shinji). Scholars tend to agree that this inscription refers to Kasuga, since the area thus described corresponds exactly to the present site of the shrine, but, curiously, the name Kasuga does not appear on the map, and no building is indicated.[13]

In the Yamato period (fourth to seventh century) the site on which the Kasuga Shrine was built belonged to a branch of the Wani house named Kasuga (hence the name of the shrine), and there is reason to believe that Mount Mikasa and its immediate surroundings were hallowed grounds for the Kasuga house, whose fortunes were declining at the time of the creation of the capital. During the Yamato period the Kasuga house regularly provided women as the spouses of emperors in a pattern similar to what became central to the Fujiwara house. Legend says that the kami that then owned the land was integrated into the Kasuga Shrine after its completion: that is, in the Enomoto Shrine located in the western part of the outer corridor now encircling Kasuga.[14] It is not known how the Fujiwara house came to own the land on which it built its shrines and temples. At a time that is not possible to ascertain with any precision, the Fujiwara house was granted, took possession of, or bought the large area on which the shrine and the temple were built during the eighth century.

The generally accepted date of the foundation of the Kasuga Shrine is 768 C.E. The problem with this date is that it is extremely late: nearly a century after the death of the founder of the Fujiwara house and fifty years after the creation of the new capital. This problem hinges on the interpretation of the word foundation, as was suggested by Nishida Nagao, whose views are outlined in the following pages.[15] The date 768 is inferred from a text supposedly written in 780, but the only copy extant dates from 1283. The relevant part of that text states as follows:

In its move from its august residence in Hitachi Province to its present abode on Mount Mikasa the *kami* mounted a white deer and used a branch of persimmon as a whip. On the twenty-first day of the sixth moon of the year 767 it reached the village of Natsumi in the district of Nabari in Iga Province. Upon undergoing purification in the Segawa River, the *kami* stuck its whip into the ground near the shore to mark off the area. The whip turned into a persimmon. The *kami* then moved to Mount Komou in the same province, where it took up residence for a few months.
Then it gave roasted chestnuts to [its attendants], Tokifū and Hidetsura, declaring: "I shall be worshiped forever by your descendants. If you plant these chestnuts, they shall grow into trees."
That is why those attendants took the name Ueguri [chestnut grower] within the Nakatomi lineage. From the seventh day of the twelfth moon of the same year the *kami* resided on Mount Abe in the Shirokami District of Yamato Province. The following year [768], the *kami* finally made its imprint on Mount Mikasa in the Sounokami District of the same province, on the ninth day of the first moon. Thereafter offerings were made to the *kami* Ame-no-koyane, Iwainushi, and Himegami. The *kami* chose Mount Mikasa as its abode because there is no space of higher renown in the entire province. Then the *kami* formulated its vow to protect the imperial lineage, the chieftains of the Fujiwara house, and the priests charged with its worship. It also vowed to protect the great vehicle of the Hossō lineage of Buddhism.
Empress Shōtoku received the following oracle: "I wish to reside there and to face south."
Struck with awe, the empress sent a messenger to inspect the configuration of the land, whereupon a pillar was firmly erected, and a shrine was completed in the hour of the Tiger [4:00 A.M.], on the ninth day of the eleventh moon of the year 768. After the *kami* had been enshrined, Tokifū and Hidetsura declared: "This *kami* resides in the *sakaki* tree. This tree shall therefore be its symbol for generations to come and shall be an object of continued worship."
Signed: Tokifū, on the third day of the eighth moon, eleventh year of Hōki [780].[16]

This text poses a number of problems. The first one concerns the identity of Tokifū and Hidetsura; the name that they took, Ueguri, appears in the *Shoku-Nihongi* in a segment dated 739, but it is not associated with the Kasuga Shrine, and the offering of chestnuts to the *kami* of Kasuga did not become an important practice until the Heian period.[17] Furthermore, Tokifū and Hidetsura are regarded as the ancestors of the Chidori and Imanishi sacerdotal lineages, which were responsible for the Wakamiya Shrine of Kasuga. Because that shrine was built in 1135, there is a strong possibility that this text was not written in 780. There is no reason related to the creation of Kasuga for choosing those two figures—even if they existed at the time of the foundation of the shrine—as the ancestors of a specific sacerdotal branch whose duties were related to a different shrine. A further indication that something is amiss in this text is the fact that the signs *kinoe-inu* for the year 768 do not accord with those found in the *Shoku-Nihongi*. This cannot be a simple mistake, for the day *kinoe-inu* (which would correspond to the ninth day) does not occur at all in the moon in question. These reasons alone would justify rejecting the entire text as pure fantasy and dismissing its purported date of the foundation of Kasuga.

The *Sandai-jitsuroku*, which is a text that cannot be rejected as easily, however, states the following for the year 884: "Two new *koto* were made for the Kasuga Shrine, to replace those that had been offered on the ninth day of the eleventh moon of 768."[18] There is no doubt that the *koto*, a musical instrument of great importance in Kasuga rituals, would be offered at the time of rituals commemorating the foundation of the shrine. Thus the tradition that the shrine was erected in 768 appears to have some validity. The foundation of the shrine must be understood in terms of one of the functions of ritual: a *matsuri* (commemorative rite) is performed at a sacred time in which a return to the past is accomplished. This return is effected through a solemn liturgy, food offerings, and the performance of various gestures and dances grounded in symbols and myths. These utterances, gestures, and dances form the main body of the *matsuri*, and it is only natural that a return to the origins be associated with the date of the foundation of the shrines. Therefore, concludes Nishida Nagao, the date "9–11–768" is indeed that of the foundation of the Kasuga Shrine.

This does not imply that the Fujiwara house did not worship any *kami* before 768, nearly a century after its ancestor's death. The text translated above indicates that the date 768 is that of the arrival at Kasuga of the *kami* Takemikatsuchi-no-mikoto, and it seems to imply that the three other *kami* had been there before. Furthermore, the creation of a shrine is not equivalent to the creation of rites for a *kami*. It is clear that permanent shrines appeared rather late in Japan, and that they owed something, on the one hand, to the need for institutionalization (especially in the case of ancestral *kami*) and, on the other hand, to the appearance of Buddhist temples. It is almost certain that the *kami* did not originally abide in permanent structures but in sites that were prepared at the time of the performance of rituals. When agriculture developed and communities tended to settle in one area and form close territorial bonds, the forces of nature that oversee the cycles of fertility were propitiated in the fall and the spring. In time, these nature *kami* and those that protected the community merged with ancestor worship. That is why ancestral *kami* are more often than not worshiped according to the agricultural timetable, and why those rites show definite traces of nature worship. The ritual actions by which those *kami* are invoked do not require the presence of permanent buildings. What is needed, rather, is a site for ritual action, that is, a ritually defined and purified area entered only by specialists of ritual who have prepared themselves through the observance of specific taboos. Such a site may be located on or at the foot of a mountain, at the entrance to a valley, near a spring, or in a forest. At such sites the focus for ritual is a rock abode or a tree that serves as the support for the *kami*. It is when objects other than natural ones, such as swords, are regarded as supports that a building designed to house them is needed. In Japan that was usually a storehouse closely connected with granaries.

Even when there was a permanent shrine, sometimes a temporary shrine would be erected for the duration of the ritual and destroyed immediately after it. This is, in fact, the case at Kasuga for the Wakamiya Shrine, the temporary building of which (erected every year at the time of the *On-matsuri*) is seen by most Japanese scholars of ritual and architectural history as the original structure of the shrines of Kasuga before they were established permanently. It is easy, therefore, to imagine that the Fujiwara house did not need a shrine for the worship of its ancestral and tutelary *kami*: what was needed was a sacred ground (*shinji*), which is precisely what can be seen on the map dated 756. Archaeological excavations have revealed the existence of a fairly large number of ritual sites around the Kasuga Shrine, all apparently dating back to the Nara period (eighth century).

There is yet another view on this matter. According to a document entitled *Kasuga-sha honji gotakusen-ki*, which is kept by the Ōhigashi sacerdotal lineage, the Kasuga Shrine was not originally in its present site. Though the document does not specify the original location of the shrine, it states that the shrine was moved to its present site by Fujiwara no Nagate in the second year of the Jingo-Keiun era (766), on the first day of the monkey, and hence the use of the term *monkey rite* to refer to the Grand Rite of Kasuga. According to a government decree (*kampu*) issued in the seventh year of the Tempyō-Shōhō era (755) and contained in the *Kasuga-*

sha shi-ki,[19] the shrine would have then become a state-supported institution, possibly on an order by Kōmyō Kōgō, who was the first Fujiwara-
born imperial consort. Until the year 766 all expenses for the Kasuga rituals
would have been borne by the Fujiwara house as a private matter. These
documents, if worthy of belief, demonstrate that the Kasuga Shrine was
established even earlier than has been thought, and that it was quickly
supported by the state so as to ensure its proper inscription within the
dominant structural modes of society.

According to Nagashima Fukutarō and Kuroda Noriyoshi, during the
Nara period the Kasuga Shrine consisted of only three shrines, which were
dedicated respectively to Takemikatsuchi-no-mikoto, Iwainushi-no-mikoto, and Ame-no-koyane-no-mikoto and his consort, Himegami. This last
shrine was called *aidono*, a generic term designating a shrine dedicated to
a *kami* and its consort. It was not before the middle of the ninth century
that, according to Kuroda, a separate, fourth shrine was added for
Himegami, and that Kasuga took the basic form it has kept through history
(see figure 1). The ritual text contained in the *Jōgan-gishiki*, which was
promulgated in 869–71, states clearly that at Kasuga there were four
shrines in front of which food offerings were to be made. In addition to
the fourth shrine, other buildings were added over the course of the Heian
period. It was probably around 859 that the *jingūji* (literally: "[Buddhist]
temple for a *kami*") was erected within the compound of the shrine, to the
south of the four shrines and facing west. Very little is known about the
jingūji, as about all buildings of that type in other places in Japan.[20] It was
probably used to store the scriptures that were chanted by monks in front
of the *kami* and may have contained statues and paintings. There is no
document whatever concerning the existence of administrative and residential buildings at Kasuga during the Nara and Heian periods.

It is not clear why it took such a long time for the Kasuga Shrine as we
know it to appear, but as will be seen shortly, the reason might be associated
with the question concerning the relation between the liturgical and political functions of clans in the emerging state, and its corollary, the need
to erect shrines. In order to clarify this issue, an analysis of the character
of the four *kami* enshrined at Kasuga—Takemikatsuchi, Futsunushi, Ame-
no-koyane-no-mikoto, and Himegami (the consort of Ame-no-koyane-
no-mikoto)—is needed.

ENIGMATIC IDENTITIES

Even though the Fujiwara house was Japan's leading aristocratic lineage,
and even though the Kasuga Shrine was one of the country's most im-

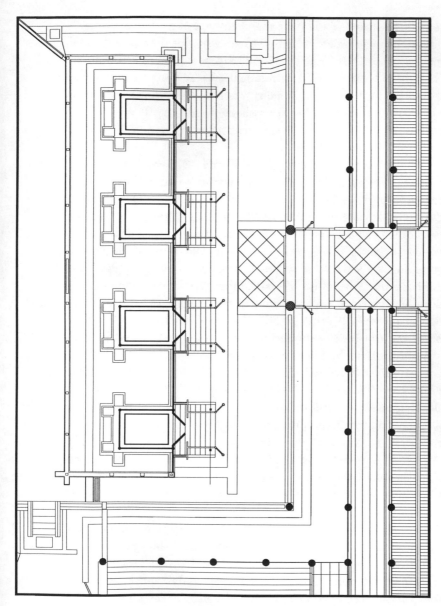

Figure 1. The Kasuga Shrine after the 859 Reconstruction. Computer-assisted rendering of Kuroda Noriyoshi, *Kasuga taisha kenchiku-shi ron* (Kyoto: Sōgeisha, 1978), plate no. 32.

portant shrines, the identity of three of the four *kami* of Kasuga is unclear. Japanese scholars are divided on this issue, and even the Kasuga priests can offer no conclusive evidence as to their identities.

The first two *kami* worshiped in Kasuga are said to have been enshrined originally in Kashima and Katori, which are located on what was in the Nara period the far eastern edge of the area under the control of the Yamato court. Documents dealing with this issue are extremely scarce and unreliable, and to complicate matters, although the more important *kami* enshrined in Kashima are mentioned in local documents of the time, those documents do not identify the *kami* of Kashima. A further difficulty is presented by the fact that even if we are to assume that the *kami* of Kashima is indeed Takemikatsuchi-no-mikoto, there is no explanation as to how that *kami*, who is mentioned in the *Kojiki* first in relation to the mythology of fire and later in relation to the conquest of Izumo in the western part of the islands, came to be enshrined in such a distant place. Yet another difficulty is that the *kami* enshrined in Katori, which is located a short distance from Kashima, is identified by documents belonging to Yamato as either Futsunushi-no-mikoto or Iwainushi-no-mikoto, but no explanation or indication of what, if anything, these two names have in common is provided. Finally, there is no explanation of the reason for which those *kami* would have been moved in the eighth century from their distant abode to the center of Yamato, or why they came to be seen as the tutelary *kami* of the Fujiwara house.

The Pyroclastic Birth of Takemikatsuchi

According to the myths contained in the *Kojiki* and the *Nihon shoki*,[21] the last divine couple to appear spontaneously in the cosmos was Izanami (female) and Izanagi (male). Given the order to consolidate the world, they descended to a heavenly bridge and churned the ocean below with a bejeweled spear, thus creating an island upon which they established residence. There they engaged in sexual intercourse, and Izanami eventually gave birth to a leech. Wondering how this could have happened, the couple asked the council of the *kami* in Heaven for an explanation and learned that the production of a leech resulted as a "mis-conception" of the socially acceptable role of women. Izanami, it seems, had initiated intercourse, which is a male prerogative. To ignore this code could only cause a birth defect, what might be termed a miscommunication between the genetic codes of the couple, or an incoherence: the birth of a leech, which is deprived of either articulated members or language. Strengthened by this new knowledge of socially acceptable codes, the couple returned to the island where, upon the invitation of the male, they resumed their sexual union. They then gave birth to the Eight Islands of Japan and procreated *kami* related to seas, rivers, winds, trees, mountains, plains, a *kami* called "Heavenly-Bird-Ship," the moon, and, finally, fire.

In giving birth to fire Izanami was burned to death. Izanagi, angered by the loss of his spouse, then killed fire. When he did so, the blood of fire spurted forth and splashed on various parts of his sword, thus giving birth to new *kami*. The blood of fire splashing against the tip of his sword caused the *kami* Iwasaku, Nesaku, and Iwatsutsuno-o to appear. Two *kami*, Kura-okami and Kura-mitsuha, appeared when the blood of fire splashed on the hilt of the sword and ran through Izanagi's fingers. Finally, the blood of fire splashing on the sword-guard and on the rocks caused the *kami* Mikahayahi, Hihayahi, and Takemikatsuchi (which also received the names Takefutsu and Toyofutsu) to appear. It is this last *kami* that would be enshrined in the highest position in Kasuga.

Saddened by the death of his spouse, Izanagi then cried and his tears gave birth to *kami* called Nakisawame, which, we are told, reside in a pond located at the foot of Mount Ama-no-kagu (Fire of Heaven) in Yamato, a major sacred hill for the Nakatomi sacerdotal lineage. Then Izanagi entered the netherworld to search for his spouse. Upon finding her he was told that he could regain her only if he led the way out of the netherworld and did not look at her condition, but, unable to remain patient, he made some light and saw her body in decomposition. Upset by Izanagi's breach of promise, Izanami pursued him, but Izanagi reached the surface of the earth before her and closed the entrance to the netherworld. The couple then pronounced words of separation, and Izanami vowed to kill a number of Izanagi's children every day, to which Izanagi retorted that he would then give birth to many more.

At this point, polluted by his contact with decay, Izanagi decided to purify himself. He went to the mouth of a river, discarded his clothes, and cleansed his body. In this process he caused many *kami* to appear: first were the *kami* of Watatsumi, which were worshiped by the Azumi clan, the naval force of Yamato Japan, and second came the Sumiyoshi *kami*, which are related to strategy and to seafaring. Then, standing in the water, Izanagi purified his face; cleansing his left eye he gave birth to Amaterasu, the solar emblem of the imperial lineage; cleansing his right eye he gave birth to Tsukuyomi, the lunar emblem of the agricultural world; and cleansing his nose he gave birth to Susano-o, a *kami* whose character is difficult to define and that may be related to land conquest.

This cycle of Japanese mythology is extremely important because it offers in a most succinct manner notions held by sacerdotal lineages in the eighth century. The key to the cycle is the position of fire: before fire's appearance various *kami* of Earth (*chigi*) were born through sexual intercourse and from the lower part of Izanami's body, and after fire's appearance various *kami* of Heaven (*tenjin*) appeared in a process of purification of the erect body and the face of a male demiurge. Although everything before the birth of fire belongs to the world of nature, everything that follows and has to do with the control of fire belongs to the world of culture. Fire thus dances between nature and culture and shows two faces: on the natural side it is violent and dangerous, since it kills its mother; on the cultural side it is also violent, but it can be controlled and then prefigures, in its relation to swords, the advent of symbols upon which the classical Japanese state rests. Furthermore, the female *kami* Izanami stands decidedly on the side of nature, which is symbolized by natural processes of procreation, decay, and putrefaction, which are equated with natural birth, menstruation, and death. The male *kami* Izanagi, in contrast, is on the side of culture, which is symbolized first and foremost by processes of purification that are equated with the production of sociocosmic emblems. Fire is both natural and cultural, pure and impure; when used for preparing food for the dead it is impure, but it is pure when it is ritually prepared for the *kami*. Fire is hot: it was born from the womb of nature, which is lukewarm and the site of digestion and warm decomposition, but it is tempered or controlled by water, which symbolizes the cold aspect of culture that is the site of manipulations and symbol making. Japanese scholars suggest that the eruption of fire from the womb of the earth should be equated with a volcano, while the killing of fire by its father should be equated with the tempering of swords.[22] On the natural side fire is a volcano, and on the cultural side it is a sword made from earth and fire and tempered by Izanagi, who is a sort of Vulcan who masters (kills) fire.

It would seem, therefore, that the *kami* Takemikatsuchi, which is enshrined at Kasuga, is a sword spirit closely related to fire and born in violence at the very junction of the realms of nature and culture. That is, indeed, how Takemikatsuchi appears later in the myths; namely, as a *kami* seated atop the tip of an erect sword that surfaced over the sea in Izumo and was then used for the "pacification" of Japan.[23] Takemikatsuchi's presence in Kashima is still unexplained, however, and further investigation of Japan's early history is in order to solve that problem.

The only source that offers some details on the settlement of what became the eastern province of Hitachi is the *Hitachi Fudoki*, which will be quoted extensively in the following pages.[24] The *Fudoki*, a remarkable collection of documents commissioned by Empress Gemmei in 713, contains for each of the provinces controlled by the Yamato court at that time descriptions of the land and of its natural and man-made products, as well as historical notations, legends, and various reports related to place names. Although too few in number, the extant documents are tantalizingly rich and suggestive. According to them the province of Hitachi formerly consisted of several independent districts that had been settled by conquest in a distant past:

> An elder said: In olden times the land situated west from Mount Yamasaka in the province of Sagamu was called Azuma. In those times one did not say Hitachi [the current name of the province]. Instead, one spoke of the districts of Niibari, Tsukuha, Ubaraki, Naka, Kuji, and Taka, each of which was ruled by a local official [*kuni no miyatsuko*] and an assistant sent by the court. Later, under the reign of Emperor Kōtoku [r. 645–54], orders were given to the *omi* of Takamuko and to the *muraji* of Nakatomi and Hataori to govern this area. It was then that the Eight Provinces were formed and Hitachi Province came into existence. Isn't this the country that in the past used to be called the Land of Tokoyo? . . . The district of Ubaraki was pacified by the *omi* of Ō and is headed by a certain Kura-osaka-no-mikoto.[25]

This passage is important because it reveals that Hitachi Province was formed shortly after the Taika Reform, which was masterminded by Emperor Kōtoku, Prince Naka no Ōe, and Nakatomi no Kamatari, and because it states that the province came to be governed by subbranches of the Nakatomi and Hataori lineages, to which we shall return. It is also of the greatest interest to read later in the text that Kamatari was granted some land in one of the six districts that came to form Hitachi:

> District of Kuji. In the time of Emperor Tenji [Prince Naka no Ōe] a certain Satomaro of Karu was sent by the court to inspect the land that had been granted to the Fujiwara grand minister [Kamatari]. This man [Satomaro] built a dam and a lake for irrigation. North of this lake is the site called Taniaiyama.[26]

This short statement explains in part why the province of Hitachi remained of great importance to the Fujiwara house in subsequent centuries; namely, it is the site of the house's first estate. This may also be the reason why by the end of the Heian period, people believed that Kamatari was born in Hitachi.

Let us now turn to the *Fudoki*'s account of the conquest of the land by Ō no Kura-osaka's forebear:

> Under the reign of Emperor Sūjin, Take-Kashima-no-mikoto was sent to pacify the land in this district of Namekata. At the head of an army he defeated various rebels and came to stop at the

island of Aba. As he was looking over in the direction of the east, he saw some smoke and wondered whether it was caused by humans. Then Take-Kashima-no-mikoto made a test [*ukehi*]: facing Heaven he declared, "If this smoke is caused by Heavenly Men [= friends of the court], let it come over my head. If it is caused by rebellious brigands, let it go over in the other direction." The smoke went in the other direction, out over the sea. Thus Take-Kashima-no-mikoto knew these were enemies, and he went to fight them.[27]

And, further in the document:

[Meeting with resistance on the part of the native residents who had entrenched themselves, Take-Kashima-no-mikoto invents a stratagem:]
Preparing weapons, he arranged them in awe-inspiring fashion upon the waves, and had the boats close ranks and thus form a floating platform. He let exquisitely decorated umbrellas flutter in the breeze and displayed banners of all hues of the rainbow. The "Heavenly-Bird-*koto*" and the "Heavenly-Bird Flute" played harmonies in the Kishima style, accompanied by the sound of waves and the rhythm of the tides, for a duration of seven days and seven nights. [Whereupon the natives left their fortifications out of curiosity and were massacred.][28]

The complex information in this short passage will receive detailed analysis later, but for the moment let us investigate Take-Kashima-no-mikoto. The *Kojiki* states that he was a descendant of Emperor Jimmu (the first "emperor" of Japan, according to the mythology) and, more precisely, of a certain Kamu-ya-wi-mimi-no-mikoto, who was a son of Jimmu's and who had ceded his birthright to his brother, who had been unable to engage in killing. This son was the ancestor of nineteen "families" that were spread all over Japan: the first of these was the Ō clan, and the fifteenth was initiated by Take-Kashima-no-mikoto, the ancestor of Ō no Kura-osaka, who ruled the district of Naka in Hitachi.[29] Donald Philippi offers the following information about Kamu-ya-wi-mimi-no-mikoto's family: "Opo (Ō); an extremely large family including all the sub-families mentioned as the descendants of Kamu-ya-wi-mimi-no-mikoto. The family of the *omi* of Opo (*asomi* after 685) is the main line of the clan and is said to have originated in a village called Opo in Towoti [Tōchi], Yamato (today Ō, Tawaramoto-chō, Shiki-gun, Nara-ken), although Ota thinks that they originated in Hizen in Kyushu."[30]

One of the compilers of the *Kojiki* was a certain Ō no Yasumaro, and members of the Ō "clan" played a great role in the evolution of the culture of the Yamato court, as has been demonstrated by Yamagami Izumo.[31] But Yamagami goes further than Philippi and suggests that the Ō "clan" might have come from Korea around the fourth century and might have conquered much land from Kyushu all the way to Hitachi, while leaving some of its members and cultural patterns in every conquered area, particularly in Kyushu, Yamato, and Hitachi. The conquest of Hitachi must have been initiated from the sea, as the *Fudoki* recalled, and was pursued during the Yamato period by the Mononobe clan and its allied Nakatomi and Urabe lineages. That is why the *Fudoki* repeatedly refers to those lineages in Hitachi, specifically in connection with the shrines of Kashima and Katori. At the beginning of the eighth century these shrines were already of great importance, as the *Hitachi Fudoki* emphasizes many times:

> There is a harbor at E-no-ura. A station was established there,
> because this marks the beginning of the Hitachi Road that
> branches off the Eastern Sea Road. Whenever officials enter the
> province they stop here, purify their mouths and hands, and turn
> toward the east to worship the Great *kami* of Kashima. Only
> then are they allowed to proceed.[32]

It is unlikely that any other shrine was treated with the same awe anywhere in Japan at that time. Indeed, the language used in the *Fudoki* to refer to the *kami* of Kashima and Katori is charged with the highest respect:

> Before the pure and the impure were separated and before
> Heaven and Earth were created, the various ancestral and Heav-
> enly *kami* (people of the area refer to those as *kamirumi* and *ka-
> miraugi*) called for a great assembly of all eight hundred myriads
> of *kami* in the High Heavenly Plain, and declared: "The Land of
> Luxuriant Reeds shall be ruled by our descendants."
>   The name of the *kami* who descended from Heaven to rule
> this land is the Great Heavenly *kami* of Kashima. In the realm of
> Earth it is called Shrine of Kashima of the Sun, while in the
> realm of Heaven it is called Kashima of Abundance. . . . Under
> the reign of Emperor Sūjin offerings were made that consisted of
> ten swords, two halberds, two iron bows, two sets of iron arrows,
> four *koro* [= quivers?], one set of flattened iron, one set of
> forged iron, one horse, one saddle, two decorated mirrors, and
> one roll of woven silk. . . . Messengers were sent under the reign
> of Emperor Tenji with orders that a shrine be erected. Ever since
> then, repairs and periodic reconstructions have taken place with-
> out interruption.[33]

According to this document, the *kami* of Kashima is obviously treated as one of the major members of the heavenly pantheon, and yet, curiously, its name is not mentioned. It is directly related to the conquest of the eastern seaboard of the islands and is granted offerings of swords and the gear of warriors; it must, therefore, be a sword spirit that was worshiped at that time by the Nakatomi and Urabe lineages. The identification of this Great *kami* of Kashima with the sword spirit Takemikatsuchi appears in documents only in the Heian period and, surprisingly enough, in the *Kogoshūi*, which is a document compiled by the Imbe sacerdotal lineage in order to show its disagreement with the Nakatomi sacerdotal lineage on various matters related to the *Kojiki*, in the redaction of which the Nakatomi had participated.

The fact that swords were forged in the vicinity of the shrine of Kashima should be stressed:

> District of Kashima, beach of Takamatsu. A spring surges at the foot of a pine tree; the spring's circumference is about eight or nine feet. The water is pure and limpid, and its taste is extremely good. In 704 the administrator of the province gave orders to the *asomi* Uneme, to a smith, and to a certain Ōmaro of Sabi to take iron ore from the beach of Takamatsu and to make swords. . . . However, since this site is a sacred hill belonging to the Kashima Shrine, people are not allowed to cut down the pine trees or to take iron as they wish.[34]

It is possible that the Great *kami* of Kashima is indeed the Takemikatsuchi spirit of the sword used by Take-Kashima-no-mikoto of the Ō clan at the time of the earliest conquest of the east. The documents, however, raise doubts about this: if that sword was used by the Ō clan, one might expect the *Kojiki* to mention the Ō clan in the context of Takemikatsuchi's appearance in Izumo, but nothing of the sort is mentioned. And, if the shrine of Kashima had always been dedicated to that sword spirit, then the *Fudoki* would not state the following:

> An elder said: In the year 649, under the reign of Emperor Kōtoku, Nakatomi no ——ko [missing segment in the name] and Nakatomi no Unoko requested that the governor general of the eastern provinces establish a district for the regular support of the shrines. . . . What is called the Great Heavenly *kami* of Kashima is actually a group of three shrines: the shrine of the Great *kami*, the shrine of Sakato, and the shrine of Numao. (People of the area are used to saying: "the hail-ridden country of Kashima.")[35]

Japanese scholars over the past have focused intensely on the brief statement in the *Fudoki* that the Kashima Shrine is actually a composite of three distinct sites of cult.[36] Opinions on this question vary a great deal and revolve on the point whether Kashima was always a composite, or whether the shrines of Sakato and Numao were extremely ancient sites of cult near which, at a later date, the *kami* that symbolized conquest and Yamato court supremacy were enshrined by Nakatomi and Urabe sacerdotal lineages. Although the paucity of extant records makes the resolution of this problem impossible at present, the ubiquitous presence of the Nakatomi and Urabe lineages in the area is strongly felt:

> On the tenth day of the fourth moon of each year a ritual feast is held and rice-wine is served. Members of the Urabe sacerdotal lineage assemble men and women, and day after day, night after night, people deport themselves in drinks, songs, and dances. One of the songs says:
>
>> Divine new rice-wine!
>> Is it because I was told:
>> Drink!
>> That I lost my spirit?
>
> These Urabe dwell in the immediate surroundings of the shrine. The configuration of the land is ideal: high and flat, sea to the east and to the west, regular arrangement of hills, valleys, and villages. Trees on the mountain and grasses on the plain form natural hedges, and water is plentiful, running in the streams and from springs in the cliffs. Houses are built on elevations, with hedges of pine trees and bamboo to protect them. Wells are dug on the side of hills covered with abundant vegetation. Passing through these villages in spring, one is met by fragrances emanating from a hundred plants; passing through in autumn, one can see the natural brocade offered by the leaves of the trees. One must admit that this region is the natural obscure residence of the *kami*, the natural site of their miraculous manifestations. It is impossible to describe in detail the bountiful and delicate character of this land. . . . To the north is the sacred lake of Numao. An elder reports that its water came from Heaven at the time of the *kami*. The taste of the lotuses that grow in it is so extraordinary and so sweet that nothing can compare to it. Whoever eats the lotus when ill is cured in no time in a miraculous manner.[37]

Thus it would appear that the presence of the Nakatomi and Urabe lineages in the Kashima district of Hitachi Province, combined with the need of the political center to keep in contact with the periphery, might account for the grant of land to Kamatari, for subsequent Fujiwara interest in the area, and also for that house's claim of the Kashima *kami* as its tutelary divinity. Leaving aside other problems raised by the documents translated above, we can now turn to the second *kami* enshrined at Kasuga.

Futsunushi, Master of Radiance

The second tutelary *kami* of the Fujiwara house is Futsunushi-no-mikoto, who is enshrined in Katori. The *Hitachi Fudoki* is clear as to its identity:

> District of Shida. . . . An elder reports that at the beginning of Heaven and Earth, when the vegetal world was speaking words, a *kami* came from Heaven. Its name is the Great *kami* Futsu. In its rounds of the Central Plain of Reeds [Japan], it pacified various rebels. Once this Great *kami* had accomplished its work of civilization, it conceived in its heart the desire to return to its celestial abode. It therefore left its weapons and gear on earth, and, mounting a white cloud, returned to Heaven.[38]

Futsunushi is definitely a sword spirit, for the term *futsu* is derived from the Korean *pur* ("radiance"), which Mishina Shōei has shown to refer to the aspect of lightning that was associated with swords from very ancient times.[39] It may be that the swords used for the conquest of Izumo and later of Hitachi were of Korean manufacture and, therefore, the tutelary *kami* of the Fujiwara house were of continental origin, although that may have been forgotten by the Nara period. Futsunushi is also the name of the *kami* enshrined at Isonokami, south of Kasuga, where it is worshiped as the spirit of a sword symbolizing the power and identity of the Mononobe house, which used to be the main military arm of the Yamato court. This explains why during the medieval period, the *kami* of Kasuga and Isonokami were confused with each other. It appears that the Nakatomi often worshiped *kami* associated with the Mononobe in the Kinai area.[40]

In the *Fudoki* the Katori Shrine is also associated with another type of *kami*:

> During the seventh moon every year boats are made and offered to the shrine of Tsu. An elder reports that, under the reign of Emperor [sic] Yamato-Takeru-no-mikoto, the Great *kami* of Heaven instructed Nakatomi no Osayama in the following manner: "You now shall take responsibility for the boats."
> To which Osayama replied, saying: "I humbly acknowledge the august order and shall not defy it."
> The following morning the Great *kami* of Heaven declared: "Your boat is in the sea."
> When Osayama went to see for himself, he saw the boat on a hill. Then the *kami* said: "I put your boat on the hill."

And as Osayama went then to see for himself, the boat was, that time, offshore. This was repeated a number of times, whereupon Osayama was struck with awe, built anew three boats ten *tsue* in length, and offered them.[41]

This legend offers in a cryptic manner the origin of the famous boat festival of Kashima/Katori, which consists of placing the support of the *kami* into a boat and then crossing the river that separates Katori from Kashima. Thus it appears that in the cases of both Kashima and Katori there were several historical and ritual layers, at the top of which the sword spirits of Takemikatsuchi and Futsunushi were positioned once it became crucial to establish in the distant province of Hitachi the supremacy of the Yamato court and, subsequently, the Nara and Heian courts. This served the geopolitical purposes of the Fujiwara house.

Another problem is raised by the alternate name of the *kami* worshiped in Katori, Iwainushi-no-mikoto. The term means "Master of Worship," and that name, together with the other name, "Master of Radiance," was carried over to Kasuga. The question is vexing; it is thought by Miyai Yoshio that as Iwainushi, the *kami* is a hypostatic form of the sacerdotal figure charged with the worship of Takemikatsuchi, and it is that character that comes to the fore in the Katori shrine's boat festival, which is sometimes called the "helmsman" (Kajitori) festival. The solution of this problem requires further investigation of the sacerdotal lineages that were originally responsible for the sword spirits Takemikatsuchi and Futsunushi.

The Kyushu Connection

The foregoing discussion points to a process of assimilation of the national territory at a conscious level on the part of the rulers, and to the formation of a geopolitical sphere of influence in the east on the part of the emerging Fujiwara house in the eighth century. These processes entailed the formation of symbols and the establishment of major shrines, as well as their appropriation by the center in Yamato. It is not only elements of the far eastern parts of Yamato-controlled territory that were involved in these processes, for elements from the westernmost parts of that territory, namely Kyushu, also played an important role.

The first connection between the center and Kyushu concerns the *kami* Futsunushi and is contained in the *Hizen Fudoki*:

Province of Hizen, district of Mine. . . . There is a village called Mononobe. The shrine in this village is dedicated to a *kami* called "Futsunushi of the Mononobe." A long time ago, under the reign of Empress Suiko [r. 592–628], Imperial Prince Kume was made a general, and he passed through this village on his way to conquer Korea. He had the Wakamiya-be of the Mononobe clan come here in order to erect a shrine for this *kami* and worship it. Therefore, this was called Mononobe village.[42]

This passage provides evidence of the presence of the sword spirit Futsunushi, Master of Radiance, which symbolizes the Mononobe armed forces in Kyushu and which is also enshrined in Yamato at the Isonokami Shrine and in Hitachi at the Katori Shrine, as well as in Kasuga's second shrine. Undoubtedly, the establishment of these shrines, which symbolized military conquest, followed the eastward movement of Yamato forces (or whatever they may have been in fact) from the western confines of the Japanese isles to their eastern parts.

A second and more complex connection is established by statements in the *Hitachi Fudoki* to the effect that Take-Kashima-no-mikoto tricked indigenous residents with songs "in the manner of Kishima,"[43] and that the residents of Kashima refer to that area as "ridden with hail" (*arare-furu*).[44] Kishima, a sacred mountain of Kyushu, is described in the fragments of the *Hizen Fudoki* as follows:

> District of Kishima. South of the district office there is a mountain that stands alone. It is composed of three peaks oriented on a southwest/northeast axis. Its name is Kishima [Mallet Island]. The southwestern peak is called Hikogami [Male *kami*], the central peak is called Himegami [Female *kami*], and the northeastern peak is called Mikogami [August Child *kami*]. Another name for Mikogami is Ikusagami [Army *kami*]: when the mountain shakes it is said to mean that an army is on the move. Every year in spring and autumn men and women of the region take rice-wine and *koto* and, holding hands, climb the mountain in order to contemplate the landscape. There, they drink, sing, and dance. When the festivities end, they return to the plain below. Here are the words of their song:
>
> > Mount Kishima,
> > Steep slopes
> > Ridden with hail!
> > Losing hold of the grass,
> > I take my beloved's hand.
>
> This is called song in the manner of Kishima.[45]

This Mount Kishima is located near a coastal village that is now called Kashima but that was called Fujitsu (Wisteria Harbor) by virtue of the growth of wisterias on the rope of Yamato-Takeru-no-mikoto's boat anchor. The *Fudoki* reports that when an emperor's boat landed in the area of Kishima and the anchor (*kashi*) was thrown onto the land, a spring surged from the hole thus made. Another version of that event has it that the landing site of the imperial party became "of itself" an island (*shima*), and that, therefore, it was named Kashi-shima (anchor-island), of which, we are told, Kishima is a phonetic corruption.[46] In other words, ancient documents expressly associate Kishima in Kyushu and Kashima in Hitachi with a specific type of ritual chant through a kind of popular etymology of the term *Kashi-shima*, which mediates the phonetic difference between Kishima and Kashima.

Interestingly, the same chant appears in the *Manyōshū*, where it is associated with a mountain called Kishimi,[47] and it is also associated with Mount Tsukuba, the most sacred mountain in Hitachi Province.[48] Yamagami Izumo, an authority on Japanese ritual and the performing arts, states that this song belonged to the Ō clan and that it can be found in Kyushu, Yamato, and Hitachi.[49] Evidently it was picked up by the Nakatomi and Urabe sacerdotal lineages who followed the conquerers—Mononobe or others—in their journeys and took care of their symbols.

Other important connections between Hitachi and Kyushu in regard to the Kasuga Shrine of Yamato will be analyzed in chapter 3, under the heading "Echoes of Camphorated Maritime Music." For the present, it is important to recognize that the establishment in Kasuga of *kami* related to military conquest in Kyushu, Izumo, and Hitachi, and their appropriation by the Fujiwara house as its tutelary *kami* in Yamato, were most astute geopolitical acts.

Ame-No-Koyane-No-Mikoto and the Mirror

The third *kami* enshrined at Kasuga is Ame-no-koyane-no-mikoto, who is regarded as the ancestral *kami* of the Nakatomi sacerdotal lineage and consequently of the Fujiwara house, which emerged from that lineage in 669. There is no doubt about the identity of that *kami*, for its role is clearly defined in the *Kojiki* and the *Nihon shoki*, where it appears in what may be the most famous scene in Japanese mythology.

The Great *kami* Amaterasu, born from the left eye of Izanagi, was granted rule over Heaven, but her brother Susano-o, born from Izanagi's nose, was jealous of her prerogatives and went to her palace. Fearful of her brother's character and intentions, and protective of her territory, Amaterasu waited for him, poised for battle. Upon realizing that he could not easily storm her palace, Susano-o claimed that he had come with good intentions and consented to undergo a test (*ukehi*) to prove it. Separated from his sister by a well, he purified his emblem (a sword) in the water of the well and turned it over to his sister, who, taking her emblem (a pearl), did the same. Then, putting each other's emblems into their mouths, they spat out water in a fine mist from which there appeared new *kami* whose gender would by preestablished contract determine the truth of Susano-o's claim. Winning that contest, Susano-o became rampant: he desecrated a weaving hall and infuriated his sister to such a degree that she hid away in a cave and blocked the entrance with a boulder that nobody could remove. Consequently, darkness pervaded the world. In the words of the *Kojiki*:

> Then the eight hundred myriad deities assembled in a divine assembly in the river bed of Ame-no-yasu-kawa. They caused the child of Takamimusubi-no-kami, Omohikane-no-mikoto, to ponder. They gathered together the long crying birds of Tokoyo and caused them to cry. They took the Heavenly Hard Rock from the upper stream of the river Ame-no-yasu-kawa; they took iron from the mountain Ame-no-kana-yama. They sought the smith Amatsumara and commissioned Ishikoridome-no-mikoto to make long strings of myriad *maga-tama* beads. They summoned Ame-no-koyane-no-mikoto to remove the whole shoulder-bone of a male deer of the mountain Ama-no-kagu-yama, and take heavenly *hahaka* wood from the mountain Ama-no-kagu-yama, and (with these) perform a divination. They uprooted by the very roots the flourishing *ma-sakaki* trees of the mountain Ama-no-kagu-yama; to the upper branches they affixed long strings of myriad *maga-tama* beads; in the middle branches they hung up a large-dimensioned mirror; in the lower branches they suspended white *nikite* cloth and blue *nikite* cloth. These various objects were held in his hands by Futo-dama-no-mikoto as solemn offerings, and Ame-no-koyane-no-mikoto intoned a solemn liturgy.[50]

Thereafter an enticing dance performed by Ame-no-Uzume caused the assembly to laugh and Amaterasu to move the boulder of the cave and inquire of the reason for such merriment in her absence. At that point Ame-no-koyane-no-mikoto and Futo-dama-no-mikoto brought out the mirror and tricked Amaterasu out of the cave, thus restoring light to the world.

The universe of meaning surrounding Ame-no-koyane is fundamentally different from that associated with the preceding *kami*. In the case of those *kami* we were confronted with armed conquest, fire, and swords, but we are now entering the world of liturgy, purification, and divination. Ame-no-koyane-no-mikoto is regarded as the ancestral *kami* of the Nakatomi sacerdotal lineage and, at the same time, he is considered to be the patriarch of scapulimancy, that is, divination by way of scorching the shoulder bones of male deer. He is symbolized by the mirror, which he used to trick Amaterasu out of the cave, and we thus understand why mirrors and swords figure prominently not only as the regalia of the imperial lineage but also as the symbols of the Fujiwara house, and why they are prominently displayed in Kasuga at the time of ritual assemblies.

The mythological scene presented above is central to Kasuga and the Fujiwara house in several distinct ways. First, the role of Ame-no-koyane in helping to restore solar light through the performance of ritual and the intonation of a solemn liturgy not only has become a basic structure of Japanese liturgy but has stood for centuries as a metaphor encoding Fujiwara behavior. Indeed, the role of the Fujiwara house has been to ensure that the imperial lineage, which was believed to have descended directly from Amaterasu, is constantly upheld: it is as if the Fujiwara house understood that its sociocosmic duty was to act, so to speak, as a mirror that attracts imperial (solar) rule out of the darkness of time and onto the stage of a history of mythical (sacred) character. Because the Fujiwara house emerged from the Nakatomi sacerdotal lineage, that lineage was charged with the worship of the *kami* of Kasuga, and since Ame-no-koyane is the ancestral *kami* of the Nakatomi, he represents the purely ancestral dimension of the *ujigami* of the Fujiwara house, in contradistinction to the two sword spirits, which represent the tutelary, military aspects of the *ujigami* of the house. Second, the fact that Amaterasu was lured from her concealment by dances determined that dance would have a sacred role in the Kasuga cult, which is regarded as one of the origins of Nō drama during the medieval period.

The fourth *kami* of Kasuga, Himegami, who is the consort of Ame-no-koyane, was worshiped originally at Kasuga in the same shrine as Ame-no-koyane but was given a separate shrine in 859, most likely when female *kami* consorts came to be seen as symbolizing female imperial consorts of Fujiwara birth.

Although the identity of Ame-no-koyane is quite clear, that of his descendants is shrouded in darkness. Naturally, the Nakatomi sacerdotal lineage claims him as their ancestor, but so does the Urabe sacerdotal lineage, which specializes in divination on turtle shell (plastromancy), and the opinions of Japanese scholars on the relations between the Urabe and Nakatomi sacerdotal lineages are as varied as can be imagined.[51]

THE ORGANIZATION OF THE SHRINE

The eighth century was a time of institutionalization and crystallization, and the major result of those processes was the creation of the imperial city.

That development was reinforced by other movements, most notably the production of texts in 712 (the *Kojiki*) and 720 (the *Nihongi*), which established once and for all the legitimacy of the imperial lineage, and the compilation shortly thereafter of the *Fudoki*, which witnessed to the control of a vast geopolitical sphere by the government. In these texts the various *uji* collected the legends and myths whereby their position vis-à-vis the imperial lineage and their connections with each other were fixed. In this process of urbanization and centralization the creation of shrines played a major role, particularly when it was accompanied by the formulation of genealogies and forms of ancestor worship that were increasingly influenced by Confucianism and Buddhism. A new map of Japan, on which were depicted the geopolitical spheres of influence of the centralized state and of its supporting clans, was also produced in the course of the eighth century. Those spheres were symbolized by the erection of shrines and temples that grounded the legitimacy of the state's and the clans' power. As the aforementioned texts indicate, these processes of institutionalization were rather swift, pervasive, and, by the middle of the Heian period, definitive.

The organizational features of the Kasuga Shrine are a prime example of these processes. Indeed, that shrine evolved not only as a symbol of and for the Fujiwara house but of the entire state as well. Kasuga could be called a ceremonial center, which is defined by Eric Wolf as follows:

> Operationally, ceremonial centers were instruments for the generation of political, social, economic, sacred (and other) spaces, at the same time as they were symbols of cosmic, social, political and moral order. . . . Above all, they embodied the aspirations of brittle, pyramidal societies in which, typically, a sacerdotal elite, controlling a corps of officials and palace guards, ruled over a peasantry whose business it was to produce a fund of rent which could be absorbed into the reservoir of resources controlled by the master of the ceremonial center.[52]

The Kasuga Shrine and, subsequently, the Kōfukuji came to form a ceremonial center as defined by Wolf, and the organization of these sites of cult symbolically reflected the various components of what was the object of ceremonial behavior.

The Kasuga Shrine is dedicated to four *kami* that together form the *ujigami*—which means literally "house-*kami*" but is best rendered in English as "ancestral and tutelary *kami*"—of the Fujiwara house. *Ujigami* is a complex term because it contains several historical and ritual layers and because ancient Japanese *uji* were not necessarily blood lineages but territorially related groups. An *ujigami* is ancestral only when the accent is put on direct lineage for legitimacy purposes; in all other cases it is tutelary, even though this tutelary aspect may have been covered over later by an ancestral claim. To consider the *ujigami* to be purely ancestral is a mistake often made, one that has been made in the case of Kasuga.

The *kami* of the Kasuga Shrine are enshrined in a set of four shrines that are situated next to each other, facing south, and in decreasing order of importance from east to west. The easternmost shrine, which is dedicated to the *kami* of Kashima, Takemikatsuchi-no-mikoto, is therefore the most important, as is demonstrated at the time of ritual and by the fact that it is slightly larger than the others. The second shrine is dedicated to the Katori *kami*, alternatively called Iwainushi-no-mikoto and Futsu-nushi-no-mikoto. The third shrine is dedicated to the *kami* of Hiraoka, Ame-no-koyane-no-mikoto, and the fourth shrine is dedicated to that *kami*'s consort, Himegami. The first two of these *kami* are tutelary, whereas the second two are ancestral. The appropriation of the *kami* of Kashima and Katori allowed the Fujiwara house to be grounded in a different (though related) realm than that of the main branch of the Nakatomi. Such appropriation of *kami* was by no means exceptional: the Nakatomi themselves used to worship the territorial *kami* of the land on which they came to reside in the provinces of Settsu and Yamato. The conquest of land was not accompanied by the destruction of preexisting shrines but rather by their assimilation, a process in which the name and character of the *kami* were often changed. This accounts for the complexity of tutelary *kami*.[53]

The two tutelary *kami* of the Fujiwara house had a double function: first, they expressed the importance attributed to the periphery by the center at the time under consideration. As the center grew in power, the periphery came to be considered part of its geopolitical sphere of influence, and the Fujiwara house nurtured that development by sending offerings to the Kashima and Katori shrines in a systematic way. Second, those *kami* allowed for the creation of a distinct identity for an *uji* that was born at the end of the seventh century. It may be because those *kami* were related to the birth of an *uji* that they came to be seen as ancestral, but that must have been a rather late development. The other two *kami*, because they were the ancestral *kami* of the Nakatomi sacerdotal lineage, represent the purely ancestral part of the Fujiwara *ujigami*. Thus the *ujigami* of the Fujiwara house is half-tutelary and half-ancestral, half-peripheral and half-central, as well as half-military and half-liturgical.

The distinction between the political and liturgical components of the concept of rule that appeared during the *Kofun* period can be seen both in the character of the imperial person and in the structure of the institutions of government and liturgy that were created after the Taika Reform of 645. The distinction of rank between members of the Office of the *Kami* of Heaven and Earth and those of the Department of State paralleled the distinction between liturgical and political duties, and there was yet another distinction of level: namely, the political function was more important than the liturgical one, in spite of what is written in the documents. This was clearly the reality of the time. Even though the Fujiwara were issued from the Nakatomi, the Nakatomi headed the Office of the *Kami* of Heaven and Earth, whereas the Fujiwara were determined to head the Department of State and thus to rule the country, which they eventually did. The rank of the Fujiwara was therefore superior to any position the Nakatomi could ever hope to reach, and these crucial distinctions between the two lineages are precisely those found in the arrangement of the Kasuga Shrine: the tutelary *kami*—whose character is military and political—are ranked above the ancestral *kami*, whose character is primarily liturgical.

The organization of the Kasuga Shrine is, therefore, a spatial reflection of the structure of the concept of rule that was embodied in the other institutions of government. In a word, the Kasuga Shrine displays in its architectural arrangement a miniaturized representation of the world held by the Fujiwara house and the state at large, and it is, therefore, a socio-cosmic symbol. It is no wonder that with the development of the Kōfukuji, the area on which the shrines and the temples stood came to form an Outer Capital.

It could be argued that the arrangement of the shrines at Kasuga was purely accidental and bore no relation to the arrangement of the two main institutions of the new state, but a look at the architectural organization of the Hiraoka Shrine, which is dedicated to the ancestral *kami* of the Nakatomi sacerdotal lineage, invalidates that argument. The same four *kami* that are enshrined in Kasuga are also enshrined in Hiraoka, but in exactly the reverse order: that is, the liturgical *kami* Ame-no-koyane and Himegami are first in rank and order, and the military-political *kami* Takemikatsuchi and Futsunushi are second. Such was the sociocosmic view proposed by the Nakatomi, which reflects the organization of the state established by the System of Codes, according to which the Office of the *Kami* of Heaven and Earth ranks above the Department of State.

The Hiraoka Shrine is situated on the western slope of Mount Ikoma, directly west of Kasuga. Thus seated on an east-west axis that runs through the northern part of the Yamato Basin, the architectural settings of the Kasuga and Hiraoka shrines conceal and at the same time reveal the vision of society held by the Fujiwara and Nakatomi houses. Furthermore, whereas the Hiraoka Shrine faces west, the Kasuga Shrine faces south, a clear indication of the imperial ambitions of the Fujiwara house.

THE CREATION OF THE KŌFUKUJI

To understand the universe of the Fujiwara house in the eighth century requires an examination of the organization of the Buddhist "house-temple" (*ujidera*) that was erected by its leaders next to the Kasuga Shrine or, at least, next to the sacred grounds where rituals were performed and where, later, a shrine was built.

That Buddhist temple was built over a period of exactly one hundred years. The origins of the temple are said to have sprung from Nakatomi no Kamatari's Buddhist beliefs, which the tradition remembered better than his ancestor worship. One of the aspects of Kamatari's interest in Buddhism is related to his first son, Mahito, who became a Buddhist monk at a very young age and was sent to China in 653, when he was only eleven years old. His ordination name was Jō-e. There is no doubt that Kamatari had ambitious hopes for his son, who would have studied under the greatest masters of the time in China and might have brought back new knowledge not only of Buddhism but also of Chinese culture in general. Shortly after Jō-e returned from China in 665, however, he was poisoned by a person from Paekche. At that time, Silla, Paekche, and Koguryō were vying for control of the Korean Peninsula: in the conflict Japan sided with Paekche and T'ang China sided with Silla, which finally unified the peninsula in 668. It is possible that Paekche representatives in Japan were afraid that Jō-e would influence his father in favor of the T'ang position, and therefore he was killed.

Whatever the details of this little-reported event may have been, it is hard to imagine that Kamatari would have done nothing about his son's death, and since he had been a monk, it would have been appropriate to perform Buddhist rituals in honor of his spirit. It is not known what was done for the dead in Japan at the time: corpses were either put into plain graves or simply abandoned in the mountains, and it is likely that Buddhist funeral ceremonies would have been immediately welcomed if only for their contribution to the cult of the dead. The tradition states, erroneously, that Dōshō, who was one of the early leaders of the Hossō lineage (which came to be housed in the Kōfukuji) and who traveled to China together with Jō-e, was the first person cremated in Japan. According to the texts that describe the origins of the Kōfukuji, Kamatari pledged to make representations of the Buddha if he succeeded in eliminating the Soga leaders and establishing Prince Karu (Emperor Kōtoku) on the throne.[54] These images would have been a large bronze statue of Śākyamuni and smaller ones of his two bodhisattva attendants and the Four Celestial Kings. They would have been installed by Kamatari's spouse in his private residence in Yamashina, which became the Yamashina Chapel and is claimed by the Kōfukuji to be its origin. While accepting the possibility, if not the probability, that Kamatari did worship the Buddha or was interested by Buddhism, we might have to reject as spurious the story concerning these statues because it bears too many resemblances to the legend according to which Shōtoku Taishi made a vow to erect a temple if he won his battle with the Mononobe. Furthermore, there is reason to believe that Kamatari might have been against the formation of "house-temples" (*ujidera*).

Whatever representation of the Buddha that may have been kept at Kamatari's residence would have been taken to a temple named Umayazaka-dera near the Fujiwara capital at the end of the seventh century and transported to the new capital, Heijō-kyō, when it opened in 710. There is no information available concerning the structure of the Umayazaka-dera or its sacred images. The claim that that temple's origins are to be found in Kamatari's residence in Yamashina is an indication of the private character of the Umayazaka-dera as well as the desire to locate the temple's origins in the lifetime of the founder of the Fujiwara house. Both Yamashina and Umayazaka are place names, but the name Kōfukuji, "Temple to Promote Posthumous Felicity," indicates that the temple's function was to take care of the dead.

Work began on the Kōfukuji between 714 and 717 on the orders of Fuhito, Kamatari's second son. Although the Kōfukuji was a private institution, in 720 the government placed an official in charge of its construction, thus giving the impression that from its inception on this institution had a semiprivate, semipublic character.

The general layout of the temple compound at the beginning of the ninth century appears to have been a mixture of arrangements found at the Asuka-dera (the Ch'onggamni-sa model), the Shitennōji (the Kunsuri-sa model), and the Yakushiji (the Hwangnyong-sa model), all of Korean origin. Whether this was planned from the outset or not cannot be ascertained.[55] Like most temples built in Nara, the Kōfukuji faces south. In all probability the site, which was outside the capital itself, was chosen because it is adjacent to the sacred ground on which the Kasuga Shrine was later erected.

The erection of the Kōfukuji in combination with Kasuga, as well as the erection of the Tōdaiji north of these sites of cult in 745–51, gave birth to the Outer Capital. The structure of those sites depicts the view of the world that was held by the aristocracy of the time in a much clearer way than that portrayed by the structure of the capital itself, which is essentially

Chinese and therefore could not totally satisfy the needs or the realities of Japan. Chinese capitals were symbolic constructs in which views of the world were architecturally encoded; Japanese capitals, even when built on Chinese models, necessarily encoded Japanese conceptions. The exact processes leading to the choices made for the creation of this Outer Capital are not known, but it is difficult to imagine that the Fujiwara house first chose a site for the temple and later chanced upon a neighboring site on which to erect its shrine. There is little doubt that the land between the capital and the foothills was theirs to use and that the building of the temple and the shrine was a concerted effort. Nor was it simply by chance that the temple and the shrine are situated on each side of the Tōdaiji and just south of it.

Work on the Kōfukuji was carried on regularly between 714 and 772, after which it stopped until 813. This gap corresponds precisely to the period during which there occurred the events leading to Dōkyō's exile, events that caused the capital to be moved from Heijō to Nagaoka and subsequently to Heian. During these years the fortunes of the Fujiwara house were uneven, as it took some time for the house to regain its power following the death of Fuhito's four sons (Muchimaro, Fusasaki, Umakai, and Maro) in 737 in an epidemic of smallpox. The construction of the famous Southern Round Hall (Nan'endō) at the Kōfukuji in 813 marked the resurgence of the house to power. Thus, the main core of the temple was created during the Nara period.

The Kasuga Shrine and the Kōfukuji, situated side by side, fulfilled complementary roles: the Kasuga Shrine served to establish the foundation of the Fujiwara house through the worship of tutelary and ancestral *kami*. It also enhanced the unity of the house and enforced its hierarchy through the observance of the protocol that will be discussed in chapter 3.[56] The Kasuga Shrine was not, however, established for the worship of the dead of the Fujiwara house; that service was performed exclusively by the temple. It was not that shrines necessarily shied away from death for ritual reasons, but, rather, that before the Taika Reform the *kofun* (funeral tumuli) had played this role. After the *kofun* were prohibited for economic and sociopolitical reasons, their role was taken over by Buddhist temples.

One interesting corollary to this development is that not only did the temples take care of the dead after the *kofun* had disappeared, but they also performed the *kofun*'s function of aggrandizing the legitimacy of the ruling houses. Therefore, an important point in regard to the early role of Buddhism in Japan is not that temples took care of the dead because shrines did not do so, but that temples were in fact the new *kofun*. That is why under the Buddhist pagodas there were chambers that contained the paraphernalia that in earlier times were stored in *kofun*. Moreover, the

Kasuga Shrine was dedicated to entities symbolizing a whole living house, whereas the Kōfukuji's buddhas and bodhisattvas were dedicated to the deceased members of that house.

Thus the Kōfukuji and the Kasuga Shrine were not at all in competition, and no conflict between "Shinto" and Buddhism—in this case, between shrine and temple—would have been expected by anyone. Each institution fulfilled a different need, and there was no mistake about which institution fulfilled which need. In a sense, then, the Kasuga Shrine did not represent "Shinto" any more than the Kōfukuji represented "Buddhism," at least not before the temple became the center of a particular Buddhist lineage. "Shinto" and Buddhism were not in opposition to each other during the Nara period; they were neither conceived of nor organized, at least at the house level, in such a way. The Kasuga Shrine and the Kōfukuji were two aspects of a single sociocosmic reality, which the use of the term *Shinto* prevents us from adequately perceiving. Kuroda Toshio's statement that Shinto was a medieval creation is correct.[57]

According to the earliest documents on the history of the Kōfukuji, the first building erected there was the Golden Hall (*kondō*), which was called subsequently Central Golden Hall (*chūkondō*) to distinguish it from the Eastern and Western Golden Halls, which were constructed later (see figure 2). It is sometimes called Central Pavilion of the Buddha of the Unique Vehicle (*chū-butsuden-ichijō-in*) and Pavilion of the Central Golden Hall (*chūkondō-in*). It was built in 714, reportedly to house the representation of Śākyamuni made on the wishes of Kamatari before his plot against the Soga clan. This is the statue that, together with the images of the Four Celestial Kings, would have been installed in the Yamashina Chapel and later in the Umayazaka-dera. Representations of an eleven-headed Kannon (*Jūichimen-Kannon*; Skt.: Ekadaśamukha) and of two attendant bodhisattvas to Śākyamuni, *Yaku-ō* and *Yaku-jō*, would have been added in 714. Upon the first anniversary of Fuhito's death in 721, his spouse, Lady Tachibana no Michiyo, donated a group of statuettes representing the Pure Land of the Buddha of the Future, and they were also installed in the building.

The other buildings that formed the core of the Kōfukuji were added over the next twenty years. The Northern Round Hall (*hokuendō*), actually an octagonal building, was also built in 721 on the occasion of the first anniversary of Fuhito's death on an order given to Prince Nagaya by the retired Empress Gemmei and Empress Genshō. This building housed an image of the Buddha of the Future, as well as statues of two attendant bodhisattvas, two arhants (sages in the early Buddhist tradition), and the Four Celestial Kings (see figure 3).

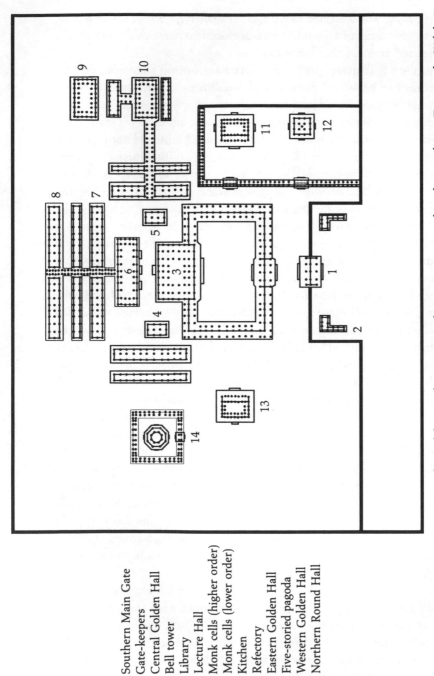

1. Southern Main Gate
2. Gate-keepers
3. Central Golden Hall
4. Bell tower
5. Library
6. Lecture Hall
7. Monk cells (higher order)
8. Monk cells (lower order)
9. Kitchen
10. Refectory
11. Eastern Golden Hall
12. Five-storied pagoda
13. Western Golden Hall
14. Northern Round Hall

Figure 2. The Kōfukuji in the Nara Period. Computer-assisted rendering of Aiga Tetsuo, ed., *Kōfukuji*, vol. 5 of *Meihō Nihon no bijutsu* (Tokyo: Shōgakkan, 1981), 121, figure no. 105.

The Eastern Golden Hall (*tōkondō*) was built in 726 by Emperor Shōmu for his aunt, Empress Genshō, in order to cure a disease that she had contracted. The building of votive temples of that type is characteristically Buddhist. As might be expected, a triad of the Buddha of Medicine and his two attendants was installed there. It is reported that a painting of the Buddha in nirvāṇa, which was originally in the Yamashina Chapel, was also installed in this building.

The Five-storied Pagoda (*gojūnotō*) was erected south of the Eastern Golden Hall in 730 on the wishes of Emperor Shōmu's consort, Kōmyō Kōgō, and together the two buildings formed one single unit surrounded by a wall cut by two gates on the western side. Though this pagoda was completed in only one year, work on the four groups of statues installed in it was completed a few years later. One of those groups of images, which depicted the Pure Land of Maitreya, was placed on the northern inner side of the pagoda; a group installed on the eastern side represented the Pure Land of the Buddha of Medicine; the one placed on the southern side represented Śākyamuni, and the western group represented the Pure Land of Amitābha. The four groups, which were arranged in the same manner as those still seen in the Hōryūji, contained as many as eighty-three figures.

The Western Golden Hall (*nishi kondō*) was built on the wishes of Kōmyō Kōgō for her mother, Tachibana no Michiyo, who died in 733. Ceremonies held on the first anniversary of her death in 734 took place in front of the following statues: a large statue of Śākyamuni flanked by two attendant bodhisattvas and surrounded by his Ten Great Disciples, and representations of Rahula, Brahma, Indra, the Four Celestial Kings, and the Gods and Demons of the Eight Kinds (*Hachibu-shū*).

The Refectory (*jikidō*) was built some time before 744, but no other details are available on it. The same is true for the bathhouse (*ōyuya*).

It is not known when the Lecture Hall (*kōdō*), on which work was initiated shortly before Fuhito's death in 720, was completed; that may have been in 746, when statues were installed in it. On the occasion of the first anniversary of the death of Fujiwara no Fusasaki's spouse, Muro no Ōkimi, in 746, her son Matate dedicated a statue of Amoghapāśa (*Fukū-kensaku Kannon*) to the Lecture Hall, but the main image was changed in 791 when a triad of Amitābha and his attendant bodhisattvas was dedicated on the occasion of the first anniversary of the death of Fujiwara no Oto-muro, Emperor Kammu's consort. It has been thought that the statue of Fukū-kensaku Kannon that had been installed in the Lecture Hall was transferred to the Southern Round Hall in 813, but recent evidence calls this into doubt.[58] What seems clear is that the Southern Round Hall was

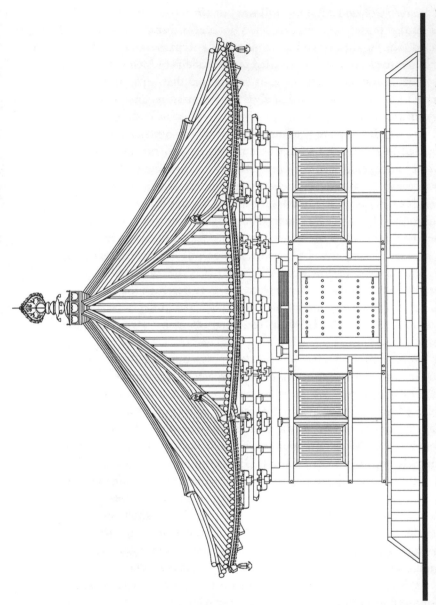

Figure 3. The Hokuendō (Northern Round Hall) of the Kōfukuji. Computer-assisted rendering of a figure contained in Nishikawa Kyōtarō, "Kōkei to Unkei," in Nishikawa Kyōtarō and Tsujimoto Yonezaburō, ed., *Hokuendō to Nan'endō no shozō* (Tokyo: Iwanami Shoten, 1974), 1.

built and dedicated in 813 (the ceremony of dedication was probably performed by Kūkai) and that its main image was *Fukū-kensaku Kannon*, which was surrounded by representations of the Four Celestial Kings. Later, the latter statues were replaced by representations of Zeju and Gembin, to which were added four other effigies of famous monks. This group of statues came to be known as the "Six Patriarchs of Hossō."

In 761 a building called Bark-roofed Hall of the *Tō-in* was erected for the repose of the spirit of Kōmyō Kōgō on an order issued by Emperor Junnin to Fujiwara no Nakamaro. This building housed a statue of Kannon, and some time later Nakamaro dedicated a weaving that represented the Pure Land of Kannon and a woven representation of the Pure Land of Amitābha (Japanese, Amida) for the repose of the spirit of Emperor Shōmu. The *Enryaku-ki* states that there was also installed a triad of Amitābha and his two attendant bodhisattvas. In 760 the court ordered that representations of the Pure Land be made in each province and dedicated in each provincial nunnery (*kokubun-niji*).

A building of the same type but with a tiled roof was erected in 764 to house one hundred thousand small clay stupas and a triad of Amitābha for the repose and "rebirth in the Pure Land" of Fujiwara no Momoyoshi's spouse. At the same time a copy of the scriptures (*Issai-kyō*) was ordered to be made for the repose of the spirit of Fujiwara no Toyonari, of the former spouse of Nakamaro, and of Momoyoshi's mother, Lady Taima.

Finally, a building called Hall of Kṣitigarbha (*Jizōdō*), which was erected in 772 and dedicated to Fujiwara no Nagate, housed a triad of Amitābha and a representation of Amoghapāśa. Unless one acknowledges that the Buddha represented in the crown of that bodhisattva was mistakenly thought, at that time, to be Kṣitigarbha (as the *Keiran-shūyōshū* states), there is no explanation for the name of this hall.[59] Nagate was the central figure in the creation of the Kasuga Shrine.

The construction of the walls and gates that surround the main core of the Kōfukuji is not recorded in any extant document. All work on the temple compound apparently ceased betwen 772 and 813, the period that started with the events surrounding Dōkyō's exile, the move of the capital from Heijō-kyō to Nagaoka and, finally, to Heian-kyō (Kyoto) in 794.

Thus the main core of the Kōfukuji was built during the Nara period. Texts of the Heian period and thereafter refer to this core as the Main Temple (*honji*), to distinguish it from the other major parts of the Kōfukuji that were added subsequently. All buildings and all major representations of the various buddhas and bodhisattvas were dedicated in commemoration of deceased leading figures of the Fujiwara house, as were also the ceremonies and ritual assemblies, the most famous of which is the Ritual

Assembly of Vimalakīrti (*Yuima-e*), which is dedicated to the spirit of Kamatari.

The classical documents describe these undertakings as manifestations of filial piety, but it is also apparent that sociopolitical hierarchy was observed, because not all members of the house were treated in the same manner. The statues that were offered on various occasions give us direct information about the Buddhist flavor of the universe of meaning of the Fujiwara house of the time. There are several such flavors: representations of Maitreya (*Miroku bosatsu*) indicate that there was belief in the Buddha of the Future on the part of the Fujiwara house from the very beginning, a belief that was to remain a salient feature of its creeds for centuries. The same can be said of the other images dedicated during the early stages of the history of the temple: Amitābha (*Amida*), Avalokiteśvara (*Kannon*), Kṣitigarbha (*Jizō*), and also, interestingly enough, Śākyamuni (*Shaka-muni*), whose cult was not celebrated in other parts of Japan before the medieval period. Bhaiṣajyaguru (*Yakushi*), the Buddha of Medicine, was also represented in the temple; this was a characteristic of Fujiwara creeds in particular and of Buddhist cults in Japan in general.

These buddhas and bodhisattvas were seen as residents of a Pure Land, a transcendent realm toward which it was hoped that the deceased would move and into which they might be reborn. This suggests that the belief of the Fujiwara house of the time with regard to the Pure Land was very different from later Pure Land beliefs. The belief was always held on behalf of someone else who had passed away, and it was only during the Heian period that the Fujiwara began to build chapels for themselves and were moved by personal and fervent devotion to this or that member of the Buddhist pantheon. During the Nara period, people did not hope that they themselves might be reborn after death in the Pure Land; rather, they performed rites and offered prayers that their deceased parents or spouses might do so. The concern of an individual Fujiwara with life after death for his or her own sake did not appear before the political position of the Fujiwara house as a whole or its various branches were threatened with destruction and intense individual competition arose within the house.

The Kōfukuji was ranked by the government as a *daiji,* "Great Temple." There were Seven Great Temples, all located in Nara: Gangōji, Hōryūji, Daianji, Kōfukuji, Yakushiji, Tōdaiji, and Saidaiji. During the Heian period there were Five Great Temples (Tōdaiji, Kōfukuji, Enryakuji, Onjōji, and Tōji); another classification was that of the Fifteen Great Temples, which included the seven listed above and the eight following ones: Shin-Yaku-shiji, Honganji (a Kyoto temple that was sometimes replaced by the Hok-keji of Nara), Tōshōdaiji, Shitennōji, Sufukuji, Gufukuji, Tōji, and Saiji.

The term *daiji* has its equivalent in India (*mahāvihāra*) and in China (*t'ai-ssu*), and although in India the term was applied to important monasteries, in China and Japan it was applied exclusively to monasteries and temples having a specific connection with the emperors.

These temples should not be confused with the state temples or provincial temples, because they tended, originally, to be private temples associated with specific lineages. The concept became somewhat blurred in Japan after the practice arose whereby certain private temples were funded by the state in virtue of the political positions of given lineages within the imperial system. It is clear, however, that most of these *daiji* were based on the concept of "Posthumous Felicity" and were built to take care of the spirits of deceased fathers, mothers, and spouses.

These temples played major social and political roles in the history of Buddhism in China and Japan: they were marks of filial piety, a "Confucian" virtue, inscribed onto the practice and understanding of Buddhism, and politically their establishment signified the evolution of the control of the state over Buddhism. In Japan, Buddhism confronted a society with an established structure of legitimacy and ritual, and Buddhists had to accommodate themselves to that structure if Buddhism was to survive. This is why it is necessary to look for organizational patterns that on the surface appear to be Buddhist but are in fact hidden patterns of organization that belong to pre-Buddhist Japan.

CEREMONIES AND RITUAL ASSEMBLIES OF THE MULTIPLEX

Although it is known that a number of ceremonies, rites, and rituals were performed at the Kasuga-Kōfukuji multiplex from its establishment, most of them were not recorded in detail, or else those documents have been lost. Sumptuous ceremonies were performed at the temple long before rituals came to be performed at the Kasuga Shrine; in fact, even if 768 is accepted as the date of the foundation of the shrine, it is likely that the rites performed at the shrine for some period were rather small in scale and totally house oriented. It is only after the Fujiwara house established its political superiority at the beginning of the Heian period that rituals were codified and unified, not only for Kasuga, but for all major shrines that came to be sponsored at that time by the imperial house.

The Kasuga Shrine developed spring and autumn rites during the Nara period. These rites were organized by the leading member of the Fujiwara house (the position of chieftain had not yet been created), with funds from the Kashima and Katori shrines in Hitachi. During the early Heian period two major developments occurred: first, a reformulation of the ritual processes by the Jōgan Codes (*Jōgan-gishiki*) and the Procedures of the Engi era (*Engi-shiki*), and second, the sponsorship by the state of shrines that originally belonged to individual lineages but that were put under the aegis of the imperial household for the purpose of unification. This might seem to be a straightforward phenomenon, but the Fujiwara house was behind these formulations and its purpose was to establish almost complete control over the political and liturgical institutions of the state.

The Jōgan Codes, which were promulgated in 869 and 871, reveal marked changes in the ritual world of that time. Their formulation of the ritual process in the Kasuga Grand Rite (*taisai*) is as follows:

At dawn on the day of the Rite, a member of the Office of the *kami* of Heaven and Earth, accompanied by a young girl whose duty is abstention and purity [*mono-imi*], cleans the interior of the shrine. Priestly officials [*kambe*] decorate the shrines, placing the shrine-treasures in front of the four shrines as well as near the fence running in front of them. The various officials [*shoshi*] make offerings as usual.

The Chieftain of the House enters the sacred area of the shrine through the Southern Gate in the western corridor, and goes to his seat in the Outer Area [*ge-in*]. Following him, members of the Fujiwara house who hold the sixth rank and below approach and take their seats, and write their names on the tablets [*fuda*]. Tablets, brushes, and inkstones must be prepared in advance by the officials.

During that time the sacral woman [*saijo*] leaves her carriage and approaches the shrine. She passes through the Northern Gate in the western corridor. By then those who hold the rank of *tayu*, and who preceded her, have formed a single line. . . . After the sacral woman reaches her seat, those holding the rank of *tayu* leave, while those who hold the rank of *naishi* go to their seats.

At this point the head of the *uchi-kura* orders that the pendant strip offerings [*nusa*] be displayed on a shelf outside the gate, and he waits there for the Elders of the house and of the court. Those who hold the rank of *naishi* take their seats by the shrines and inspect the offerings.

Then the sacral woman removes her travel garments and puts on a ceremonial dress. She then enters the sacred area of the shrine and goes to her seat. The head of the *uchi-kura* takes the pendant strips, enters the shrine area, and displays them on a high shelf in front of the fence. He withdraws after bowing twice. Then the two palace emissaries do the same, whereupon the members of the Fujiwara house take the strips and display them on lower shelves, each member of the house bowing twice and then retiring.

At that point four priests advance, take the pendant strips from the *uchi-kura*, pass them over to the *mono-imi* girl, and retire. The girl then advances to offer the strips in front of the shrines, and withdraws. The four priests each take a straw mat, which they spread on the ground in front of the shrines, and withdraw. Thereafter, the members of the Fujiwara house who hold the fifth rank and below take, two by two, the tables containing the food offerings, and form a line starting at the Eastern Hall. The priests, two by two, take casks of rice-wine, pass beyond the fence, and display them in front of the shrines: one in front of the first shrine, one in front of the second shrine, and one between the third and fourth shrine. Members of the court who hold the fifth rank and below withdraw and return to their seats in the Outer Area, while those of the *naishi* rank and below enter the sacred area and remove the covers from the food offerings. They then pour rice-wine and offer two cups for each shrine. This being done, they withdraw to their seats within the fence in the courtyard in front of the shrines.

At this point the Chieftain and members of the house, as well as the emissaries of the court, advance and take their seats. Then four sacred horses and eight race horses are aligned in front of the shrines. The Major-General (*shōshō*) of the Palace Guard, as well as the Head of the Palace Stables, walk in front of the horses. Then the head-priests put on cotton wigs, take their seats to intone the *norito*, do double reverence in front of the shrines, and clap their hands four times. This being completed, they go to their seats in the Naorai Hall. Then the priests perform the rite [known as] *sansai*. At this point the Officer of the Stables leads the horses eight times around the shrines. . . . Thereafter the sacral woman returns to the Inner Room at the Western Gate and changes her clothes. The ceremony of return to her Pavilion [*ton'ya*] is the same as at that of her entry.[60]

This is the oldest extant account of the Grand Rite of Kasuga, which is still performed today according to the same rules, with the major exception that both the sacral woman and the *mono-imi* girl have been removed, which has been the case, apparently, for several centuries. It is not possible, at this point, to offer a date for the cessation of the presence of women in the Grand Rite, but it is quite certain that sacral women played an important role at Kasuga in the early period. The main figure in the Grand Rite was the chieftain of the Fujiwara house, who was represented by a symbol of purity linked by blood; in other words, the sacral woman played for that house the same role as the role customarily played by *mono-imi*, or that role might have been directly related to the accent that came to be put, in the Heian period, on the Fujiwara mothers of emperors. The *mono-imi*'s role, the observation of absolute purity, is relatively easier to understand because it is still widely observed in several parts of the country. She must be pure, having known neither menstruation nor sexual contact. It may have been under the influence of Buddhism that women disappeared from such rites, because the Buddhist tradition considered women to be essentially impure.

The *Engi-shiki*, which was compiled in 927, provides the text of the ceremonial formula (*saimon*) that was chanted by the head priest during the Grand Rite. It is reproduced below in Felicia Bock's translation:

> By the august decree of the Sovereign, in great awe, we humbly speak in the awesome presence of the four mighty *kami*, Takemi-kazuchi-no-mikoto who resides in Kashima, Iwainushi-no-mikoto who resides in Katori, Ame-no-koyane-no-mikoto and Himegami, who reside in Hiraoka, thus: In the manner in which the mighty *kami* have ordained, we have planted firmly the pillars of the shrine in the rocks deep under Mt. Mikasa of Kasuga. The crossed beams thereof reach toward the heavens, offering a shelter from the gaze of heaven and from the blazing sun. And in it we have prepared and offered these treasures for the *kami*: august mirror, august sword, august bow, august spear, and august horse; and for sacred raiment, we offer up bright cloth, shining cloth, soft cloth, and coarse cloth. And we place in rows the first-fruits sent in tribute from the provinces in all directions as offerings: the products of the blue sea, things wide of fin and narrow of fin, seaweeds from the deep and seaweeds from the shore, and even unto the sweet herbs and the bitter herbs from mountain and moor. Let the offering jars be filled with *sake* to their brims, yea, let the bellies of the rows of jars be full, and let all manner of goods be heaped up like a range of hills.
>
> Let the surname, clan-rank-title, Court rank, and position of those who are shrine-chiefs be made known. May the choice of great offerings which we present be pleasant offerings, be abundant offerings, and may they be received in tranquillity and pleasure. So we pray as we raise our words of praise to the four mighty *kami*. Since we serve thus by our worship, we pray that now and in the future our Sovereign may reign in tranquillity and be blessed with a prosperous reign. May it be firm like a solid rock, eternal as an enduring rock, and be caused to flourish. May all the princes and court nobles of all the families from each locality who have participated and served here be at peace. May the August Sovereign flourish in his palace more than the plants

and trees which grow, for a reign that prospers, thus we pray as we humbly raise our words of praise.[61]

The contents of this text reveal with no ambiguity that by the Engi era (901–21), the Grand Rite had come to be sponsored by the state and was no longer simply an *uji* ritual for ancestral and tutelary *kami*. Not only do the words ancestral *kami* or tutelary *kami* never appear in it, but the main purpose of the text is to ensure a prosperous reign for the emperor. Furthermore, the relation between the center and the periphery is made quite clear: food offerings may be of a religious nature, but they also symbolize the power of the state and of the Fujiwara lineage. Indeed, the "four mighty *kami*" also form a body that needs to be fed and clothed by tribute from the nation, just as the imperial body and that of its main supporting lineage must receive tribute from all provinces. The Kasuga Grand Rite functioned unequivocally as an index of relations between the state and the Fujiwara lineage, and between the center and the periphery.

The Kōfukuji and the Kasuga Shrine became state institutions on the condition that they reciprocate by supporting the imperial institution. This relation of reciprocity was grounded in a system of metaphors that associated the center and the periphery, the imperial lineage and the Fujiwara house, the ranks of members of the house and those of their *kami*, the spheres of influence of *kami* and those of ruling houses, and later, *kami* and members of the Buddhist pantheon. The purpose of this system of metaphors was to intimate that the pantheon and the state were structurally similar, mutually supporting, and sustained by ritual. Moreover, the function of this system was to legitimize power.

Grounded as it was in metaphors regenerated by ritual in a cyclical manner, the cult could not—and would not—change as swiftly as the structures of the state and the economy did. Thus the cult tended to perpetuate itself in the forms laid in the late Nara and early Heian periods and to perpetuate imperial rule as well as certain modes of relations between the center and the periphery.

If the Kasuga Shrine symbolized the identity of the Fujiwara house and its relations with the imperial lineage, the Kōfukuji, by contrast, formulated notions regarding the salvation of individuals within the Indian-Chinese cultural contexts. It should be emphasized, however, that many of the ritual assemblies that were held at the Kōfukuji came to be performed with the specific purpose of protecting the state. Thus, the shrine and the temple formed a single multiplex in which one can identify complementary components of the sociocosmic system represented by the classical Japanese state, at the head of which the Fujiwara house attempted to maintain itself by rationalizing its position as something that it held by divine right.

Perhaps afraid that Buddhist institutions might end up sponsored solely by individual lineages, in 783 the Japanese government issued a decree forbidding the further construction of private temples. Indeed, the fact that those temples had a private financial base turned out to be an obstacle to the spread of Buddhism in Nara Japan; that is, Buddhism had few chances of surviving in a foreign culture as an *uji* phenomenon, especially if its main purpose was to take care of the dead. The question was, therefore, to decide who should support Buddhism. The major houses supported it originally for reasons that had everything to do with the creation of ceremonial centers: indeed, as has been discussed, the Outer Capital of Heijō-kyō was the result of the creation of the Kasuga Shrine, the Kōfukuji, and the Tōdaiji. When the capital was moved from Heijō to Heian, one of the salient differences to appear was that thereafter Buddhism was supported exclusively by the state. It was as members of that state that houses continued to support Buddhism in general, while, at the same time, they continued to develop their own house temples. In this light, at the level of the state Buddhism played exactly the same function that had been played by shrines at the house level.

Buddhism could not develop fully within such narrow walls, and that is why heterodox figures like En-no-gyōja and Gyōki appeared and spread other forms of Buddhism to the people. Those forms of Buddhism, however, were repressed by the state orthodoxy, because as forms of popular Buddhism, they were seen as proponents of views that did not mesh structurally with those advanced by the various houses or by the state, an institution that was after all little more than a conglomerate of those houses.

When the house-oriented character of the Kōfukuji cult evolved toward a state-oriented one, a supralocal coloration appeared in its rituals. These rituals were dedicated to the welfare of the state in general, or of the emperor, who was the symbol of the state. Indeed, rituals dedicated to the Buddha of Medicine were mostly performed on request to cure a disease of the imperial person "in the name of the protection of the state."

Returning to Eric Wolf's definition of the ceremonial center, "Ceremonial centers were instruments for the generation of political, social, economic, sacred, and other spaces, at the same time as they were symbols of cosmic, social, political, and moral order,"[62] it might be argued that the Kasuga-Kōfukuji multiplex fit that definition almost too well. That is, it generated the Outer Capital, which was bordered to the north and the east by temples and shrines, and contained the residences of members of the Fujiwara house and its retainers, and when the Fujiwara left, they were replaced by those who would take care of the sites of cult. It is this part of the capital that remained alive throughout history under its new name, Nara.

The Fujiwara house claimed for centuries that its political legitimacy was grounded in the myths that defined the *kami* that it worshiped, and thus the Kasuga belief system evolved as an intensely political reality. The Kasuga-Kōfukuji multiplex was generative of a social order first, because it was dedicated to ancestral and tutelary entities related to the definition of Japan's primary social division and second, because it supported that house structure as well as a particular vision of Japanese society it developed during subsequent periods of history. The multiplex also generated specific economic practices that will be discussed later in this study and are best represented by the system of landholdings and by the control of merchants' associations. The multiplex also generated a sacred space, which was suggested earlier and will be discussed later.

Yet another aspect of the role of Kasuga as a ceremonial center is that it generated a "space" for political and symbolic action on the part of the Fujiwara: if the role of Ame-no-koyane had been to attract the solar entity out of its cave of darkness, the descendants of that *kami* were destined to attempt to do the same, at a metaphorical level, in society: that is, to support the continued governance of Japan by the imperial lineage. Had the Fujiwara house dreamed of any other possible sociopolitical arrangement, it would have been prevented from realizing its implementation because of the very nature of the cult. Encoded as it was by myth and ritual, Fujiwara behavior was also grounded in blood, a symbol of direct importance, because marriage into the imperial lineage was the guarantor of continued political power; the Fujiwara house requested children from its *kami*. The cult was, therefore, thoroughly committed to a particular vision of the structure of power in classical Japan.

Finally, the multiplex was also the generator of "other spaces." First and foremost, the Kasuga belief system generated a cultural space. That is, it became a center for ritual, dance, music, poetry, and other aesthetic-ritual expressions of a general quest for meaning; and it also generated a space for the scholarly study of specific systems of Buddhist thought and practice. Because of these various "spaces" or arenas of behavioral definition, Kasuga also generated its own antithetic spaces: that is, its visions caused divisions.

IDEATION-ONLY AT THE KŌFUKUJI

"Ideation-Only" is the translation of the Japanese term *yuishiki*, which refers to a doctrine of the Yogācāra school of Indian Buddhism, the Japanese form of which was based at the Kōfukuji under the name *Hossō*.[63] The lineage of transmission of this school originated with the monk Maitreya, whose dates are unknown. Maitreya's disciples were from the Kashmir region of India, and two of them are especially famous: Asaṅga (Mujaku, 310–90), who authored a treatise entitled *Mahāyāna saṃparigraha śāstra* (Japanese, *Shō-daijō-ron*),[64] and his brother Vasubandhu (Seshin, 330–400), who wrote the treatise entitled *Vimśatika-karikā* (Japanese, *Yuishiki jūniron*).[65] Asaṅga's teachings were brought to China by Paramārtha (499–590), and those of Vasubandhu and several of his famous disciples— Dignāga (Jinna, 400–480), Asvabhāva (Mushō, 450–530), and Dharmapāla (Gohō, 530–61)—were brought to China by Hsüan-tsang (600–664), an eminent scholarly monk who came to be regarded as the main Chinese patriarch of the Yogācāra lineage. In 659 Hsüan-tsang's brilliant disciple K'uei-chi (Kiki, better known in Japan as Jion Daishi, 632–82) helped his master translate into Chinese the *Vijñaptimātratāsiddhi-śāstra* (Chinese, *Ch'eng wei-shih lun* and Japanese, *Jōyuishikiron*), a text that became the basis for the Hossō school and remained as its central scripture in Japan.[66]

The transmission of that school of thought to Japan occurred in successive stages that the Japanese tradition remembers as the "Four Transmissions." The first one was when the monk Dōshō (628–700), having studied in China under Hsüan-tsang, returned to Japan and took up residence in one of the major temples of Asuka, the Gangōji. Little is known about Dōshō, including the date of his ordination, even though a number of documents contain legendary accounts of his life, especially his death. He left for China in 653, together with Kamatari's elder son Jō-e, and studied under Hsüan-tsang for a duration of maybe six years, after which he returned to Japan with many scriptures and documents. He is said to have resided in the Gangōji, where he erected a meditation hall in one corner of its compound, but he left the temple for a life of wandering, during which he helped build bridges and roads, dug wells, and established river crossings. One legend says that he rebuilt a famous bridge over the Uji River. An imperial order recalled him to temple life and services at court. As was the case for Gyōki, who might have been one of his disciples, legends about Dōshō—which are found, for example, in the *Nihon ryō-i-ki* (completed around the year 822)—appear very soon after his death. According to that text, toward the end of his life Dōshō closed his room, turned his seated body in the direction of the west, and passed into the Pure Land as a great luminescence irradiated the room.[67] Dōshō is said to be the first monk to have been cremated in Japan, but archaeological excavations prove otherwise.

The second transmission of the Hossō school took place in 658 at the hands of Chitsū and Chitatsu, who also studied under Hsüan-tsang but about whom even less is known. These first and second transmissions are referred to as the southern, or Gangōji, transmissions, because before the creation of the Heijō capital all the monks initiated into the Hossō lineage by then resided in the southern part of Yamato Province. These southern transmissions were represented during the late Nara and early Heian periods by various monks, including Gyōki (668–749), Shōgu (n.d.), and Gomyō (750–834). Gomyō wrote a large number of treatises on the doctrine of the Hossō school and was one of the opponents of Saichō at the time of the debates concerning the superiority of the Hossō or Tendai vehicle of salvation.

The third transmission took place in 703 when Chihō, Chihan, and Chiyū went to China, and the fourth transmission occurred in 735, when Gembō (?–746) returned from China and subsequently settled in the Kōfukuji. These last two transmissions are known as the northern transmissions and are also called the Kōfukuji or Mikasa transmissions.

Of the four transmissions, the northern transmission by Gembō is the most important, because it was directly linked to the Kōfukuji and because it was in direct line from K'uei-chi's teachings. For several reasons the Hossō doctrine did not have much impact during the Nara period. First, the Japanese of the time did not have, and could not have had, a clear understanding of the relative positions of the diverse systems of Buddhist philosophy expressed in the massive body of scriptures that by then had been in existence for more than a thousand years. Second, the doctrine of Ideation-Only is complex, and generations passed before a comprehensive understanding of its system was realized. Even then the extent of that understanding has been questioned. Third, there remains the question of exactly what the Japanese government and intelligentsia expected from Buddhism. There is no doubt that Buddhism was a political tool as well as a cultural storehouse to the Japanese, but the exact reasons why a particular school of thought was supported by the government or by its satellite lineages are still unexplored. Although further studies are necessary before answering these questions satisfactorily, there is a possibility that the

Hossō school developed in the Kōfukuji as the result of a conscious choice on the part of the Fujiwara for two reasons, one political and the other philosophical.

On the political side, it is clear that the highest members of a society that was modeling itself on China would, upon sending their sons to Chinese monasteries, ensure that they would receive their training in monasteries governed by monks who enjoyed direct relations with members of the Chinese court, if not with the emperor himself. Hsüan-tsang, who was one of the most respected monks at the time, was very close to the Chinese court, and for that reason Kamatari sent his own son to study under him. The reason why Dōshō accompanied Jō-e may also have been political: it is reported that Dōshō's father saved various chronicles and state documents from destruction by fire when the Soga were attacked by Prince Naka no Ōe and his ally Nakatomi no Kamatari. In subsequent decades the monks who left for China were supported by the government and by Fujiwara or other aristocrats, and therefore they studied under the same masters or their disciples.

The philosophical reason for the choice of Hossō by the Fujiwara has to do with one of the central notions of the school, which is that only certain types of beings were considered to have Buddha-Nature. This elitist doctrine appealed to the aristocrats of the time.

Several eminent members of the northern transmissions who were all logicians must be mentioned, namely Gien (?–728), Gembō (?–746), and Zenju (723–97). Gembō stands out as particularly worthy of note. A member of the Ato family, he studied Hossō doctrine under Gien and left for China in 716 with an embassy headed by Abe no Nakamaro and Kibi no Makibi. He achieved some fame in the Chinese Buddhist establishment, for he received the third rank and a purple robe, which were signs of achievement at court. He returned to Japan in 735 with five thousand scriptures. In consideration of his achievements, in 736 Emperor Shōmu, a strong supporter of Buddhism, granted him ten *chō* of wet land, the revenue from one hundred households, and the services of eight lay followers. He was even allowed to go by horse to official functions and ceremonies.

Gembō was a clever politician; he allied himself with Kibi no Makibi in favor of the Tachibana house, which was then in competition with the Fujiwara house. Tachibana no Moroe was then Minister of the Left. Because Fujiwara no Fuhito's four sons died in 737, the fate of the Fujiwara house was most uncertain, and this may have been one of the reasons Gembō sided with the Tachibana and Kibi houses. The other reason was personal; that is, Gembō had gone to China with Makibi. Fujiwara no

Hirotsugu, a grandson of Fuhito, recognized, however, that the alliance between Gembō and other houses was extremely dangerous and, while in Kyushu, requested that the government remove Gembō and Makibi from office. Obtaining no satisfactory response to that request, Hirotsugu rebelled in 740, but he was defeated and put to death. Gembō continued to enjoy the support of the court for a while, and he assisted it in its efforts to build the Tōdaiji in spite of the economic difficulties that it met at that time.

In the meantime, Tachibana no Moroe failed in his attempt to move the capital from Nara to Kuni and thus secure political preeminence. Fujiwara no Nakamaro (of the southern branch of the family) became counselor in 743; he enjoyed the support of Emperor Shōmu's consort (Kōmyō Kōgō, of Fujiwara birth) and worked to remove all opposition to his family at court. Moroe's power thus vanished, and Gembō, suddenly without influence, was sent to Kyushu in 745 under the pretext of being given the honor of heading the Kanzeonji; however, he was dispossessed of all the gifts given to him earlier by the court. Later the government recalled Gyōki from his semidisgrace to replace Gembō, in order to gain popular support for the erection of the Tōdaiji, which, thanks to the unexpected discovery of gold, was completed in 752. We have no information concerning Gembō's exile; the *Shoku-Nihongi* states simply that Gembō behaved in a manner that did not befit his ecclesiastic position and that he died in 746 as he was trying to escape. Legend says, however, that he was killed by the angry spirit of Fujiwara no Hirotsugu, who tore off Gembō's head and threw it onto the roof of the Kōfukuji.[68]

Thus, even though Gembō had been instrumental in establishing some of the deep links between Buddhism and the state, links that profoundly marked the history of Japan, his relation with the Fujiwara house had been extremely bad. It is an irony that he was one of the transmitters of the Hossō doctrines at the Kōfukuji.

The case of Gembō, a prelate who nourished political ambitions, was not unique to those times, precisely because of the type of sociopolitical and liturgical structures that were defined earlier in this chapter. Shortly after Gembō's time, Dōkyō, who was also a Hossō monk, attempted to turn Japan into another type of theocracy and backed his claim with the authority of no less a divinity than Hachiman. Fujiwara no Nakamaro saw in Dōkyō's support by Empress Kōken exactly the same danger that Hirotsugu had seen some twenty years earlier in the case of Gembō. Nakamaro rebelled in 764, but he was forced to flee and was killed, together with his family, on the shore of Lake Biwa.[69] It took a counteroracle from the Usa Hachiman Shrine—which was delivered to Wake no Kiyomaro, who was allied with Fujiwara no Momokawa, one of Hirotsugu's brothers—to deny Dōkyō any chance of usurping the throne. Dōkyō was exiled after the death of the empress who had given him her favors, and he died in 772.[70] Twelve years later, the capital was moved to Nagaoka, and then to Heian.

Thus, in order to consolidate their position within the state, various branches of the Fujiwara house had to fight—at least twice during the short Nara period—the political power of Hossō monks. Both Hirotsugu and Nakamaro rebelled against them and lost their lives. Gembō and Dōkyō, who were versed in a doctrine that states that the world is nothing but a construct of the mind, ended their lives in exile.

CONSTRUCTS OF THE MIND

Characterized by scholars as idealistic, the Hossō school is grounded in scriptures and commentaries that are exceedingly obscure and difficult.[71] Since the Japanese lineages did not add any significant developments to Hossō philosophy over the centuries, a brief exposition of its main tenets as they are offered by the school's central scripture, the Ch'eng wei-shih lun (Jōyuishikiron) of Hsüan-tsang, is adequate to the present consideration.

The Hossō school places itself squarely in the middle area between what it considers to be two opposite and wrong views: one is represented by the "realistic" schools, which hold that phenomena exist entirely on their own and are independent from the mind that perceives them, and the other is represented by the school of Emptiness, which holds that both phenomena and the mind that perceives them are devoid of any reality or self-nature. Objecting to those radical (as it saw them) conceptions, the Hossō school claims to take a median view according to which the phenomenal world is based on a transformation and manifestation of consciousness and is considered to be a mere subjective elaboration that is not different from a dream. Hence the name Ideation-Only.

Much of the doctrine is an attempt to elaborate a philosophy of consciousness and its correspondent epistemology, and in that effort it posited three major distinctions: six "consciousnesses" that perceive spheres of objects and correspond to the five organs of perception, plus a center that provides gross analysis of data; one "consciousness" that cogitates and deliberates; and a final "consciousness" that acts as a storehouse that contains all the seeds that mature into the realistic illusion that all people share according to their deeds and that they call existence. This view of consciousness was linked to the theory of moral retribution, and thus it was intimately related to a philosophy of action. Indeed, the storehouse consciousness, said to manifest itself perpetually like a torrent and to be influenced by passions and attachments, is renounced when one attains the state of a saint who enters nirvāṇa. It is also called "maturation," because it holds the fruit of retribution that will determine which of the three spheres of existence, which of the six destinations, and which womb an individual will be reincarnated into.

It can easily be imagined that a brief description such as that offered above would have attracted aristocrats who believed that they were born into a higher realm of existence by virtue of their own or of their ancestors' past deeds, and who had an aesthetic inclination to consider existence to be an ephemereal phenomenon that was like a dream. Indeed, that is the view of life that was most often pronounced in their poetry, their art, and their spiritual life. It is not surprising, then, that they seemed to live, especially in the medieval period, in a dreamworld. This is seen clearly in the *Kasuga gongen genki*, a magnificent painted scroll that was dedicated by the Fujiwara house to its *kami*.[72] The text that accompanies the paintings is structured around forty-two dreams depicting "reality." To the minds of many members of the Fujiwara house, dreams were so real that reality deserved to be called a dream.

And yet the Hossō school, while claiming to belong fully to the doctrinal body of Mahāyāna Buddhism, held the notion that few human beings possess the seed that germinates into Buddhahood. This belief clashed with the teaching that the other schools of Mahāyāna thought considered to be the *sine qua non* for inclusion in that branch of Buddhism: namely, the belief in possession of the seed of Buddhahood not only by all animate beings, but also by all inanimate beings. At the end of the eighth century this point of doctrine caused serious debates between scholarly representatives of, on the one hand, the Hossō tradition, and, on the other, Saichō (767–822), the founder of the Tendai lineage. As noted earlier, several Nara clerics had become so deeply involved in politics that they met a fierce resistance on the part of the members of houses such as the Fujiwara, who were afraid that the imperial system and, consequently, the status of the houses that supported that system, might be replaced by a theocracy centered at Buddhist institutions. The events that led to the exiles of Gembō and Dōkyō were somewhat reminiscent of those that had led to the downfall of the Soga clan earlier in history, and there were good reasons to fear that the structure of the state, as it had been envisioned by the politicians who introduced the System of Codes, might crumble, unless the position of Buddhism in society were clearly defined and the tradition subjugated to the state.

Thus, as has often been pointed out, one of the reasons for the decision to move the capital from Heijō to Nagaoka and from there to Heian-kyō

was to reorganize the state's relation with the Buddhist clergy and institutions. Indeed, even though the general population of Heijō moved to
Heian-kyō, the temples were ordered to remain in Heijō, and the emperor
of the time, Kammu, did not build any temples in Heian. He did have
religious counselors, however, among whom was Saichō (767–822), who
had been trained in Heijō but who abandoned the city for the same reasons
for which the capital was to be moved a few years later. Saichō also opposed
the doctrinal views held by the prelates of the Heijō temples. There is little
doubt that as Saichō gained influence at the Heian court, the rejected
Buddhist establishment viewed him with jealousy, and when he attempted
to mark his complete independence from the Heijō temples by requesting
the creation of a platform of ordination based on Mahāyāna principles,
those temples mounted a major and bitter opposition to him. Indeed, the
platform of ordination for monks and nuns, which was at the Tōdaiji, not
only served to ensure the proper training of the clergy but it also played
an important political role: it was a means whereby the state controlled the
number of monks and nuns. The Heijō temples realized that if a new
platform was created on Mount Hiei, their control over the clergy would
vanish. The new platform was granted shortly after Saichō's death in 822.[73]

From the Nara period, rituals performed in major shrine-temple multiplexes were funded by the state for the express purpose of protecting the
state structure. This is most evident in the Kasuga-Kōfukuji multiplex, in
which a close relation between the shrine—which symbolized the structure
of the state under the System of Codes—and the temple developed for the
specific purpose of protecting the state and the Fujiwara house, and at which
rituals were structured to symbolize that protection.

The move of the capital to Heian-kyō, however, marked a fundamental
change of attitude toward Buddhism on the part of the state. The Tendai
and Shingon schools, which were established in Heian around the beginning of the ninth century, were forced to present arguments showing that
their establishment was needed not only for the pursuit of spiritual matters
but also for the protection of the state (*chingo-kokka*). To that end, Kūkai
(774–835) offered, in several of his writings, forceful arguments in favor
of sponsorship by the state. The Heian period, however, marked the
beginning of a long and complicated relationship between the imperial
system and the Buddhist establishment.[74]

2 Kasuga *Daimyōjin*
Protector or Ruler?

> My abode is located
> Where the deer live,
> South of the Capital
> Amid floating clouds
> Over Mount Mikasa.
> *Kasuga gongen genki*, Scroll #1

As the years passed after the creation of the Kasuga Shrine and the Kōfukuji, the cultic centers evolved into a major unified institution in which the relation between the shrine and temple components of that multiplex was symbolized by associations established between the *kami* of the shrine and the buddhas and bodhisattvas of the temples. The production of those associations was accompanied by the development of a complex, stratified bureaucracy within the multiplex, the population of which grew to form a major city. Concomitantly, the character of both the institution and the Kasuga cult were substantially transformed: in addition to the role of protector of the Fujiwara house the multiplex came to govern the entire province of Yamato, and at the same time, the cult changed from being an aristocratic one to a popular one. The evolution of the cult is evidenced in part by the decreasing number of significant references that were made to the various divinities of Kasuga in distinction from the buddhas and bodhisattvas of the Kōfukuji; instead, a different numinous entity called Kasuga *daimyōjin* appeared. This entity, the character and identity of which are at least at first sight elusive, became the overall symbol of the multiplex, the cult, and Yamato Province. Its manifestation was coeval with the unification of the multiplex, which oversaw the unity of Yamato Province, the Hossō lineage of Buddhism, and some affairs of the Fujiwara house. It also presided over the development of Nara as a sacred city.

This chapter will investigate the processes whereby these developments came about. Beginning with a brief analysis of the function of temples that were built within the compounds of shrines (*jingūji*), the chapter will examine the nature and significance of the associations of the *kami* of the shrines with the buddhas and bodhisattvas of the temples and then consider the entity called Kasuga *daimyōjin*. This will be followed by a discussion

71

of the organization of the shrines and temples in the Kasuga-Kōfukuji multiplex and the members of that institution.

THE *JINGŪJI* PHENOMENON

The establishment of Buddhist temples within the compounds of shrines represents an early stage of the relations between Buddhism and the indigenous tradition. Those relations, which seem to have been clearly defined, differed qualitatively from subsequent relations between "Shinto" and "Buddhism."

During the eighth century a large number of temples were built on the grounds of shrines, some by monks who had relations with the Kōfukuji. As early as 749, for example, a *jingūji* was built at Kashima by an itinerant monk (*yūgyō-sō*) named Mangan, who also built the *jingūji* of the Tado Shrine. Little is known about this figure, whose name appears mostly in the context of the creation of this type of institution. Intriguingly, he seems to have had some rapport with the Kōfukuji. Subsequently, a certain Kenkei, who was originally from the Kōfukuji, erected a three-storied pagoda in Tado in 780. This Kenkei wrote the biography of Fujiwara no Muchimaro, and therefore he belonged in all probability to the Buddhist establishment (it is reported that he was among those who welcomed Ganjin upon his arrival in Japan), but apparently he left established Buddhism to become an itinerant monk. He reported in the aforementioned biography that Muchimaro erected the Kehi *jingūji*. According to Miyai Yoshio, the *jingūji* of the Taga and Okushima shrines were built by monks who had some relation to the Kōfukuji and the Fujiwara house.[1] Tokuitsu (dates unknown), a Kōfukuji monk famous for his debates with Saichō, most likely built the mountain temple of Tsukuba in Hitachi Province.

Though there are precious few, if any, documents on the structure and functions of *jingūji*, it appears that they were built by powerful families that ruled local districts and that Buddhist clerics came to administer the affairs of many of the shrines at which *jingūji* were built. It also appears, on the basis of stories contained in the *Nihon ryō-i-ki*, that the *kami* worshiped in those shrine-temples were regarded as beings that were inferior to the buddhas and in need of salvation, just as human beings were to be saved by the doctrines and practices of Buddhism.[2] The practice of reading Buddhist scriptures for the benefit of local indigenous *kami* (*shinzen-dokkyō*) may have arisen in the *jingūji*. The role of the *jingūji* was very different from that played by the *kokubunji*, the provincial monasteries for monks and nuns: whereas the *kokubunji* focused their efforts on the education of the populace and were created by the state, the *jingūji* applied their energies to the salvation of the *kami* and were built by individual families. The *kokubunji* and other Buddhist monasteries, in turn, set up shrines dedicated to the divinities, spirits, and demons that protected their compounds, but those beings, which were referred to by the generic name *chinju* ("protectors"), should not be confused with the *kami* worshiped at *jingūji*, because they are not of the same origins or character. It appears that administrative responsibility for the *jingūji* was held by district offices, not by the provincial government or the main temples in the capital, even though the Kōfukuji and other major temples may have played a role in the early development of the *jingūji*. The *jingūji* were, therefore, essentially local phenomena that represented early efforts on the part of Buddhist monks to control worship and unify creeds. In any case, many *jingūji*, even those erected on the grounds of major shrines, fell into disrepair during the Heian period. This indicates that the original role of these institutions did not develop to any important degree, for reasons that remain yet to be determined but that may be related, on the one hand, to the slow emergence of combinatory rituals and, on the other, to the efforts on the part of shrines to take some distance from the temples.

A *jingūji* (the Fukai-den) was built in the compounds of the Kasuga Shrine perhaps in the early Heian period, but it did not play a significant role even though it remained in the main shrine enclosure until the end of the nineteenth century. One tradition has it that the Fukai-den was built by Fuhito, and another claims that it was erected by Kūkai, but both traditions seem to be spurious. The Kōfukuji's role in relation to the Kasuga Shrine was not that of a *jingūji*, nor should Kasuga be thought of as a *chinju* shrine of the Kōfukuji. The relations between Kasuga and the Kōfukuji were based on the principle of reciprocity. Statements to this effect were repeatedly made in the course of history. For example, the *Fusōryakki* states the following for the year 1093: "Kasuga *myōjin* protects the Kōfukuji, and the temple supports Kasuga *myōjin*. Though one uses here the term shrine and there the term temple, they are one and the same. A misfortune for the shrine is inevitably one for the temple."[3]

The practice of reading Buddhist scriptures in front of representations of the *kami*, for which documentary evidence is available for the year 794 in Kyushu, developed in Kasuga as well: the *Vimalakīrti-nirdeśa sūtra* was read as early as 859 in front of the four shrines of Kasuga. That date is important, for it is at that time that the four Kasuga shrines were erected as we know them today and state-sponsored rites were instituted. The *jingūji* of Kasuga must have been erected for that occasion. It may be a mistake, however, to look for the rationale for the relation between the shrine and the temple in this type of religious phenomena alone, because the role of the Kasuga *daimyōjin* as it emerged during the Heian period seems to have been to protect a certain vision of the Fujiwara house as well as the Hossō lineage of Buddhism housed in the Kōfukuji. Had it been forced to survive on its own doctrinal and ritual merits, the Hossō lineage might have disappeared, for the Fujiwara who ruled Japan from the capital of Kyoto (Heian-kyō) were more interested in Tendai and Shingon doctrines and rituals, and later in Pure Land practices, than they were in the abstruse teachings of Hossō. Because of the Kasuga Shrine's function of legitimating the structure of the Fujiwara house, however, and because of the importance of the Kōfukuji's cults dedicated to the deceased leaders of that house, the shrine-temple multiplex continued to receive the political and economic support of the Fujiwara. The Kōfukuji claimed that the Kasuga Shrine was to serve a function that might be termed "protective" vis-à-vis the temple, a function in which one may see traces of the *chinju* and *jingūji* phenomena but that evolved well beyond their original limits.

THE ASSOCIATIONS BETWEEN *KAMI* AND BUDDHAS/BODHISATTVAS

The Japanese term *shimbutsu-shūgō* is frequently translated into English as "syncretism," but it is better translated as "associations between *kami* and buddhas/bodhisattvas." This technical term, which indicates the association of the particular *kami* of a shrine to a specific buddha or bodhisattva of an adjacent temple, is a territory-specific phenomenon that varies with each cultic center of Japan. The component *shin* does not refer to Shinto but to *kami*, which is the Japanese reading of the graph read *shin* in Chinese, and the component *butsu* does not refer to *bukkyō* (Buddhism), but to a buddha or a bodhisattva. The word *association* is used not only because it is the precise translation of the term *shūgō*, but also because connections between the members of the native and foreign pantheons were more often than not grounded in linguistic associations in which the rationale for the relation was sought. The Japanese reading of the term *gō* in *shūgō* is *awase*, a term found very frequently in Heian literature: for example, *e-awase* (painting associations), *uta-awase* (poetry associations), *kō-awase* (incense associations), and the like. The component *shū* (*narai*) means "assimilation."

It is crucial to be aware that the expression *shimbutsu-shūgō* does not designate a syncretic blending of abstract entities such as Shinto and Buddhism, whatever those may have been in the early days, nor does it designate loose mixtures without rationale. Unfortunately, some scholars understand it in that way. For example, Edward Seidensticker declares flatly in his introduction to *The Gossamer Years* that the religion of the Fujiwara house was "a hopelessly incoherent mishmash of Shinto, Buddhism, Confucianism, necromancy and witchcraft," and a "curious jumble."[4] With due respect to this eminent scholar of Heian literature, his statement is not only an exaggeration but is quite false. What is found in Japanese cultic centers is not a hopeless incoherence but an extremely concrete combinatory phenomenon in which the various elements of the combination retained some of their pristine identity, their fundamental characteristics, but also gained, by accretion and interplay (it is tempting to say, by dialectic), a mass of meaning that they did not have as independent entities. Thus, for example, in some cases a *kami* gained an anthropomorphic status, while a buddha gained a specific territory in which to ground its identity and activity; and "Buddhist" monks retained essential characteristics of the native tradition, such as purification practices and attitudes toward nature, while the members of sacerdotal lineages in shrines listened to sutras. Similarly, shrines gained architectural, economic, organizational, and ritual features from temples, and vice versa.

The associations between *kami* and buddhas/bodhisattvas represented a fundamental aspect of the Japanese cultural discourse in which Indian, Chinese, and Japanese elements were combined in a subtle, complex, and structured manner. In this combinatory way, a new world of meaning and practice was created: namely, Japanese medieval culture. Furthermore, these associations served the establishment of a rationale for the state in the medieval period: they were a central aspect of the political discourse, the concept of rule, and the practice of power subsumed under the term *chingo-kokka*, "protection of the state."

Ideally the multifaceted character of the Kasuga *daimyōjin* should be studied from a variety of perspectives—historical, ritual, religious, philosophical, economic, administrative, and political—in order to do justice to it. And yet at the present level of analysis it is necessary to impose an artificial division on that phenomenon and to study the economy of the Kasuga cultic center separately from its religious functions. It should be remembered, however, that the pictures that will be drawn successively are in fact on a single canvas.

The preceding chapter suggested a rationale for early connections between shrines and temples, indicating that some functions of Buddhist ceremonies and rituals might have been similar—in intent if not structurally, in some cases—to the functions of the rituals that had been performed in earlier times near funeral tumuli (*kofun*): "Buddhist" ceremonies were primarily matters of protocol and the enhancement of specific lineages. The major celebration of the ancestral and tutelary *kami* of the Fujiwara house, the Kasuga Grand Rite, was not originally attended by monks, not because Kasuga was "Shinto" whereas the Kōfukuji was "Buddhist," but because prelates of the Kōfukuji were, in terms of the Fujiwara house, outsiders. As outsiders they were not allowed to participate in the worship of Fujiwara ancestral *kami,* but they could organize rites for the spirits of departed members of the house, and such was in fact their major function.

This situation changed when members of the Fujiwara house began to take Buddhist orders and became the major prelates of the Kōfukuji, at which they organized combinatory rituals in newly built edifices dedicated to Kasuga *daimyōjin.* The best example of this type of ritual performance is the *On-matsuri* of the Wakamiya Shrine, which was originally, in part, a peasant ritual that the Fujiwara clerics co-opted. It was organized by the temple's lay members (the *shuto*) and the shrine's lay members (the *jinin*), but it was administered and ritually governed by Fujiwara-born ecclesiastics of the Kōfukuji.[5] It seems that the creation of the Wakamiya in 1135 served, at least in part, to unify the *shuto* and the *jinin* and to allow monks to penetrate the ritual affairs of the shrines. The sponsorship of ritual was always associated with power. If one of the major functions of the Grand Rite of Kasuga in the early days was the unification of the Fujiwara house by way of rituals dedicated to its ancestral and tutelary *kami,* then a central function of the Wakamiya celebration was the unification of the populace of Yamato Province by way of rituals directed to a divinity related by a "family" tie to the combined entities that were worshiped by the Fujiwara. Viewed in this light the Wakamiya cult and the processes of its popularization, which cannot be understood without an exposition of the character of the associations between the *kami* of the shrine and the buddhas/ bodhisattvas of the temple, become more clear.

The first penetration of the grounds of the Kasuga Shrine by Kōfukuji monks had to do with a ritual matter for which precedents had been set in the eighth century in other shrines and *jingūji,* namely the recitation of Buddhist scriptures inside the shrine compounds. The earliest documented incidence of this occurred in 859, when a ceremony called *Chōgō-e,* an "Expanded Lecture" on the topic of the *Vimalakīrti-nirdeśa sūtra,* was performed by Kōfukuji monks in the Naorai Hall of the main shrine. This hall came to be known also as *Hakkō-no-ya* because *Hokke-hakkō* ceremonies based on the *Lotus Sutra* were held there as well.[6] The *Vimalakīrti-nirdeśa sūtra* is the scripture on which the Kōfukuji's major ritual assembly, the *Yuima-e,* was based. That ritual is dedicated to Nakatomi no Kamatari, the human ancestor of the Fujiwara house.

The recitation of Buddhist scriptures at Kasuga began at exactly the same time the reorganization of the shrine's major rites took place, which is also when the architecture of the shrine was redefined in Chinese style, a phenomenon not limited to Kasuga but characteristic of all major shrines supported by the state. No attention has been paid to date to this point, despite the fact that the creation of "Shinto" rites, such as those depicted in the *Jōgan gishiki*, indicates that the concept of rule and its relation to *kami* and buddhas/bodhisattvas were undergoing major changes at the time.

Originally, Buddhist scriptures were simply chanted in front of the shrines, but during the Heian period, ceremonies, including debates that turned into ritualized discussions of those scriptures, were held as well. There are no extant descriptions of such rituals at Kasuga, but descriptions of the same type of assemblies held in the Hie Shrines at the foot of Mount Hiei, the center of the Tendai lineage, do exist.[7] The lectures on the Lotus Sutra that were held in the Kasuga Shrine by Kōfukuji monks from the year 947 on were probably similar to those that were held at the Hie Shrines. These lectures became a regular event at Kasuga and were held on the ninth day of the fourth moon and the fourth day of the ninth moon, thus paralleling the spring and autumn rites at the shrine. Furthermore, readings of the main scripture of the Hossō lineage, the *Jōyuishikiron*,[8] also came to be held in front of the shrine, and are still held today. The Fujiwara held this scripture in high esteem and offered copies of it to the Kasuga Shrine and the Kōfukuji on private and public occasions.

A major practice of the Kōfukuji monks that evolved during the Heian period and had a substantive impact on the development of the *kami*-buddha/bodhisattva associations and of the cult at large is known as *komori*, or *sanrō*. Those terms, which could be translated "ascetic seclusion," refer to a practice that involved all scholarly monks (*gakuryo*) who participated in ceremonies and rituals at the temple and the shrine. Some time before a ritual was to be held, the monks would leave their temple and seclude themselves, for a period that varied according to the nature of the rituals or to personal inclination, in various buildings that had begun to be erected on the plain that separated the temple from the shrine toward the end of the Heian period. In those pavilions, or huts, which were called by various names (*Hannya-ya, Hondangi-ya, Nishi-ya, Kawara-ya*, and the like), Buddhist scriptures marked by seals bearing the inscription "Kōfukuji Shrine-temple of Kasuga" were kept for perusal by the monks and for ritual purposes. The *kami* of Kasuga were considered protectors of the Hossō lineage, and this protection was symbolized in part by the printing of Buddhist scriptures known as Kasuga Prints, which were kept in those huts and halls. The oldest extant edition bearing this inscription is dated 1088; others are dated 1202, 1213, and 1221.[9]

In 1148, buildings called *Hakkō-ya*, which were erected on the Tobihino

Plain, were used for preparations for the *Hokke-hakkō* ritual assemblies that were held on the basis of the Lotus Sutra and in memory of Fujiwara no Uchimaro. In those buildings, the monks underwent strict mental preparation, engaged in meditation, chanted scriptures, and waited for dreams or visions. All scholarly monks trained at the Kōfukuji were required to perform these austerities on the grounds of the plain, and it was there that associations may have been first envisioned and the mystical character of Kasuga *daimyōjin* may have originated. It seems that several buildings erected on the Kasuga Plain contained effigies of divinities, for a document dated 1133 (Chōshō 2) states: "West Pavilion. Jizō *bosatsu* enshrined."[10]

When monks had some doubts about their way of life, their careers, or other matters of importance to them, it became a normal practice for them to visit a major multiplex and wait fervently for a sign from some divinity. This practice took place in the major cultic centers from the middle of the Heian period throughout the medieval period.

The various phenomena mentioned above indicate a slow but steady association of the shrine with the temple, which was followed by the identification of associations between their respective divinities. In 1060 the Kōfukuji issued a prohibition against killing deer and other animals on the grounds of the cultic center, even if the killing was done for the purpose of making an offering to the *kami*. This indicates that in earlier days deer (which became the theriomorphic emblem of the cult) were offered at Kasuga. Members of the Fujiwara house who wanted to visit the shrine had to undergo a strict purification before departing from their residences, and this practice came to be marked by Buddhist influences: for example, it came to be forbidden to eat fish for three days before the departure. These ritual preparations for visits to the cultic center, which were known as Kasuga *shōjin* ("Kasuga ascesis"), are mentioned in various journals of the Fujiwara. For instance, the *Taiki*, the journal of Fujiwara no Yorinaga, offers the following entry for 1145: "Today I began ablutions, chanting the name of Amida. For several days, due to illness, I have been unable to chant the Name [of the Buddha], but I have refrained from approaching women and from eating fish."[11]

The way in which systematic associations were made between particular *kami* and particular buddhas and bodhisattvas at Kasuga is somewhat problematic because documents on that topic are scarce and sometimes unreliable. A great many documents disappeared in the fires that reduced the temples to ashes in 1046, 1060, 1096, and 1180, with the result that the history of the cultic center during the second part of the Heian period is difficult to reconstruct. The oldest extant classification of the associations between the main Kasuga *kami* and the main buddhas and bodhisattvas of the Kōfukuji dates from 1175, but the associations must have been established long before that date.

In evidence of this, a number of documents mention the existence of "Avatars of the Four Shrines" (*shisho gongen*) earlier in the Heian period; the *Kasuga gongen genki* states that the title of bodhisattva was given to the Kasuga *daimyōjin* as early as 937;[12] and the *Sadanobu-kō ki* (Journal of Fujiwara no Tadahira, which covers the period from 907 to 948) states that in 924 the Grand Minister of State (Tadahira) requested that a painted representation of the Kasuga "Bodhisattva" be made, and in 927 he ordered that rites dedicated to it be held.[13] The same rites were dedicated in 935 at the time of the rebellion of Taira no Masakado, and again in 938, for a reason that is unclear. The chieftain of the Fujiwara house in 1016, Michinaga, states in his diary that the only *kami* qualified as a bodhisattva was Hachiman; this statement suggests that the divinity of Kasuga was not called, by Michinaga's time, bodhisattva. Indeed, all subsequent references to that divinity are in the form of *Kasuga-daimyōjin*, "The Great Divinity of Kasuga." In contradistinction, Hachiman was called a *daibosatsu*, "Great Bodhisattva," while the *kami* of Ise came to be called Amaterasu *kōdaijin*, "Imperial Great Divinity." These different denominations represent subtle but important distinctions concerning the religious and political character of these entities.

In any case, the oldest documents that associate the Kasuga *kami* with buddhas and bodhisattvas date from the end of the Heian period, a time of extreme political and economic insecurity. At that time, the Fujiwara aristocracy was losing its control over the affairs of the state: warrior families were making their opposition to the government increasingly manifest, and two of those families, the Minamoto and the Taira, were at war. Popular unrest reached epidemic proportions, and natural disasters and pestilences reinforced the already widespread notion that the world was entering a period of general decline (*mappō*). In this context, the shrines and temples of the cultic centers considered it necessary to formalize systematic relations between the *kami* and buddhas/bodhisattvas, because those relations symbolized the unification of doctrinal, political, and economic factors. Thus, the establishment of those relations would enable the cultic centers to survive the crises befalling the country. Grounded in the rationale that supported the ideology of the state during the Heian period, these associations between *kami* and buddhas/bodhisattvas thus became an important aspect of the general state of affairs in Japanese society and culture at the end of the Heian period and throughout the medieval period.

The oldest case of a *kami*-buddha/bodhisattva association in Japan seems

Table 1. Associations according to the Ōnakatomi
Sacerdotal Lineage

Shrine Position	Kami Enshrined	Associated Buddha or Bodhisattva
First	Kashima Take-ikazuchi	Fukū-kensaku Kannon
Second	Katori Iwainushi	Yakushi *nyorai*
Third	Hiraoka Ame-no-koyane	Jizō *bosatsu*
Fourth	Aidono Hime-gami	Jūichimen Kannon
Wakamiya	—	Monjushiri *bosatsu*

Source: Miyai Yoshio, *Fujiwara-shi no ujigami-ujidera shinkō to somyō saishi* (Tokyo: Seikō Shobō, 1978), 387.

to have occurred in the Hachiman cult.[14] Hachiman received the title bodhisattva in 798 in Heijō-kyō, and it appears that the practice of giving a bodhisattva title to a non-Buddhist divinity originated there. The Hachiman cult originated in Usa in Kyushu, but Hachiman came to be the protector of the Tōdaiji as well as of the Yakushiji, a major temple of the Hossō lineage in Nara. This explains in part the subsequent linkages that evolved between the Hachiman and Kasuga cults. The Kasuga *daimyōjin*'s early bodhisattva name was *Jihimangyō bosatsu* ("Bodhisattva Rounded Practice of Compassion"), a name that would have been revealed to a monk in an oracle. *Kami* that were regarded as bodhisattvas came to be called *gongen* ("avatar"), a term that was first used in 1004 for Atsuta Shrine, in 1007 for Yoshino Shrine, and in 1083 for the Kumano Shrines. It is likely that the same practice took place in Kasuga as well as in other shrines around that time, but the term *Kasuga gongen* appears for the first time in the surviving texts only in 1170.

The documents designating specific associations between each *kami* of a shrine and each buddha or bodhisattva of an adjacent temple were set against a background of economic superiority on the part of the temples. And yet, the oldest extant reference to Kasuga in this regard was authored by the sacerdotal lineages of the shrines. That document, which is dated 1175 and signed by Ōnakatomi no Tokimori, the head-priest of the Fourth Shrine, and Nakatomi no Nobunaga, the head-priest of the Wakamiya Shrine, makes the following associations (table 1).

In this document the name of the *kami* of the first shrine is written with ideograms meaning "Valiant Thunder" and pronounced *take-ikazuchi*, which appears to indicate that the *m* of Takemikazuchi might be an ep-

Table 2. Associations according to the *Daijō-in jisha zōjiki*

Shrine	Daijō-in Transmission	Ichijō-in Transmission
First	Shakamuni	Fukū-kensaku Kannon
Second	Yakushi	Yakushi
Third	Jizō	Jizō
Fourth	Jūichimen	Jūichimen
Wakamiya	Hachiji Monju	Shō-Kannon

Source: Suzuki Ryōichi, *Daijō-in jisha zōjiki* (Tokyo: Soshiete, 1983), 61–62.

enthetic consonant, and that the *kami*'s name is pronounced Takemika-zuchi and not Takemikatsuchi. It is also noteworthy that the second *kami* is named Iwainushi, not Futsunushi; that the fourth *kami* is characterized as *aidono* ("combined shrine"); and that the name of the Wakamiya *kami*, which is designated later to be Ame-no-oshi-kumone-no-mikoto, is not specified. In the fifteenth century, when the Kōfukuji was a tripartite organization consisting of the Main Temple (*honji*), the Ichijō-in mon-zeki,[15] and the Daijō-in *monzeki*, each *monzeki* proposed a different list of associations (table 2).

The choice of the particular buddha or bodhisattva that was associated with each *kami* appears to have been the result of processes that are unclear if not baffling, but it is safe to assume that the people who were responsible for these associations did employ some type of rationale. The two sets of associations listed above (tables 1 and 2) shed some light on this question simply because the directorship of the *monzeki* was a lineage matter. That is, specific branches of the Fujiwara house were always in control of these institutions, and one has to identify which figure of the Buddhist pantheon was worshiped by which forerunner of this or that branch of the house in order to understand the *monzeki*'s varying sets of associations. In the Kasuga-Kōfukuji multiplex the associations could occur only between divinities already installed in the shrines and temples, and thus the choice was not free, nor could the associations be copied from those established at other cultic centers.

Furthermore, the rationale governing the *kami*-buddha/bodhisattva associations was grounded in the Heian aristocracy's favorite game, namely, that of making associations, which allowed an interplay between originally unrelated objects. This may have something to do with the fact that the Japanese language—often called "vernacular" in distinction from

"Chinese" (*kambun*)—itself came about as the result of systematic associations of indigenous and foreign streams, and thus the process of associating indigenous and foreign divinities was modeled on the processes of assimilation found in language. Consequently, the associations between divinities of a given cult obeyed linguistically grounded modes of combination such as association, metaphor, palindrome, anagram, and anagogy. No single theory alone elucidates the nature of the choices made in associating a given divinity to another one, and therefore research on these phenomena must be conducted cultic site by cultic site. The well-known *honji-suijaku* theory, which advocates that the *kami* are hypostases of buddhas and bodhisattvas, is sometimes inadequate, and in any case, it is so little discussed that it can hardly be considered important. It was, in fact, a practice not a theory.

/ The language in which the *kami*-buddha/bodhisattva associations were expressed is Buddhist and therefore does not necessarily reflect what must have been complex psychological, philosophical, and ritual realities. In fact, iconographic directions that were appended to lists of associations often state whether a *kami* ought to be represented in lay attire (*zoku*), in Buddhist garb (*sō*), or in feminine shape (*nyokei*), thus indicating that some *kami* came to be thought of as anthropomorphic, a development that occurred under the influence of Buddhism. The *honji-suijaku* practice suggests what could be called a parental relationship, in which the buddhas and bodhisattvas were the parents, and the *kami*, their children. That relationship echoed the character of the administrative and economic relations between temples and shrines, in which the temples usually had the upper, "parental" hand. It would seem, however, that not all associations were of that nature to begin with: some of them were simply tautological. In all probability, reasons related to the definition of the divine were involved.

THE KASUGA ASSOCIATIONS

Takemikatsuchi

Fukū-kensaku Kannon (Skt., Amoghapāśa) is the major deity of the Nan'endō of the Kōfukuji, a building erected at the beginning of the Heian period by the northern branch of the Fujiwara, which was then the dominant branch of the house. This bodhisattva was chosen as the original nature (*honji*) of Takemikatsuchi-no-mikoto by virtue of an association grounded in symbolism and iconography: Takemikatsuchi-no-mikoto was believed to have reached Kasuga mounted on a white deer, hence the choice of that animal as the sacred theriomorphic symbol of the cultic center. Ritual treatises of Buddhist iconography state that Amoghapāśa wears on its shoulders a deerskin, and thus the association was immediate, logical, and irrefutable.[16] Various painted or sculpted representations of the combined divinities of the multiplex during the Kamakura and Muromachi periods show Amoghapāśa mounted on a deer, and the symbolism of the Deer Park—the site of the first sermon of the Buddha in Benares—was used by the multiplex to indicate that Kasuga was in fact the Deer Park in Japan. Associations of this type, ruled as they were by metaphor, had tremendous consequences, especially when the metaphor was forgotten and replaced by a direct relation of identity: if Kasuga "was" the Deer Park, why bother going to India? This is what Myō-e learned through an oracle from Kasuga *daimyōjin*, and he thus decided not to travel there.[17]

Other branches of the Fujiwara house saw the original nature of Takemikatsuchi-no-mikoto as *Shaka Nyorai* (Skt., Śākyamuni), the main deity of the Central Golden Hall and the Western Golden Hall of the Kōfukuji. This choice did not exclude the association with the deer in any way, since the Deer Park symbolism was still valid. The choice of *Fukū-kensaku Kannon*, however, is clearly related to the northern branch of the Fujiwara house, whereas the choice of *Shaka Nyorai* might be related to Kamatari, the founder of the house. The latter choice may have been founded on a tradition according to which the Kōfukuji claimed to have originated in Kamatari's chapel at Yamashina, where a statue of *Shaka Nyorai* was installed. Painted "shrine mandalas" (*miya mandara*) of the Kamakura period show Takemikatsuchi-no-mikoto flanked by both *Fukū-kensaku Kannon* and *Shaka Nyorai*, thus avoiding possible conflicts between separate branches of the Fujiwara house. The documents that assign the associations put *Fukū-kensaku Kannon* first and add *Shaka Nyorai* with the caption: "one version says." These decisions might have been based on which branch of the Fujiwara house was in power at the time they were made, and since power shifted from branch to branch the emphasis on this or that buddha also shifted. On the other hand, both *Fukū-kensaku Kannon* and *Shaka Nyorai* are directly related to Fujiwara no Uchimaro: he erected the Nan'endō, and the *Hokke-hakkō* ceremony of Kasuga was dedicated to his spirit.

Futsunushi

The second association was established between Futsunushi-no-mikoto— sometimes also called Iwainushi-no-mikoto—and the Buddha of Medicine, *Yakushi Nyorai* (Skt., Bhaiṣajyaguru vaiḍūrya-prabhārāja), which is one of the more popular forms of the Buddha in classical Japan. It was widely worshiped by the aristocracy and the imperial family as the reliever of pain and suffering and was also the object of highly combinatory cults related to disease and curing. This buddha was a major feature of Fujiwara religiosity and was the main deity of the Eastern Golden Hall, in which it was flanked by its attendants—*Nikkō bosatsu* (Skt., Suryaprabha) and *Gakkō bosatsu* (Skt., Candraprabha)—which are emblems of the sun and the moon.[18] It was also surrounded by the *Jūni-shinshō* (literally, the Twelve Divine Generals: that is, Kumbhīra, Vajra, Mihira, Aḍira, Majira, Śaḍira, Indra, Pajra, Makura, Sindūra, Catura, and Vikarāla), which is a group of entities that look like warriors that protect and assist it in fighting various ailments afflicting the world. These twelve figures were also represented in the temple.

The rationale for the association of *Yakushi Nyorai* with Iwainushi-no-mikoto is different from the previous case; here, the second most important buddha of the Kōfukuji was associated with the second most important *kami* of the Kasuga Shrine. No text of any period, to my knowledge, links the Katori *kami* to medicine. During the Muromachi period a number of confraternities (*kō*) that formed in the villages of Yamato Province developed a cult to Kasuga *daimyōjin,* and some of them engaged in a cult dedicated to the twelve warrior assistants of the Buddha of Medicine. It may have been that these figures were associated in the minds of the members of the confraternities with the warring spirit of the age and with the sword spirits of Kasuga and Isonokami. In any case, the rationale for the association of the Buddha of Medicine with the second *kami* of Kasuga is obvious when one considers that the rituals dedicated to the Buddha of Medicine and ordered by the imperial house were celebrated for the sake of protecting the body of the emperor, by which was meant the metaphorical body of the state, and that was precisely the role of the sword-spirit of Katori. The *Kasuga gongen genki* states that Futsunushi-no-mikoto was associated with the Buddha of the Future, probably because of the importance of this bodhisattva in the creeds of the Fujiwara house and its presence in the Northern Circular Hall (Hokuendō) in the Kōfukuji. This appears to be an exception to the generally admitted list of associations.

Ame-No-Koyane

The third *kami,* Ame-no-koyane-no-mikoto, was associated with *Jizō bosatsu* (Skt., Kṣitigarbha). The cult dedicated to Jizō is perhaps Japan's most popular: more than half of all Buddhist statues represent this deity.[19] This "Buddhist" deity is in fact a member of the ancient Hindu pantheon, in all probability Prithivī, who symbolized the earth. As Buddhism developed in India, a number of divinities mentioned in the Veda were absorbed into the Buddhist pantheon according to specific trends and rationales. The divinity that represented earth in the Buddhist pantheon came to be called Kṣitigarbha, and the divinity that represented heaven came to be called Ākāśagarbha (*Kokuzō bosatsu*). Both are well represented in the body of Buddhist legends and rituals in China and in Japan, but Kṣitigarbha was by far the more popular of the two. There are several reasons for this popularity, but only the main one will be discussed here.

Each bodhisattva resides in a specific transcendental space, a "Pure Land" that is reached after incalculable eons of practice and after making the vow that one will put off final extinction so that one will be able to continue to save living beings. For the latter reason bodhisattvas came to be seen as the embodiments of compassion, Mahāyāna Buddhism's first and foremost virtue. Although most bodhisattvas lived in transcendental realms and manifested themselves under various guises in this world in order to save all living beings, Jizō abandoned his transcendental realm (Kharādīya) and made the Six Destinations (the various realms of existence) his abode. Nobody prayed to be reborn in his Pure Land. Furthermore, his telluric origins linked him to the forces that the Chinese and Japanese cultures associated with the earth, whether paths, territories, or underground realms. This is one of the reasons why in China this bodhisattva was regarded as a judge in hell. When hell and paradise imagery became popular in Japan, so did the cult of Jizō.

The Buddhist canon contains eight scriptures related to Jizō, five of which belong to the exoteric branch of Buddhism and three to the esoteric branch. Three of these, which are considered to be central to the Jizō cult, are called the "Three Scriptures of Jizō." They are the *Daijōdaishū Jizō jūrin-gyō*, the *Jizō-bosatsu hongan-gyō*, and the *Senzatsu zennaku gohō-kyō*.[20] The first of these was translated into Chinese by Hsüan-tsang in the seventh century and was introduced to Japan in the early eighth century. The second scripture was introduced to Japan in 738. The third scripture is an apocryph, the origins of which were said, as early as 594 in China, to be obscure; it was banned in China in 593 under the pretext that it encouraged sexual rites but was finally added to the Buddhist canon in 695. The text teaches various divinatory practices that allow people to know their past, present, and future faults and their chances of salvation. In Japan this scripture was not high on the list of readings required for monks who received state-sponsored ordinations, but it was given some importance by self-ordained monks. The text lost prominence not long after its introduction but was rediscovered in the Kamakura period.

The *Daijōdaishū Jizō jūrin-gyō* was the most important and by far the most widely read of the "Three Scriptures of Jizō." It states that Jizō's role was to appear in the interval of time between the death of the historical Buddha and the coming of the Buddha of the Future and, by way of taking various forms, to help sentient beings both during their lifetimes and in the afterlife. Jizō was invoked by many people because of his promises to provide food, clothing, treasure, medicine, and the like. His special role as the reliever of the pains of hell is established by his Fundamental Vows, which are recounted in the second scripture. That text describes the origins of this aspect of the Jizō cult in the following story: a woman whose mother had fallen into hell built a temple for the repose of her spirit, and subsequently, when she went to hell to visit her mother, the ruler of hell told her that her prayers had been efficacious and that her mother had left hell and gone to heaven. The woman then vowed to do the same for all human beings, and consequently, in her next lifetime she was reborn as Jizō.

Unlike other bodhisattvas, Jizō is considered to have been an Auditor of the Buddha (Skt., śrāvaka) and is depicted iconographically as a monk holding a wish-fulfilling gem and a staff. The oldest extant representation of Jizō, which is found in Lung-men, dates from 664, and thus the Jizō cult appears to have developed simultaneously with the cult of Amitābha (*Amida*). The first Japanese references to Jizō, which date from the latter half of the eighth century, are associated with the Kōfukuji, which seems to have introduced the Jizō cult to Japan: the Jizō Hall there was built on the orders of Fujiwara no Nagate (of the northern branch) in 771, and the first statue of Jizō was made for the Kōfukuji between 782 and 805. According to documents kept in the Shōsō-in, the first copies of scriptures related to Jizō were made between 733 and 747. None of the representations of Jizō that might have been made during the Nara period are extant; the oldest statue of Jizō, which is kept at the Kōryūji in Kyoto, is said to date from the beginning of the Heian period. The *Nihon ryō-i-ki*, which was compiled around 820, is the oldest document to identify the relation between Jizō and the Fujiwara house: Fujiwara no Hirotari, who went to hell to meet his deceased spouse, was told that in Japan the king of hell (*Emma*) was called Jizō.[21]

The Jizō cult spread quickly among both aristocrats and commoners and gradually changed in character. By the middle of the Heian period Jizō's role as savior from hell and guide to the Pure Land was emphasized, and it is in that role that Jizō is represented in some Kasuga mandalas. In other depictions of the cult, he is represented as standing on a deer.[22]

The Fujiwara house established the Jizō cult in Japan and introduced into it new elements whenever contacts with China brought new insights or practices. The association of Jizō with the ancestral *kami* of the Fujiwara house was made quite naturally, especially in the context of the beliefs in "angry spirits" (*onryō*), in which Jizō played a role, and it must be pointed out that the popularity of the Jizō cult enhanced the cult dedicated to Ame-no-koyane-no-mikoto. The main emphasis in the Jizō cult among the aristocracy was on hell and the afterlife, and in that regard it was related to the cults dedicated to the deceased members of the Fujiwara house. It is in this context, as well as in the beliefs of Fujiwara no Nagate, that the rationale of the association between Jizō and Ame-no-koyane-no-mikoto can be found.

The valley at the southern foot of Mount Mikasa came to be regarded as the "Valley of Hell," probably because corpses were discarded there from very early times. Monks went to this valley to practice penance, and along the paths of the valley they sculpted representations of Jizō, some of which are still to be seen today. Kasuga, which was seen as a Pure Land on Earth, was located directly over a hell, and Jizō was an intermediary agent between these realms of the afterlife.[23]

Himegami

The fourth *kami*, Himegami, has multiple identities: some traditions describe her as the consort of Ame-no-koyane-no-mikoto and others identify her with the solar *kami* Amaterasu. Divine consorts are rarely identified in Japanese religious texts. Some scholars suggest that divine consorts originated as symbolizations of the priestesses charged with the cult of *kami*, but there is little evidence to this effect. It is probable that the identification of Himegami as Amaterasu in Kasuga appeared after an imperial prince of a Fujiwara mother was placed on the throne, a phenomenon that led to an emphasis on Fujiwara mothers and, concomitantly, on divine consorts in state-sponsored shrines and the "sacral women" (*saijo*) of imperial blood that played a role in their major rites. The divine consorts thus symbolized the blood relationship between the Fujiwara house and the imperial lineage.

The identity of the buddha or bodhisattva that is believed to be Himegami's original nature (*honji*) was also subject to fluctuations. Some traditions consider it to be *Dainichi Nyorai* (Skt., Mahāvairocana), the central buddha of the pantheon of esoteric Buddhism and an emblem of the light of heaven, but others say that it is *Jūichimen Kannon* (Skt., Ekadaśamukha), the eleven-faced Bodhisattva of Compassion, which is the object of an early cult in Japan and is represented in one of the main statues in the Kōfukuji's Central Golden Hall. Though it is not known where a representation of *Dainichi Nyorai* was kept in the Kōfukuji, the rationale for the association of the fourth *kami* of Kasuga with Mahāvairocana is obvious as long as that *kami* is thought to be Amaterasu, for both Mahāvairocana and Amaterasu are divinities related to the phenomenon of light. It is probable that the fourth *kami* was worshiped by some members of the Fujiwara house who had personal devotion to the eleven-faced Kannon, though it is not known who dedicated the statue at the Kōfukuji. To solve the problems indicated above, more research on the history of the infiltration of the Kōfukuji by Shingon practices and on combinatory ideas is necessary.[24]

In any case, the buddhas and bodhisattvas that are associated with the *kami* of the four shrines are the main deities represented in the oldest buildings of the Kōfukuji, and they are clearly represented in the various shrine mandalas of the medieval period.[25]

Wakamiya

Finally, by the middle of the twelfth century the Wakamiya *kami* was assigned a Buddhist counterpart, but curiously, either the *kami* of that shrine was not given a specific name, or else the name has been lost. Documents dating from the Muromachi period indicate that the Yoshida sacerdotal lineage identified the Wakamiya *kami* as Ame-no-oshi-kumone-no-mikoto, and earlier records state that this divinity manifested itself in 1003 as a small snake. Ame-no-oshi-kumone was the *kami* charged with fetching "Heavenly Water" from the wells atop Mount Futagami for the enthronement ceremony of emperors and was symbolized by a snake or dragon. It also had a high position in the pantheon devised by Yoshida Kanetomo, which fact may explain the choice expressed in the Muromachi period. In any case, the term *Wakamiya* means "young deity," which, in Kasuga, was thought to be the child of Ame-no-koyane and his consort, Himegami.

Two Buddhist divinities are associated with the Wakamiya *kami*, *Monju bosatsu* (Skt., Mañjuśrī) and *Shō-Kannon* (Skt., Avalokiteśvara). In either case a rationale can be suggested. When the Wakamiya *kami* is represented as Monju, who is often depicted in Buddhist iconography as a youth, it is represented as a youthful entity: the importance is the youthful character of the divinity. Furthermore, Monju is the interlocutor of Vimalakīrti in the main scripture read at the *Yuima-e* ritual assembly, which means, metaphorically, that the Wakamiya Shrine was the interlocutor of the Kōfukuji. Indeed, a painting dated 1273 and recently discovered inside a statue of Monju that was sculpted by Kōen depicts Monju as a child dressed in Japanese court attire but forming a *mudrā* with his hands and standing in the plain at the foot of Mount Mikasa between a prelate of the Kōfukuji and three priests of the Kasuga Shrine.[26]

The identification of the Wakamiya *kami* as Avalokiteśvara might demonstrate the psychological ambivalence of the Wakamiya phenomenon, which may be related to youth initiation or to the feminine character of young men who were the object of romantic attachments on the part of some aristocrats and monks of various temples, though the first possibility appears to be more likely. It is also possible that the identification of the original nature of the Wakamiya *kami* varied with the audience: if the Bodhisattva of Wisdom seems to be compatible with the elite, the character of the Bodhisattva of Compassion seems to have more popular appeal, and this would fit the interests of the general population of the multiplex. A systematic investigation of the links between the various branches of the Fujiwara house and their construction of certain temples, and of their devotion to particular buddhas and bodhisattvas, might provide more rationales for these associations. These divinities are all represented in various buildings of the Main Temple of the Kōfukuji; none of them originated in the *monzeki*.

It appears that a metaphorical structure was at work in the associations, one based on interactions between different cultural realms that were linked to linguistic structures and to patterns of anagogical interplay through which a metameaning was achieved. The associations between *kami* and buddhas or bodhisattvas were first and foremost a system of communication between shrines and temples that represented widely divergent systems of thought and practice. Associations expressed by puns and metaphors allowed a sort of communication between cultural systems and their identification, which led to the consideration of all associated entities of the multiplex as aspects of a single symbol called Kasuga *daimyōjin*. A global entity made up of combinations of *kami* and buddhas/bodhisattvas, Kasuga *daimyōjin* became the representative of a cultural system of great complexity.

Kami that were absorbed into the Kasuga cult over time were given specific shrines and a Buddhist counterpart. The zone immediately surrounding the four main shrines was divided into three sections: the Outer Area (*ge-in*), the Intermediate Area (*chū-in*), and the Inner Area (*nai-in*). Various subshrines (*sessha* and *massha*) that were built in those areas reflect the cultic influences that pervaded Kasuga. Lists of these subshrines were made in 1133, 1216, 1269, 1593, 1663, 1704, and 1973. There were thirty-four subshrines in 1133, and sixty-one in 1973. The names of those shrines and the *kami* enshrined in them varied over time. In 1133 the Inner Area of the main shrine contained seven shrines, four of which were very Buddhist in character even though their names were written with graphs that gave them a native appearance. Of the Intermediate Area's eight shrines, one was predominantly Buddhist. The Outer Area had ten shrines dedicated to native or combined deities. The Wakamiya Shrine was divided into an Inner Area, which had two shrines, and an Outer Area that had seven shrines, one of which was dedicated to *Kishimo* (Hārītī).

The main shrines and their subshrines became the objects of popular tales and legends that were enriched by all types of accretions characteristic of medieval culture, as well as the objects of combinatory rituals and celebrations in which can be seen the popularization of aristocratic culture and the emergence of particular art forms, such as Nō drama. These cultural productions show the nature of the interactions that took place between, on the one hand, shrines and temples and, on the other, cultural systems. In other words, the associations between various *kami* and buddhas or bodhisattvas in cultic centers such as Kasuga were in-depth phenomena at the surface of which one can see the interactions that gave Japanese medieval culture its specific character. Had these associations not taken place, it is possible that the culture of Japan would not have been the result of systematic interchanges, accretions, and substitutions to the extent that it was.[27]

The associations between the *kami* and the buddhas and bodhisattvas of the multiplex were recorded in documents passed secretly among members of sacerdotal lineages and among scholarly monks. They were also inscribed or codified in paintings of the temples made by the Bureau of Painting and shown by prelates to leaders of the Fujiwara house for devotional purposes, or used by those prelates in their own rituals. The oldest documentation of what was to become a generalized practice in medieval Japan was mentioned earlier, that is, the visit of Fujiwara no Tametaka to the cultic center, where he offered a devotion to a representation of the numinous entity Kasuga *daimyōjin* in the Kōfukuji. Another practice surfaces in the *Gyokuyō*, the journal of Kujō no Kanezane, in the entry for the seventeenth day of the fifth moon of the third year of the Tōei era (1184). The short excerpt that follows was written four years after Taira warriors attacked the multiplex and set it ablaze, reducing Nara to ashes. That disaster caused near panic among the aristocracy, but the entire cultic center was quickly rebuilt and soon began to produce some of the finest treasures of Kamakura culture. A new page was being turned in Kasuga. The *Gyokuyō* reads:

It is raining. I have received from the Monacal Rector of Nara a scroll representing the August Shrine of Kasuga. Having taken a bath and thus purified myself, I put on my belt (adding as usual my sword), took the purifying wand (a small one made of six streamers) and, in front of the shrines, I performed my devotions as usual by making a repeated double bow.[28]

The practice of making representations of the shrines and temples of a cultic center and performing devotions in front of such a representation as though one were in the cultic center itself was a new factor in the Japanese tradition. Not only did that practice allow one to worship from afar, but there is little doubt that these representations were supports for meditation and mental pilgrimages. The representations of shrines and temples were formally connected to mandalas, pictorial representations of the universe of the buddhas and bodhisattvas in Esoteric Buddhism. These are spatial representations, and it is significant that cultic centers such as Kasuga came to be seen as mandalas, for this indicates that the sacred space of cultic centers was associated with the transcendental space of the cosmos of the buddhas and bodhisattvas. It also indicates the tendency to think spatially and visually, a good example of which is found in a statement concerning the Nan'endō in the *Kōfukuji ranshō-ki*:

During the fourth year of the Kōnin era, in the reign of Emperor Saga (the fifty-second generation of human sovereigns), a statue of Fukū-kensaku Kannon was commissioned by the Minister of the Left, Fuyutsugu, and ordered by his father, the Nagaoka Minister of the Right, Uchimaro, in accordance with indications provided by Kōbō Daishi. This statue was first installed in the Lecture Hall, but it was later removed to this Pavilion [the Nan'endō] by Fuyutsugu in accordance with the will of his deceased father. This Pavilion, built in consultation with Kōbō Daishi, was also the first one that monk dedicated in this Country. The Kannon statue that is enshrined in it was ordered by Uchimaro, together with statues of the Four Heavenly Kings and paintings of the Eight Patriarchs of the Hossō Lineage, that were made by Kōbō Daishi himself. The main divinity is Fukū-kensaku Kannon. Its height is six *jō*. It was created by the Master of Sculpture Kōkei during the Kenkyū era [1190–1199]. The *Shun'ya-shinki* states: "At the time of the construction of this altar two Elders among the people present chanted these poems in the Japanese manner:

On the southern shore of Mount Potalaka, this Pavilion; To the north, waves of wisteria are in full bloom now.

The Elder in question was the Great *kami* of Izakawa. The other
Elder was the *kami* of Enomoto, who chanted the following
poem:

> Mount Potalaka. . . . On its southern shore a residence,
> In full bloom now the northern waves of wisteria.

The two Elders then vanished."

Mount Potalaka is a place where the wisteria blooms in profu-
sion in all seasons. The Pavilion originated when parts of that
mountain were displaced from their original location and appeared
in this country. Hence the poems. The phrase "northern waves
of wisteria" was used because, of the four branches of the Fujiwara house, the northern branch is the most successful. At the
time of the dedication of this building, six members of the Minamoto house passed away; that is why, at the time of Imperial
visits to this cultic center, the Minamoto do not attend.

Fukū-kensaku Kannon wears on its left shoulder a deerskin.
Since the First *kami* of Kasuga came from Kashima mounted on a
white deer, this animal became its messenger; it was decided that
these two divinities would be associated through this communication device. This is a most profound rationale for the relation between the two divinities.[29]

This text is typical of the medieval reasoning concerning associations.
A metaphor would bind the divinities, and the result of that binding was
a single entity whose character transcended either divinity taken alone,
though neither was forgotten or abandoned: combination implies separation. As a consequence of that kind of reasoning an important element of
the relation between the Fujiwara universe of meaning and society came
to the surface: that is, the notion that this world is a Pure Land, a paradise
on earth, the residence of the associated buddhas and *kami* and their
descendants.[30] Mandalas painted toward the end of the medieval period
depict the Kasuga Mountains above the shrines and temples, with Mount
Potalaka floating on an ocean above the mountain range.[31] Such paintings
are direct representations of the poems attributed to the Elders of Izakawa
and Enomoto, in which we are told that the Nan'en-dō stands in the middle
of Mount Potalaka, a metaphysical space located south of the world in
which humans dwell, and where the Bodhisattva of Compassion resides.

The Fujiwara believed that their cultic center was a transcendental space,
a cosmic zone of dwelling, part of a metaphysical land that had flown to
and landed in Japan.[32] Thus the cultic center of the Fujiwara house was an
otherworldly "isle" set in the midst of the ocean of transmigration, against
the shores of which waves of blue wisteria exuded heavenly fragrances and

broke in ecstatic silence. Myō-e *shōnin* once dreamt that boats careened in the sky and landed on Mount Mikasa. The auspicious sight of the deer roaming freely caused the aristocratic visitors to the cultic center to believe that they had left behind them the confines of a spoiled world and had set foot on an undefiled realm that was symbolized and lit by the full moon, which is itself an emblem of Awakening and of purity.[33] The Fujiwara made pilgrimages to Kasuga in a quest of visions of the Pure Land.

KASUGA *DAIMYŌJIN*

Originally the Kasuga *kami* were worshiped separately, and each had a structurally and functionally different character. A double process appeared rather early in history, however, the first of which was the development of associations as described above. The second process was one whereby the five *kami* and their associated buddhas and bodhisattvas became a conglomerate referred to as "Kasuga *myōjin*" and later as "Kasuga *daimyōjin*." The term *myōjin* appears for the first time in records dating from the year 848 and is found in the *Shoku-Nihon-kōki*. In those records the term refers to a *kami* that was worshiped at the Yamazaki Shrine in the district of Otokuni, province of Yamashiro. *Myōjin* is a highly ambiguous term: at first sight, it is unclear whether it indicates a single divinity, several divinities, or a unified group of divinities. English prevents us from communicating the same ambiguity, for in English one has to speak either of a Kasuga divinity or Kasuga divinities. The term Kasuga *daimyōjin* entails the notion that the five *kami* of Kasuga and their associated divinities at the Kōfukuji formed a single coherent unit. The term, then, ought to be understood to mean something like "the numinous unit of the associated *kami* and buddhas/bodhisattvas of the Kasuga-Kōfukuji multiplex." The Fujiwara ecclesiastics who worshiped that entity addressed it with the formula *Namu Kasuga Daimyōjin,* which was copied on the *Namu Amida Butsu* or *Namu Myōhōrenge-kyō* formulas of the Pure Land and Nichiren lineages.

The term Kasuga *myōjin* appears for the first time in a document written by a monk of the Enryakuji on Mount Hiei in 859. In this document, the term *myōjin* is charged with Buddhist connotations and refers to a divinity of high rank and prestige. The term Kasuga *daimyōjin* first appears in documents authored by members of the Fujiwara house in 1152, though there is little doubt that it was in use before that date. By the year 1152 the entity known as Kasuga *daimyōjin* had become much more than the protector of the interests of the Fujiwara house and, concomitantly, of the state under imperial rule: it had become the de facto "governor" (*shugo*) of the entire province of Yamato, and its character as a tutelary deity that protects a territory had come to full fruition. The complex processes whereby the various *kami* and buddhas/bodhisattvas merged to form this single entity paralleled the processes whereby the rule of the cultic center came to encompass a large geopolitical and spiritual sphere of influence.

It is possible that this combinatory process was related to the emerging custom of enshrining the divinities of the Kasuga multiplex in the private residences of the high nobility. This custom originated, according to existing documents, in the twelfth century, but it is probable that it was practiced earlier. Some monks of Fujiwara origin erected shrines dedicated to the Kasuga divinities in their private residences during the Kamakura period. That was the case of the "Buddhist" monk Jōkei (Gedatsu *shōnin*, 1155–1212), who erected a shrine for Kasuga *myōjin* in his temple on Mount Kasagi in 1192; and of Myō-e *shōnin*, who practiced a Kasuga cult at his residence at the Kō-zanji in Takao, Kyoto. Non-Fujiwara people also erected shrines and formed confraternities (*kō*) for the practice of the Kasuga cult in Yamato Province during the late part of the Kamakura period and during the Muromachi and Edo periods. The transfer of the Kasuga divinities to private residences was executed according to fixed ritual patterns: first a shrine was erected on purified ground, and the transfer itself was performed by a Nakatomi priest of high status who invoked the *kami* to take temporary residence in a branch of *sakaki*, the sacred tree of Kasuga. This branch was then placed in a portable palanquin and moved from Kasuga to the shrine in the private residence. Treasures symbolizing the *kami*'s normal surroundings at Kasuga were provided. They included a sword, a mirror, a halberd, a bow, two arrows with a container for each, a half-mat, and a folding seat.

The first recorded instance of a transfer of the Kasuga divinities to a province other than those immediately adjacent to Kyoto was in 1100 when the *kami* were transferred to a domain owned by the Kasuga Shrine in the northern province of Echigo. This transfer may have been requested by the governor of the province, who was a member of the Fujiwara house. In any case, it became customary to erect Kasuga shrines on all domains owned by the main Kasuga Shrine or the Kōfukuji. Earlier, when the capital was moved from Heijō to Nagaoka, the Kasuga *kami* were transferred to a shrine that received the name of the site where it was built, Ōharano. Subsequently, when the capital was moved to Heian, the new Kasuga Shrine was called Yoshida, which is also a place name. Shrines that were erected on lands owned by the multiplex were always called Kasuga *jinja* (Kasuga shrine), not Kasuga *taisha* as in Nara, and their structure was also combinatory. A good example is that of the Kasuga shrine of Minoo, where the *kami* were associated with the same buddhas and bodhisattvas as in Nara.

By the twelfth century Kasuga *daimyōjin* formed a single entity as protector of land in various provinces, and it was becoming the protector of the entire province of Yamato. The development of combinations of the divinities of the Kasuga multiplex into a single entity, which was paralleled by developments in cults in other parts of Japan, took place against the ideological backdrop of the relation of multiplexes to the state, in which major shrine-temple multiplexes organized themselves in a structurally identical manner and established new relations with each other. A foremost aspect of these relations was the formation of the unity of the "Three Shrines": Ise, Kasuga, and Hachiman. These three major shrines (and temples), which were conceived of as a single entity that protected the state, were themselves above yet another group of shrines (and their temples) called the "Seven Shrines": Ise, Iwashimizu, Kamo, Kasuga, Hie, Gion, and Kitano. These, in turn, stood above the classical arrangement of the "Twenty-two Shrines."[34] The term "Three Shrines" (*sansha*) appears in documents dated 1147, then again in the *Gyokuyō* of 1180, in which the following phrase is found: "When reflecting upon the matter, is it not evident, at this time, that the peaceful destiny of our country rests upon the Grand Shrine of Ise, the Shrine of Hachiman, and Kasuga *daimyōjin*?"[35]

As in the realm of religious language, Kasuga *daimyōjin* was an ambiguous entity in the sociopolitical and economic realms. Though Kasuga was supported by the Fujiwara house, which claimed the System of Codes as the main organizing device of the sociocosmic system of classical Japan, the cultic center's economic organization was diametrically opposed to the structure portrayed in these codes. Thus, the interests of the Fujiwara house and those of its cultic center were in direct conflict, a conflict in which the cultic center was often victorious. When the multiplex became a major military power in Yamato Province during the Heian period, its requests were made known to the capital through the symbolic and ominous use of the sacred tree (*sakaki*), a branch of which was customarily carried by Kōfukuji monks and Kasuga priests from Nara to Kyoto. The clergy of the Kōfukuji alone would never have had any power over the Fujiwara house members; a symbol of the Kasuga divinities that could be used as a threat was needed, and this explains the presence of Kasuga priests in arguments that developed between the court and the Kōfukuji.[36] Even though the prelates of the Kōfukuji had the power to exclude members of the Fujiwara house from their family's lineage, they exercised that power in the name of Kasuga *daimyōjin*, not in the name of a buddha or a bodhisattva.

One of the better sources for the identity of Kasuga *daimyōjin* is the *Kasuga gongen genki*. This illustrated text is one of the finest examples of Japanese medieval literature and painting.[37] It consists of twenty scrolls that were presented to the shrine in 1309 by Saionji Kin'hira, then Minister of the Left. The text was written by the former regent Takatsukasa Mototada and three of his sons: Fuyuhira (current regent in 1309), Fuyumoto (major counselor), and Ryōshin (who had been and would again be the abbot of the multiplex). Though it is not the purpose of this chapter to examine this work in detail,[38] the identity of Kasuga *daimyōjin* and the character of the cult as they are represented in this classic work will be briefly discussed.

Ample proof that the identity of Kasuga *daimyōjin* ought to be expressed as "the numinous unit of the associated *kami* and buddhas-bodhisattvas of the Kasuga-Kōfukuji multiplex" is provided by the *genki*, in which Kasuga *daimyōjin* manifests itself thirty-five times, all but two of which are described in detail. The thirty-five manifestations occurred in dreams, visions, or through possession. These were fundamental aspects of the Kasuga cult during the medieval period and were related to the belief of the Hossō lineage of Buddhist philosophy that reality is nothing but a mental construct. Dreams were seen as the prime example of reality considered as a figment of the imagination, and "reality" was seen as a dreamlike, ephemeral concoction of the mind. In this context, then, Kasuga *daimyōjin* appears in the *Kasuga gongen genki* under various guises: as a woman of noble appearance (seven times), as a young boy (eight times), as an old man (twice), as an aristocrat of noble composure and dress (seven times), as Jizō *bosatsu* (twice), and as an angry spirit (four times). In every case we are told that this is Kasuga *daimyōjin*; we are also told from which of the five shrines it appeared, and in some instances which buddha or bodhisattva is its original nature. In the first scroll we are told the "Fourth Shrine is Amaterasu conjoined in perfect union with the Third Shrine" (Ame-no-koyane-no-mikoto), and in the seventh scroll we are told, "A single utterance of the formula *Namu Kasuga Daimyōjin* manifests the powers of the Five Shrines."

It is obvious, therefore, that Kasuga *daimyōjin* is a composite entity. Its residence is described in one passage as Mount Mikasa, and in another as the Mountain of the Numinous Eagle, with an intermediary space (the multiplex itself) that separates the hell that lies beneath the Kasuga Plain from a Pure Land that hovers above it. Kasuga *daimyōjin* is combinatory in several instances: it chants parts of the *Jōyuishikiron* with "a lovely feminine voice," and it appears as Jizō, who promises to stand in hell, where he would pour drops of liquid from his bowl into the mouths of those who suffer torture under the Kasuga Plain and thus relieve their pain until they could be pulled from hell and taken to the Pure Land. In another passage Kasuga *daimyōjin* promises that the sufferings of hell will be avoided by those who practice filial piety, and in yet another context it appears as the manifestation of Jūichimen Kannon and declares, "My abode is in the West."

Sometimes Kasuga *daimyōjin* demonstrates its bias in favor of the Hossō lineage: for instance, on one occasion it set fire to a house and burned the *Makashikan* (a major text of the Tendai lineage) while sparing the *Jōyuishikiron* that was set beside it. In another case, Kasuga *daimyōjin* is said to have appeared as a young child seated on the knees of a prelate, its hair "wet with tears because, even though I like the Lotus Sutra, I would prefer that you chant the *Jōyuishikiron*."

The most famous case of Kasuga *daimyōjin's* possession of a person occurs in the seventeenth and eighteenth scrolls of the *Kasuga gongen genki*, in which it is related that the divine entity took possession of a Tachibana Lady in order to prevent Myō-e *shōnin* from going to India. That event was both frightening and wonderful: the lady's face became as transparent as crystal and her body exuded a fragrance of such sweetness that people who suffered from various ills licked her feet and were cured.

In other words, Kasuga *daimyōjin*, as it appears in the *Kasuga gongen genki*, is a combinatory entity in which one may discern various layers of meaning and practice: it includes different trends of Buddhism, shamanistic trance and possession, and traces of the original indigenous cult. The text contains popular versions of aristocratic notions and aristocratic versions of popular creeds, a phenomenon characteristic of the medieval period. In the sixteenth scroll we are told, "Kasuga *daimyōjin*, in both its original nature [*honji*] and its hypostasis [*suijaku*], is worthy of trust." This divine entity was thus a perfect expression of the structures of interaction that animated the Kasuga cultic center through much of its history. And, as one might expect, it supported the arts and letters, either as a divine inspiration for treatises on prosody, as an apparition dancing in a pine tree, or as a stern figure who reminds a prelate that music and dance are heard in the Pure Land and therefore should not be prohibited in the shrine-temple multiplex, even if they distract the mind from study.[39]

It was under the protection of this complex divine entity that the city devoted to its cult, Nara, grew to large proportions.

FROM CEREMONIAL CENTER TO SACRED CITY

After the capital was moved from Heijō to Heian at the end of the eighth century, the abandoned city, once a grandiose Chinese-style capital, became a desolate landscape covered with weeds and debris. Former residents who returned to the city for brief periods composed poignant poems about the beauty that had vanished. Fields reclaimed the sites of noble mansions. Originally a complex of vermilion and white buildings, the imperial palace gradually fell into disrepair and became prey to people who needed building materials or firewood. Recent archaeological investigations, which have yielded official tablets and pieces of jewelry or plates strewn over a large area, show that the departure from Nara was sudden. Though the demarcations created by the grid of the streets are still visible today, the city was gone forever. Only the temples remained. Over a period of several centuries each of the major temples in the former capital became the center of small concentrations of inhabitations. But if the Heijō capital died completely, the "Outer Capital" did not.

Around the Tōdaiji and its Tamuke Hachiman Shrine, and the Kōfukuji and its Kasuga Shrine, a city that was to become Nara as we know it today slowly grew. This city, like Heijō before it, remained a ceremonial center; its character evolved in such a way that it must be called a sacred city.

Cities that developed around cultic centers are called in Japanese *monzenchō*, a term that means literally "Gate-Front-City." The development of such cities is a phenomenon that was common to both Japan and Europe in the medieval period: Nara reminds one of Mont Saint-Michel, Canterbury, and other European cities that developed according to a more or less similar pattern. Nara, however, was much more than a *monzenchō*. Under the spiritual, economic, and political protection of Kasuga *daimyōjin* and Hachiman *daibosatsu*, it became the ceremonial center of Yamato Province and the largest landholder in the country during the medieval period.[40]

Finally, at Nara there developed a specific culture that gradually pervaded the Japanese sensibility. That culture had two major traits: first, like the Kasuga belief system, it was characterized by associations between native and foreign elements that were meshed structurally; and second, it contained similar structural combinations of elements of the aristocratic culture of the Fujiwara house and elements of popular culture. It is in those two sets of combinations that the processes of the popularization of the cult and the development of the identity of Kasuga *daimyōjin* can be discerned.

In the medieval period the Kasuga Shrine gained a large population that was dedicated to its maintenance and to the cult of various *kami*. Those people, who were called *jinin* ("*kami*-men"), resided in specific areas near the shrines in Nara as well as in those provinces where Kasuga shrines had been erected. Similarly, the Kōfukuji temples also gained a large population that was dedicated to their maintenance and to the cult of various divinities as well. Those people were divided into three groups. First were the *gakuryo*, who were scholarly monks not issued from aristocratic blood. Below them were the *dōshū*, "hall-men," a term that originally referred to the residents of the Western and Eastern Golden Halls, and finally, the *shuto*, a term that defies translation but refers to a group or class of people related to specific temples via those temples' land possessions, of which they were the caretakers. The *shuto* might have been the original owners or caretakers of plots of land that at some point were offered by the imperial lineage to the multiplex, at which time many of them moved to the Kōfukuji and slowly gained a position of authority there. These *shuto* bore arms but wore monastic garb and lived in quarters around the various temples with which they were affiliated. Other *shuto* continued to live on the provincial domains of the multiplex, in which case they were called *kokumin*, "provincials," and they identified themselves more readily with the shrines than the temples.

The *jinin* and *shuto* shared a common culture: the former, though related primarily to the shrines, also worshiped the buddhas and bodhisattvas associated with the *kami*; and the *shuto*, though related primarily to the temples, worshiped the *kami* as well as the buddhas/bodhisattvas of their temples. Thus, even though it is tempting to separate the two groups on the basis of their administrative affiliations, it is incorrect to do so, for their associations reflected the associations of the buddhas and the *kami*. When a branch of the sacred tree of Kasuga was carried to Kyoto at the time of their frequent protests to the court, the *jinin* and *shuto* did so together under the auspices of the combinatory entity Kasuga *daimyōjin*, and in the main rites of the multiplex, the *shuto* of the temples organized the dances and Nō performances of the *jinin*. The superior status of the *shuto* reflected the administrative superiority of the temples.

The growth of Kasuga's land possessions was a decisive factor in the evolution of the belief system and it led to a major transformation of the multiplex, whose prelates came to rule the province. These developments could be expressed in a simple formula: instead of ruling a symbolic realm of relationships within a house that was not territorially based, the multiplex returned to the pre-Taika structure that was characterized by the primacy of territory. In so doing it went against the government policies as they stood on paper, but the economic, political, and spiritual power of the ceremonial center grounded in territory was so great that the center resisted successfully any intrusion into its affairs on the part of the state, and even on the part of members of the Fujiwara house who were active in the central government. Such posturing was based partly on a sense of total security on the part of the multiplex, but also on the fact that its administrative organization was immense. Other elements—especially those concerning the definition of the state and of power and legitimacy in general—were directly involved in the growth and activities of the multiplex. A description of this organization based on the meager documents presently available follows.[41]

THE MEDIEVAL ORGANIZATION OF THE KASUGA SHRINE

The Kasuga Shrine was established during the Nara period as a ceremonial center for the legitimation of power on the part of a new house that was attempting to symbolize the particular type of relationship that it had with the imperial lineage. This was effectively achieved when the shrine began to be supported by the state, when its rituals were reorganized during the early Heian period along lines that were structurally similar to those of the main state rituals, when the shrine was granted land, and when institutional and other ties were established with the temples.

From at least 1150, the people referred to as *jinin* were organized separately from the *shuto* of the Kōfukuji and were put under the authority of the "Three General Offices" (*sansōkan*), which were under the jurisdiction of the Kōfukuji and administered the population of the four shrines and the Wakamiya Shrine. The first of those three offices was that of the head-priests, which was originally a single office for the Nakatomi sacerdotal lineage. It was originally called *jingū-azukari* (shrine custodial office), or *zōgū-azukari* (custodial office for the construction of the shrine), but at some point in the Heian period it was renamed *shō-no-azukari* (head custodial office), or *shugyō-shōyo* (office of management and custody).

Had it not been for a ritual matter, it is probable that the Kasuga Shrine would have remained under the control of a branch of the Nakatomi family that had ruled it from the beginning. In 965, however, a mourning taboo prevented all members of the Nakatomi branch at Kasuga from participating in the Kasuga Grand Rite, and they were replaced by Ōnakatomi no Tsunetaki, who went down to Kasuga from Ise for the rite. The Ōnakatomi lineage held important positions in the Office of the *kami* of Heaven and Earth and customarily accompanied the chieftain of the Fujiwara house at the time of the Kasuga Grand Rite. In 965 the Fujiwara chieftain designated Tsunetaki to be the main sacerdotal figure at the shrine. This arrangement led to the development of a second office, the *kannushi-gata* (office of the head-priests).

Although the aforementioned *shō-no-azukari* was controlled by members of the Nakatomi lineage, the *kannushi-gata*, which took precedence over it, was controlled by members of the Ōnakatomi lineage. In 1135, 170 years after the establishment of the *kannushi-gata*, the Wakamiya Shrine was created by the Kōfukuji and a separate office for its administration was set up. This was the *Wakamiya kannushi-gata,* the office of the priests of the Wakamiya Shrine. The directors of these Three General Offices were nominated by the chieftain of the Fujiwara house, and each of them headed a sacerdotal house whose members had different functions and vied with one another for nomination to the top positions. Those who were successful in that competition created their own subhouses and took different names. By the middle of the medieval period these groups, in conjunction with the houses and subhouses of the *shuto* of the Kōfukuji, ruled Nara, and all of them were under the control of the *monzeki,* temples that were run by Fujiwara-born clerics.

These sacerdotal lineages lived in clearly designated territorial units around the shrine compounds, and they came to be known by the names of those sites. The Ōnakatomi lineage resided in the northern area bordering the Third Ward of the ancient capital, an area that was called Noda and that later on was commonly referred to as Hokugō, the Northern District. The main subhouse that issued from the Ōnakatomi lineage was the Nakahigashi family, which controlled the *kannushi-gata* office until the Meiji period. The Nakatomi lineage resided in the southern area bordering the Third Ward of the Outer Capital, an area that was called Takabatake and that later on was commonly known as Nangō, the Southern District. Over time two main subhouses of this Nakatomi lineage emerged, each claiming descent from the original priests of Kasuga: one of those subhouses, the descendants of Tokifū, took the name Tatsunoichi, and the other, the descendants of Hideyuki, took the name Ōhigashi. These two lineages vied for power until the Meiji period. The first priest of the Wakamiya Shrine was a certain Tatsunoichi no Sukefusa, who was, as his name indicates, a member of Tokifū's line, and the administration of the Wakamiya Shrine was headed by a subbranch of that line that took the name Chidori. Thus, even though the names differed, the lineage was always the same. The Chidori lived in the Wakamiya District.

Under the authority of the Three General Offices were people who came to be called *ujibito,* or "house members." The *ujibito* were not members of the Fujiwara house but of the four lineages mentioned above. They held some kind of position within the administration with regard to ritual matters of the shrines and had the title of *shashi,* "shrine officials." The more promising *ujibito* could make a career in the offices of the shrines: in the case of the *kannushi-gata,* they could rise to the positions of *shin-gon-kannushi* (junior assistant head-priest), *gon-kannushi* (assistant head-priest), and *kannushi* (head-priest); in the case of the *shō-no-azukari-gata,* they could rise to the positions of *kanin-azukari* (adjunct

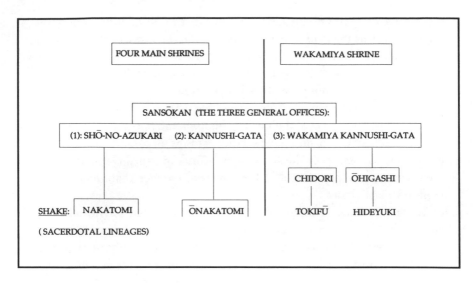

Diagram 1.   The Organization of the Kasuga Shrine's Sacerdotal Lineages.

custodian), *jingū-azukari* (shrine custodian), *shin-azukari* (junior custodian), *tsugi-azukari* (senior custodian), *gon-azukari* (assistant custodian),
and shō-no-azukari (head custodian). In the case of the Wakamiya Shrine,
the highest office was hereditary. (The organization of the Kasuga shrines
is represented schematically in diagram 1.)

The Three General Offices and the *ujibito* belong to what the tradition
refers to as *shake* (shrine-houses, or sacerdotal lineages). A large number
of caretakers, workers, and artisans put themselves under the protection
of the *shake* and attempted to secure permanent jobs through the traditional pattern of clientage. People who worked for the main houses became
jinin, and they were commonly known as "Yellow Garments" (*kō-e jinin*),
for they wore yellow clothes. This distinguished them from the "White
Garments" (*shiro-e jinin*), the *jinin* who belonged to Kasuga subshrines in
Yamato and other provinces and whose social status was relatively less
elevated. The Yellow Garments *jinin* thus corresponded to the *shuto*, and
the White Garments *jinin* to the *kokumin*, though their respective social
status was different. Whenever a shrine was erected on land owned by the
Kasuga Shrine, an administrative infrastructure was set up, and it was the
White Garments *jinin* that were responsible for the shrine's rites, the
upkeep of its grounds, its protection, and its relations with the main
multiplex, such as the regular payment of revenues.

This practice evolved to large proportions; the shrine-temple multiplexes gained so much economic power that complaints began to appear in documents rather early. As early as 1156, Emperor Go-Shirakawa, who unlike his predecessors or successors was not willing to let the shrine-temple multiplexes wield great power, issued a restraining order in which the following is stated: "Recently, calling themselves subshrines of ancestral shrines or domains of temples related to the state, some shrines have set up organizations of several thousand *jinin,* and some temples have assembled huge numbers of *shuto,* and both make improper shows of authority."[42] A similar prohibition was issued in 1212 but with little effect, for by then the shrine-temple multiplexes had become the largest landowners in the country, and their awesome economic and political power made them either a formidable ally of the state or an indomitable foe. The main shrine-temple multiplexes that the government tried to control, to little avail, were Gion, Hie, Ise, Iwashimizu, Kamo, Kasuga, and Sumiyoshi—all members of the Twenty-two Shrine-Temple Multiplexes sponsored by the imperial house. These multiplexes were major social, political, economic, and cultural institutions, whose power rivaled that of the noble families and the major warrior houses.[43] It is among the *kokumin* and *shuto* that the powerful warrior clans of the medieval period appeared: the Tsutsui clan emerged from the *shuto* of the Kōfukuji; the no less powerful (and opposing) Ochi clan arose from the *kokumin* of Yamato.

Like the aforementioned sacerdotal lineages, the groups of *jinin* that served the Three General Offices of Kasuga were also referred to by the names of the area of their residence. Thus, the *kannushi-gata jinin* were known as *jinin* of the Northern District; the *shō-no-azukari jinin* were known as *jinin* of the Southern District; and the *Wakamiya-gata jinin* were known simply as *jinin* of the Wakamiya Shrine. Although these *jinin* were generally of low social extraction, they could acquire some status in the shrine administration; the best among them might become *shinden-mori* (shrine-guardians), an office that they hoped to be able to transmit to their descendants. This was rare but it did happen, and some Nara families who had this charge over several generations were legally entitled to take a name, such as Ōmiya in the Northern District, and Umeki in the Southern District.

The first name of all *jinin* included the word *haru* (spring), which is the meaning of the first of the two graphs with which Kasuga is written. Thus, such names as Masaharu, Haruo, Yoshiharu, Harunobu, and the like would immediately reveal that their bearers were Kasuga *jinin.* There were some ranks among the *jinin,* but little is known about them; evidently they were related to the type of function or profession the *jinin* specialized in, such as police, porcelain makers, earthenware makers, utensils makers, and so forth.

It is nearly impossible at this time to discover how this large social system developed around the shrines of Kasuga, for the available documents are neither very old nor very detailed. We know that by the end of the fifteenth century there were several hundred *jinin*, and documents produced in 1720 show that the shrine community had the following numbers at that time: 13 shrine officals, 16 *ujibito*, 45 "main shrine priests," 111 "priests" (*negi*) of the Southern District belonging to sixty-six houses, 119 "priests" of the Northern District belonging to sixty-one houses, and 64 "priests" belonging to the Wakamiya Shrine. Thus, a total of 368 people held posts in the administration and rituals of the shrines.[44] If children, spouses, and related family members are included, all together there were several thousand people whose livelihood depended directly on the shrines. If monks and *shuto* of the Kōfukuji are added to that number, it is clear that an impressively large citizenry lived around the cultic center. It is little wonder that the rest of the citizens of Nara functioned exclusively as members of the support system for this population, and that the various artisans and merchants in Nara were under the control of the multiplex.

The White Garments *jinin* sought economic and spiritual support from the cultic center, but they lived outside its precinct either in Yamato or one of the other provinces. Most of them were caretakers of the Kasuga subshrines that were built on the lands granted to the multiplex, but some became priests of those shrines. Their main task was the military protection of the shrine's domains, the overseeing of tax payments, and the transportation of the various in-kind offerings that were regularly sent to Kasuga. Some of them came to own land and thereby attained a higher status in society. The White Garments *jinin* carried out their military and economic duties under the spiritual protection of Kasuga *daimyōjin*. Sometimes the White Garments called themselves *negi* (priests), but this practice drew criticism because it confused public and private levels of identity and authority. This usage of the term *negi*, however, was generalized in the premodern period.

In addition to the *jinin* of the main shrines of Kasuga was the population of the Wakamiya Shrine, whose administrative structure was dependent upon the Kōfukuji. The Wakamiya Shrine differed from the others in that it had been created by the temples and its priestly organization was structurally different. The main reason for these differences is that the cult of the Wakamiya *kami* was a popular one. The Wakamiya Shrine's priests belonged to the aforementioned subbranch of the Nakatomi lineage that took the name Chidori. This shrine governed groups of female shamans (*fujo*, or *miko*) and groups of male dancers called *kagura-otoko*. The female shamans were divided into several groups: the *jōju-fujo* (permanent female shamans) served at the Veneration Hall in front of the Wakamiya Shrine and were usually either spouses or daughters of the priests of the shrine. Below them were two groups of female shamans who resided in different parts of the city: there were the *Kuni-fujo*, who lived in the Furuichi District, and the *Yashima-fujo*, of the Yashima District. Those who specialized in the performance of sacred dances (*kagura*) were organized into two major groups called the Northern League (*kitaza*) and the Southern League (*minamiza*), each of which had about fifteen dancers who held various ranks. Also, there was a group of some twenty male dancers who were sometimes referred to as Yellow Garments. These ritualists did not belong to the *shashi* and *jinin* groups, which, it will be recalled, were affiliated with the main shrines, for they were directly under the control of the Western Golden Hall of the Kōfukuji and were nominated to their function by a two-part document, half of which was issued by the master of ceremonies of the Western Golden Hall and the other half by the head-priest of the Wakamiya Shrine.

Finally, the Wakamiya Shrine apparently took care of a group of blind people whom it used for ritual purposes such as communication with the dead, and for medicinal purposes such as massage. The earliest mention of such a group in Japan was made in connection with Saichō, who seems to have organized a group of "blind monks" in Chikuzen Province. That group may have been the predecessor to those groups of blind monks who transmitted the epics orally to the accompaniment of the *biwa*, that is, the Biwa *hōshi*. Because those monks were blind they were associated with the *kami* of the earth and, later, territory, and thus the most important function of the blind community may have been related to notions of territory. The blind monks, whose main object of worship was Jizō, went on pilgrimages dedicated to the *kami* enshrined around the boundaries of districts and provinces, the *sai no kami*.[45]

The Kasuga administrative structure also included several bureaus that performed some functions with regard to the shrines but that were under the authority of the Kōfukuji. These were the bureau of painting, the bureau of music (which was run by the *jinin*), the bureau of carpentry, and groups of artisans whose connection to the administrative infrastructure of the cultic center was not always clearly determined. Many people attempted to put themselves under the control and protection of the multiplex because it assured them employment and gave them a measure of authority, which they did not hesitate to display in the provinces in order to have their way, obtain contracts, or acquire and manage land. Such people wanted to be protected by Kasuga, a protection that they symbolized by erecting Kasuga subshrines on their lands. The Kasuga main shrines were built anew every twenty years; if a shrine was in good condition it was transferred to another site and rebuilt. If an entire shrine could not be moved in a block, those parts of it that were in good condition were added to existing shrines in the provinces. Bidding took place in the Three General Offices before any decision was reached as to who would be awarded the shrines that were no longer in use. Several of these still exist today.

The entire province of Yamato was under the control of the Kasuga multiplex and was administered by the groups discussed above. In that context it is easy to understand how the cult of Kasuga *daimyōjin* slowly went beyond the confines of the Fujiwara house and spread through the province in successive layers. Those *jinin* who lived in the province and managed to secure the "seal" of the Kōfukuji, whereby they acquired special privileges of an economic character, naturally came to worship Kasuga *daimyōjin*. Villages located on the land domains of the multiplex organized confraternities (*kō*) of worship through which local social organization and political control from the main cultic center were reinforced.

THE MEDIEVAL ORGANIZATION OF THE KŌFUKUJI

If during the Nara period the Kōfukuji had been a semiprivate, semipublic temple dedicated to the spirits of the departed leaders of the Fujiwara house and a ceremonial center that symbolized the structure of the classical state through the performance of rites and ceremonies dedicated to its protection, during the Heian period the temples became a cultic center whose main concern was the appropriation and control of land in Yamato Province.

As this transformation took place, the character of the cult underwent substantive change in two main ways. First, there was the development of associations between the *kami* and buddhas/bodhisattvas, a process that, as discussed above, gave rise to the combined divine entity Kasuga *daimyōjin*. Second, there was the popularization of the belief system, a process based partly on the emergence of the Wakamiya Shrine and partly on the growth of a large population under the control of the prelates of the shrine-temple multiplex.

The associations between the *kami* and the buddhas and/or bodhisattvas were grounded in a triple rationale. First, the Fujiwara house and its sacerdotal lineages demanded a rationale for the coexistence of different divine entities, rituals, and philosophical tenets. Second, the gradual enlargement of the land possessions of the shrine-temple multiplex required a unified administration, which came to be centered in the temples because some members of the Fujiwara house were the head-priests of those temples and could control the land. And third, multiplexes like Kasuga, Iwashimizu, Hiei, Gion, and others developed in their internal interactions and through their external rapports a new ideology for the state. During the medieval period this ideology and its concomitant practices were inseparable from the associations between *kami* and buddhas/bodhisattvas, from ritual, and from the economic and social structure of multiplexes.

Through these processes the Kasuga-Kōfukuji multiplex became a major ceremonial center that controlled the province of Yamato as if it were a possession of the Fujiwara house under the tutelage or spiritual protection of Kasuga *daimyōjin*. The province thus became a quasi-theocracy, a "sacred land" (*shinkoku*) that was symbolized by the sacred city of Nara, itself administered by aristocratic clerics who believed that society functioned in the way in which the political and religious domain they had created was supposed to function.

In order to govern Yamato, the Kōfukuji and the Kasuga shrines developed vast administrative capacities, built up military forces to protect their interests in the province, and employed political resources in order to perpetuate their rule. This was partly realized by the systematic accretion of buildings and by stimulating the growth of a large population directly controlled by the multiplex.

In 758 authority in the Kōfukuji was centralized in the office of abbot (*bettō*), to which was added, in 869, the office of assistant abbot (*gon-bettō*) and others. As the power of the Fujiwara house grew to immense proportions during the Heian period, and as the possessions of the temples and shrines reflected this success, two entirely new units were created and added to the older unit of the Main Temple: the Ichijō-in *monzeki* and the Daijō-in *monzeki*. The Kōfukuji thus became a tripartite institution.

A *monzeki* is a major temple run by an aristocratic lineage. The oldest institution of the kind in Japan is the Ichijō-in *monzeki*, which was created at the Kōfukuji between 978 and 983 by Jōshō, who was a son of the Minister of the Left, Fujiwara no Moroyasu, and who had become abbot of the Kōfukuji in 970. The second *monzeki* of the Kōfukuji, the Daijō-in *monzeki*, was created in 1087 by Ryūzen, who was a son of Fujiwara no Masakane and became assistant abbot of the Kōfukuji in 1096. From the twelfth century on these two *monzeki* came to be controlled exclusively by members of the *sekkanke* of the Fujiwara house who took Buddhist orders. Only men of Fujiwara blood could aspire to rule these institutions, and thus the possessions of these institutions remained, at least ideally, within Fujiwara control. These men came to be called *kishu* (noble seeds).

The two Kōfukuji *monzeki* became the model for other temples: for

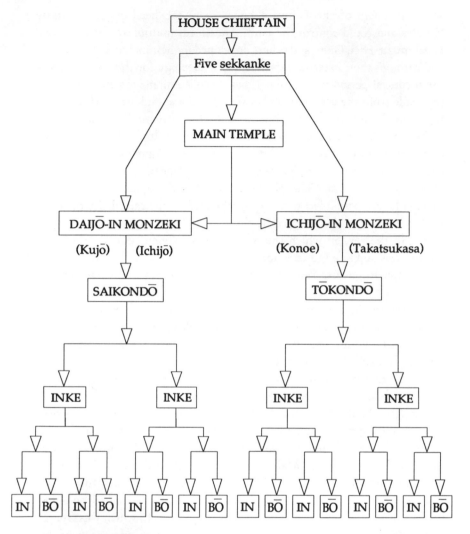

Diagram 2.   The Organization of the Kōfukuji.

instance, the Enryakuji, the center of the Tendai lineage, created the Shōren-in *monzeki* in Kyoto in 1150, the Sanzen-in *monzeki* in Ōhara in the middle of the twelfth century, and the Myōhō-in *monzeki* in 1203.

The two *monzeki* of the Kōfukuji became, over time, the central administrative units of the entire multiplex. Each was symbolically attached to the older buildings of the Main Temple of the Kōfukuji: the Ichijō-in was connected to the Eastern Golden Hall, and the Daijō-in was connected to the Western Golden Hall. The *monzeki* controlled lands as well as the temples on those lands, which became their subtemples; they also controlled all subpavilions on those lands and the people who lived on them. As time passed the Kōfukuji *monzeki* grew to large proportions and their dependences came to form the bulk of the city of Nara. Besides the *monzeki* there were other major institutions that were run by members of noble houses other than the Fujiwara house. These institutions were called *in*, the lineages that could claim entrance into these were called *inke*, and the nobles-turned-monks who ran them were called *ryōke* (members of good houses). These temples were also controlled by the *monzeki*.

Under these major institutions were residences called *bō* (lodges), which were run by ecclesiastics who could not claim aristocratic birth and therefore could expect only little advancement in the hierarchy of the multiplex, no matter what their abilities and qualifications were. The abbot of the entire Kasuga-Kōfukuji multiplex came to be chosen from among the *monzeki* and the fifteen *inke* under their supervision. Toward the end of the Kamakura period the diversification of the branches of the Fujiwara house was reflected in the cultic center; thus the Ichijō-in *monzeki* came to be headed exclusively by members of the Konoe and Takatsukasa branches of the Fujiwara house, while the Daijō-in *monzeki* came to be headed by members of the Kujō and Ichijō branches. The same was true for the *inke*, in which rules of succession were intimately related to the inheritance of land possessions by the various temples and their subtemples. During the Edo period the abbot of the multiplex was chosen in alternation from each *monzeki*, and the assistant abbot was chosen from the Kita-in *inke*, which was created in 949 by Kūsei. (The organization of the Kōfukuji is represented schematically in diagram 2.)

Below the office of abbot, who was the overall superior of the multiplex, was the important office of the five masters for special ceremonies (*bechi-e goshi*). The main duty of the five prelates who held that office, which had a duration of one year, was to organize those ceremonies of the Kasuga shrines in which temples had a major part. The most prominent of these ceremonies was the *On-matsuri*, which was held at the Wakamiya Shrine, but there were many other ceremonies that were organized by "monks" in the temples and dedicated to Kasuga *daimyōjin*. A list of such major ceremonies in the fifteenth century is found in the *Daijō-in jisha zōjiki* (table 3).

Table 3. Ceremonies Organized by the Kōfukuji at Kasuga

Ceremony	Date
Kasuga-sai mōke-goto	1st day of the monkey of 2d month
Kasuga saitō yuishiki-e	15th day of 3d month
Kasuga-sha sanjukkō	From 15th to 29th day of 3d month
Kasuga-sha gohakkō	9th day of 4th month
Kasuga-gosha ango	From 10th day of 4th month to 9th day of 7th month
Wakamiya sairei joshi	7th month
Kasuga-sha gohakkō	19th day of 8th month
Wakamiya On-matsuri	9th month
Kasuga-sha godokkyō	10th month

Source: *Daijō-in jisha zōjiki* (Ōnin 1, 4th month, 10th day).

These ceremonies required preparations of some complexity, not only in ritual organization and performance but also in offerings, ritual implements, the training of monks, and the like. The staggering expenses incurred in these ceremonies and rites were provided by special land domains that were controlled by the Main Temple.

According to a document sent by the Kōfukuji to the Muromachi shogunate in 1348, the administrative office of the multiplex, which was directed by the abbot, consisted of an elder (*jōza*), two directors (*jishu*), four vice-directors (*gon-jishu*), and three administrative officers (*tsuina*), all of whom were "members of good houses." Under that office were departments known as the "four supervisors" (*mokudai*), which specialized in repair work, ritual matters, official documents, and other duties.

The abbot of the cultic center had a private secretary known as *shusse-bugyō,* a term perhaps translatable as "overseer." Each office under him had a group of specialized functionaries known as *sento,* whose duties ranged from the protection of domains to matters related to music and dance. Each of the seven main temples of the Kōfukuji was directed by an official (*dōshi* or *daigyōji*) who supervised its affairs and was assisted by several aides who were known by various titles: *shōshin, dōtatsu,* and *dō-dōji.* There were also, as discussed earlier, the bureaus of painting, carpentry, and sculpture. The list of the various bureaus of the cultic center would not be complete without mention of the Bureau of Yin and Yang, which was staffed by members of a subbranch of the Kamo sacerdotal lineage and specialized in the calendar and various intricacies related to it, such as direction taboos and the choice of auspicious days for the performance of ceremonies. Orders were issued from the higher to the lower echelons of this administration; in the reverse direction, only appeals from the various members of each social group, written after collegial approbation, could be heard.

The various temples, subtemples, and residences of the Kōfukuji population were organized geographically, like the Kasuga Shrine residences but in the form of a cosmic diagram composed of "Six Directions," or zones. In fact there were eight and at times ten areas of residence. The first four were called, in relation to their orientation in regard to the Main Temple, the *inui* zone (N.W.), the *ushitora* zone (N.E.), the *tatsumi* zone (S.E.), and the *hitsujisaru* zone (S.W.). The fifth zone was called Ryūge-in, and the sixth Bodai-in. In these six zones resided the *waka-gakuryo*, the lower-ranked "scholarly monks" of the Main Temple who were not under the direct control of the *monzeki* (see map 4).

In the seventh zone, which was known as the "Four Lodges," were the residences of the *shuto* of the Western Golden Hall only, and in the eighth, which was called Rentai-in, were the residences of the *shuto* of the Eastern Golden Hall. In other sections of Nara were the temples, pavilions, chapels, and various halls that housed the immense population of the Kōfukuji. The residents of these halls were known as *kōshū* (priests), who were assisted by their retainers called *dōshū*, who were for the most part local landowners who had come to Nara to settle near the Kōfukuji to share more closely in its power. Furthermore, each of the seven major buildings of what had been the core of the Kōfukuji in the eighth century had its own *shuto*.

Some of the *shuto* and *dōshū* were ordained priests, others were lay devotees, and some bore arms of various kinds (sticks, swords, halberds, bows and arrows). The latter became the infamous *sōhei* (literally, monk-soldiers). This term is somewhat misleading because it suggests that ordained monks bore arms, but it seems that that was rarely the case. Most of the *shuto* who bore arms but dressed as though they were monks were in fact lay devotees who gradually came to live in the temples and whose duty it was to enforce the peace on the temples' land possessions and to police the city of Nara. The ordained priests came from the lower aristocracy or the provincial landed gentry. The exact nature of the *sōhei* is not clearly understood: this topic requires further research on the social structure of the medieval period, and comparative studies of cultic centers. The term *sōhei* does not appear in documents before the end of the medieval period.

As the city of Nara came increasingly to be seen as a sacred space under the spiritual protection of Kasuga *daimyōjin*, the *shuto* of the Kōfukuji and

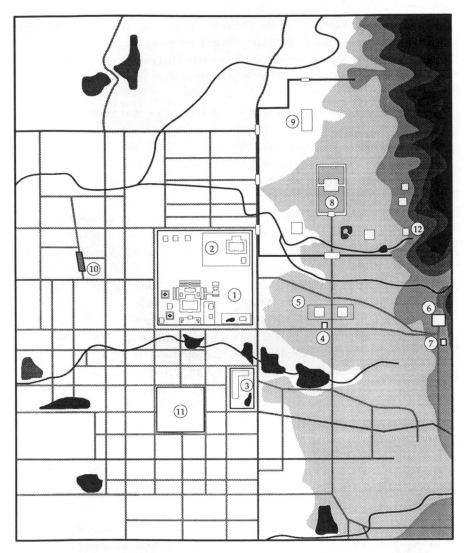

Map 4.   Nara in the Fifteenth Century. Computer-assisted rendering based on
Nagashima Fukutarō, *Nara* (Tokyo: Yoshikawa Kōbunkan, 1963), 171.

1. Kōfukuji (main temples)
2. Ichijō-in *monzeki*
3. Daijō-in *monzeki*
4. Wakamiya *otabisho*
   (temporary shrine)
5. Site of the "Kasuga pagodas"
6. Kasuga Shrine
7. Wakamiya Shrine
8. Tōdaiji
9. Shōsō-in
10. Market
11. Gangōji
12. Tamuke Hachiman Shrine

the *jinin* of Kasuga came to view themselves as semireligious figures: the *shuto* began to wear religious garb, and the lay people who put themselves under the control of the shrines began to dress in yellow or white garments to indicate their affiliations. The *shuto* were strictly organized in hierarchic structured cells. Some *shuto* were literate, and the most successful among them came to own their residences and the lands on which they were built. Some *shuto* married in secret or had women in some other part of town, and the children that they sired were euphemistically called "true disciples" (*shintei*). The *shuto* left their possessions either to their disciples or to their children. Those *shuto* who managed to gain a post in the administrative infrastructure of the Kōfukuji and to make a name for themselves tended then to transmit their posts hereditarily. In the late medieval period each major administrative unit of the temple had a group of approximately twenty *shuto* who were called *kampu-shuto*, that is, "government-appointed *shuto*." They were appointed for four years and their duties were mainly police matters. Many of the *shuto* who lived on the temples' land possessions in Yamato or some other province became wealthy, and eventually they gave birth to warrior clans that claimed the temples' lands as their own and challenged the authority of the *monzeki*. The most famous of these clans in Yamato was the Tsutsui clan, mentioned earlier.

The population that supported the multiplex resided in the zones mentioned above. Temples were built in each of these zones, and that population came to own or govern them. These administrative units, which were called *gō* (district), were the forerunners of the districts (*chō* or *machi*) created during the early Edo period. Apparently residents of these districts had a tendency to build their houses within the compounds of the temples, for a document dated Karyaku 3 (1328) bemoans the fact that the ceremonies for entering and leaving sacred compounds were not observed by those who had set up their houses there.

The districts controlled by the Kōfukuji developed mainly south of the central gate of the temple, which faces south. Subsequently they grew to include the area in which the Gangōji is located, and finally others developed on the western side of the temple. In time, the southern and northern districts of residence of the Kasuga *jinin* came to be controlled by a *monzeki*: the northern district came under the control of the Ichijō-in *monzeki* and the southern one under the Daijō-in *monzeki*. Thus the three major areas controlled by the Kōfukuji corresponded to its tripartite structure, that is, the Main Temple and the two *monzeki*. Each district comprised smaller units that were also called districts but that we shall call "subdistricts" in the following discussion. All in all the Kōfukuji controlled a total of 106 subdistricts: the Main Temple controlled 52 of that total; the Daijō-in *monzeki* controlled 41; and the Ichijō-in *monzeki* controlled 13.

Some documents issued early in the Muromachi period indicate that a subdistrict was composed of about fifteen to twenty households, most of which had adjacent fields. If those figures are reliable, then the Kōfukuji's 116 subdistricts included approximately sixteen hundred to twenty-one hundred households. If the average household had between five and ten members, then the population of the Kōfukuji's districts was at least eight thousand and possibly as high as twenty thousand people. Several thousand of those people would have been adult males, some of whom would have been monks, and the rest of the population either peasants or merchants and artisans and their families, some of whom might or might not have taken the tonsure. To this number must be added the population of the districts controlled by the shrines, which Nagashima Fukutarō estimates to have been about fifteen hundred adult men at the end of the Muromachi period. By the end of the medieval period the population of the city of Nara probably numbered about thirty-five thousand people, the great majority of whom were under the total or partial control of the Kasuga cultic center, some of whom were under the control of the Tōdaiji, and all of whom were related to the Kasuga-Kōfukuji multiplex in one way or another.

ECONOMIC CONSIDERATIONS

The districts and subdistricts of Nara varied economically, some specializing in agriculture and others in commerce. Many of the men who engaged in those occupations became *jinin* or *shuto*. For example, the district called Abura-zaka (Oil-hill) was under the control of *jinin* of Kasuga who specialized in the lucrative oil business; these oil merchants gained *jinin* status by offering to provide oil free of charge to the multiplex. This status was highly valued for several reasons: first, those who had it were exempt both from having to pay taxes to the multiplex and from the corvee services that were required of the common people. Second, *jinin* obtained special privileges for the establishment of markets in Yamato Province and elsewhere: they received from the multiplex a "seal" that allowed them to do business controlled by the cultic center. This was an extremely lucrative situation. In one case, Kyoto oil merchants who were Kasuga *jinin* managed to evade the taxes and corvee services that were levied by the Hie Shrines; when, at one point, the question of that exemption arose, discussions took place between the leaders of Mount Hiei and the dignitaries of the Kōfukuji, the latter of whom won the case. This shows the power of the cultic center and how close the connection between merchants and the multiplex became. Some temples established money-lending houses and amassed great fortunes through the levying of exorbitant interest rates.

A somewhat typical district of the Kōfukuji was Mochidono (Rice-cakes Hall), which is famous for its merchant street and its role in the preparation of the *On-matsuri*. Its name is said to have originated in the fact that this area specialized in preparing food offerings of rice cakes for the divinity Benzaiten. In 1570 this district had the following specialized households: a maker of bamboo screens (*sudare*), a locksmith, several carpenters (*banshō*) who had a part-time position in Kyoto and one who resided full-time in Nara, a maker of waistbands (*haramaki*), a preparer of noodles, a brewer, a public bath owner, two silversmiths, and a number of officials (*kunin*). Documents indicate that the population of Mochidono almost doubled in the space of twenty-five years at the end of the sixteenth century. Today it is one of the major merchant areas of Nara.

By the end of the Kamakura period the multiplex ran two major markets: the southern market, which belonged to the Daijō-in *monzeki*, and the northern market, which belonged to the Ichijō-in *monzeki*. The southern market was created in 1302, when the old Fukushima market was transferred to that site. The northern market, which was created in 1414, was owned by the scholarly monks (*gakuryo*) of the temples but was administered by the *shuto*. The markets were held for a duration of three days each ten-day period and were open alternately. Each market was protected by the divinity of prosperity, Ebisu, which was worshiped in its own shrine. These Ebisu shrines are still present in Nara today.

Nara's merchant associations (*za*), the oldest of which was an association of sake brewers that is first mentioned in documents written in the early Kamakura period, might have originated in these surroundings. Other associations quickly developed around that time and put themselves under the partial control of the temples. In 1407, for example, the southern market had as many as thirty associations for the following products: rice, cakes, yams, radishes, birds, lotus roots, fish, salt, soybeans, pines, charcoal, ramie, silk, wadded-silk garments, indigo, cloth, cotton, paper, small articles, hats, caps, straw seats, buckets, nails, gold, kettles, arrows, clay pots, noodles, and gruel.

The markets were used not only by the city residents but also by rural peasants and other people who came to the city for purchases until markets were created in other cities. In the late medieval period, warriors, worried that the multiplex had too much economic strength, forcibly removed merchants and artisans from Nara and had them settle in other cities, such as Kōriyama, the stronghold of the Tsutsui clan.

The economic well-being of Nara fluctuated considerably: some times were undoubtedly harsher than others, with little possibility of a reduction of the economic and in-kind tax burden imposed on the populace by the multiplex. Movements of liberation from the tutelage of the cultic center arose in the sixteenth century, first among the artisans and merchants of the city and later among the peasants. Some measure of self-government was granted by the multiplex to the main districts, and regular meetings as well as procedures for grievances were established. These were probably based on the grievance and meeting procedures developed over time by the *shuto* of the cultic center, in which some historians locate the origin of the self-governed groups (*jichikai*) that characterize contemporary Japan.

Finally, it should be mentioned that several areas, mostly in the northern part of Nara, were reserved for what were known in the medieval period as "nonpersons" (*hinin*) and for beggars and poor people (*senmin*). Extremely little is known about the *hinin* and the *senmin*, whose status seems to have varied and had to do with notions of purity and pollution and with brushes with the law. Some monks specialized in helping those people by dispensing medicine, food, and spiritual help to them. Some *hinin* and *senmin* played an important role in the festivities of the multiplex as jugglers, acrobats, and actors.[46]

GOVERNANCE AND POLICE

The only documents on the organizational structure of the districts are records that were made by the *jinin* and *shuto* when funds were requested from each household for rituals and ceremonies. The little information we have reveals that there were elders (*tone*) who, either alone or in groups, decided local matters in cooperation with various officials of those local subtemples that specialized in contacts with the high administration of the multiplex. Apparently the elders had some degree of autonomy because they held meetings apart from those officials in separate buildings.

Police and legal matters in the district were supervised by the abbot but were taken care of by certain *shuto* and *jinin* who were called *kunin* (officials). These men, who survived as local authority figures up to the nineteenth century, were charged with reporting on district matters to the authorities of the various temples and with assigning the various duties to be fulfilled for the cultic center. The *kunin* were also charged with ensuring the proper payment of taxes, originally in produce and later either in money or professional services. If an incident occurred in one of the districts, the officials of the temple to which the district belonged would investigate and summarily decide on the case. If the incident was a criminal offense, they would burn or otherwise destroy the houses of the culprits.

The *shuto* charged with this grim duty were always accompanied by *jinin* of Kasuga, so that purification of the site could be swiftly performed. All these matters were supervised by the "supervisors" (*suten*, or *jichō*) of the districts. Toward the middle of the Muromachi period police matters, which during the Heian period had been in the hands of the *shuto* and during the Kamakura period in the hands of the *kunin*, fell under the jurisdiction of the Tsutsui warriors who traced their origins to the *shuto* of the Kamakura period but who worked in concert with the *bakufu*.

The district around the Gangōji represents a special case: this originally powerful temple lost its economic strength during the Heian period and fell under the rule of the Tōdaiji and the Kōfukuji. When the Daijō-in *monzeki* was destroyed by fire at the end of the twelfth century, however, the Zenjō-in pavilion at the Gangōji was used for the residence of the abbot and came to be considered a part of the Daijō-in *monzeki*. Thus the district of the Gangōji fell under the control of that *monzeki*. Jurisdictional problems in that district remained, however, and the abbot of the Gangōji kept the right and duty to investigate criminal matters. This abbot was chosen for one term from the Tōdaiji and one term from the Kōfukuji. This led to the following compromise when a criminal matter was investigated in the district: namely, emissaries of three parties (the Tōdaiji, the Daijō-in *monzeki*, and the Main Temple) arrived on the scene in a prearranged order. The Main Temple was represented because of the claim that the Kōfukuji, as the governor of Yamato Province, had the right to investigate such matters.

The Tsutsui warriors were given police authority by the Ashikaga *bakufu* in the sixteenth century; they were the "government-appointed *shuto*" (*kampu-shuto*) mentioned earlier, whose rule came to encompass the entire city and parts of Yamato Province during the Edo period. At that time, some of them became *daimyō*, and the main Tsutsui figure in the sacred city became the Nara *bugyō*. The main cause of the transformation of the organization of Nara during the premodern period was the appearance of these local warriors, who gradually penetrated the city and took over the responsibility for the police and justice; they increased their control after the multiplex lost much of its economic and political power at the hands of Oda Nobunaga and Toyotomi Hideyoshi.

In conclusion, we have examined the type of community that the Kasuga-Kōfukuji multiplex developed during the Kamakura and Muromachi periods and the factors that pushed the Kasuga cult out of the aristocratic world into the world of the commoners. The multiplex stood in the center of Nara surrounded by the districts and subdistricts it controlled. It commanded a population of men whose status was not exactly that of laity nor exactly that of clergy, who bore arms or were ready to bear them when necessary, and who identified themselves directly in relation to the shrines (*jinin*) or the temples (*shuto*) and therefore viewed themselves as a sociocosmic community. This community, which was strictly organized according to notions of purity and pollution, included people who ranged in status from aristocratic ecclesiastics to nonpersons, all of whom resided in strictly defined zones.

The population of the sacred city worshiped divine entities that ranged from protectors of the land to demonic spirits, as well as the *kami* enshrined in the various old cultic sites of the city, such as the Izakawa Shrine or the Ebisu Shrines. They also participated in rituals at the various temples and subtemples as well as in the shrines and subshrines that were opened to them, such as the Wakamiya Shrine for Kasuga or the Hachiman Tamuke Shrine for the Tōdaiji. These *kami* were worshiped in the light of their associations with various buddhas and bodhisattvas of the large pantheon represented in the temples, and the population of the province shared a sense of importance, legitimacy, and identity provided by the immense power of the multiplex. Various confraternities of devotees of Kasuga *daimyōjin* developed in the villages. It was in the midst of these conditions that Nara developed its unique culture.

3 Protocol
The Sociocosmic Organon

Protocol: a rigid long-established code prescribing complete deference to superior rank and strict adherence to due order of precedence and precisely correct procedure.

Webster's Third New International Dictionary

This chapter will analyze the various elements of the "universe of meaning and practice" exhibited during the medieval period by the Kasuga-Kōfukuji multiplex. To that end it will examine the multiplex's economic base, ceremonies, and rituals and will attempt to delineate the understanding of the multiplex held by Jinson, abbot of the Daijō-in *monzeki* during the second half of the fifteenth century and author of the *Daijō-in jisha zōjiki*, perhaps the most important diary of the period. One can find in the relations among these elements the overarching principles whereby the multiplex defined itself and was inscribed within the larger cultural discourse of Japan during the classical and medieval periods. Also, an examination of protocol and hierarchy ("the procedural imperative") will provide insights into the nature of rituals seen as tools of social organization and disseminators of cultural information, and an examination of ritual ("the ritual imperative") will reveal the intricacies of the relations between state and house, house and province, rite and protocol, and between Buddhist and non-Buddhist ideologies. These two imperatives were connected in a fundamental manner by way of claims to territorial possession ("the territorial imperative"), which are evidenced in part by the fact that food and money offerings for the shrines were drawn exclusively from certain land domains, as well as by the fact that land possessions were claimed in virtue of a sociocosmic status.

THE PROCEDURAL IMPERATIVE

George Sansom wrote of the Fujiwara:

> Sources of information. . . . [are] concerned with what at first sight seems to be the most trivial detail of Court life, points of

ceremonial and the niceties of etiquette. But their very existence bears witness to a significant feature of metropolitan life under the rule of the Fujiwara; and therefore a brief description of their contents may properly serve as an introduction to the study of Japanese society. . . . [O]ther works . . . seem on cursory examination to pay excessive attention to matters of ceremonial. In the *Shōyūki* are to be found descriptions of a wrestling match, a poetry contest, prayers for harvest, and the correct form of documents. The *Gonki* deals largely with etiquette and ceremonies. The *Chūyūki* treats of rules for Court dress, for the conduct of horse races as part of religious festivals, for precedence at official functions, and similar matters.[1]

George Sansom was right: protocol, hierarchy, and ceremony were an important part of court life in the Fujiwara house. It is necessary, however, to go beyond the mere recognition of the importance of protocol to point to its central function in the organization of the universe of meaning and practice that the Fujiwara constructed and its generative aspects in the form of Japanese society.

In Japan, sanctity has tended to function as an equivalent of power, with a peculiarly medieval twist in which those who possessed authority had little real power but staked their survival on the claim that their authority had originated in a sanctified realm. Not only was this an almost perennial condition in the case of the imperial lineage (emperors reigned but rarely ruled), but it was also the case with respect to the Fujiwara house after the twelfth century and with respect to the Kasuga-Kōfukuji multiplex from the sixteenth century, when it lost much of its economic and political power but continued to claim divine status.

This sanctity was legitimated by claims of divine origin, rituals at the multiplex, the social hierarchy, and the establishment of shrines on domains owned by the multiplex. The expression of sanctity took, at times, the extreme form of procedure and protocol, which are the dominant aspects of the performance of ritual, and ritual itself served to legitimize power. In this intricate web of interdependency, several factors could directly threaten the internal coherence of the system. A breach in etiquette or protocol could negate the efficacy of a ritual; the loss of a land domain could challenge divine status; and historical conflicts eventually threatened a legitimacy based on an ancient myth. The Fujiwara house therefore insisted on the periodic renewal of its shrines and the regular performance of rituals to be witnessed by those whom the house claimed to govern. The Fujiwara paid an incredible amount of attention to the most minute details of rite, protocol, and performance. Their noble lineage took on a priestly role in order to reaffirm their divine status, and members of the Fujiwara lineage became the leading ecclesiastics of the Kasuga-Kōfukuji multiplex.

The combination of ritual, protocol, and land possessions reveals the existence of tensions between the concepts of political and religious authority. If for some of the Fujiwara the secular and the sacred merged in practice, and if this fusion was legitimized by the Buddhist doctrine of "non-twoness," they in fact lived according to a double standard whereby this doctrine applied to them but not to others.[2] In other words, ideology and practice clashed. Notions of protocol and rank were also attached to the *kami*: food offerings were given by rank (the first shrine received food first), and the shrines were all structurally connected to social order by ranking. As the importance of the Fujiwara house grew, the ranks of the shrines affiliated with it were elevated, and when the shrines of Kasuga received a higher rank to reflect the higher status of the Fujiwara, the ranks of the Kashima, Katori, and Hiraoka shrines were also elevated.

Little research has been conducted on the nature and function of the ranking of shrines, and thus it is premature to make definitive statements in that regard. It is probable, however, that this ranking was an index of the amount of offerings made by the court to the shrines, the nature of the relation of the Fujiwara house to the imperial house, and, finally, a direct indication of the way the early Japanese conceptualized their society. The ranking of shrines was identical in style, order, and denomination to the ranking of the nobility at court. The consequence of this identity was the construction of a hierarchy at the level of *kami* that matched that of humans; and, since these two hierarchies mirrored each other, the human order, grounded in protocol, reinforced the principle on which it was based through the performance of rites in which protocol and hierarchy played a major part. This was a sociocosmic system.

The ascent of the Kasuga *kami* to the highest ranks among the divinities took place rather swiftly. On the fifth moon of 836, the following ranks were granted:

Takemikatsuchi-no-mikoto: Senior Second Rank
Iwainushi-no-mikoto: Senior Second Rank
Ame-no-koyane-no-mikoto: Senior Third Rank
Himegami: Junior Fourth Rank

Just three years later, the following ranks were granted:

Takemikatsuchi-no-mikoto: First Rank
Iwainushi-no-mikoto: First Rank

Ame-no-koyane-no-mikoto: Second Rank
Himegami: Senior Fourth Rank, lower class

In 850, the following ranks were granted:

Takemikatsuchi-no-mikoto: Senior First Rank
Iwainushi-no-mikoto: Senior First Rank
Ame-no-koyane-no-mikoto: Junior First Rank
Himegami: Senior Fourth Rank, upper class

The Kashima and Katori tutelary *kami* (Takemikatsuchi and Iwainushi) always held a higher rank than the ancestral *kami* (Ame-no-koyane and Himegami). This indicates the respect in which the former two were held by the Fujiwara house and suggests that the cult had, from its inception, a particular coloration in which the periphery played a large role, as is evidenced by the custom of the "Kashima emissaries" and by the fact that the first economic support of Kasuga was derived from Kashima.

The notion that the divine and human orders were two aspects of a single reality had important consequences. First, there was a parallel between mythology and history: the aristocrats claimed to be the descendants of *kami* whose exploits are described in the myths, so that the distinction between the mythological past and the present was blurred. This, in turn, gave history (time) a sacred character, evidenced by the claim that human actions are ultimately determined by the *kami;* and it also gave land (space) a sacred character, evidenced by the claim that "Yamato is a sacred land" (*Yamato wa shinkoku nari*). The relation of myth to a history imbued with a sacred character was affirmed in rituals in which those myths and the symbols that sustained them were reactivated, and the relation of myth to space imbued with a sacred character was affirmed in ritual and the periodic reconstructions of shrines. Second, these rituals were rites of renewal in which two distinct binary orders—divine/human and myth/history—communicated and reinforced each other in the interplay of proper procedure, performance, and food offerings. And third, all these served to ground the legitimacy of the Fujiwara house, first in the context of Japanese society and later in relation to the imperial house and power.

In every instance it is obvious that in early Japanese ideology the divine and human orders were inseparable and that the ceremonial center acted as a catalyst and model for the stabilization of a certain form of society within a culturally determined universe of meaning. It is also obvious, especially during the medieval period, that the binary myth/history construct was central to formulations of history writing and the ideology of the state. Finally, the vision of Yamato, and later Japan, as a sacred land was also central to the formulation of the ideology of the state.

THE TERRITORIAL IMPERATIVE

In early Japanese history a territory seemed to be a central characteristic of the formation and organization of clans. The creation of Heijō-kyō and new houses as the result of political or other achievements signaled the appearance of a different type of social organization, one uprooted from what might have been its original territory (if it had any). This was a significant change: instead of an insistence on territory as the main aspect of cohesion in the clan, there was increased insistence on blood relationships and protocol, together with the possibility of allowing outsiders into the group through adoption. This marked the appearance of the "house," the identity of which was grounded in ancestral and tutelary *kami* rather than in predominantly territorial *kami*.

A case in point is that of the Fujiwara house. The Fujiwara appeared originally as a somewhat abstract political and social entity separated from direct contact with any particular territory but attached by blood to the imperial lineage as soon as it succeeded in having an emperor born of a union between one of its women and a member of the imperial house. This became a major practice of the Fujiwara: Japanese traditional history counts 125 emperors and empresses, 61 of whom had Fujiwara mothers (66 if one includes the emperors of the Northern Court). To realize their ambitions the Fujiwara used all possible means at their disposal—from exiling competitors to employing religious rituals to ensure the birth of male children. The tight relationship between the Fujiwara house and the imperial lineage was motivated at least in part by the fact that, according to the new System of Codes, all land belonged to the state/emperor and the closer one was to the imperial house, the greater the possibility of acquiring land possessions and, therefore, power.

If, however, at the time of its inception the Fujiwara house did not possess any land (except that which had been granted to Kamatari), it soon came to receive extensive domains that were granted to it for its services to the state. In other words, although the Fujiwara house was not originally a territory-bound social unit, it soon became one. Of course it did not own all the private estates (*shōen*) in the country, and, in fact, only a portion of the total revenue of its estates was earmarked for transmission to the Fujiwara. Very soon, however, possession claims began to be made, especially on the part of shrine-temple multiplexes run by the Fujiwara house. One of the reasons for this development is that it was becoming extremely difficult to ensure the proper payment of taxes, especially after the disturbance of Jōkyū in 1221.

The *kami* that were to become those of the Fujiwara house did not own a territory, though they were related to the conquest and pacification of "Japan" in the provinces of Izumo and Hitachi, as described in the *Kojiki* and *Nihongi*. As discussed earlier, however, from the middle of the Heian period the combinatory divine entity Kasuga *daimyōjin* was seen as the protector of the entire province of Yamato and of all domains claimed by the cultic center and the Fujiwara house throughout Japan. Through the use of estates granted to its shrine-temple multiplexes, and through the appointment of some of its members to the positions of highest authority in those cultic centers, the Fujiwara house managed to become, by the beginning of the medieval period, a full-fledged territory-bound social, political, and religious unit.

This would not have been possible without the development of the *shōen* system, without the preservation of the past in the form of rituals and the regular reconstruction of ritual buildings, and without extensive worship of the divine entity of Kasuga as protector of the Fujiwara house, Yamato Province, and the state. This worship entailed, in a prominent manner, food offerings drawn from land domains, through which offerings relations between the center and the periphery were reinforced. These are the main reasons why rituals, land possessions, and protocol must be discussed in relation to each other.

The Fujiwara house had evolved early into four separate lineages, each originating with a son of Fuhito: Muchimaro's lineage was called the Southern lineage (*nanke*); Fusasaki's the Northern lineage (*hokke*); Uma-kai's the Ceremony lineage (*shikike*); and Maro's the Capital lineage (*kyōke*). These four lineages gave birth, in turn, to sublineages, such as the *Kanjūji-ryū* and the five *Sekkanke*. Each of these was in turn subdivided into households. During the course of the Heian period the Kasuga-Kōfukuji multiplex became a symbol of unity for the entire Fujiwara house, and at the same time, it organized its affairs as if it were itself a house. In so doing, it created a discourse of power that is representative of the entire medieval period, in which specific relations obtained between rank and status, purity and pollution, and sanctity and power.

The person responsible for the main rites of the Fujiwara house at the Kasuga-Kōfukuji multiplex was the house chieftain (*uji no chōja*). It is generally thought that the custom of choosing a house chieftain began with Mototsune (836–91), but Nagashima Fukutarō thinks that the practice may have existed before that time.[3] Its origin corresponded exactly with the changes that came about in the Kasuga Grand Rite in 859 and with the last elevation of the rank of the *kami*. This indicates that Mototsune was a pivotal figure in the history of the Fujiwara house. In any case, the position and power of the house chieftain were directly related to the Kasuga-Kōfukuji multiplex because ritual matters served to unify the house behind the chieftain, recall the identity of the social group, and reaffirm its hierarchy.

Pointedly, the legitimacy of the chieftain was directly associated with land. At the time of his investiture the chieftain was granted the following emblems of legitimacy: a seal, a red lacquered dish, a plate for food offerings, and four land domains (*doryō shisho*), namely, Shikata, Katakami, Kusunoha, and Sahodono. These domains provided revenues for specific rituals. The Sahodono domain in Yamato provided finances for the lodging of the Fujiwara chieftain during his visits to the Kasuga-Kōfukuji multiplex. The Shikata domain in Bizen provided funds for the *Hokke-e* and *Chōgō-e*, ritual assemblies that were held at the Nan'endō in the Kōfukuji, as well as for the ritual feasts of spring and autumn at the Ōharano Shrine. The Katakami domain provided funds for the *Yuishiki-e* ritual assembly held at the Eastern Golden Hall and for a ceremony called *Shiji-busshō*. The Kusunoha domain provided the sacred horses that were traditionally offered by the house chieftains at the time of the Kasuga Grand Rite. These four domains, with their exclusive relation to fundamental rituals that took place in the multiplex, together with the other emblems of legitimacy that were transmitted to each generation of Fujiwara chieftains, indicate that the legitimacy of the chieftain as head of the entire house was grounded in the cult. It is clear that the function of the chieftain of the house was a matter of protocol embodied in ritual and grounded in land domains that were related in a specific manner to the multiplex. It should also be emphasized that the rituals connected to the house chieftain were performed at both the Kasuga Shrine and the Kōfukuji, which means that from the middle of the ninth century on, Japanese concepts of power and legitimacy were grounded in both *kami* and buddhas/bodhisattvas.

When the new chieftain was to use his seal for the first time he sent emissaries to the Kashima and Katori shrines in the northeast and informed the Kasuga, Ōharano, and Yoshida shrines that this was being done. Apart from the symbolic reference to the original site of the tutelary *kami*, the origin of this custom is unclear, but the rationale is clearly based on territory and center-periphery relations. This practice is mentioned for the first time in the journal of Fujiwara no Michinaga (966–1027) in the year

995, but it might have occurred as early as 859. The priestly heads of the Kasuga, Kashima, and Katori shrines were always nominated by the house chieftain and were appointed by government decree.[4]

At the time of the Kasuga Grand Rite, messengers were again sent to Kashima; dispatched by the Office of the *kami* of Heaven and Earth (*jingikan*), they were always chosen from the pool of house members who were students at the Kangaku-in. This particular event lasted about a month, during which time elaborate offerings were made at Kashima and Katori. One of the functions of these messengers to the distant province of Hitachi was to relay to the *kami* all information deemed important, such as nominations to high office, requests for male children, announcements of births, and other matters of direct relevance to the welfare of the Fujiwara house. This practice became central to the cult during the Heian period and remained so through history. In general, members of the Fujiwara house would address their personal requests to the *kami* at Kasuga, but they made offerings of gratitude—if their wishes were realized—to the Kashima and Katori shrines. Rites accompanying requests by imperial consorts that they bear male children were often made, and always at Kashima. There is no evidence that this type of request was addressed at Kasuga; this may indicate that the Kasuga and Kashima *kami*, although identical, had different functions in the minds of the house members. Sometimes the Fujiwara addressed their requests to the Sannō divinities of Mount Hiei rather than to the Kasuga divinities.

In addition to the benefits it enjoyed from the four domains that symbolized the position of the Fujiwara house chieftain, and from the land possessions of the Fujiwara house in general, the cultic center itself began to accumulate land. From the middle of the Nara period the Kōfukuji had been a *daiji* (Great Monastery), that is, one funded by the state for the purpose of protecting the state, and the funds for ceremonies commissioned by the state came from domains earmarked for this specific purpose.[5] Gradually the government abandoned that practice and began to grant domains rather than funds; the Fujiwara house followed suit, offering domains to the multiplex. The temples were then held responsible for the development of these parcels of land.

The Kōfukuji did possess some land in the Nara period: approximately one thousand *chō*, from which it received a revenue of 1,200 *ko*.[6] As Nagashima Fukutarō explains:

> The exact extent of the possessions of the Kōfukuji during the Nara period is unknown. According to the *Ruki*, besides the land granted when the temple was founded, Kōmyō Kōgō gave seventy

chō of wet land in the provinces of Yamashiro and Echizen to provide funds for the memorial services dedicated to the spirit of her deceased father Fuhito. By imperial decree a donation of one thousand *chō* of land in Echizen and Kaga was made in 749. In 757 Fujiwara no Nakamaro donated one hundred *chō* of land—the domain of Namazue in Ōmi—to provide funds for offerings. In 762 an imperial grant of thirty *chō* of land was made to provide funds for the *Brahmajala-sūtra* rites dedicated to the spirit of Kōmyō Kōgō; to these, fifty more *chō* were added in 765. This land was granted to provide funds for buildings, sacred images and rites. It is not clear whether those lands were *kaiden* (tilled fields) or *konden* (reclaimed land). . . . In any case it seems that the economic base of the Kōfukuji during the Nara period was of a small scale. Of all the documents of the Nara period concerning the temple, not a single one contains information on those matters.[7]

Originally the Kasuga Shrine received support thanks to a decree issued in 768 that ordered the Kashima Shrine of Hitachi to provide Kasuga with revenues from the landholdings of twenty households for every yearly ritual. This practice was abandoned in 820 when Kasuga and the Kōfukuji were granted domains by the government and members of the Fujiwara house. Shortly after the death of Kōmyō Kōgō, Fujiwara no Nagate (714–71) devised strategies to consolidate the Northern branch and unify the house. The Northern branch, which was the strongest of the four, supported the Kōfukuji and forced the other branches to separate themselves from the temple. For instance, Muchimaro, a member of the Southern branch, was not given memorial rites at the Kōfukuji but was buried on Mount Ada in the district of Uchi, and the Eizanji was erected there for the repose of his spirit.

At the beginning of the Heian period, Fuyutsugu, a leader of the Northern branch of the Fujiwara house, built the Nan'endō at the Kōfukuji. This building and its dedication by Kūkai symbolically marked the ascendance of the Northern branch, reinforced the centrality of the Kasuga-Kōfukuji multiplex, and led to the architectural enlargement of the Kasuga Shrine during the Jōgan period (858–77). Because the multiplex thus became the Ceremonial Center for the Fujiwara house, and because the house blossomed during the Heian period, the cultic center remained strong. This was in stark contrast with the other shrines and temples of Nara, which, with the exception of the Tōdaiji, fell into disrepair. Toward the end of the Heian period it became difficult for the Tōdaiji to administer land domains situated in distant provinces, so it turned its attention toward

Yamato Province, only to discover to its dismay that most of the province was under the control of the Kōfukuji.

Every time the Fujiwara house was granted land for services that it rendered the state, it was customary to offer part of that land to the multiplex in gratitude to the *kami* and the buddhas. Because most of that land was located in Yamato Province, the multiplex had a major advantage over other temples whose lands were located in various parts of the country and were therefore more difficult to administer and control. Furthermore, because a Kasuga subshrine was erected on each parcel of land owned by the multiplex, the people of Yamato Province came to be associated with the cultic center in a unique way; and when the cultic center became the governor of the province, it appointed functionaries in each district. The multiplex thus became a political and economic entity.

As the Fujiwara climbed higher in the government and attributed their power and success to their *kami* and the spirits of their forefathers, they enlarged the multiplex. In 859, for example, the Kasuga Shrine was considerably enlarged: it was then that the four main buildings were built and numerous other buildings added, thus giving the shrine the appearance it has today. The periodic reconstruction of the shrines, which takes place every twenty years on the model of Ise, may have come into effect by that time. The position of abbot of the Kōfukuji was created in Jōgan 11 (870), as was that of assistant abbot; by then the shrine-temple multiplex had become a major institution on a par with the most powerful temples of Kyoto.

It was at that time that the major rites were reorganized to fit the state character of the cult. The participation of a sacral woman (*saijo*) by imperial order in the Grand Rite became a major part of that rite also around that time. Among the major rites that came to symbolize Nara, the *Tegai-e* of the Hachiman Tamuke Shrine of the Tōdaiji and the Kōfukuji's *Jōgaku-e* and *Shūni-e* of the Western Golden Hall were instituted in 860. The *Jōgaku-e* became famous for its performance of music and the *Shūni-e* for its performance, during the medieval period, of *takigi-Nō*.[8]

Land was granted by the government and members of the Fujiwara house to pay for the maintenance of the buildings and for those immensely expensive rites. In 881 the temple received grants of 600 *chō* of land in the districts of Niu, Ono, Sakai, and others in Echizen Province. In 883 it received 216 *chō* in Kaga and another 112 *chō* in Echizen. When the office of Regents (*sesshō* and *kampaku*) was established by the Fujiwara in the middle of the Heian period, that office came to rule the country in fact, and the five branches of the Fujiwara house (the five *sekkanke*), from whom the Regents issued, amassed a large number of land domains, parts of which they granted to the multiplex. Some lands were "commended" directly to the multiplex in order to be put under its spiritual protection (and to be tax free). Examples that can be gleaned from the records are:

In 986, Emperor Shirakawa donated 1,384 ha.

In 1021, on the occasion of a visit by Emperor Go-Ichijō, the district of Sounokami in Yamato was donated.

In 1083, fields immediately surrounding the multiplex were donated by imperial decree.

In 1100, Retired Emperor Shirakawa donated the domain of Kawaguchi to provide funds for the reading (*tendoku*) of the complete canon of Buddhist scriptures (*Issaikyō*).

In 1104, on the occasion of a pilgrimage to the shrine, Fujiwara no Munetada donated five fields from a domain in Noto and five others from a domain in Kibi.

In 1108, Fujiwara no Tadazane ordered that special rites be performed "for the longevity of the house" and donated the domain of Nakagawa in Yamato Province.

In 1122, the domain of Ōshima in Settsu Province was donated.

In 1183, Fujiwara no Motomichi donated the domain of Tarumi in Settsu Province.

And in 1286, Retired Emperor Go-Fukakusa offered 690 ha.

These recorded gifts yield an exceedingly poor representation of the actual state of affairs. In fact, domains were granted to the multiplex in such vast quantitites that the *Heihanki* reports the following complaint as early as 1158: "The province of Yamato has become the possession of the Kasuga Shrine and of the Kōfukuji: not one single square foot of public fields is left in the province."[9] It had become customary to put land under the spiritual protection of the multiplex, and the Kōfukuji gave local notables the position of domain official on those lands. Very early in the Heian period these officials became in effect powerful landowners whose relation to the multiplex was ambiguous, if not outright antagonistic. A good example is provided in the middle of the Heian period: Minamoto no Yorichika, a close attendant to Fujiwara no Michinaga, was appointed governor of Yamato Province. He used his position to establish a number of private estates in the southern part of the province. His descendants settled there as local powerful landowners who became "Provincials" (*Kokumin*), such as the Uno and Ochi Yamato Warriors. They did not hesitate to display their independence from the multiplex.

Thus the Kasuga-Kōfukuji multiplex was transformed from an *uji*-related institution into a jealously independent entity, an *état dans l'état* ("state within the state"). In 1135, Minamoto no Shigetoki, who was named governor of Yamato Province, attempted to go to Nara to "worship the *kami* and the buddhas," but the *shuto* of the multiplex were so aggravated that they refused to let him enter the province. The reason for their anger was twofold: first, the multiplex, remembering only too well the example of Yorichika, felt that a Minamoto had no business worshiping the *ujigami* of a house that was not his own (even though the Fujiwara adopted some Minamoto men when they had no sons); and, second, this refusal was an attempt on the part of the multiplex to prevent governmental interference into its affairs. The multiplex became thenceforth the de facto governor (*shugo*) of the province and received legal authority to prevent government officials from entering its land domains (*funyū-ken*). Those domains, which were exempt from taxation, provided the revenue for the development and maintenance of the multiplex and its rituals.

During the medieval period food offerings that were made daily at the shrines in the morning and evening, and special offerings that were made every ten days, were drawn from specific land domains in the following manner. The morning offerings, which consisted of five *to* and eight *masu* of rice (34.56 quarts U.S.) and four hundred copper coins (*mon*), were requested from domains in Yamato and Settsu that belonged to the *sekkanke* but were administered by the Kōfukuji.[10] The evening offerings, the amount of which we do not know, were requested from domains of Yamato Province by the sacerdotal houses of the shrines. The special offering that was made every ten days consisted of two *koku* of rice (89.6 gallons U.S.) and six thousand *mon* and was drawn from Settsu domains by the *gakuryo* (scholarly monks). Products of the sea and the mountains that were also offered were secured by granting the status of *jinin* to merchants' associations (*za*) in areas bordering the sea, especially in Settsu and Izumi.

In order to ensure payment of the taxes it levied on its domains, the multiplex installed *jinin* and *shuto* to take care of the Kasuga subshrines (*massha*) and of the Kōfukuji subtemples (*matsuji*) built on those domains. The *jinin* and *shuto* were responsible for the upkeep of the buildings, the performance of ceremonies, the forwarding of tax revenues, and the police. One of the symbols of ownership of land domains was the establishment of a transit fee that was levied on people and goods passing through the domains.

There are few documents on the land possessions of the Kasuga-Kōfukuji multiplex during the medieval period. Proofs of ownership either did not exist, even though they were required by the government, or else

Table 4. Subtemples and Subshrines Controlled by
the Saishō-in of the Kōfukuji in 1441

Province	No. of Temples	No. of Shrines
Yamato	16	9
Yamashiro	44	17
Settsu	3	0
Iga	4	2
Ōmi	69	17
Kawachi	6	0
Total	142	45

Source: "Kōfukuji kammu chōsho," in *Dai Nihon Bukkyō Zensho*, vol. 84, no. 673.

they were lost in the many fires and attacks that befell the cultic center over the years. Some information on the extent of the landholdings of the multiplex in the late medieval period is available. For instance, in the late sixteenth century the Kōfukuji held a grand total of 344 land domains. Of these, 271 were in the province of Yamato (in contrast, the Tōdaiji had only 52 domains in that province), and most of the remaining 73 domains were in the Kinai area: 12 in both Yamashiro and Settsu, 9 in Ōmi, and 7 in Kawachi. The last 33 domains were located in other provinces from Kyushu in the west to Dewa in the north.

Three documents contained in the *Dai Nihon Bukkyō Zensho*—the first is dated 1441, the second 1666, and although the third one has no date, it seems to belong to the sixteenth century—offer detailed information on some of the multiplex's landholdings. The first document, entitled *Kōfukuji kammu chōsho*, contains a list of all the temples and shrines administered by the Saishō-in of the Kōfukuji in six provinces. It also offers some information concerning the official population of the subtemples and subshrines, though this type of information is lacking for a number of places. The numbers provided below are, therefore, an extremely pale reflection of the reality. Some numbers may have been underestimated, depending on whether the shrines and temples felt that the information would be detrimental or beneficial.[11]

In 1441 the Saishō-in of the Kōfukuji controlled a total of 187 branch institutions in six provinces, 142 of which were temples and 45 were shrines. The breakdown is shown in table 4. It should be noted that the numbers for Kawachi are said to be "abridged," and that the claim that

Table 5. Population of Subshrines and Subtemples Controlled by the Saishō-in of the Kōfukuji in 1441

Province	No. of Bō (halls)	Kōshū	Shuto	Jinin	Shasō (shrine-monks)	Kannushi (priests)	Shōji (servants)	Kenzoku (depen-dents)
					No. of Residents			
Yamato	373	129	23	45	22	3	50	—
Yamashiro	784	324	99	54	10	7	539	226
Settsu	188	—	—	—	—	—	—	—
Iga	35	10	—	—	—	—	—	—
Ōmi	1,762	66	342	67	29	42	2,058	26
Kawachi	74	—	—	—	—	—	—	56
Total	3,216	529	464	166	61	52	2,647	308

Source: "Kōfukuji kammu chōsho," in *Dai Nihon Bukkyō Zensho*, vol. 84, no. 673.

there were only sixteen temples and nine shrines in Yamato is prepos-terous.

The population of these sites of cult was divided into various groupings: the priestly and semipriestly residents of the temples (*kōshū, shuto, jinin,* and *shasō,* "shrine-monks") who lived in buildings called *bō*; and *kannushi* (shrine priests), *shoji* (menial workers for the temples and shrines), as well as *kenzoku* ("dependents"), whose status is unclear. The breakdown is given in table 5.

Obviously, something is amiss in those numbers. It may have been that the 4,227 people mentioned in table 5 all lived in the 3,216 buildings, but that was probably not the case, for each building was the residence of a priestly family and its dependents, including servants. Indeed, given that many statistics are missing, it is likely that the population of these sub-temples was at least twice as large as the numbers noted above.

The undated document, entitled *Kōfukuji matsuji chō*, is a list of all the subtemples that were under the supervision of the two *monzeki* and the Main Temple, but it provides no detailed information about them.[12] Ac-cording to that list, the Ichijō-in *monzeki* had 24 subtemples (5 in Ya-mashiro and 19 in Yamato), the Daijō-in *monzeki* had 28 (1 in Yamashiro and 27 in Yamato), and the Main Temple had 87 (76 in Yamato, 9 in Yamashiro, and 2 in Kawachi). That list does not include a single subtemple in Ōmi, which is strange when one recalls that this province had the largest number of subtemples according to the document dated 1441. The total number of subtemples mentioned in the *Kōfukuji matsuji chō* is 139, which

Table 6. Repartition of Revenues of the
Kasuga-Kōfukuji Multiplex in 1666

	Amount	
Recipient	Koku	To
Priestly (shake)	1,554	2
Priestly (negi)	1,651	8
Ichijō-in monzeki	1,495	2
Daijō-in monzeki	951	7
Kitai-in (inke)	280	0
Inke	290	0
Various bō (residences)	7,721	0
Five Masters (On-matsuri)	3,475	9
Study (Five Masters)	1,000	0
Repairs	1,071	0
Funds for kitō rites	1,195	3
Residences of negi	33	2
Shuto	380	0
Residences of shōji	19	9
Total	21,115	42
Total value[a]	21,119	2

Source: "Kōfukuji-ryō shuin," in Dai Nihon Bukkyō Zensho, vol. 84, no. 677.
[a]1 koku = 10 to.

is close to the number of 132 claimed in the *Kōfukuji kammu chōsho* of
1441.

The third document is of a different nature from the other two in that
it lists the assessed revenue of land domains (by rice production calculated
in *koku, to,* and *masu*) claimed in the governmental requests (*sashidashi*)
of 1596 and 1666.[13] The multiplex reported in 1596 a total assessed revenue
of 15,028 *koku,* six *to,* and nine *masu,* and in 1666 it reported a total
revenue of 21,119 *koku* and two *to.* It should be borne in mind that these
figures belong to a time following major losses of domains by the Kōfukuji
and that the figures were requested by the Tokugawa government. In 1666,
the revenues of the Kasuga-Kōfukuji multiplex were shared between the
various administrative branches of the cultic center (table 6), and the
revenues of the entire Kōfukuji were distributed by temple (table 7).

Table 7. Repartition of Revenues of the Kōfukuji in 1666

Recipient	Amount			
	Koku	To	Masu	Gō
Ichijō-in *monzeki*	1,495	2	0	0
Daijō-in *monzeki*	952	7	0	0
Kita-inke	280	0	0	0
Shōrin-inke	105	2	7	6
Shunan-inke	74	7	4	9
Tōboku-inke	74	6	2	7
Daiki-in	102	7	5	3
Hōshō-in	134	1	4	6
Seijō-in	88	6	8	4
Watenkyō-in	84	4	5	1
Enjū-in	56	7	0	7
Daiji-in	66	6	1	1
Hōtoku-in	51	2	8	1
Kongō-in	95	8	9	5
Sōjū-in	114	8	9	5
Fukujō-in	55	2	6	2
Saihosshi-in	85	2	2	7
Kanzen-in	154	8	9	4
Renge-in	51	7	3	7
Chikurin-in	59	9	7	4
Shōgan-in	73	8	4	9
Monju-in	88	7	2	0
Jimon-in	70	6	9	9
Ryūun-in	152	3	1	8
Kisshō-in	58	1	0	0
Jison-in	174	9	5	4
Amida-in	57	8	8	5
Fukujū-in	61	7	7	1
Godai-in	126	4	4	1
Shinnyo-in	76	0	0	0
Fudō-in	127	6	9	9
Jūfuku-in	31	7	5	7

Table 7 (*continued*)

Recipient	Amount			
	Koku	*To*	*Masu*	*Gō*
Saion-in	52	1	8	1
Shōkaku-in	34	8	0	0
Gyokuzō-in	40	8	7	7
Konshō-in	72	7	2	4
Aizan-in	30	7	0	0
Shōbō-in	32	1	3	0
Myōon-in	8	8	0	0
Tō-in	164	6	8	8
Hōun-in	49	0	6	5
Kannon-in	96	3	5	5
Hōzō-in	35	3	5	0
Jihō-in	49	9	0	0
Fukushō-in	27	5	5	2
Shōchi-in	92	5	7	2
Muryōjū-in	130	2	0	0
Myōki-in	69	1	2	0
Myōtoku-in	180	2	6	2
Manijū-in	88	6	0	0
Bucchi-in	50	8	0	8
Sanzō-in	67	8	4	4
Chūzō-in	69	7	3	0
Chisoku-bō	88	4	4	4
Jigen-in	97	8	6	7
Gyokurin-in	86	7	0	0
Jimyō-bō	60	2	0	7
An'yō-in	30	4	9	0
Daishō-in	49	4	4	7
Kanshū-bō	84	2	0	0
Kegon-in	79	0	3	5
Jion-in	34	6	9	6
Jakkō-in	83	0	0	0
Saishō-in	84	9	0	1
Zōkō-in	24	8	0	0
Kudoku-in	48	0	2	2

Continued on next page

Table 7 (continued)

Recipient	Amount			
	Koku	To	Masu	Gō
Tokuzō-in	85	4	8	3
Ryūtoku-in	29	4	5	8
Hōjū-in	97	0	0	0
Hōkō-in	37	5	3	9
Myōshō-in	42	0	8	1
Anraku-in	52	9	3	5
Miroku-in	51	8	2	2
Kenshō-in	134	3	4	3
Sangaku-in	36	2	4	9
Kōzen-in	75	0	0	4
Renzō-in	40	9	1	2
Myōkō-in	63	7	9	6
Hōjū-in	22	7	8	7
Jōmyō-in	77	6	0	9
Enjō-in	82	3	5	0
Eshin-in	60	7	6	0
Shōrō-in	51	5	3	2
Myōgyoku-in	114	7	0	3
Ekai-in	159	5	8	3
Enmyō-in	58	3	7	6
Mitsugon-in	46	8	8	1
Renjō-in	60	6	3	1
Tamon-in	67	0	0	0
Jōnyo-in	60	2	3	5
Jōshin-in	305	4	7	8
Yōken-in	50	0	5	7
Seson-in	105	5	6	2
Enman-in	47	9	4	6
Chishaku-in	82	2	1	2
Okuzō-in	29	2	0	0
Total	9,761	458	372	333
Total value[a]	9,810	8	5	3

Source: "Kōfukuji-ryō shuin," in Dai Nihon Bukkyō Zensho, vol. 84, no. 677.
[a]1 koku = 10 to; 1 to = 10 masu; 1 masu = 10 gō.

During the Kamakura and Muromachi periods the multiplex controlled its land domains by means of an organizational structure that was similar to the one whereby the multiplex itself was administered. At the top of the structure was the house chieftain, who oversaw the possessions of the *sekkanke*, which included domains owned by the Kōfukuji and by Kasuga as well as those possessions of the *sekkanke* that were independent of the multiplex. What domains the temples actually controlled is a complicated issue compounded by the fact that the temples administered some land possessions of the shrines. For the land possessions of the temples proper, there was a triple organizational structure: one branch of that structure dealt only with the land possessions of the various temples, pavilions, and halls; a second one dealt solely with the possessions of the two *monzeki*; and a third branch dealt only with the possessions of the Main Temple. The third branch had two subbranches, one of which controlled the expenses related to combinatory rituals and repairs to the buildings, and the other administered the expenses related to the personnel of the Main Temple itself. These expenses were provided by what was known as the abbot domains. Thus the administrative offices of the cultic center were concerned mostly with economic affairs and, to a lesser degree, with ritual affairs and such juridical matters as rules of inheritance, taxation, and justice. (The administrative separations of domains are represented schematically in diagram 3.)

A good example of the way in which ritual, protocol, and land domains were part of a single reality is found in the symbolic behavior of the multiplex's *shuto* and *jinin* on those occasions when they expressed grievances against the government or other multiplexes. The *shuto* of Kasuga were famous for backing their grievances with a most symbolic and ominous act: they placed the sacred tree of Kasuga (the *sakaki*), which was the emblem of the belief system, on a palanquin and carried it to Kyoto. They did not refrain from using violence whenever that suited their purpose, and thus they came to be feared. Their obstinate and violent behavior came to be known as *Yamashina dōri*, the "Yamashina method." Yamashina, it will be recalled, was the site of the private chapel of Nakatomi no Kamatari, which the Kōfukuji claims as its origin. The Yamashina method was in stark contrast to the scholastic debates that took place regularly in the temples; but then, land was at stake.

THE SACRED TREE: GROWTH OF RITUALIZED VIOLENCE

Almost every facet of human activity was ritualized during the Kamakura and Muromachi periods, and this development gave rise to set patterns of behavior and crystallized modes of action characterized by strict protocol

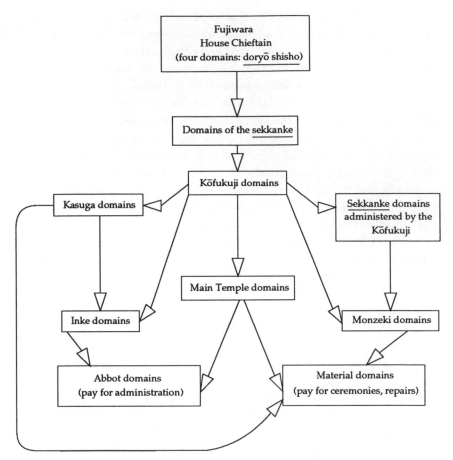

Diagram 3. Administrative Separations of the Land Domains of the Multiplex.

and proper procedure. A number of examples of this cultural tendency in Kasuga, such as the ritualization of theological debates in which the formalization of patterns reached an almost unbelievable level, might be studied from this perspective. Here we will consider the surprising example of conflict.

The economic and political power of the Kasuga-Kōfukuji multiplex took peculiar forms that can be explained in terms of the fundamental ambiguity of the concept of rule in Japan. This ambiguity is found in the understanding of the nature of power and its legitimation through sanctity. Whenever the multiplex was dissatisfied with decisions made by the court, or when it was in conflict with other cultic centers such as Mount Hiei and Iwashimizu, it would organize a column of armed *shuto* who, preceded by *jinin* carrying the sacred tree, would march from Nara to Kyoto. This tree was then taken to the court or to other buildings related to the Fujiwara house and was left there until the multiplex received a satisfactory resolution of its problem. The immense religious authority of the sacred tree, which symbolized the sanctified aspect of the power of the Fujiwara, was much revered and feared by them. If its presence at the doors of the imperial palace was not sufficient to move the court, then the multiplex would send an armed militia and use force. Between the eleventh and sixteenth centuries the tree was taken from the shrine at least seventy times. Similarly, the Hie-Enryakuji multiplex of Mount Hiei took to Kyoto the palanquins of the Hie Shrines.

Distinctions ought to be made concerning the way in which the sacred tree was used on those occasions. Sometimes it was removed from the shrines and placed in the Utsushi-dono, which is situated next to them in the main compound of the shrine. News of that move was then sent to the capital. On some occasions this action alone was enough to move the court, especially if it felt that the multiplex had a legitimate claim, so it would grant the claim and thus calm would be restored. If the court's answer to that news was not satisfactory, the tree was then put on a carriage and installed in front of the Western Golden Hall of the Kōfukuji. Another period of waiting would then ensue. If satisfaction was still not given, the tree was brought in a procession by the *shuto* to the Byōdo-in, where it was placed in a pavilion on the bank of the Uji River. There the *shuto* would wait for signs from the court. The next step was to take the tree to the capital and leave it in front of the imperial palace or by the entrance of the residence of the highest members of the Fujiwara house, or in the Kangaku-in.

The removal of the tree either to the Utsushi-dono of Kasuga or to the front gate of the Kōfukuji was called *dōza* (change of station), and the transfer of the tree to the capital was called *nyūraku* (entrance into the capital). The first move of the tree from Nara to Kyoto occurred in 1007, and the last one in 1501. The event related below, which took place in 1281, midpoint in the history of the phenomenon, had to do with land. The *shuto* had been quarreling over the boundaries of the contiguous Takigi district and Ōsumi estate ever since the year 1106, and the time for settling the issue had come.[14]

It was decided, probably after consultation between the *shuto* and the *jinin* of the multiplex, that the tree should be moved on the twenty-fifth day of the ninth moon of the fourth year of Kōan (1281). A ceremony in which the doors of the five shrines would be opened was scheduled, and duties were distributed among the priests and their *jinin*. The head-priest of Kasuga at the time, a certain Sukezane, overviewed the entire matter. A supplication invoking the *kami* to move into the tree was chanted by Haruaki, a *jinin* who was a permanent resident of the Southern District. Other priests and *jinin* took positions in front of each of the five shrines. At the first shrine was Tsuneyo, a *kannushi* who was a permanent resident of the Northern District. At the second shrine was the aforementioned Haruaki. At the third shrine was the assistant *kannushi* Hikotsugu. At the fourth shrine were several *jinin*: the second assistant Sukeie, Ōmiya-dono, who was a shrine-guardian and a *jinin* of the Southern District, was charged with the torches (*taimatsu*); and various minor duties were given to a certain Haruhisa of the Southern District and Morimasa of the Northern District. The Wakamiya Shrine was represented by its head-priest Suke-masa. The duty of removing the sacred tree was usually assigned to a *jinin* named Harusumi, who was a permanent resident of the Wakamiya Shrine, but because he was absent on the occasion in question, a man named Toshiharu was designated as his representative.

When the arrangements were made, Haruaki recited the orally trans-mitted secret formula of invocation, and Toshiharu did the same for the Wakamiya *kami*. The sacred tree was then taken to the Southern Gate of the Kōfukuji by the *jinin*, in a procession arranged from front to back as follows: two servants (*chōshi*) carrying long sticks (*o-suwai*) at the end of which the petition was affixed; the monks of the temple; the sacred tree set on a palanquin; carriers of halberds that symbolized the shrines; carriers of bows and arrows and of the mirror symbolizing Kasuga *daimyōjin*, which was wrapped in votive paper strips; various members of the sacerdotal lineages; and a number of their *ujibito*. A figure called in the document "holy monk" (*seisō*), who was probably the abbot of the multiplex, waited by the Eastern Gate while representatives of the sacer-dotal lineages brought up a horse for him. As the procession began, the *shuto*, who had assembled in front of the Kōfukuji, blew their conch shells. The procession left the city, and arrived at the hour of the rat (midnight) at the Kizu Pavilion. The marchers remained there for one week, until the hour of the wild boar (10 P.M.) on the second day of the tenth moon, when they moved on to Uji, arriving at the hour of the tiger (4 A.M.). Food offerings were immediately made in front of the palanquin: eight sorts of sweets (*kashi*), eight dishes of vegetable "follow-ups," three *masu* of rice, and rice-wine, all of which were "offered with the greatest care" according to formal procedure.

The procession left for the capital on the fourth day, and upon reaching the bridge over the Uji River, it met with resistance from the government warriors who guarded the capital. Undaunted, the priests cut through the ranks of warriors with branches of the sacred tree, against which the warriors did not dare to make a move. Further on other warriors attempted to prevent the progress of the procession beyond the Inari Shrine. The procession stopped there, and the sacred tree was installed in the Lower Shrines of Inari. Screens for its protection were sent by the Kujō branch of the Fujiwara house. The procession left Inari on the sixth day at the hour of the boar (4 P.M.) and reached the Hōjōji in central Kyoto on the hour of the rat (midnight). The same procedures as before for food offerings were strictly followed, and the sacred tree was then placed in the eastern room of the main hall of the Hōjōji. On the eighteenth day the emblem of the Katte Shrine arrived and was put in a separate room; later, the emblem of the Furu Shrine (Isonokami) arrived and was put in another room. Ten *jinin* were charged with the security of the precincts.

Three months later, the matter having been settled with the court, the procession returned to Nara on the thirteenth day of the first moon of the following year and arrived on the hour of the dragon (8 A.M.). The same people were at hand for the return ceremonies, with the exception of the head-priest, who could not participate for his mother had just passed away. The last sentence of the document states, laconically: "The matter of the domains of the temple has been settled with victory on our part."

Thus the infamous "Yamashina method" of settling claims seemed to work wonders; at other times, however, it caused the destruction of the entire multiplex. The striking characteristic of the Yamashina method is its ritualization of behavior: it involved a procession, food offerings, cutting across rows of government warriors with branches of the sacred tree, and a discussion (about which no details are given in the document). In all probability, the matter in contention had already been settled by the very presence of the sacred emblem that stood in stead of an army, if, indeed, it had not already been settled earlier by a threat of excommunication from the Fujiwara house directed at a member of that house by the multiplex "in the name of Kasuga *daimyōjin*." The multiplex had the power to take away rights or privileges of membership in the house, and it exercised that power a number of times during the late Heian and Kamakura periods.

THE PRICE OF TIME RENEWED

Another example of the way in which land, economic behavior, ritual, protocol, and hierarchy were part of a single reality is provided by the details of the rite of periodic reconstruction of the shrines. One of the central aspects of the psychology of time that characterizes ritual practices in a specific sociocosmic arrangement grounded in myth and land is cyclicality. Even though the Fujiwara harbored an overwhelming sense of impermanence, cyclicality and impermanence were in fact two poles of the same psychological reality: the desire to control time. It was thought possible to manipulate time ritually in order to ensure a regular renewal, a purification, as it were, or an atonement, all of which are, in the Japanese context, interrelated notions.

The periodic reconstruction of shrines may have been necessitated by the materials with which they were built and by the climate, but there is no doubt that the practice was inscribed within a larger framework of meaning, as the very regularity of the practice suggests. As soon as Kasuga had become a state-supported institution with the highest ranks accorded to its *kami*, the shrines came to be reconstructed periodically and ritually every twenty years, on the model of Ise. The first such reconstruction is said to have occurred in 766, though scholars have serious doubts concerning that claim. The date 803 (Enryaku 22), which is often offered as an alternative to 766, seems to be acceptable to Kuroda Noriyoshi, the main historian of Kasuga architecture, though that claim entails the idea that the major architectural features of the shrines existed before the enlargement of the compounds and the initiation of state ceremonies in 859.[15]

Funds for those periodic reconstructions of the shrines were drawn originally from the domains of Sounokami and Yamanobe and were administered by the sacerdotal houses. In 1079 Tamba county came to be held responsible for the funding of these reconstructions. That practice lasted, according to Kuroda, until the eleventh reconstruction, which occurred in the Eishō era (1046–53). Nagashima Fukutarō, an historian of Nara, however, suggests that documents issued before the Kamakura period are not reliable in this regard.[16]

The position of official supervisor (*zōkokushi*) was created in 1162 to supervise the reconstructions; this office lasted until 1344, when the shogunate took over the expenses. Finances for the reconstructions were gathered from all the provinces by order of the Muromachi shogunate from 1367 on. At the beginning of the Edo period the Tokugawa shogunate took over that responsibility and set aside the sum of twenty thousand *koku*, a staggering amount, for each reconstruction. This system lasted until the Bunkyū era (1861–64), when the last reconstruction in the premodern period took place.

History and buildings were renewed regularly, but for a price. Very little information about that price is available, but a document concerning the 1427 reconstruction, the *Kasuga Wakamiya kantono-mori no ki* (Notes of the Kasuga Wakamiya Shrine Guardian), does provide some insights.[17]

According to this document, a messenger of the shrines was sent to Kyoto on the twentieth day of the ninth moon of the thirty-third year of the Ōei era, that is, 1426, to inform the shogunate of the impending start of the Initial Ceremonies (*koto-hajime*) of reconstruction. Two days later the messenger returned with the approval of the government and also with an order for reconstruction from the chieftain of the Fujiwara house. The Initial Ceremonies began in front of the main Kasuga shrines at the hour of the snake (10 A.M.) on the twenty-sixth day of the ninth moon, with the following shrine notables officiating: the head-priests Ōnakatomi Morohisa (Northern District) and Nakatomi Nobumoto (Southern District); the assistant head-priests Ietsugu and Tokimoto, the latter of whom was newly appointed; the shrine custodian Sukehodo, and the assistant custodians Suketoki and Sukenori, the latter of whom was from Ihara; and five other high-ranked officials of the shrines.

The *ujibito* stood in the corridor surrounding the shrine, while the head-priest of the Wakamiya Shrine took his position. Representatives of the "Five Masters" (monks who organized the *On-matsuri*) and other prelates of the Kōfukuji stood in front of the *Jingūji*, and the *jinin* lined up outside the shrine compounds. Also present in ceremonial attire was the administrator of the temple carpenter's office, who was accompanied by four assistants and four carpenters from Kyoto, as well as by one thatcher and his five assistants, who were dressed in white. The four August Pillars of the Wakamiya Shrine, the main pillars of the shrine-to-be, were aligned outside the fence surrounding the main shrine: with their upper ends facing north, and with the first one to be erected placed to the east of the others, they were ceremonially cut so that they were all of the same length.

This completed, all in attendance proceeded to the Wakamiya Shrine in front of which the carpenters ceremoniously placed the pillars so that their upper ends now faced east. The pillars remained on the ground through that night, and a vigil was kept in the compounds. At that time a high-ranked prelate of the Butsuji-in began a week-long ascetic seclusion. A dispute arose concerning the impropriety of the absence of food offerings, so money with which to purchase such offerings was sent for; rice-wine was then distributed in the order in which the dances of the *jinin* of the three residential zones (Southern, Northern, and Wakamiya) were arranged, and congratulations were exchanged.

Actual work on the shrine did not start until the fourth moon of the next year. When a problem arose concerning the proper procedure, the attribution of duties, or the necessity of the presence of monks or priests, the records of preceding reconstructions were fetched and discussions on those matters took place. This occurred several times in 1427. Because each major group of *jinin* of the aforementioned three zones kept such documents, comparison could be made. In the case of conflict, the head-priest of Kasuga was consulted. All the sacerdotal lineages, and all the clerics of the shrines and temples, were on call during the reconstruction, as were the *shuto* who supervised the *jinin* of the Wakamiya Shrine, in addition to a number of artisans, carpenters, metalworkers, swordsmiths, papermakers, silk and cloth weavers, and sake brewers. Hundreds of people, ranking from the lower echelons of the society of the multiplex to the highest-ranked prelates, figured in the undertaking.

The record of this reconstruction is filled with details of precedence and propriety, but this aspect comes second to that of money and various other offerings. The reconstruction of the shrines proved to be an expensive matter for the economy of the multiplex at the time, especially since support from the *bakufu* was not immediately forthcoming. Consequently, special levies were forced on people of the province, and most of the funds they provided were in the form of copper coins, rice, food, and labor.

The *Kasuga Wakamiya kantono-mori no ki* contains some details about the expenses incurred in the course of the fourteen months of reconstruction activity, though not all are recorded in full, especially in the case of food offerings. The recorded expenses totalled 134,464 *mon* (copper coins), a sum that in itself does not tell us much until we translate it into some meaningful referent. At the time, a *kan* (a string of one thousand *mon*) paid for approximately 1 *koku* of rice, which probably amounted to about 5.2 bushels of rice. Because there was no unified measurement of rice in Japan at the time, the amount contained in one *koku* varied from province to province. Still, historians tend to agree on the figure presented above. It is also generally agreed that one *koku* of rice was more or less the amount that one person needed to live for a whole year. Thus, 134,464 *mon* would purchase roughly 700 bushels of rice (or 135 *koku*), which was approximately 1 percent of the entire assessed revenue claimed by the cultic center sixty years later when it was requested by Oda Nobunaga to declare its economic power. This amount does not include the in-kind offerings nor does it include many items whose price is not recorded.

The *Kasuga Wakamiya kantono-mori no ki* records a list of items for the reconstruction of the Wakamiya Shrine, with their date of purchase and their cost, if known (table 8).

The *Kasuga Wakamiya kantono-mori no ki* is interesting in several respects: it provides information about the length of time needed for the reconstruction of the shrine (seven months); it tells us what kinds of rituals were involved in the reconstruction, though not in any detail; and it indicates the number of *jinin* that were involved in the protection of the shrine. In its account of the horse offerings made by the carpenters at the time of the completion of its reconstruction, it offers clues to the impor-

Table 8. Reconstruction of the Wakamiya Shrine, 1426–1427

Year/ Month	Day	Gift or Income	Value (in mon)
1427			
8th	1st	Sacred horse offered by Ochi Ikejiri	—
	23d	Old Wakamiya Shrine purchased by Tsutsui Imasato	7,000
11th	1st	*From head carpenter:* 1 saddled horse, 1 horse, 1 set of food offerings, 10 *tan*[a] of indigo fabric, 20 *tan* of white fabric	—
		From each of the four carpenters of Kyoto: 1 sacred horse, food offerings, 10 *tan* of white fabric, 1 roll of plain silk	—
		From carpenters' team head: 1 horse, food offerings, 5 *tan* of white fabric	—
		From paint master: 1 horse, food offerings, 10 *tan* of white fabric	—
	2d	Gift by superior of Lumberyard Office to *jinin*	3,000
	25th	Offering of rice-wine by metalworkers	600
		Offering of rice-wine by railing ornaments artisans	200
Subtotal			10,800

Year/ Month	Day	Type of Work or Offering	Value
1426			
9th	20th	Messenger to Kyoto and back	—
	26th	Food offering from *jinin*	3,000
	27th	Contributions to Permanent *jinin* of the Three Zones	100
1427			
4th	7th	Offerings of rice-wine, eel, and bonito	—
	29th	[Decision to begin fund-raising drive]	
7th	10th	Various expenses (*zōjiryōsoku*)	107,716
		Clothes	2,800
	11th	Cloth for drapery	1,200
		Funds for dances, wine, and fish	120
	15th	Funds for "hot water" (purification rites)	500
	17th	[Beginning of work by carpenters]	

Continued on next page

Table 8 (*continued*)

Year/ Month	Day	Type of Work or Offering	Value (*in* mon)
7th	18th	Funds for purification and exorcism	1,100
	19th	Rice offerings	100
		1 *masu* (1.98 U.S. quart) of white rice, paper for wands	—
	20th	130 spits for drapes, 1 eight-legged table, 3 high tables, 4½ mats (*tatami*), 30 strings for mirrors, 12 strings for screens, 8 Iyo screens, 82 *mon*, screens for a corridor of six yards, 5 rush mats	—
	22d	2 pails, 5 spikes, 2 nail sets, 1 pincer, 1 bucket, 12 bamboo poles	—
		Various mirrors in covered boxes	—
		Rice offerings on eight-legged tables	—
		5 straw mats from the lumberyard of temple	—
	23d	Expenses for guards paid by carpenters	20
		General expenses for 100 guards	—
		1 sacred horse	—
	24th	Food offerings	50
	25th	1 shelf for temporary shrine	100
8th	11th	[Beginning of thatching work]	
	22d	[Visit by abbot of Ichijō-in *monzeki*]	
9th	12th	1 sword	2,800
		Pendant paper strips for a scroll	50
		1 skewer for same	25
		1 octagonal tray for rice offering	33
		Food offerings	500
		Fabric	1,400
10th	1st	[Begining of painting of shrine]	
	14th	[Beginning of construction of *torii*]	
	30th	Food and beverage for ceremony of *mune-age* (main beam installation)	3,000
11th	1st	[Ceremony of *mune-age*]	
	5th	Rice-wine for shrine-guardians	600
	15th	Offerings for 7 subshrines	1,900
	16th	Clothing, rice-wine, gloves, socks	1,800

Table 8 *(continued)*

Year/ Month	Day	Type of Work or Offering	Value (in mon)
11th	19th	20 scrolls of paper for doors, 135 pieces of thick paper, 1 scroll of same for masks of *jinin*, 3 bundles of seaweed, 25 strips of dark leather, and 1 *jō*,[b] 3 *shaku*[c] of silk	—
		Rice-wine	125
	20th	20 bunches of scouring rush	—
	22d	130 spikes for drapes	—
		Rice-wine	75
		Congratulatory rice-wine	75
	24th	[Grand cleaning of shrine]	
		Kasina (ritual plate)	—
		Rice-wine	150
	25th	[Cleaning of corridor, installation of new mats]	
		Rice offerings	50
		Candles	—
		[That night, grand dedication ceremony between the hour of the tiger and the hour of the hare (3 A.M.)]	
Grand Total			134,464

Source: "Kasuga Wakamiya kantono-mori no ki," in *Zoku-Gunsho-ruiju*, Jingi-bu 37, 256–80.

[a]1 *tan* equals about 8.6 meters as a unit of length for textiles.

[b]1 *jō* equals about 3.8 meters as a unit of length for textiles.

[c]1 *shaku* equals about 30.3 centimeters, also for textiles.

tance of the carpenters, because only wealthy people could make such an offering. The text also tells us that the shrines contained several mirrors and a *kasina*. The Sanskrit word *kasina* originally designated a round earthern plate used by Buddhist monks to concentrate their minds when meditating.[18] To my knowledge, the mention of a *kasina* at the Kasuga Shrine is the only one in the literature, but it would not be surprising that they were commonly used in shrines during the medieval period. The *kasina* might have served as an object of meditation for the divinity, or it might have been used by Buddhist monks in the shrines as an emblem of sorts.

The dominant impression one receives from this document is the enormity of the funds required to reconstruct the shrine. This was one of the reasons the multiplex requested that the government bear the financial obligation; the multiplex's only source of funds was its domains, over which control was far from complete during the Muromachi period, and the population of those domains was already so heavily burdened by regular levies that it would revolt if special levies were ordered. Nonetheless, the periodic reconstruction of shrines was considered to be so crucial that it was carried out even in times of dire poverty: the realm protected by the *kami* and buddhas needed that protection even more when it was afflicted by droughts or epidemics, and all shogunates made sure that proper care was given to the shrines of the Fujiwara house, partly for political and partly for cultural reasons.

The completion of the reconstruction undoubtedly brought a sense of achievement and probably relief, for numerous indeed had been the periods of ascetic confinement and the strict observances of taboos concerning food, clothing, sex, and cleanliness. The amount of sake ingested by the participants was staggering. Tsutsui Imasato bought the old Wakamiya Shrine for about 5 percent of the price of the new one; he probably moved it to Kōriyama, where the shrine became an emblem of his power and of his relationship to the province of Yamato.

The last sentences of the document read: "When Haruo carried the Octagonal Mirror from the Storehouse to the Wakamiya Shrine, a strong rain began to fall. It was ordered that Harutane carry an umbrella. . . . The final ceremony took place at night. There was a heavy rain again. A large number of fireflies could be seen along the slopes of the mountain. The rain soon stopped." The mention of fireflies corresponds to the closing lines of the *Kasuga gongen genki*, which describe the mood following the return of the stolen emblems of the *kami*: the *kami* were back in their abode, peace and prosperity were ensured, and time started anew.[19]

Two days later, the Wakamiya Rite was performed.

THE RITUAL IMPERATIVE: RITES OF THE SACRED CITY

By the end of the Heian period the Kasuga-Kōfukuji and Hachiman-Tōdaiji multiplexes had become huge institutions of religious, political, and economic control. They grounded their power in complex, multilayered claims of legitimacy embedded in an early rationale for relations between ritual and government, which was exemplified in mythology and by the state support of temples and shrines and enlarged later by the ideology of the protection of the state by multiplexes.[20] These claims are manifest in ritual, in the structure of which are overwhelming concerns with time and space in the form of the territory; in that context the territory was the stage on which human relations, which were the object of protocol, were acted out.

The theory of the protection of the state by combined *kami* and buddhas and/or bodhisattvas, and its implementation through the regular or extraordinary performance of rituals, gained strong political overtones, especially after the loss of hegemony by the aristocrats and the emergence of the warrior class. Generally speaking, the rationale of the protection of the state was conservative and proimperial; the associations between *kami* and buddhas were politically relevant because they defined and upheld a vision of the state that even the warrior elites of the Kamakura and Muromachi periods did not dare oppose. The warriors wanted power; they never wanted to reject the traditional concept of the state or the rites that sustained it. In fact, they upheld that concept according to the same traditional principles: the Taira developed the Itsukushima shrine-temple multiplex, the Minamoto developed the Tsurugaoka Hachiman shrine-temple multiplex in Kamakura, and the Ashikaga developed the Gozan system of Zen temples; but all the warrior regimes continued to support Kasuga and other shrine-temple multiplexes.[21] Even the Tokugawa, who inherited a considerably different situation, developed the shrine-temple multiplexes of Nikkō and of the Tō-Eizan in Edo.

According to Émile Durkheim, "religious phenomena are naturally arranged in two fundamental categories: beliefs and rites. The first are states of opinion, and consist in representations; the second are determined modes of action. Between these two classes of facts there is all the distance which separates thought from action."[22] Although some of Durkheim's assumptions concerning ritual have been called into question,[23] his views are of great use in the case of Japan, where the relation between social structure and ritual is so tight, and particularly in regard to the Kasuga multiplex, where *in thought* the world of representation was given precedence according to the Hossō tenet that the world was nothing but representation, but where *in practice* modes of action and political battles took precedence over everything else. The beliefs that characterized Kasuga had to do with supernatural realms and specific divinities, but they also had to do with the structure of society and its grounding in a system of purity and pollution and proper procedure.

The relation of the Fujiwara house to the state figured preeminently in Fujiwara representations of the structure of society, which were given form in the rites performed at the Kasuga-Kōfukuji multiplex and other centers of cult. Of course the Fujiwara participated in various rituals besides those

performed in Nara; much of their time was also spent at grandiose ceremonies and at rituals performed at the many temples and shrines they
built in and around Kyoto and by which they reaffirmed the legitimacy of
their power.

During the Nara period the Kasuga Shrine developed its main spring and
autumn rites, which were dedicated to the ancestral and tutelary *kami* of
the Fujiwara house. As the shrine came to be sponsored by the state,
however, the rites changed greatly in structure and scope and became an
affaire d'état, especially after the participation of the sacral woman had
been added. Similarly, the Kōfukuji's *Yuima-e* ritual assembly, which was
dedicated to the spirit of Kamatari, the human ancestor of the Fujiwara
house, also became a state-sponsored event. Many other rites and ceremonies were created during the Heian period, when combinatory rituals
also came to be performed. In the Kasuga-Kōfukuji multiplex this process
culminated with the appearance of Kasuga *daimyōjin* as the overall emblem
of the belief system. Some of these rituals were called by imperial decree
and were attended by imperial envoys and court members. The major rites
of Kasuga-Kōfukuji and Hachiman-Tōdaiji, which were all in some way
interconnected, provided the major timetable for the clergy and the population of Yamato Province and served as reinforcers of the identity of the
sacred city. They were organized by the government, the aristocracy, the
clergy, and the populace of the province. Funded in part by domains
belonging to the cultic centers, they were immensely expensive events.
They were also the cradle of much cultural life: many different facets of
thought and practice, and many different trends of philosophy and ritual,
were crystallized in them. Elements of aristocratic culture and Buddhist
orthodox rituals merged with popular culture and with heterodox forms.
The grand rites served also as steps on the ladder of the career of prelates
and were thus important political events for the cultic center itself.

Some of those rituals are still performed today with great pomp and are
attended by large gatherings of people. The *On-matsuri* has become an
Intangible Cultural Property (*mukei bunkazai*) and as such is supported by
the government for cultural reasons; prime ministers of Japan make money
offerings at the time of the *Omizutori* Grand Rite of the Tōdaiji's Nigatsu-
dō. In 1973, for example, the name of Tanaka Kakuei, the prime minister
of that time, and the amount that he donated were contained in the list
(*kanjinchō*) of sponsors and donors that is solemnly recited by the priests.
Imperial envoys are still sent at the time of the Kasuga Grand Rite. These
celebrations are grounded in symbols, myths, and legends of great antiq-

uity and provide a royal avenue to one of the structures of the Kasuga cultural system.

ECHOES OF CAMPHORATED MARITIME MUSIC

Although it is impossible in the present context to analyze in detail all symbols and myths that bear directly on the conduct of rituals in the multiplex, the *koto* musical instrument must be given some attention if only because it is played at the most important times in the performance of the Kasuga Grand Rite. The search for the origins of the place of that instrument in Japanese culture reveals fascinating associations. It will be recalled that the *Sandai jitsuroku* stated that two *koto* were offered in 884 to replace those that had been offered to the *kami* of Kasuga in 768, the purported date of the foundation of the shrine.[24]

The first mention of the *koto* appears in the *Kojiki* under the reign of "Emperor" Chūai, who is said to have ruled in the fourth century C.E. Chūai's consort was Okinaga Tarashi (Jingū Kōgō), the mother of a son who eventually became "Emperor" Ōjin and was deified subsequently as Hachiman.[25] In that *Kojiki* reference the *koto* was used at the time divination was performed and was played by the emperor, whose spouse, becoming possessed, made utterances that were interpreted by a sacerdotal figure known as *saniwa*.[26] Although the *Kojiki* does not indicate the material out of which the *koto* was made, it is likely, for the following reasons, that it was camphor wood. The *Nihon shoki*, in its record of "Emperor" Ōjin, and the *Kojiki*, in its record of the next emperor (Nintoku), relate that an offering was made to the court of a boat that was made in Izu out of camphor wood. This boat, known by the name of Kareno, had been famous for its great speed. After wood taken from that boat had aged for thirty-one years, it was treated with fire and a *koto* was made out of it. The sound of this *koto*, we are told, was so pure and powerful that it could be heard from as far as seven leagues.[27]

Subsequently, in its report of legends related to the first Buddhist statues in Japan in the sixth century, the *Nihongi* tells us that these statues were made out of a camphor tree that had come floating over the sea and emitted light and a music audible when the tree was still no more than a point on the horizon, and that these statues were slightly burnt.[28] The *Nihongi* reports that in the year 553, "Sounds of the law were heard like thunder coming from the sea, and a light as brilliant as the sun was seen." On hearing of that the emperor dispatched a messenger, who discovered the floating trunk of a camphor tree irradiating light. He took it and offered it to the emperor, who ordered that two statues of the Buddha be made from it; these statues were placed in the Yoshino-dera.[29]

The Nihon ryō-i-ki, which dates from around 820 and is Japan's first compilation of edifying Buddhist stories, offers a slightly different version of the incident: it states that the sounds were at times like that of musical instruments and at other times like that of thunder. A messenger who was sent to investigate discovered a trunk of a camphor tree that had been hit by lightning. He took it back with him, and statues were made out of it and placed in the Toyura Temple before they were moved to the Hiso-dera of Yoshino.[30] The Fusō ryakki, compiled toward the end of the Heian period, states that in the year 595 a great light accompanied by sound was perceived near the province of Tosa and landed on the shores of Awaji Island; that light exuded a strange scent (camphor?). The object was offered to the court but peasants, who did not know better, "burnt" it. Nevertheless, the story continues, a statue was made out of the scorched wood and was placed in the Hiso-dera of Yoshino. A related anecdote appears in the Nihongi for the same year.[31]

These records are corroborated in an interesting way: in 1976 archeologists unearthed on the shores of Lake Biwa a nearly complete koto dating from the fifth century, and in the following year three more koto were unearthed near the mouth of the Ado River where it empties into Lake Biwa. Not only were these koto made out of camphor wood, but they also bore traces of scars left by fire.[32] It seems that camphor wood taken from boats to make musical instruments would have to be dried with fire. More importantly, in reference to the realm of symbols, camphor was treated with fire because of the role played by that element in mythology, namely, the fact that it facilitates passage from the realm of nature to that of culture. Camphor wood was taken from boats for the same reason that Stradivarius violins were treated with brine. The binary opposition of fire and water is central to the myths related to the forging of swords, which are also associated with lightning. The type of koto mentioned in the documents and unearthed in Shiga Prefecture is called Yamato-goto or wagon, "Japanese koto," because it has a different number of strings (five) than the same type of instrument found in China and Korea. It is represented in haniwa figurines dating from the latter part of the Kofun period and has retained a prominent place throughout Japanese history.[33] Legends associating the coming of Buddhism to Japan with the koto allowed the country to readily accept the Buddha as if he were a kami whose will was ascertained through the medium of music, an emblem of divination and ordered rule.

The Fudoki are highly informative in the present context. In its record of the conquest of Hitachi Province, the *Hitachi Fudoki* states that Take-Kashima-no-mikoto used a stratagem that entailed the performance of dances and music to lure the natives away from their fortifications. That music, in the Kishima style, was played on board a boat on a "Heavenly-Bird *koto*."[34] There is little doubt that the term "Heavenly-Bird" refers to a shaman,[35] and that the *koto* was used primarily for divination and as an emblem of power. The connection between camphor and boat is indicated by the *Fudoki*:

> During the fifth year of the reign of Emperor Ōjin, in the tenth moon, an order was given to the province of Izu to build a boat. That boat, though of a length of ten *tsue* [ca. 30 meters], was as light as a leaf on the water and had a great speed. It is reported that it was made from the trunk of a camphor tree of Okino, a site near the foot of Mount Higane. This was the first boat built in our country.[36]
>
> Under the reign of Naniwa-no-Takatsu-no-miya-no-sumera-mikoto [Emperor Nintoku], a camphor tree grew above the well of Komade in Akashi. In the morning sun its shade stretched all the way to Awaji Island, and in the evening sun all the way to Shimane in Yamato. A boat was built out of the trunk of this camphor tree; it was as swift as a bird and cut across seven waves in one instant, and was therefore called *Hayatori* [Swift-Bird]. This boat was used to transport water for the repast of the emperor.[37]

Camphor trees, which were considered sacred at the time, are mentioned quite frequently in the *Fudoki*. For example:

> A long time ago, there grew a large camphor tree in the village of Saka. It branches reached a great height and its foliage was luxuriant. In the morning sun its shadow stretched [15 kilometers] to Mount Kamakawa in the district of Kishima, and in the setting sun it stretched [20 kilometers] to Mount Kusayoko in the district of Kabu. When Yamato-Takeru-no-mikoto saw the foliage of this tree, he declared: "This country shall henceforth be called Luxuriance (*saka*)."[38]

The sacred camphor trees that were used to build boats were taken from places as diverse as Kishima in Kyushu, Akashi in Harima, and Izu. Another report that a *koto* was made from camphor occurs in the *Hizen Fudoki*:

> There is a site called Koto-ki-no-oka [Hill of the *koto* tree]. However, today this site is flat, and there was originally no hill there.

Here is what happened: Ōtarashi-hiko-sumera-no-mikoto
["Emperor" Keiko] declared: "This place should have an elevation." Subsequently orders were given and an artificial hill was
erected. The emperor ascended it and a banquet was served. When
the festivities ended, the *koto* that had been used for the music
was planted vertically into the earth, and from it grew a camphor
tree. Hence the name of this site.[39]

This event is said to have taken place shortly before the reign of Chūai
in the fourth century. Whereas the *Kojiki* states that Chūai played the *koto*
to enquire of the will of the *kami*, the *Sompi bunmyaku* indicates that he
used a professional corps of diviners to whom he granted the name Urabe
for that purpose. The person who was first given that name, a certain
Ikatsu-omi of Tsushima,[40] was, according to the *Nihongi*, the interpreter
of oracles for Chūai's consort.[41] Ikatsu-omi, who appears a number of times
in documents, is regarded as a descendant of Ame-no-koyane-no-mikoto,
and he was claimed as ancestor by a certain Sugao no Suetsugu, who played
the *koto* at the time of the Yasojima ritual that was held at the Sumiyoshi
Shrine during the enthronement ceremonies for Emperor Montoku in
850.[42] He also has a prominent role in the *Fudoki* in a story that is at the
basis of the Hagoromo legend and takes place on Lake Ikago, near Lake
Biwa.[43] All this indicates that the Urabe and Nakatomi sacerdotal lineages,
both of which specialized in divination, may have been responsible for
transmitting the symbolic world of the *koto* through the centuries and for
giving it an important place in Kasuga. Indeed, still today the *koto* is played
at Kasuga when the *kami* are called upon to manifest themselves and reveal
their will.

Yet another association that must be mentioned concerns the deer,
which became the theriomorphic emblem of Kasuga and is also related to
divination. A text of the medieval period, the *Hachiman gudōkun*, states
that the *kami* of Kasuga are the same as those enshrined in Kashima in
Hitachi, and in Shika-no-shima in Kyushu.[44] These *kami* may have been
associated simply because Kashima and Shika-no-shima are written with
graphs meaning "deer-island," but the *kami* worshiped at Shika-no-shima
belongs to a complex universe of meaning related to the sea and to divination, and thus may have been associated with the ritual world of Kasuga
for deeper reasons. Indeed, that *kami* was worshiped by the Azumi lineage,
which made up the naval force of the government during the Yamato period
and later became responsible for procuring imperial food.[45] It is also said
that it is that *kami* that originated the famous *sei-no-o* dance, which was
regularly performed at Kasuga, Tōnomine, and other centers of cult.[46]
Furthermore, the *Fudoki* states that the naval forces of ancient Japan were

known as *kako*, "deer-children," because they wore deer hides and deer antlers.[47] Thus many harbors of Japan situated all along the coast from Kyushu to Kashima and from Kyushu to the Noto Peninsula bear names related to the deer: Shika-no-shima, Kashima, Kagoshima, and so on. Naturally, therefore, the Yamato warriors liked to sport antlers on their helmets during the medieval period.

Finally, the aforementioned camphor *koto* of the fifth century were unearthed at the mouth of a river, the Ado, which is written with graphs usually read Azumi. Thus, medieval authors reinforced the sense of ritual and national unity by cleverly recalling myths and legends that associated, in the universe of Kasuga, boats, deer, *koto*, camphor, and Buddhist statues, and they combined the symbolic and mythical realms of the Kasuga and Hachiman universes of meaning. Even though the use of camphor wood for crafting *koto* was discontinued in the Heian period, because its grain made it extremely difficult to sculpt, and was replaced by the more versatile paulownia, the ancient connections were long remembered in Kasuga. For instance, at the beginning of the sixteenth century, Jinson, the abbot of the Daijō-in *monzeki* of the Kōfukuji, sculpted a statue of *Daikoku-ten* from a piece of the camphor trunk that had been used, allegedly, to sculpt the Kannon statues of the Hase-dera in Yamato and the Hase-dera in Kamakura.[48]

Such are the reasons why the *koto* is so important in ritual performance at Kasuga.

THE KASUGA GRAND RITE

The Kasuga Grand Rite (Kasuga *taisai*) became a state-sponsored event as early as the middle of the Nara period. This means that imperial messengers were sent to attend it, and that the nature of the ritual had changed in such a way as to be in accordance with the new structure of society and power. It also means that the bulk of the financial burden for the holding of the ritual was assumed by the government, which may be one of the early reasons for the granting of land domains that would provide funds twice a year. These domains may have been related to the shrines from an earlier period, when it was decided that they would specialize in sending special food offerings (either from the mountain or the sea) or horses for the rituals. As time passed, other domains, which also specialized in sending either natural goods or funds, were added. Like the other rituals that were restructured during the first part of the Heian period in order to support the new state, there was added to the Kasuga Grand Rite a liturgical figure of imperial blood, the sacral woman (*saijo*), whose primary function was based on the double symbolism of blood (she had to be of imperial lineage) and purity (she had to undergo strict ritual preparations), for blood and purity were central aspects of the vision of government and social status. The presence of this female figure was marked not only by the complex ceremonies surrounding her but by a display of magnificence characteristic of the aesthetic sense of the high nobility of Heian and what has been called its rule of taste. This display served, in fact, to obfuscate the real political world of the Fujiwara house and hid the ideological framework that sustained its power.

The Kasuga Sacral Woman, who lived in Kyoto, observed various taboos, interdictions, and strict ritual purity measures for a period of several weeks before the Grand Rite. The day of her travel to Nara was decided by divination, for in those days travel was still strongly connected to divination, which ensured freedom from directional taboos (*kata-imi*) and designated directional alternatives (*kata-tagae*).[49] On the day of travel the sacral woman would undergo final purification rites and then set out on the road with a large following. Arriving by the end of the day at the Utagoe Pass north of the ancient capital, she would then pass in front of the Hokkeji, a major Buddhist temple placed on what might have been the former residence of Fujiwara no Fuhito, and went to a residence especially established for her for the duration of the rite. This special residence was created with funds from the domain of Saho that were granted for that purpose and thus came to be called the "Saho Residence." The Saho domain was administered by the chieftain of the Fujiwara house, since it was one of the four domains granted to him at the time of his investiture: this gives some indication as to how important the Kasuga Grand Rite was. The sacral woman would stay overnight in the Saho residence, and early the following morning she would go toward the Kasuga Shrine and stop in another building made up of several rooms where she could change attire. She would then enter the grounds of the shrine through doors used only by her and oversee the proper course of the rite. At the end of the rite she changed clothes again, because her contact with the divine entity of Kasuga had rendered her dangerous.[50]

During the Heian period the funds for the Grand Rite of spring, originally issued from Kashima, were provided by the state and various specified domains. During the Kamakura period, the domains administered by the two *monzeki* provided most of these funds. During the Muromachi and Edo periods, as the multiplex lost more and more domains and rites became increasingly complex and expensive, the government set up special fields throughout the country for this particular purpose. These were known as "Fields for the Kasuga Rite" (*Kasuga-sai den*), and during the Edo period they came to be called "Funds for the Kasuga Rites" (*Kasuga sairei-ryō*).

We have provided earlier a description of the Kasuga Rite, so will now turn our attention to the *On-matsuri*.

THE *ON-MATSURI*: A PROVINCIAL MATTER

The main ritual of the Wakamiya Shrine, the *On-matsuri*, was instituted upon imperial authorization in 1136 by Fujiwara no Tadamichi to call for an end to a famine and for a bountiful crop. It was then put under the supervision of five Kōfukuji ecclesiastics known as *bechi-e goshi* (the Five Masters of the Special Rite), whose main duty was to organize the *shuto* and the *jinin* of the entire province of Yamato for the performance of this festive ritual. The *On-matsuri* soon became a pageant of such extravagance that an edict restricting its excesses was promulgated as early as 1181, barely fifty years after its creation. The primary target of this edict was the performance of *dengaku*, that is, field songs and dances. Enormous amounts of money were poured into the event with the purpose of aggrandizing the spiritual authority of the Wakamiya *kami* and its local sponsors, and it may well be that there was some competition with the pageantry of the aristocratic but secretive Kasuga Grand Rite, which was reserved exclusively to the Fujiwara lineage. In stark contrast, the *On-matsuri* involved the entire province, whose population rallied around its performance.

Documents do not indicate the participation of the Fujiwara house in that ritual, except for those Fujiwara who had become priests of the Kōfukuji and were therefore involved in it. The *On-matsuri* was funded by all the domains in the province of Yamato and was organized by the *shuto* of the *monzeki* and the *jinin* of the shrines under their supervision. Thus from its inception the *On-matsuri* was a rite dedicated to a new divinity and organized by the province and was therefore totally different from the state-sponsored Kasuga Grand Rite. Because of its festive character the *On-matsuri* was so popular that people of other areas began to imitate it. For example, in the fifteenth century Nara accused the city of Sakai of making "copy-cat" festivities based on the *On-matsuri*, and requested that these be stopped.

The *On-matsuri* progresses according to strict conventions, three of which stand out as particularly significant: the performance of music and dances, the procession, and the food offerings. The core of the rite is the performance of music and dances among which the *dengaku* (field dances) used to be the most lavish. The various *inke* of the *monzeki*, which were responsible for overseeing the preparation of these performances, nominated directors of dance and music. These appointees, called "head of field dances" (*dengaku kashira*, or *dengaku tōnin*), held a coveted position.

During the medieval period the expenses incurred by those people were so stupendous that special taxes called *dengaku-kashira dansen* were levied specifically for their use. In the thirteenth century Myō-e *shōnin* was stunned by these expenses, and he cast on the *On-matsuri* the stern eye of an ascetic and philosopher:

> Since people in this age of decadence do not possess the wisdom of rational thinking, they adorn their faces and wallow in the profane world, thinking that the development of the Buddhist Law is based on the performance of *dengaku* and *sarugaku*, the adorned magnificence of which they pay for with astounding amounts, spending all their lifetime thinking about these.[51]

Myō-e's sense of history was such that he could not see the immense role that the *On-matsuri* played in the unification of Yamato Province and in its culture.

Regenerative Performance: Recreation, or Re-Creation?

The modern performance of the *On-matsuri*, which will be described below, is based on procedures specified in a document of the Edo period.[52]

The *On-matsuri* starts officially on the first of October. That day is marked at 11 A.M. by a short visit to the site of the temporary shrine by the priests and artisans who will erect it. The ropes that delimit the sacred grounds are affixed to poles, the site is purified, and the artisans receive their first purification. Food is then offered on a table at the site of the future building, and votive offerings of paper-strips are made. A litany is then recited in which the *kami* is invoked and requested to accept the food and extend its protection to the various aspects of the rite. Bowing twice and clapping their hands, the artisans and the priests leave the newly consecrated ground. This short ceremony marks the *koto-hajime*, or initial moments of the ritual. The stage is now clear, and work can begin in all areas of preparation.

An important aspect of these preparations is the contruction of a temporary shrine (*kari no miya*) on the site called *otabisho* (literally, "travel-site") to which the *kami* will be carried at the time of the main rites. There is no explanation for this practice; one theory has it that the *otabisho* is the site of a former shrine where a *kami* originally manifested itself. In the case of Kasuga, little can be said with any certainty, but it is noteworthy that the *otabisho* is located at a point nearly equidistant from the Main Temple and main shrine and next to the former site of two major pagodas that were erected on the Kasuga Plain during the Kamakura period. These five-storied pagodas were destroyed by fire and never rebuilt. It was probably in them that the specialists in combinatory practices lived and performed rites dedicated to Kasuga *daimyōjin* and to the Wakamiya divinity. Only the stone foundations of these pagodas exist today, and no text of the time is extant to provide any detail.

The temporary shrine is erected on a grassy knoll consisting of two grades: a high level for the shrine itself, and a slightly lower one for the performance stage. The construction of the shrine, which lasts one week, is initiated on 11 December after a ritual called *chōna-hajime* (literally, first use of the foreplane). Facing south, the shrine is built according to what is thought to be the archaic model of Kasuga-style architecture (*Kasuga-zukuri*): four pillars of unpeeled logs joined by mud walls on three sides, open in the front (the entrance is covered by a screen), and topped by a simple inverted **V**-shaped roof made of beams covered with green branches of cryptomeria. The shrine is completely surrounded by an open corridor made of wood roughly peeled and mounted in the front of a simple staircase. None of the wood is squared: the trunk and branches are left as close as possible to their natural state. Both the open corridor and the staircase are covered with rush.

In front of the shrine two cone-shaped piles of sand have branches sticking up out of them to mark the sacredness of the building. Two pillars are planted in the ground on each side and slightly to the front of the shrine. At the top of the pillars banners of five hues are hung, and below them are affixed the regalia of the *kami*: a mirror and *magatama* stones on one side, and a sword on the other. The positions of these emblems are the opposite of what they are in the main Wakamiya Shrine. As soon as the *kami*, taken from the main shrine by the priests and moved to this temporary shrine, is installed, the priests reverse the positions of those emblems. The Wakamiya *kami* is believed to be sensitive to the correct positioning of regalia and must have them set properly with the mirror always on its left side and the sword on its right.

An intriguing feature of the walls of the temporary shrine is that triangular blocks of white paper are set into the mud before it solidifies, with the result that the design of the walls thus closely resembles the dragon-scales pattern found in brocade costumes of Nō drama. The priests and artisans are unwilling to divulge the meaning of those blocks of paper, assuming that they themselves know it. It has been suggested that the blocks might contain words inscribed on a sheet of paper set in their middle, but there is no indication of what these words might be. Potent utterances (*dhāraṇī*)? Japanese poems? Names of divinities? Requests? Divinatory formulas? It has also been suggested that the triangular blocks represent dragon scales, since the Wakamiya *kami* first manifested itself in the form of a snake. Indeed, the Wakamiya *kami* is, like the two tutelary *kami* of the main shrine, related to thunder and its associated theriomorphic emblems, one of which is a salamander. Significantly, there is a salamander pond next to the Wakamiya Shrine.

The temporary shrine reminds one of other temporary structures found here and there in Japan, especially parturition huts (*ubuya*). This suggests that the temporary shrine is the site in which the *kami* is going to be reborn (regenerated) through food offerings and the performance of dances and songs. The overall impression conveyed by the setting and the architecture is that of rustic, aged simplicity, of elements of nature barely worked upon so that the flavor of the natural world can be exhibited. The setting is one in which nature and culture are going to stand in oppositions and combinations out of which a *kami* shall be brought back into being, its energy renewed.

On the first night of the *On-matsuri*, 17 December, takes place what must be characterized as one of the most mystical and impressive rites of the Japanese tradition, the *Senkō no gi* (Rite of Transfer). On that night, the "support" (*mishōtai*) of the Wakamiya *kami* is transferred from the Wakamiya Shrine to its temporary building. This transfer is preceded by the "Rite of Dusk," which may not be seen by the general public, in which the head-priests announce to the *kami* of the third and fourth shrines the imminent birth of their progeny and install a branch of *sakaki* in the Wakamiya Shrine. The priests then return to the main shrine and purify themselves before consecrating a new fire. From about ten-thirty at night, at about thirty-minute intervals, they send to the Wakamiya Shrine priests who shout the words "first notice," "second notice," and "third notice," while a number of musicians play bamboo flutes at the foot of the large camphor tree growing in front of the shrine.

Then, around midnight, the head-priests and their followers leave the main shrine, preceded by torches lit with the newly consecrated fire, and advance to the Wakamiya Shrine. Having requested complete silence, they cover the torches so that absolute darkness envelops the precincts. Upon reaching the Wakamiya Shrine the head-priest climbs the stairs to the inner sanctum, opens its doors, chants silently a secret *norito*, and withdraws the support of the *kami*, which is put into a paulownia box. That box is then carried to the temporary shrine in the company of fifty priests in white garments who, as soon as the shrine's doors were opened, had entoned a long, loud monotonic chant, a mark of awe that they continue to utter during the one-mile walk to the temporary shrine. The musicians in the procession play a melody called *Keiun-raku*. The procession is led through the woods of the Kasuga Plain by priests who carry long burning torches and walk approximately thirty yards in front of the group of priests who huddle protectively around the box, holding branches of the sacred tree and chanting. The support of the *kami* is thus carried over two parallel trails of smoldering, scented ashes that both indicate and purify its path. At the temporary shrine, which is in total darkness, the musicians revert to playing the flute. The priests recite a secret *norito*, open the screen at the front of the temporary shrine, and install the *kami* in its temporary abode. After the screen is lowered, the position of the regalia is inverted, and light is immediately restored outside.

In front of the temporary shrine the priests start the "Rite of Dawn": they offer food and recite a *norito*, whereupon the priestesses dance *kagura* to music of the *koto*. The food offerings are retrieved by the assistant head-priest and his accolytes. The various participants then perform some of the finest dances created or transmitted by Japanese culture, such as the *sei-no-o* dance mentioned earlier.

The Procession

The second main aspect of the festivity is the procession in which socio-political order is reaffirmed. At the time of the Nambokuchō dynastic crisis (1366–92) the participation of the *shuto* and the *kokumin* in the On-matsuri became overwhelming and ostentatious. By that time these powerful houses had come to control various domains of the *monzeki* in the province and were the main sponsors calling for the performance of the rite, which became an *affaire de province*. This was one of the main reasons for the popularization of the Kasuga belief system in the province.

Local political leaders and the ecclesiastics of the multiplex figured prominently in the procession. Today they are still represented in their traditional attire, but the shrine has added various contemporary officials such as the governor of the prefecture of Nara, the director of the bureau of tourism, and other worthies to the procession.

Two days before the *On-matsuri* begins the local officials come to Nara and stay in a special residence in the Mochidono area called Ō-jukusho (the Great Lodge), where the procession is formed and where it starts on its way to the temporary Wakamiya Shrine. These events are still marked today by rites conducted on the site of the Great Lodge, where food offerings placed in a temporary structure covered with cryptomeria branches are prominently displayed. The food offerings consist of salted fish, raw fish, pheasants, ducks, and rice-wine. In the *On-matsuri* of 1981 as many as thirty salted fish, five ducks, and five pheasants were offered, but in the past the food offerings were considerably larger and included wild boar and rabbit. The contemporary leaders of the *Kasuga-kō* (the lay association of the Kasuga cult) meet in the Lodge, the entrance hall of which has been turned into a shrine also decorated with food offerings. The assistant head-priest of Kasuga and his accolytes (both male and female) conduct a short rite and perform *kagura* dances. The main room of the Great Lodge serves as a repository for the various emblems and for the masks, weapons, and clothes to be worn by the participants the next day.

On the afternoon of 17 December the procession gathers and proceeds slowly through the streets of Nara toward the shrine. Passing in front of the main Southern Gate of the Kōfukuji, it then goes through the first *torii* of the Kasuga compound and advances to the first large pine tree bordering the path on its southern side. This pine tree has been the object of a complex cult associated with the Sumiyoshi pines (the Takasago Pines);[53] it is represented on the back wall of all Nō stages and thus symbolizes the Nō drama, for the following reason. Tradition has it that some time during the Kamakura period the Tendai abbot Kyōen was reciting the *Jōyuishikiron*, the main scripture of the Hossō lineage, near that pine when Kasuga *daimyōjin* manifested itself and danced in it. Thus, at the time of the *On-matsuri*, special reverence is paid to the tree, at the foot of which performances of Nō chant and dance take place. Following a short dedicatory rite at the pine tree, the procession advances to the area of the temporary shrine and enters its compounds where buildings have been erected to shelter the various officials, priests, monks, warriors, *shuto*, *jinin*, and performers. The temporary shrine, erected over an elevation of the ground, looks down on a grassy knoll that serves as the stage. The stage is surrounded by torches; near it are two large dragon and phoenix drums that are beaten at the time of *bugaku* performances. Once the entire procession has entered the site of the temporary shrine, the assistant head-priest and his assistants proceed to present elaborate food offerings to the *kami*.

Food Offerings

The Wakamiya *kami*, as the symbolic body of the province of Yamato, must be fed. The food offerings made to that *kami* are famous throughout Japan for their complexity, exquisite appearance, and evocation of the Heian aristocratic ways of preparing food. Furthermore, since the *On-matsuri* is said to have been created for the purpose of placating the forces that caused two years of extreme famine in 1135 and 1136, it is natural that such offerings have a central place in the rites. Food offerings for the *On-matsuri* and a fire made from sticks of *hahaka* wood are prepared in secrecy in a building designed for that purpose, the Cauldron Pavilion located to the west of the main shrine compound.[54] The priests who prepare the fire and food undergo strict purification, observe behavioral taboos, and wear white masks over their mouths and noses. Food for the *kami* cannot be polluted by human contact, by breath or spittle, even from those who have accumulated purity through austerities and various observances. In the case of the *On-matsuri*, four full days of preparation of the food offerings are needed, for the displays are intricate. The overall preparation takes much longer than that, for the rice for the offerings is grown in sacred fields of the shrine tilled by the priests, and from that rice the *miki* (rice-wine) is also prepared by the priests. The symbolic connotations of each food item are known to but a few priests.

The food offerings of the *On-matsuri* consist today of ten kinds:

1. *Kikyō-date.* This refers to four clay dishes that are displayed on a single wooden tray; in each dish is a delicate paper reproduction of a violet bellflower (*kikyō: Platycodon grandiflorum*). In the center of the tray is another clay dish containing yet another dish filled with rice-wine. Since originally the rites were held during the ninth moon, fresh bellflowers would have been available, but when the rites were moved to December, paper representations of the flowers came to be used.

2. *Shō no gohan* (literally, "smaller [portion of] rice"). This is three *gō* of cooked white rice shaped into a cylinder and placed on a flat piece of wood that is set on a wooden tray.[55] White chopsticks are placed on a clay holder in front of the rice.

3. *Dai no gohan* (literally, "greater [portion of] rice"). This is five *gō* of white rice placed on a single tray in the same manner as above.

4. *Sue go sai.* A tray containing six kinds of offerings, each placed on a single flat piece of wood. Five round turnips (*kabura*). Ten sticks of burdock (*gobō: Arctium lappa*) arranged in the structure of the graph meaning "well": two parallel pieces on the bottom running north-south, on top of these two parallel pieces running east-west, on top of the latter two more parallel pieces running north-south, and on the topmost level four parallel pieces running east-west. The same arrangement is made with ten sticks of radish (*daikon*). Ten round pieces of taro (*sato-imo: Colocasia antiquorum*) are stacked in three layers of three pieces each topped by one piece and held together with fine wooden sticks. Two arrangements of incised lotus root (called *hasu* at Kasuga), finely cut to represent the feathers at the end of an arrow. An arrangement called *tonegiri* (or *taka-magari*), which consists of twelve small round Chinese-style cakes stacked in three layers of four cakes each topped with three sticks of grilled *mochi* (rice-cake).

5. *Oimono* (literally, "follow-up"). Similar to the tray mentioned above but with two piles of burdock instead of turnips.

6. *Somewake.* A tray containing four clay dishes that support cylinders made with rice paper (*washi*) onto which rice dyed (*some*) in four colors (white, green, yellow, red) has been stuck with organic glue in such manner that the cylinders are divided (*wake*) into four vertical parts.

7. *Morimono.* A tray containing four clay plates, each with a cylinder of the same size as above onto which beans are affixed individually with tiny sticks: one cylinder has black soybeans (*kuromame*) fixed to it; another soya beans (*daizu*); the third small soybeans (*komame*); and the fourth *kaya* nuts (*torreya nucifera*).

8. *Kashi.* A tray containing eight different arrangements of sweets (*kashi*), each stacked on a single flat piece of wood. The first of these eight arrangements consists of five Chinese-style cakes called *buto*, which are cakes of rice dough deep-fried in colza oil. It is said that priests who do not know how to make those cakes properly do not deserve to be called priests. The second is an arrangement of five cakes called *nashi* (pear), though they are in fact *takamagari*, a type of Chinese cake. Third, five persimmons (*kaki*). Fourth, five cakes called *mitsubaishi*. Fifth, five moon-shaped rice cakes (*mochi*). Sixth, ten *buto* cakes that are formed into more intricate shapes and called Chrysanthemum *buto* (*kikubuto*). Seventh, four sweet tangerines (*mikan*). And finally, ten chestnuts stuck on the end of long picks.

9. *Shishoku* (literally, "four colors"). A tray containing four clay plates, each holding cylinders onto which rice dyed in four colors has been glued. In the case of *somewake* each cylinder has four colors, but in this one each cylinder has only one color. Both *somewake* and *shishoku* dyed rice cylinders seem to have originated in Korean shamanistic circles.

10. *Mika.* A jug of rice-wine, the mouth of which is closed by paper sheets of five colors (light blue, yellow, red, white, and dark blue) arranged in such manner that they overlap and are constricted at the mouth of the jug by a gold string.

Most of these offerings are prepared between the tenth and the thirteenth of December. The rice cakes (*mochi*) and the *buto* are prepared on the thirteenth, and the rice and raw vegetables on the fourteenth. When the preparations are complete, the food offerings are carried in paulownia boxes to the tent of food offerings at the temporary shrine, and then they are ceremoniously transferred one at a time in "bucket brigade" style from priest to priest from the tent of food offerings to the shrine itself. Each priest bows as he is about to receive the tray from his predecessor, takes it and raises it to the height of his head, then turns around to give it to his successor, and bows again. This is done to the accompaniment of classical *gagaku* music. The same procedure is followed but in reverse order upon completion of the dances, after the Wakamiya *kami* has "eaten." The food is then disposed of, for it has been touched by the *kami* and is therefore charged with a frightening power: it has become untouchable. Extreme purity and pollution, rather than being set apart by incalculable distances, are in fact two neighboring points at the opposite ends of a line that forms a nearly complete circle.

During the festival the *jinin* artisans who build the temporary shrine and who today take care of the torches that provide the light for the performances, live in a separate building near the temporary shrine. For the duration of the *On-matsuri* they are allowed to eat only rice, pickles (*tsukemono*), and *miso* soup. On the last day of the festivities they are allowed red rice (*sekihan*).

The entire system of food offerings and the apparent status of humility on the part of the *jinin* signifies a host-guest relationship, in which the symbolic body of the province is invited by the sponsors of the rite to manifest itself and to partake of the labors of the provincial population under its rule. The *kami* is therefore treated like a visitor of great distinction and is offered the best by priests and *jinin* who function as mere intermediaries between the province and its own symbolic body, the *kami*. Sitting humbly in their wayside building, the hosts eat frugal dishes that they do not hesitate to share with visitors such as the Nō actors or this writer. The essence of offerings rituals is hospitality.

Once the food offerings are displayed in front of the shrine, the head-priest offers a branch of *sakaki* tree, recites a *norito*, and is then followed in worship by a special figure named *Hi no tsukai* ("messenger of the sun"). This envoy, who is dressed in grand classical attire, seems to represent the upper echelons of the court. He might have been an imperial envoy in earlier times, but it is no longer clear who he represents. Then officials—from the governor of the prefecture to representatives of the lay Kasuga confraternities, followed by people impersonating the *shuto*, *jinin*, and various ecclesiastics of the past—advance in strict order and display, according to rehearsed procedure, branches of *sakaki* in front of the shrine. Protocol is of the essence, because the symbolic body of the province (the *kami*) and the hierarchical social body of men must merge in a single identity.

Then the following dances are performed: *kagura* in the Kasuga style, a type of *kagura* that was invented only in the Meiji period; *Azuma asobi*, a form of archaic dance that perhaps originated in the eastern part of Japan;

dengaku and *sei-no-o* dances mentioned earlier in this study; *sarugaku,* a medieval form of entertainment that was the fountainhead of Nō; five *bugaku* dances, which originated in Central Asia and in China; *Yamato-mai,* a classical court dance; and six more *bugaku* dances.

The food offerings are then retrieved solemnly, and the Wakamiya *kami* is carried back to its main shrine according to the same procedures by which it had been taken to its temporary abode. The next morning *sumō* wrestling takes place in a consecrated ring located in front of the temporary shrine but on the side of the path away from the shrine. In earlier times there used to be horse-riding archery contests (*Yabusame*), but these have been discontinued.

In the afternoon several Nō plays are performed on a stage erected during the morning in front of the temporary shrine. This event, called the Last Day *Sarugaku,* recalls the fact that the main troupes of Nō actors were originally in close contact with the Kasuga-Kōfukuji multiplex. The dances mentioned above are performed facing the shrine (the *kami* is thus the spectator), whereas the Nō plays of the last day are performed with the shrine to the back of the actors, since the *kami* is not present in the shrine anymore.

The Wakamiya *kami* is not a child taken from its crib in the middle of the night to a place where it is offered food and entertained, nor is it a god enjoying exquisite art from the height of its pedestal. As the body of the province, it might be a youthful culture hero who undergoes regeneration in the performance of music and dance, while at the local level it is probably a snake symbolizing the predominance of land and related to fertility. During the medieval period it was both a complex indigenous *kami* and a manifestation of the Bodhisattva of Wisdom. The Kasuga belief system is thus a phenomenon in which the *kami* generate local culture and, at the same time, are generated by culture.

The overall structure of the *On-matsuri* calls to mind another possible interpretation: the fear and the purity precautions that surround the ritual seem to establish a distance between the human and divine realms, or between a social body and its symbolic form. Nonetheless, the purpose of the festive rite is to merge these two entities; this purpose is accomplished under a special light by the medium of music, which is at times disorderly and at times harmonious. It is as if chaos and order were in balanced opposition, for noise is first and foremost an indication of chaos, whereas harmonious music is an indication of ordered rule. The harmonious music is played when food offerings are made and during the dances; the cacophonic sounds are made at the time of a change in the environment of the *kami*. Thus the food offerings and the dances may be seen as magical acts aimed at placating the furor of a force that is responsible for food, itself coming from the course of seasons; that furor has often been thought to originate in a moral reaction of nature against unethical behavior on the part of people. Nature needs to be pacified, and is pacified by culture; and people need to be pacified too, for they are morally responsible for the normal course of nature. Such is indeed the fundamental structure of the *onryō* (wrathful spirit) phenomenon in Japan: if human wild behavior is seen as an agent of change in the course of nature, then human cultural production may effect the same change, in reverse.

In other words, the symbolic body and the identity of the province are regenerated through an interaction of the binary opposition nature/culture that is expressed in food systems, dances, and games, all of which are subsumed under an opposition between purity and pollution that is at the foundation of the social hierarchy. The cult appears, in this light, to have been the crux of a system whose purpose was to reinforce relations of power. Indeed, the dancers and actors were quasi-outcasts (*hinin*, literally, "nonpersons") performing for aristocrats who called themselves "noble seeds" (*kishu*). The fact that, in ancient Japan, performers of dances and narrators of stories were of extremely low social status is one that has received scholarly attention in Japan only recently and needs further examination in the future.

AESTHETICS AND ETHICS: PLEASURABLE VISIONS

This leads us to consider another rite that was performed at the Kasuga-Kōfukuji multiplex from the medieval period on and is still performed today, albeit in quite a changed form. That is the *Shūni-e* assembly, a ritual that marks the new year according to the Indian calendar and is held in Japan from the sixth to the twelfth day of the second moon. Several *Shūni-e* are celebrated in Japan, the most impressive one being the *Omizutori*, which is performed in the Nigatsu-dō of the Tōdaiji.[56]

The *Shūni-e* of the Kōfukuji is also of importance and provides some insights into the origin of Nō drama and its world, for the ceremony was completed with the performance of Nō drama in the light of wooden torches: *takigi Nō*. This form of Nō play was born in the Kasuga cult in the context of the Kōfukuji's *Shūni-e*, which was created by the *dōshū* of the Western Golden Hall during the Heian period. Later, in the Kamakura period, the conduct of the rite became the responsibility of that hall's *shuto*, to which the participation of *shuto* of other temples of the multiplex was added in the Muromachi period. In the Heian period the *dōshū* performed classical *bugaku* dances in the corridor in front of the Chōzu-dokoro, but when the *shuto* took over, the performances changed to *sarugaku*, which were performed outside the temple in front of the Southern Gate (the main entrance overlooking Sarusawa Pond), where they are still performed today. In 1027 the Eastern Golden Hall initiated the same type of ritual assembly.

The performances that took place at the end of the *Shūni-e* are associated with the creation of the four troupes of Nō actors (Komparu, Kongō, Kanze, and Hōshō) that were under the direct administrative and financial control of the Western Golden Hall. At the time, the Komparu troupe was known as "Emman'i-za" and was attached directly to the Kōfukuji; the Kongō troupe ("Sakato-za") was attached to the Hōryūji; the Kanze troupe ("Yūzaki-za") was, it seems, attached to the Kannonji; and the Hōshō troupe was originally attached to the Yamada-dera. This does not mean that the performers' guilds were owned by the cultic center; the performers lived in villages scattered through Yamato Province and performed their art at the time of local rites, but they were commissioned by the multiplex to perform at the time of rites in which aesthetics played a central role. Naturally, the four Yamato troupes lived under the influence of the multiplex and were well within the universe of meaning diffused by the Kasuga belief system. This is one of the reasons why contemporary Nō actors attribute such importance to the fact that they perform in front of the pine tree at the beginning of the *On-matsuri*, and why they still pay their respects to the multiplex. It is still the custom for all major actors of the existing lineages to come to the Kōfukuji a day before their main performance, to visit the Southern Gate and then the former emplacement of the Western Golden Hall, where they bow in supplication for success in their performing.

A document that relates the origins of the Kōfukuji's *Shūni-e*, the *Kōfukuji shūni-e engi*, sheds light on one aspect of the aesthetics of the Kasuga belief system. Speaking of the disciples of the Buddha, it says:

Origins of the rite of penance dedicated to the Buddha of Medicine and accomplished during the second moon through the recitation of the Buddha's names.

The marvelous aspect of the pearl of Awakening pervades the three worlds and leads living beings to salvation, while the attractive countenances of the golden body of the Buddha penetrate the six destinations and act according to the occasions. The moon of Awakening shines forth and dispels the clouds of ignorance, and the wind of wisdom sweeps away the misty realm of sin. How grand! It is impossible to grasp by dualistic thought the miraculous workings of Complete Awakening. The Buddha's disciples who are fortunate enough to hear the doctrine shall see their vow reinforced by the powers of the Buddha of Medicine.

In strict accordance with their ranks they shall enter the halls
of the temples and revere the pure words of the Tathāgata. On
the seventh day of the second moon of each year they shall as-
semble in the Eastern Golden Hall and recite the marvelous scripture of the Names of the Buddha, practicing regularly for six
hours at a time.

Accordingly, the sun of the Buddha will shine forth again and
the clouds bringing the rain of the Law will reappear at the
horizon.[57]

The avowed purpose of this assembly is to commemorate the advent of
the Indian New Year through a rite of penance and purification ending with
the performance of dances. Thus it is a ritual of renewal that combines rites
of penance and purification in order to let "the sun of the Buddha shine
forth again." It will be recalled that the origin of *kagura* dances is attributed
to a *kami* named Ame-no-Uzume, who danced in order to coax the solar
kami, Amaterasu, out of her hiding place. In the case of the *Shūni-e*, the
rite of penance consists in reciting a list of the Three Thousand Names of
the Buddha.[58] This recitation usually occurs as a rite of penance that
purifies the organs of perception; once they are purified, a new perception
undefiled by dualistic mental operations and accompanied by ecstatic visions and bliss takes place. This perception is referred to in the scriptures
as *rakken* (pleasurable vision).[59]

In other words, an ecstatic vision of reality is made possible through
penance and the repetition of meaningless names, the purpose of which is
to eradicate dualistic categories: thus, the penetration of the realm of ethics
leads the practitioner to a visionary realm that must be termed aesthetic.
It is only natural, then, that rites of renewal and atonement be marked by
the performance of dances and plays in which such visions and aesthetics
based on Buddhist doctrine and Shinto perceptions figure preeminently,
not only at the level of descriptions of vision but in the underlying structure
of the plays themselves.

Born partly in such surroundings, Nō drama is also an essentially
combinatory phenomenon, so much so that to look for its purely "Buddhist" elements would seem to be futile; a systematic search for structural
correlations between the purpose and form of rites in shrines and in
temples, correlations that were deemed significant and of which the drama-
turgists were most conscious, would be more appropriate and fruitful.

The site on which *takigi Nō* was performed, which was in front of the
Southern Gate to mark the end of rites of penance, is yet another grassy
knoll that came to be called "The Lawn of Wisdom" (*hannya shiba*) and,
later, "Firewood Lawn" (*takigi shiba*). Jinson, the abbot of the Daijō-in
monzeki, who noted this performance in 1475, used the term *shibai* (Being

on the Lawn) to refer to it, a term that entered the Japanese vocabulary to mean "theater."

Contemporary performances of *takigi Nō* take place on a slightly elevated stage made of planks and marked by bamboo poles at its four corners. The poles are linked by a rope, just as in ritual enclosures, to which paper strips are affixed. There is no bridge (*hashi watari*) linking the mirror room to the stage, as in contemporary Nō theaters, and the actors simply enter through curtains set in the back of the stage. Painted representations dating from the early Edo period show staggered rows of seats for the audience, but today the audience sits on the stairs of the Southern Gate and on the lawn on each side of the stage. The performances were so popular in the late medieval period that it was decided to build rows of seats for prelates, aristocrats, and common folks, and to close in the entire area with drapes so that people had to pay to view the plays. These fund-raising performances (*kanjin Nō*) helped pay for the expensive costumes that aristocratic or warrior sponsors offered to the actors before their performance to wear in their favorite plays, and for other purposes.

Today, the ceremony is initiated by the entrance of fierce-looking armed *shuto* in medieval attire carrying large torches, who climb on the stage and declare the plays open. They then set fire to the caskets that surround the stage and sit in the first row below the stage. All the plays performed in modern times in the multiplex appear to bear some connection with its realm of symbols: either a direct one, as in the case of *Kasuga ryūjin*, or an indirect one, as in the case of *Ama*, which depicts the world of the sea, or *Kaji*, which depicts the supernatural help received by swordsmiths.

The rites of the multiplex might be divided, for the sake of convenience, into the following categories: state-sponsored rites, provincial rites, local rites, and personal rites. We have examined a state-sponsored rite (the Kasuga Grand Rite), a provincial rite (the *On-matsuri*), and a local rite (the *Shūni-e*) and will examine a few personal rites in the following section on the world of the *monzeki*.

Although in early times the Fujiwara house did not participate in local rites, and the performers of local rites did not participate in Fujiwara rites, all rites associated with the Kasuga-Kōfukuji multiplex were essentially related to the sociocosmic structure of the multiplex, and the rites were intermingled in some fashion, for there were aristocratic elements in local rites and popular elements in aristocratic ones. For instance, some of the actors had an extremely low social status, and yet their services were actively sought by the prelates. As one would expect, the time at which most of these fusions occurred was the medieval period, when class struggle was the most active.

The organization, contents, and purposes of these rites are so complicated that they deserve a full historical investigation, which is out of the scope of the present study. Such an investigation would have to conduct institutional studies, economic studies, political studies, and so on, with a sharp eye to the cultural context in order to avoid producing a superficial, disjointed picture of Japanese society. As a final note in this regard, it should be apparent from our discussion so far that it is inaccurate to use the term "Buddhist" to describe Japanese rituals. Because of the nature of the context in which those rituals are performed, and because they are so pervaded by indigenous notions of protocol, power, and legitimacy, they are something other than purely Buddhist. Similarly, it is inaccurate to characterize as "Shinto" rituals in which the role of aesthetics is so profoundly associated with Buddhist doctrine, and the function of the whole ritual so deeply imbued with originally Buddhist rationales. These rituals are something other than purely Shinto in nature. They are combinatory.

DAIJŌ-IN JISHA ZŌJIKI: THE WORLD OF THE *MONZEKI*

Personal rites conducted at the Kasuga-Kōfukuji multiplex will be examined by way of an analysis of a document entitled *Daijō-in jisha zōjiki* ("Notes of the Daijō-in on Various Matters of the Shrine-Temple Multiplex"), which is the diary of Jinson (1430–1508), abbot of the Daijō-in *monzeki*.[60] In its present version this text is a collection of the diaries of Jinson, who was the twenty-seventh abbot of that *monzeki*, and of Kyōjin, the thirtieth abbot. To these diaries, which were put together in 1868, scholars added, in 1931, the diary of Seikaku, the twenty-eighth abbot. Jinson's diary, which forms the bulk of the document, is an extraordinary work, for it was simultaneously composed as a diary and a detailed account of administrative procedures. It is quite unique in the history of Japan, *a fortiori* in the history of shrine-temple multiplexes, and its discovery in 1868 rekindled studies of the medieval period in Japan.

Jinson is of great interest to us for several reasons. First, he was the son of Ichijō Kanera, a leader of the intelligentsia of his time. Second, he was a contemporary of Yoshida Kanetomo (1435–1511), head-priest of the Yoshida Shrine of Kyoto.[61] Third, Jinson was the leading figure of the Kasuga-Kōfukuji multiplex in the fifteenth century. And fourth, his diary provides us with insights into the medieval world of the Fujiwara house and the Kasuga belief system. The following is based partially on Jinson's document and partially on a study of the work by Suzuki Ryōichi.[62]

Jinson's diary is lengthy and difficult to read; it contains all the official documents and letters written by Jinson, which he produced at a rate of about thirty per month. Of these, 590 documents (31 percent of the total) are concerned with Shinto-Buddhist ceremonies and rites: 170 are requests for ceremonies; 140 are personal requests to various people to participate in certain ceremonies or in the preparations for them; 110 documents specify the duties of those participants; 120 documents concern funds; and 50 documents have to do with requests of rites by the court, the military government, or the chieftain of the house. Another 230 documents (12 percent of the total) concern promotions, decisions regarding labor, various wishes and requests. The administration of subtemples is described in some 335 documents (18 percent of the total); if we add to these the documents related to land domains, the total would be 495, or 26 percent of the total. Another 310 documents (16 percent) are related to the *bakufu*; of these, 5 percent are related to ceremonies, and 5 percent are complaints to the government regarding the loss of domains. The last 400 documents (21 percent) are concerned with various matters that cannot be put into a single category. It is apparent from a reading of the *Jisha zōjiki* that Jinson's overwhelming interest and concern was with rituals and human relationships.

Jinson was born on the seventh day of the eighth moon of 1430 in Kyoto at the residence of his father, the Ichijō-dono, which was situated at the crossroads of the First Ward and Muromachi. He was sent to the Daijō-in in 1438 and was ordained two years later, at the age of ten. He began to work in the administration of the temple at the age of twelve, by which time he had already studied the major scriptures of the Hossō lineage of Buddhism. He continued to read these scriptures every day of his life, because "such is the practice in this cultic center" and because "it will bring about good retributions." Not only was Jinson versed in Buddhist doctrine, but because he was a son of the Fujiwara house, he believed that he was related by blood to the very essence of Kasuga *daimyōjin*. Thus a phenomenal distance separated Jinson from the rest of the world: to his mind, he was a living manifestation of the *kami*, for the Fujiwara were direct descendants of Ame-no-koyane-no-mikoto. Jinson's lofty position in the *monzeki* was grounded in divine right and was part and parcel of a sociocosmic order that he was determined to uphold.

The sense that the Fujiwara leaders of the *monzeki* had of belonging to an ethereal plane of existence was mirrored directly in the administrative structure of the multiplex in that distinctions were made between members of the Fujiwara house and other lineages: those issued from the five *sekkanke* were called "noble seeds" (*kishu*), whereas the members of the *inke* were simply called "members of good houses" (*ryōke*). Only noble seeds were allowed to become abbots of the *monzeki*; the others could aspire only to positions of authority in the temples under the control of the *monzeki*. Traditionally, the Ichijō-in *monzeki* was headed by members of the Konoe and Takatsukasa branches of the Fujiwara house, and the Daijō-in *monzeki* was headed by members of the Kujō and Ichijō branches. By contrast, the *inke* were headed by "members of good houses" such as Kan'in, Hino, Murakami Genji (Koga), and others.

Naturally, the noble seeds and members of good houses were ranked well above the rest of the ecclesiastic population of the multiplex, such as the scholarly monks of the Six Directions and, needless to say, the *shuto*. They were also ranked above the sacerdotal lineages that presided over the administration of the shrines, that is, the branches of the Nakatomi and Ōnakatomi lineages and their subbranches at the Wakamiya Shrine. The noble seeds considered themselves to be above the sacerdotal lineages, not because Buddhism was thought to be superior, but because they were closer to the Kasuga *kami* in virtue of their claimed origins and their association with the imperial lineage. Aristocrats in Buddhist garb remained aristocrats. In Japan, taking the tonsure rarely meant shedding one's secular name and ties. In fact it was usually quite the opposite: for some noble seeds, the entrance into a *monzeki* meant the acquisition of a status that was sometimes envied by aristocrats.

It is sometimes thought that Buddhism failed in Japan precisely because of this practice, and the Japanese have been criticized for not "leaving the world" (*shusse*) when they entered the Buddhist community. "Leaving the world," however, was understood by the Japanese to be the way par excellence to achieve high status and power, so much so that the word *shusse* came to mean "to be successful." To criticize that situation is to fail to recognize the way in which the Japanese thought of themselves within the parameters of the sociocosmic organization that has been discussed several times in the course of this study: that is to say, those who entered the Buddhist community could not be "leaving a secular world" since that world, in the case of the aristocrats, was a sociocosmic organization of sacred character. The Fujiwara merely transposed into Buddhist terms some mythological notions that were structurally inscribed within Kasuga, and they were reinforced in those notions by the very fact that the Kōfukuji was dedicated to the spirit of their ancestors. Furthermore, Buddhist institutions could survive in Japan only as instruments of support for the state and its ideology, be that support implicit or explicit. Indeed, in the case of Yamato Province, the multiplex was the state.

During the late medieval period the Kōfukuji had about forty monks whose rank was above that of assistant master of discipline and among whom there were about ten assistant monachal rectors (*gon-sōjō*). The latter always belonged to the *monzeki* or *inke*. Very early in the history of the multiplex, even those who held comparatively low ranks (below that of *hō-in*) were members of good houses or their disciples. Some of these ecclesiastics became the heads of major temples administered by the Kōfukuji, some of which were in Nara, but others, such as the Hasedera, the Yakushiji, the Hōryūji, and the Kiyomizudera, were elsewhere. The line that separated noble seeds from good houses was a thin one; it was just a matter of one rank, but the line was never crossed, for the simple reason that the members of good houses were subordinated to the noble seeds in the same way that subshrines and subtemples were subordinated to the Kasuga-Kōfukuji multiplex. Just as it would have been incredible for a subshrine to become the main shrine, so it would have been inappropriate for a member of a good house to occupy a position assigned by divine right to a noble seed. To Jinson, the mirrorlike relation between the heavenly bureaucracy and the structure of the multiplex and of society in general was the manifestation of a preestablished harmony that could never be discussed, even less, called into doubt. Such preestablished harmony, however, grounded though it may have been in myth and supported by ritual, needed another type of reinforcement so that the postulation of the legitimacy of its power would be effected. This reinforcement was provided by economic power and, more precisely, land. Under these conditions one can imagine that the recurrent loss of domains on the part of the *monzeki* during the Muromachi period was to Jinson much more than an economic annoyance; it was a profoundly disturbing threat to the very texture of society as he conceived it. This view is demonstrated in the private, or personal, ritual life of Jinson.

Throughout his life Jinson performed rites regularly and with great seriousness. Almost every day of the month was devoted in part to one or other divinity of the pantheon surrounding Kasuga *daimyōjin,* as table 9 shows.

Jinson accompanied the performance of these regular rites with lectures, reading or chanting scriptures, making offerings, and visits to the shrines and temples dedicated to the combined divine entities. Jinson also performed various other rites on a regular basis, some on different days that rotated every nine years and were mainly dedicated to astrological divinities. Days were counted by Jinson not only according to the Chinese decimal and duodecimal systems but also the Indian-based astronomical system in its relation to astrology. Rituals based on that system had been imported to Japan by Esoteric Buddhism and were widely performed during the Heian, Kamakura, and Muromachi periods.[63]

Table 9. Monthly Devotions by Jinson

Day of the Month	Divinity Worshiped by Jinson
1st	Kasuga *daimyōjin*
3d	Bishamonten (from 1467 on)[a]
5th	Miroku *bosatsu*[b]
7th	Benzaiten (from 1461 on)[c]
8th	Yakushi *nyorai* (from 1459 on)[d]
11th	Kasuga *daimyōjin*
13th	Jion daishi[e]
15th	Amida *nyorai*[f]
15th	Relics
18th	Kannon *bosatsu*
21st	Kasuga *daimyōjin*
22d	Shōtoku taishi[g]
24th	Jizō *bosatsu*
25th	Monju *bosatsu*
25th	Temman (Sugawara no Michizane)[h]

Source: Suzuki Ryōichi, *Daijō-in jisha zōjiki* (Tokyo: Soshiete, 1983), 36.

[a]Bishamonten (Sanskrit: Vaiśravaṇa) is one of the four heavenly kings (*Shitennō*) and the guardian of the northern direction; as such, he was the object of many cults in China and Japan.

[b]Miroku *bosatsu* (Sanskrit: Maitreya Bodhisattva) is the Buddha of the Future and has been an important object of various messianic cults in India, China, Korea, Japan, and Vietnam.

[c]Benzaiten (Sanskrit: Sarasvati) was originally a deity related to water; she became in Japan the object of many combinatory cults usually related to fertility, the arts, and speech. Jinson may have worshiped her because of her ability to enhance eloquence, a quality needed in his position as debater.

[d]Yakushi *nyorai* is the Buddha of Medicine, also widely worshiped in Japan.

[e]Jion daishi (632–82) was the Chinese founder of the Hossō school, to which Jinson belonged.

[f]Amida *nyorai* is the Buddha Amitābha, resident of the Western Pure Land.

[g]Shōtoku taishi (574–622) was the imperial regent usually associated with the development of Buddhism as a political element of the Japanese government; he became the object of a specific cult during the thirteenth century.

[h]Temman is one of the titles granted upon his death to Sugawara no Michizane (845–903), who became the object of a cult dedicated to poetry and scholarship.

For instance, Jinson had a particular devotion to *Ragora* (Skt., Rāhu), a celestial body believed to cause lunar and solar eclipses. Because Ragora was ascendant at the time of his birth, Jinson performed rites dedicated to it on the eighth day of every moon. He also performed a rite to Saturn on the nineteenth day of the moon, because this planet was in ascendance at the time of his first birthday. Furthermore, he performed regular rites dedicated to the following celestial bodies: Venus (fifteenth day), comets (*Kaitsū*, or *Keitsū*: eighteenth day), Mercury (twenty-first day), Jupiter (twenty-fifth day), the Sun (twenty-sixth day), the Moon (twenty-seventh day), and Mars (twenty-ninth day).

The year 1462 corresponded to Jinson's thirty-second birthday and to the fourth ascendant passage of the planet Mars since his birth; hence, during that year Jinson performed a special rite on every twenty-ninth day of the moon, calling on Mars to prevent any harm or incident during the year. At the end of that year a comet (*Kaitsū*) appeared and Jinson commissioned from the Bureau of Painting a mandala of the comet for which he then performed the ceremony of "Eye-Opening" (*kaigen-kuyō*). He also dedicated a ritual to that mandala on every eighteenth day, which was also the commemorative day (*ennichi*) of Kannon, so he performed a double rite on that day throughout the year. In addition to these monthly rites dedicated to divinities and constellations related to time and space, Jinson performed rites on the sixteenth day of every tenth moon for the spirit of the first Fujiwara, Kamatari, and chanted the *Vimalakīrti-nirdeśa sūtra*. Of course he also attended the major rituals and ceremonies of the *monzeki* and the Main Temple, as well as the grand rite of the Wakamiya Shrine (the *On-matsuri*), about which he wrote a separate report.

If for some reason, such as illness, Jinson was prevented from performing his rites, he would not fail to catch up as soon as his condition allowed. During the five days that he spent twice a year ingesting various medicinal herbs and drugs for preventive purposes, he did not perform any rites, but he would perform them as soon as the period of five days was over. He is known to have cut short this five-day period only once in his lifetime. Much of the life of a high ecclesiastic of the cultic center was thus spent in ceremony and ritual. Because the nature of the timing of those rites was cyclical and reinforced a particular consciousness of time, it may have been an obstacle to the formation of a sense of history that might have helped Jinson to deal with his contemporary world. Instead, the prelate's consciousness was turned toward the distant past, to the origins of his lineage, or toward the future and the ineluctable time of death. In both cases these objects of consciousness were, at the same time, objects of devotion. The outstanding devotion of Jinson was directed to the *kami* and buddhas/bodhisattvas of the multiplex, but he also developed a few other ritual practices and beliefs.

It is difficult to learn from his diary how Jinson perceived the Kasuga entities, if only because he took so many things for granted and did not bother to elaborate on them, or because he held beliefs that were so widely shared at the time that they needed no special discussion on his part. For example, Jinson's understanding of the associations between various buddhas and bodhisattvas and the Kasuga *kami* is, at first sight, hard to unravel. Jinson first notes these correspondences in 1468, then again in 1469, 1471, 1472, 1476, and 1498. Had there been no problem in this regard after 1468, no further mention would have been made of them. As noted earlier, however, a problem lay in the fact that the authority of the Kōfukuji was divided between the Main Temple and the two *monzeki*. Because each of these was related to different branches of the Fujiwara house, the transmissions of the correspondences varied accordingly. The Ichijō-in *monzeki* was traditionally headed by members of the Konoe branch of the Fujiwara house, and by members of the Takanotsukasa branch when no Konoe people were available. In Jinson's time the Takanotsukasa branch ruled that *monzeki* for three consecutive generations. The Konoe branch did not manage to gather enough influence for the nomination of one of its members to that post in that period because it supported the Nichiren sect, which was, in the words of the *Kasuga gongen genki*, "abhorred by Kasuga *daimyōjin*." The Daijō-in *monzeki* was headed by a member of either the Ichijō or Kujō branch.

To Jinson, Kasuga *daimyōjin* was a complex entity that he worshiped in abstruse and various ways. He referred to Kasuga *daimyōjin* as the "Protector of the Consciousness-Only lineage of Buddhism and of the Fujiwara interests" and regularly performed daily, monthly, and yearly rites to it. His visits to the Kasuga Shrine at the beginning of the year were grandiose occasions for pomp and ceremony: he customarily organized a following of thirty prelates in grand attire, with their retinue, and commissioned vehicles to be used on temple grounds only and others to be used on shrine grounds only. His daily rites, which he performed morning and evening, were simple; they involved meditation in front of a painted representation of the multiplex (*Kasuga mandara*), and chants of various mantra (*shingon*). First he recited the *Butsugen shingon* (Mantra of the Buddha-Eye), followed by the *Dainichi shingon* (Mantra of Mahāvairocana), and then the specific mantra of each Kasuga divinity symbolized by a "seed-letter" (*shuji*; Sanskrit: *bīja*): the first shrine was symbolized by the seed-letter *mo*, the second by *bhai*, the third by *ha*, and the fourth by *ka*. He closed this daily rite with the recitation of the *Ichiji-konrin shingon* (Mantra of the One Letter in the Golden Wheel). Jinson thus worshiped the *kami* according to the prevailing Buddhist fashion, which shows how pervasive the influence of Esoteric Buddhism was on the associations between *kami* and buddhas.

Kasuga *daimyōjin* was perceived by Jinson as a numinous entity to be worshiped daily throughout the year, because it was directly related to the sociocosmic position of the Fujiwara house. The noble seeds of that house were taught, from a tender age, to believe in their divine origin. As Jinson wrote: "The *kampaku*, Chieftain of the house, is such by virtue of his being a direct descendant of the *kami* worshiped in the Third Shrine [Ame-no-koyane-no-mikoto]."

Jinson believed that the head of the Fujiwara house was such by divine right and that his position as *kampaku*, the de facto ruler of the country, had the same origin; as might be surmised, this did not allow Jinson to question the politics of the *kampaku*. Moreover, Jinson believed that the five *sekkanke* of the Fujiwara house corresponded to the five *kami* of Kasuga. Consequently, he saw his religious duties as being extremely important, for to fail to worship the divine entities of Kasuga would be a break of trust; it would rupture the contract between the heavenly bureaucracy and the human model thereof. Jinson also had a strong sense that he was the head of the *monzeki* by divine right for he was a full-fledged noble seed directly descended from the same *kami* as the chieftain of the house. Therefore, to this prelate of the late medieval period, legitimacy was grounded in lineage, heredity, and ritual, all of which were connected to land. It is obvious, perhaps, that a prelate who was master of a ceremonial center that ruled a little empire would be unlikely to question the onto-logical grounding of his position, and such was the case with Jinson, who to all appearances knew he was heir to a formidable tradition, the legitimacy of which was being threatened. His view of the organization of the realm of mythology embodied in the Kasuga-Kōfukuji multiplex was reinforced by the hierarchy that the multiplex had fostered in all parts of society and by the very organization of the cultic center and city: the distinctions between noble seeds and members of good houses corresponded to the distinctions between *monzeki*, *inke*, and the rest of the shrines and temples and their entire population. These were, to Jinson, sociocosmic facts.

Jinson's beliefs in this regard were reinforced by his understanding of history, which he and the other members of the Fujiwara house considered to be a manifestation of the will of the *kami* and buddhas. Thus, when the *shuto* and *jinin* took the sacred tree from the shrines to support their claims, they were responding to the will of the *kami*, who moved them to do so either by oracle or divine intervention of some sort, such as dreams. In

1483, for example, the *shuto* took the sacred tree on an expedition to Furu to force that district to provide funds for the periodic reconstruction of the shrines. In his diary, Jinson states that the decision to take that action was the "will of the *kami*." Throughout his diary Jinson used such terms as "divine will," "divine plan," "divine mercy," and "divine punishment." Jinson was sometimes at a loss over the turbulent events of his time, and one finds him desperately waiting for a dream that would let him know that he had taken the right step or that he should be satisfied with the turn of things. A good example of this is provided in his remarks on the *monzeki's* loss of control of the Kawaguchi domain, which was extremely important to Jinson because funds from this domain were traditionally used for the upkeep of the scriptures. When the domain was returned to the control of the *monzeki*, Jinson had a dream in which it was revealed to him that this auspicious event had been the result of an association between Amaterasu and Kasuga *daimyōjin* (the Wakamiya?). The next day he went to the Bureau of Painting and commissioned an artist to paint that dream, as he described it, at once.

Two other objects of devotion stand out in Jinson's spiritual life: the relics of Kasuga, and the Buddha of Medicine (*Yakushi nyorai*).

Jinson had a deep belief in the supernatural power of relics. He copied several scriptures, such as the ancient *Sōden-ryūki*, which describes how Hsüan-tsang brought back from India some relics "of the Buddha," and the *Ha-shari-engi* (Chronicle of the Tooth-Relic). The relics that Jinson venerated in direct connection with the *kami* of Kasuga were not those of the Buddha but relics that miraculously appeared and through which all sorts of miracles were performed because of their formidable potency. In this regard Jinson was a man of his age, for belief in the power of relics was a mark of the times. Jinson had many dreams; his diary records as many as 180 of them, about half of which are related to the *kami* and the buddhas. Among these, 30 or so are related to relics with which Jinson was so obsessed that he waited in great excitement for any opportunity to get hold of them because they had some history and were known to work wonders. For some unknown reason, he most eagerly sought after the relics that were kept at the Tōji in Kyoto; these were in the form of grainlike particles (*tsubu*), which might have been bone fragments. Of the 6,400 "grains" of relics kept at the Kōfukuji, 5,300 had come from the Tōji.

Jinson kept these relics in exquisite reliquaries that can still be seen today. The most famous, perhaps, is the reliquary dedicated to Kasuga *daimyōjin* that is kept at the Nōman-in of the Hasedera. Jinson left a detailed account of the creation of that reliquary that is so complex that it took sixteen years (between 1476 and 1492) to complete. The oldest part of that reliquary is the *gorintō* (five-storied symbol), a crystal container that was completed in 1476 and contains relics in each of the five sections that in Esoteric Buddhism symbolize the constitutive aspect of the universe (earth, water, fire, air, and ether). This container is affixed to one of the four panels that make up the reliquary, each of which is protected by two painted doors. The second container, completed in 1478, is a crystal in the form of a triple wish-fulfilling gem surrounded by flames. The third, completed in 1485, is a representation of the Kasuga deer, on top of which stands a mirror affixed to a *sakaki* tree. The mirror itself contains representations of the five buddhas and bodhisattvas associated with the five *kami* of Kasuga. The fourth panel, which was also completed around 1485, represents a pagoda over the ocean, flanked by dragons and inscribed with the name of the Sutra of Wisdom. The paintings on the doors of the reliquary were commissioned by Jinson and made by Seiken, an artist of the Bureau of Painting who resided at the Shōnan-in.

Jinson's second important object of devotion was Yakushi Nyorai, the Buddha of Medicine. Jinson performed a monthly rite to Yakushi and spent two five-day periods every year in complete seclusion in order to take various drugs. One might expect any ecclesiastic of his station to engage in these practices, but it is possible that Jinson was devoted to Yakushi because it was the original nature of the *kami* related to the branch of the Fujiwara house from which he was issued. Jinson also spent one week during the first moon of every year in devotion to Yakushi, an exercise that he performed every single year between 1452 and 1505. During that week he would abstain from ingesting salt and would chant the *dhāraṇī* (formula) of Yakushi eighty-four thousand times, a symbolic number in Buddhism that here may simply mean a great many times. The reasons he gives for doing so were "for peace of mind" and for "the prevention of disease and prolongation of life." These practices, some of which Jinson describes in detail, were typical of Esoteric Buddhism with its tenet that religious practices bring profit in this lifetime (*gense-riyaku*).

Two other devotional practices stand out in the latter part of Jinson's life, namely, dedication to *Bishamonten* (Vaiśravaṇa) and *Daikokuten* (Mahā-cāla). Devotion to Bishamonten, who was traditionally regarded as protector of the northern direction, was part of the popular cults of the time. Jinson made ten pilgrimages to Kurama in the mountains north of Kyoto, where there was a temple dedicated to Bishamonten. Kurama was not the main temple dedicated to Bishamonten north of Nara, but it certainly was the most famous. In fact, the entire road that leads north from the Kamo Shrine in Kyoto to the Japan Sea was sacred from great antiquity, and one can still see today various representations of Bishamonten in the temples and shrines along it. Especially important are the representations found in the temple of Hanase and in the impressive Bujōji, a *yamabushi* temple of the Tendai lineage. The devotion to Bishamonten at Kasuga was a specific aspect of the popular cult dedicated to that divinity: a stone in the ground immediately in front of the Southern Gate of the main shrine is said to be the site of manifestation of a divinity called *Aka-dōji* (Red Youngster), which was associated with Bishamonten.[64] Two paintings that date from the Muromachi period and are still extant today depict that cult: one shows Bishamonten seated on a rock at the foot of Mount Mikasa and flanked by two attendants standing in front of a *torii* from which wisteria branches hang, and the other shows the *Aka-dōji* standing on the aforementioned stone.[65] Those paintings may have been objects of devotion for Jinson.

Jinson offers no details about his other strong devotion to Daikokuten, but it most likely had some connection with the cult offered in esoteric circles to the *dakini* divinities, the leader of which is Daikokuten. The *dakini* are said to know in advance the time at which people will die and to feed on corpses. Oracles might reveal that time to those who are anxious to know it and who would then perform rites of intercession to the *dakini*'s superior, Daikokuten. At the age of seventy-five Jinson sculpted a statue of Daikokuten from a piece of camphor wood (one will recall the particular importance of that wood in early Japanese history) taken from the tree from which the statue of Kannon kept at the Hasedera was made. One can imagine that the Daikokuten statue, which Jinson believed was charged with extreme power, was of great importance to him. Toward the end of his life Jinson spent much time in seclusion in a hut where he installed that statue, and thus it appears that his devotion to Daikokuten was associated with his knowledge of his impending death.

Every one of Jinson's ritual duties was connected to the Fujiwara hierarchy, which ruled the multiplex and claimed some authority in the rest of the country, and that is why Jinson took great pains to oversee the education and progress of his successor (Seikaku) in the *monzeki*'s complex structure. He did this by having Seikaku participate in major ritual assemblies such as the *Hōkō-e*, the *Hokke-e*, the *Jion-e*, and the *Yuima-e*. Jinson exerted all efforts for Seikaku and wrote copious descriptions and comments on the various ceremonies that marked the official career of the head of the *monzeki*. Table 10 is a chronology of these activities.

As one can infer from this table, it took Seikaku approximately eleven years to qualify to be the discussant at the *Yuima-e* ritual assembly, by far the most important occasion at the cultic center in terms of hierarchy. Although originally this position was opened to all monks, it soon became the prerogative of the noble seeds, who gained this exalted post in less than

Table 10. Seikaku's Career under Jinson's Supervision, 1462–1491

Event	Date
Acceptance as disciple (*nyūshitsu*)	2d month, 1462
Ordination (*tokudo*)	2d month, 1463
Full ordination (*jukai*)	11th month, 1468
Discussant for ritual assembly (*Hō-e ryūgi*)	12th month, 1468
Discussant for Lotus assembly (*Hokke-e ryūgi*)	10th month, 1470
Inquisitor for Jion assembly (*Jion-e ryūmon*)	11th month, 1470
Discussant for Jion assembly (*Jion-e ryūgi*)	2d month, 1471
Discussant for Vimalakirti assembly (*Yuima-e kengaku-ryūgi*)	12th month, 1473
Lecturer for Vimalakirti assembly (*Yuima-e kōshi*)	12th month, 1475
Head of Music, Wakamiya (*Wakamiya-sai dengaku-tō*)	11th month, 1478
Overseer, Vimalakirti assembly (*Yuima-e tandai*)	12th month, 1484
Overseer, Vimalakirti assembly (*Yuima-e tandai*)	1488
Overseer, Vimalakirti assembly (*Yuima-e tandai*)	1491

Source: Suzuki Ryōichi, *Daijō-in jisha zōjiki* (Tokyo: Soshiete, 1983), 17.

twenty years, whereas it could take a lifetime for others, even those who had a better training in the scriptures. One who gained this position had a chance of becoming abbot of the Kōfukuji.

Jinson thought like a noble seed and acted—or failed to act—like one, and his life-style was similar to that of the most powerful and richest members of the Fujiwara house of earlier times. One of his main personal concerns was the reconstruction of his residence after a fire that started in the Gangōji had reduced it to ashes. Jinson was obsessed with plans for building a sumptuous residence befitting his position, and over a period of fifty years he discussed with architects, carpenters, and artists the plans and visions he saw in his dreams. His residence consisted of an L-shaped building with a corridor running in front of six rooms, the largest of which was the Veneration Hall (*jibutsu-dō*), which enshrined painted and sculpted representations of the five buddhas and bodhisattvas associated with the Kasuga *kami*. Jinson held daily, monthly, and yearly rites in this room and lived in the others. Apparently the architecture was of the *shinden-zukuri* style, which prevailed among aristocrats during the Heian period, a style of extreme refinement and supreme elegance.

He repeatedly levied taxes on all domains owned by the *monzeki*, and engaged a large number of *shuto* and *jinin* to help construct a vast garden he had envisioned, one of the finest made in the Muromachi period. The garden is usually thought to have been the work of the great artist Zen'ami (1393–?), but it must have been conceived by someone else about whom Jinson provides no detail. Contemporary Japanese scholars think that this garden's basic structure was set during the Heian period when the Zenjō-in was still part of the Gangōji and that it was largely preserved in a restructuring that took place in 1141. Thus, if Zen'ami had any hand in the design of the new garden, it was simply to improve on the already existing patterns and configurations. It is true that Zen'ami knew Jinson and visited him several times, and he may have given Jinson some counsel, for it is known that Jinson paid him.

Whatever the case may have been, the garden was a stupendous undertaking that incorporated artificial lakes and hills, paths and plains. It was so astounding that several notables from Kyoto made special trips just to view it. Jinson was clearly pleased that the important people of his time appreciated what he considered to be his own achievement. He had forty men transport a boat from the Kizu River to the lake, and on it he held music and dance parties and took many pleasure trips with the priests of the shrines. Of this he wrote in his diary, "So pleasant. I had dreamt of this for many years." His father, Ichijō Kanera, spent ten years at Jinson's estate after his Kyoto residence burned down during the Ōnin War, and Jinson invited famous poets to visit the garden before they all engaged in writing linked-verse poetry (*renga*); Sōgi, the architect and theoretician of this elegant poetic form, was a close friend of Jinson and visited him several times.[66]

Later, Jinson had a bridge built out to an artificial island in the lake. The entire garden was undoubtedly of the "borrowed landscape" style (*karikeshiki*) and may have been surrounded by white walls beyond which it was possible to contemplate the serene scenery of Mount Mikasa at the foot of the Kasuga Range. The hills of the garden being built to the east of the residence, one could walk up them to view the pagodas of the multiplex. There is little doubt that deer roamed freely through the garden, for Jinson mentioned seeing them often in his dreams. When the garden was completed, he wrote in his diary: "It is now completed. How gratifying! This must have been the wish of the Kasuga divinities."

The cost of the residence with its garden defied the imagination of the people, who were not happy about having to provide for the amusement of the prelates. Several hundred *shuto* and *jinin* worked for sixty days to build the artifical hills. Jinson managed to pay the workers regularly, but when a domain failed to provide funds within stated time limits, he proved to be ruthless and ordered the *kokumin* to harass the people of that domain.

In some cases when taxes were not paid promptly, Jinson took punitive measures and sent what he called "strong men" (*rikisha*) or "men clad as monks" (he did not use the term *sōhei*) to ensure swift payment. If the funds still did not come, he sent a heavily armed militia. The peasants protested several times, arguing that the taxes were too heavy, that the amounts demanded were added to already prescribed amounts, and that the harvests had been poor or that there had been an epidemic, but Jinson rarely relented. The peasants even rebelled a few times, but the noble seed did not think that these were serious problems and he dismissed them as "skirmishes caused by bad elements in society." He went so far as to describe the rebels as "enemies of the Kasuga divinities." The only time Jinson gained an inkling of the seriousness of the situation in Yamato Province was when the *monzeki* lost control over domains, a state of affairs that had been around for most of his lifetime and over which he felt powerless. In a few instances the Tsutsui warrior house came to his help and worked out compromises, for which Jinson complimented the Tsutsui and even made "payments of gratitude." Several times in his diary, however, he lamented making such payments, thinking it utterly demeaning to pay what might be termed protection money, and he complained that "even though the *monzeki* is the governor of the province, it has no power."

The evolution of Japanese society outside the garden of the *monzeki* rarely intruded through its thin white walls. Jinson lived in a sociocosmic preestablished harmony that allowed little or no passage of time other than cyclical and auspicious; shrines were reconstructed regularly, after all, and the ritual cycle was carefully observed. In many ways Jinson lived in the past: his father gave him, on occasion, his commentaries on classical literature; he read the *Tale of Genji*; and he dreamed. Jinson's life was a paradigm of the structures of the Kasuga-Kōfukuji multiplex.

Born an aristocrat at a time when the Fujiwara house had little power, Jinson lived like the aristocrats of old. He was their last stronghold: he had land domains and oversaw the affairs of a huge cultic center. He saw this as his sacred duty and therefore performed most seriously the many rituals that filled his life, exerting himself to find the enormous funds necessary to perform them. He found legitimacy for his actions in reflections on his divine origins. He had little say, however, in political affairs. When he visited the residence of the Ashikaga shoguns in Kyoto, he behaved in a subservient manner. He welcomed the shogun at the time of his visits to the cultic center with great pomp but always had a sense that the new ruler came to worship his own *kami*. He had power over a complex ceremonial center, but he failed to govern it effectively. Gradually he lost so many domains that there was not enough money available to repair his bath-house.

Toward the end of his life Jinson spent increasing amounts of time in another temple of the Kōfukuji, where he could feel the warmth of an understanding presence, a monk who had been his lover since that person was twelve years old and who had remained faithful to Jinson all his life. Jinson wrote in an astonishingly candid manner about his visits to the Enryakuji on Mount Hiei and about the young pages he met there; he was always welcomed there with refined dishes, much *sake*, poetry gatherings, and bathhouse parties.

All that remains of the Daijō-in *monzeki* today is a lake near the Nara Hotel and a small pillar marking its former location.

4 The Experience of Transcendence in Kasuga

The purpose of this chapter is to examine the sacred character of the Kasuga-Kōfukuji multiplex by discussing the evolution of the conceptualization of its space and time and by analyzing some of the aspects of its rituals in relation to space, time, and doctrine. Kasuga was the locus of a historical process in which Buddhist cosmology and doctrine were combined with indigenous notions and practices, thus giving birth to grand visions of Kasuga as a sort of paradise on earth, which the Japanese tradition called "the Pure Land in this World" (*gense-jōdo*). Such visions appear in the texts, paintings, rituals, and theatrical performances created at the multiplex over the centuries. Originally of a purely mystical nature in the mainstream of Buddhist practice, those visions were intricately connected to the evolution of Nara as a sacred city and to political and religious visions of Japan as a sacred land. These visions form a great part of the way the world was conceived of and lived in and represent a rich but still little-explored facet of Japanese culture in the medieval period.

The entire Kōfukuji was destroyed by fire in 1046, in 1181, and again in 1327. The subsequent reconstructions marked a renewal of religious fervor, especially in 1181 and 1327. The fire of 1181, which was set by Taira warriors, heralded the new age of the Kamakura period, and the fire of 1327 occurred shortly before the Muromachi period. It can be said that in both cases a major renewal of energy at all levels of life in the multiplex was felt throughout the province of Yamato. At those times the Kasuga belief system evolved a new world of rite and festivity, of celebration and vision, against a background of civil wars, fires, famines, and against the impending cosmic disaster of the "end of the *dharma*" that was touted by the members of the Pure Land lineages. The pervasive presence of death penetrated people's consciousness and cast its shadow over all cultural manifestations. Dreams of salvation, methods of devotion, and a host of eclectic practices characterized life in the multiplex in those times and manifested themselves in scripture, poetry, art, and theater. Amidst profound structural modifications of the Japanese social body, new cities appeared, warriors attempted to control politics and commerce, and a new ideology surfaced in the major cultic centers of the country. It was under these conditions that the Kasuga belief system ceased to be reserved exclusively for the aristocratic elite; it spread throughout the province of Yamato and became part of the general consciousness of the population.

In all these processes of change there slowly emerged a definition of the human situation that had little in common with earlier definitions. In this development of a new culture, the rites and festivities of the cultic center played a crucial role, for one can discern in them the roots of a new literature, new dramas, new visions of society and divisions over those, and new understandings of space and time. Death was hovering over all activities. But so was dance.

THE SACRED SPACE OF THE SHRINE

Beyond a basic opposition between the space of the shrine and whatever area is outside of it, three subcategories of space can be recognized within the compounds of the Kasuga Shrine itself. The first category is the cultic sites where rock abodes (*iwakura*) and various sacred stones are set; the second is the *saniwa*, a zone set in front of the shrines slightly below them and consisting of a yard covered with pebbles (*tamajari*); and the third is the shrines themselves. This third subcategory included the residences of the *kami* and their symbols; the site of the *jingūji*, which was reserved for prelates of the Kōfukuji; the site of the Naorai Hall, where members of the Fujiwara house would sit, consume festive food, and view the dances; the site of the Hei-den, where a number of ritual activities took place; and the gates through which participants in the rites were allowed to enter the compounds of the shrine according to their ranks.

The organization of space in the shrine compounds reveals two concerns: first, a ritual concern with purity, and second, a concern with hierarchy, for the physical placement of people in the shrine was a function of the separation of duties between those of the members of the Fujiwara house and those of the sacerdotal lineages, as well as a function of the organization of the Fujiwara house itself. Finally, these concerns indicate that the human body was the physical site onto which, through ritual, social information was inscribed; ritual was also the main technique through which the body was controlled.

The first of the three subcategories of space has to do with "rock abode" (*iwakura*). The rock abode seems to be one of the oldest forms of ritual sites found in Japan. It consists generally of a grouping of stones of striking shape, ritually purified and serving as the site where a *kami* manifests itself. Not only does the rock abode figure prominently in some of the sites investigated by archaeologists all over Japan, but it also figures prominently in mythology. In some cases a rock abode came to be seen as the body (*shintai, goshintai, mishōtai*) of a *kami* or even as the *kami* itself. The worship of sacred stones has a complex history, for the practice has been overlaid by many layers of ritual through the centuries. Some sacred stones are located in or near shrines; some are the objects of rain-making rituals or fertility rites, or serve to mark the sites of hierophanies or the limits of domains; some are engraved with names of *kami,* and some are sculpted so as to represent the *kami* or, under the influence of Buddhism, to represent buddhas and bodhisattvas. Stone cults remain so powerful in Japan that one may wonder whether people worship the being represented by a stone carving or the stone itself. The rock abode is, then, first and foremost the site of ritual acts.

In Kasuga there is an artificial rock abode under one of the shrines. It is not known of what that abode, which seems to have been covered with a layer of plaster, consists, for the existing photographs of it do not allow one to be more precise.[1] The Mizuya Shrine, which is located north of the main Kasuga Shrine, has a similar rock abode. It is not known why the stones in those rock abodes were covered with plaster, nor when such a practice originated. The Kasuga and Mizuya shrines appear to be unique in this respect in Japan.

Stone worship seems to be an ancient practice at Kasuga; although no text documents such worship in the Nara or Heian periods, excavations performed in 1977 indicate that it was engaged in all over the grounds of the shrines, and a number of paintings of the Kamakura and Muromachi periods show that certain stones of the compound were sacred. The most famous stone, which is set in the ground in front of the main southern gate of the main shrine, was the site of residence of a combined divine entity called "Red Child" (*Aka-dōji*), who, as was mentioned earlier, is believed to be a hypostasis of Bishamonten (Vaiśravaṇa).[2] Several extant paintings represent the "Red Child" standing on the stone, or its Original Nature sitting on a rock behind a wisteria-covered wooden shrine gate (*torii*) near which a centipede, the theriomorphic emblem of the divinity, crawls. We saw in chapter 3 that this divine entity had been the object of a special reverence on the part of Jinson, head of the Daijō-in *monzeki* during the fifteenth century.

Paintings of the shrine compounds dating back to the Edo period show all the sacred stones of Kasuga.[3] These stones can still be seen today, either within the main shrine or on the paths linking various subshrines. They are the object of little attention today, with the exception, perhaps, of the one in front of the main southern gate, which is still the object of ritual at the time of the *setsubun* in spring. Two rock abodes can be seen at the top of Mount Mikasa, the natural emblem of the Kasuga cult. They seem to represent the oldest layers of ritual related to that mountain. Many ritual sites containing rock abodes have been identified by archaeologists on the plain between the shrines and the temples.

The second subcategory of space at Kasuga is called *saniwa*. Stone worship is closely related to the *saniwa* (also called *hironiwa* or *yuniwa*), for it is an area covered with white pebbles (*tamajari*) on which a number of rites are performed. The *tamajari* may be an expansion of the rock abode ritual site. The term *saniwa* is of obscure origin; in the *Kojiki* it refers to the sacred area where the interpreter of oracles would stand, and thus the term came to indicate that person. The *niwa* portion of *saniwa* is usually translated as "garden," and, according to Ueda Masaaki, the *sa* portion of the term might mean something like "sacred," though the linguistic basis for this view is not convincing. Ueda also links the terms *saniwa* and *hironiwa* with gardens, showing that the emperors who had gardens built in their residences during the Asuka period used the word *hironiwa* (large court or garden) in their names.[4] In any case *saniwa* came to indicate a ritually defined area, and it lost its connection with the interpreters of oracles. The term seems to have come back into usage during the medieval period; it was widely used by Yoshida Kanetomo in the fifteenth century to indicate the ritual zone of his shrines.

The *saniwa* of Kasuga covers a large area set in front of and below the shrines in the main compound. An early eighteenth-century document calls it "apple garden" (*ringo no niwa*), perhaps because of the apple tree growing on its eastern side. Another *saniwa*, at which specific rites are held in spring, is located outside the main compounds below the southwestern corner of the shrine enclosure. That *saniwa* is for the Wakamiya Shrine and is set where it is because of lack of space in front of the shrine itself.

A *saniwa* is covered with white pebbles (*tamajari*) that are usually taken from riverbeds and symbolize, among other things, purity.[5] The *saniwa/ hironiwa*, regularly maintained with rakes, is a zone prohibited to common people today. Those who spent time in Japanese shrines associate the white pebbles of sacred courts with ritual; the sound of gravel crunching under the wooden clogs of priests conveys the character of the sacred. The practice of using such pebbles is grounded in mythology, in which the Heavenly River (Ame-no-yasu-kawa) is bordered with pebbles. It was on a bank of that river that the sacred dance took place, in the course of which the solar deity Amaterasu was tricked out of the cave where she had hidden. This is of some importance, for the *saniwa* is the sacred court where dances are performed in order to call on the *kami*. Even today one can see this function in Kasuga on the white sacred court: as the priestesses, seated in the middle of the court and facing the shrines, concentrate, two priests stand facing each other on the eastern side of the court, each holding an end of a *koto* waist high. A third priest, who stands behind the *koto*, starts to pluck its strings while two others play flutes and mark the rhythm with cymballike instruments. The sharp yet delicate notes of the *koto* induce the hieratic dances on the court.

It is believed that the Ise Shrine has the oldest *saniwa*, but the *tamajari* may have existed in Kyushu and other areas before it became a general feature of all main shrines in Japan. Indeed, the term *saniwa* occurs for the first time in the *Kojiki* in relation to a palace in Tsukushi, Kyushu.[6] The *saniwa* of Kasuga seems to be a late addition (perhaps as late as 859) to the shrine structure; paintings of the early Kamakura period do not represent it, though some documents mention its existence: the *Engi-shiki*, for example, uses the term *hironiwa* to indicate the court where the main rituals take place at the Kasuga Shrine.

Most rites are held in this court; it is where *koto* music is played, where food offerings are set before they are taken to the shrines themselves, and where dances are performed at the time of the Kasuga Grand Rite. The movements of priests therein are strictly organized, for the *saniwa* is the locus of ritual, protocol, and hierarchy. A good example of the *saniwa* as a symbolic space is provided by the spring rice-planting rites, which immediately follow the Grand Rite. During those rites the entire *saniwa* is symbolically treated as if it were a rice field. Priests stand on its eastern side and play music; another priest tills the land symbolically in the four directions, after which his assistants, one of them wearing a wooden mask of a bull, mimic ploughing with agricultural tools. Priestesses then dance, throwing onto the court pine branches bound together with bark and in which are inserted rice grains ("nature") and *mochi* rice cakes ("culture"). The *saniwa* represents, then, all the fields of Yamato Province.

At the time of the Grand Rite the members of the Fujiwara house sit in the Naorai Hall and face east onto the court. The dances, however, are performed as though the audience were not in that hall; the dancers face either the shrines (to the north) or the southern gate but not the west where the Fujiwara lords sit. The audience of the Grand Rite is quadruple: the *kami* on the north side of the *saniwa*, the Fujiwara on the west, the priests on the east (musicians face west), and on the southern side, members of other houses of classical Japan. Today common people are allowed to stand on the southern side of the *saniwa* during minor rites; they are not allowed in the compounds of the shrine for the Grand Rite.

Origuchi Shinobu states that the evolution of drama in Japan originated in the *saniwa* before it was taken onto a lawn (*shibai*) and then to a stage (*butai*) set up in a building.[7] Indeed, the stages of Nō drama still contain the original elements of the *saniwa*; for example, the Nō stage at the Nishi-Honganji in Kyoto is separated from the audience by a large court covered with pebbles; and the stage of the Itsukushima Shrine on Miyajima Island is separated from the audience by water. Because Itsukushima is dedicated to sea-related *kami*, the stage for dances is set over the sea, but there is little doubt that the area between the stage and the corridor where the audience sits plays the same role in both cultic centers and symbolically represents water, or at least a riverbed. The narrow area covered with pebbles that surrounds Nō stages today is called *shirasu*, a term that is usually translated as "sand bar"; that area is in all probability derived from the *saniwa*. By extension, the term *shirasu* came to refer to the pebble area set in front of the main buildings of the imperial palace and in front of the buildings where judgment was passed; hence, it has come to mean "court of justice," or "bar." Here again the symbolism is evident: the sense of respect for law is associated with the awe felt in front of the *kami*. The original meaning of *saniwa*, however, is that of a site where the *kami* come to possess a dancer or a medium, where humans and the divine associate, and where nature and culture meet.[8] Thus, the *saniwa/hironiwa/shirasu* complex represents a zone set apart from the profane, in which significant acts are performed in the name of a higher principle.

The third type of sacred space in the shrine is represented by the various buildings erected over time in the main compounds. Among these buildings, two types deserve some attention: first, the shrines themselves; and second, the Naorai Hall, which is located on the western side of the *saniwa*, as well as the Hei-den (sometimes called Mai-dono), which is located on its southern side.

The shrine buildings at Kasuga look deceptively simple. It is precisely that simplicity of architectural features that gives them their unique cachet. The specific architecture of the shrines is known as *Kasuga-zukuri*, "Kasuga construct" or "style" (see figure 4).[9] Each of the four shrines is a simple construction consisting of four pillars, three solid walls with a door in the front wall, and a thatched roof, and is surrounded by a veranda that opens to the front onto a staircase consisting of seven stairs covered by a porch formed by jutting eaves. The shrines are linked to each other by a small wall on which paintings of horses and a lion have been made. What

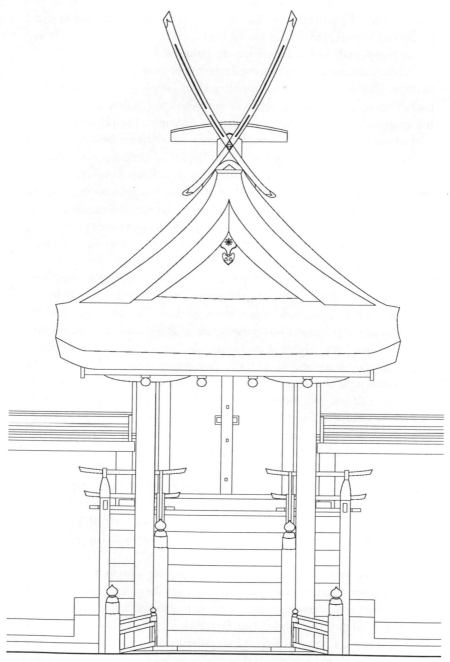

Figure 4.   The ''Kasuga Architectural Style'' (*Kasuga-zukuri*). Computer-assisted rendering of Kuroda Noriyoshi, *Kasuga taisha kenchiku-shi ron* (Kyoto: Sōgeisha, 1978), plate no. 31.

gives the Kasuga style its distinctive character is the sloped porch and the fact that the *chigi* (an **X**-shaped vertical fixture set on the beam of the roof at its front and back ends) are slightly curved instead of being straight as is the case in most shrines. The doors of the shrines are protected by screens (*sudare*) onto which mirrors are affixed. The first shrine to the east is of slightly larger proportions than the three others, a fact that indicates its higher status. The four shrines are set on stone foundations and are surrounded by a stone court. In front of that court is a bar of white pebbles crossed in its center by a path made of stone slabs. Surrounding that sandy bar is another stone court on which, in the case of the first shrine, is a stone where the head-priest sits during the Grand Rite to recite ritual formulas (*norito*). That court and the shrines are surrounded by a wooden fence, painted in red and black, which opens to the south; this opening is marked by a wooden *torii*. The fence is set immediately in front of the inner corridor of the shrines, which was built during the Heian period. Each shrine is the residence of a *kami*, and the inside of each is furnished with a chair and with paraphernalia such as mirrors and swords. The treasures of the *kami* (swords, mirrors, *tama*, and halberds), which are normally kept in the shrine repository, are removed at the time of the Grand Rite and placed ceremoniously in front of each shrine when the doors are opened so that the *kami* may partake of food offerings. The support (*yorishiro*) of the *kami*, which consists of a branch of *sakaki* tree taken from Mount Mikasa, is placed inside each shrine. The zone of the shrines set inside the inner fence is naturally the most sacred; it cannot be approached by lay people.

The Naorai Hall was built on the west side of the *saniwa* as the site of the ceremonial repast (*naorai*) shared by the leading members of the Fujiwara house and their tutelary *kami* during the Grand Rite. This is where the contract of worship on the part of the Fujiwara house is exchanged for protection on the part of the *kami*; this contract is marked by the exchange of food and the ritual drinking of rice-wine prepared by the priests. The Fujiwara leaders and representatives of the imperial house sat in the Naorai Hall, looking east during the rituals.

The sacred court is marked to the south by the Hei-den, a hall where ritual offerings were placed. Whereas the floor of the Naorai Hall is wooden, the floor of the Hei-den is made of sand. At the time of the Grand Rite, dances were performed in the Hei-den when there was rainy weather, but normally it was in that hall that representatives of the Department of State (*dajōkan*) and of the guard of the court (*Konoe no tsukasa*) sat. Members of the Fujiwara house and members of the court also sat there at the time of their personal visits to the shrines.[10] This hall is where the *sushibashiri-no-okina* dances, which played a role in the formation of Nō drama, are performed, and it also served for the reading of Buddhist scriptures, for ceremonies dedicated to the *Mahā-prajñā pāramitā sūtra*, and as a repository for the main beams at the time of the periodic reconstructions of the shrines. Until 1868 a *jingūji* (the Fukaiden) stood within the compounds of the shrine, to the east of the sacred court. The prelates of the Kōfukuji stood in front of it during rites in which they participated. To the north of the Naorai Hall stands the Utsushi-dono, which served as a repository for emblems of the *kami* at the time of their transfer to Kyoto by the *shuto* and *jinin* of the multiplex, and at the time of periodic reconstructions; it is used today for the performance of dances paid for by visitors to the shrine.

Finally, the gates located in the corridor surrounding the shrine play a role in the emphasis on hierarchy that characterizes the Kasuga ritual cycle: as stated in the *Jōgan-gishiki*, which was mentioned earlier, only certain members of the Fujiwara house were allowed to pass through the three gates set in the western side of the corridor (the Naishi-mon, the Seijō-mon or Sōjō-mon, and the Keiga-mon), and which of the three was used depended on one's rank. At the time of the Grand Rite the entire area of the shrines was ritually purified and temporary hedges of *sakaki* branches were placed outside the compounds; this is the *tamagaki*, a "sacred hedge" that prevents noxious forces from polluting the ritual area. In the Heian period, gates were made in the hedges at those points where the two main paths leading to the shrines, the northern and southern paths, which lie on an east-west axis, crossed the hedges. These "gates," which consisted of a rope strung across the openings, were ritually cut by the priests; the northern gate served for the sacral women, and the southern gate served for the members of the Fujiwara house. It is not known when the practice of erecting the hedges ceased. The southern gate of the main corridor could be used only by the chieftain of the Fujiwara house, the emperor, and the head-priests of the Nakatomi lineage to enter the precincts. It is as though, at the time of the Grand Rite, the head of the state was equal in status (though not in rank) with the head of the Fujiwara house and the head of the sacerdotal lineage. That southern gate is also used to exit the shrine in order to go to the Wakamiya Shrine; no other mode of approach at the time of ritual is allowed. Finally, there is a small shrine located within the southern part of the main corridor; called the Enomoto Shrine, it is said that it is dedicated to the *kami* that owns the land on which the Kasuga Shrine was built.

Kasuga was not only a sacred space limited by the walls of the shrine;

it was also a sacred area marked by an opposition between mountains and plains, and a physical landscape of great beauty. Archaeological investigations conducted in 1977 disclosed new information about the sacred area in which the Kasuga shrines were built.[11] They revealed the existence of a very large earthern wall, which surrounded the shrines on their southern, eastern, and northern sides, and of large beds of stones placed in a semicircular fashion around the eastern border of Mount Mikasa. The wall is, without doubt, a construction of the late Nara period; the stone beds have not been dated yet, but the presence in them of some fragments of cultic objects seems to point to the late Nara or early Heian period. The wall extended westward, south from the point where the Tsugoe River and Mount Mikasa touch to a zone close to the river again, where the wall turned north, then south again, then north across the Tobihino Plain (with one jagged area), and up to a point close to the bed of the Mizuya River, where it extended eastward in a straight line and reached the foot of Mount Mikasa on its northern side (see map 3, p. 18). The wall was, apparently, the largest of the kind built in Japan at the time, a fact that seems to indicate the authority of the state as symbolized by the shrines. It was bordered on the inside by trenches capable of carrying large amounts of rain water to tunnels built under the wall and opening onto the plain that lies between the shrines and the Kōfukuji. Gates seem to have been erected in the wall, as traces of pillars in the earth and fragments of roof tiles (as many as two hundred intact tiles were found) indicate. Furthermore, fragments of ritual implements were found near the spots where it is thought that there were gates: the gates, which opened onto the sacred area, were the object of rituals that must have been similar to those used to protect the gates of the imperial palace.[12] The main gate may have been located on the southern extension of the wall, as the excavation of a path leading to the main shrine seems to indicate. Thus the Kasuga Shrine was located in the middle of an area delimited to the north, west, and south by a large earthern wall; the main entrance to the shrine during the Nara period may have been from the south and not, as it is now, from the west, a change that may have come about because of the shrine's association with the Kōfukuji.

The stone bed around the eastern circumference of Mount Mikasa is a more enigmatic entity. Extending from the Kii Shrine north to the Mizuya Shrine, its width varies from two to thirty-five meters. Some large stones have been placed in a stairlike fashion to prevent smaller ones from running off with the rain; some bear traces of an engraving not yet identified. There is little doubt that this stone bed marks the eastern boundary of the sacred area of Kasuga, which includes Mount Mikasa as well as the shrines. Some of the stones are from nearby mountains, but others are from locations that have not been identified. In any case, the creation of this bed must have been an awesome undertaking for that era. The archaeological report does not deal with the rationale for this phenomenon, but Japan offers a few mountains (in Kyushu as well as Yamato) that are entirely surrounded by rocks.

Archaeologists call these stone beds *iwasaka* (stone enclosure), a term that may be inappropriate, because it refers to a very specific type of enclosure of ritual sites that are generally of a small scale. It is possible, however, that further studies may force an expansion of the meaning of the term *iwasaka* if it is shown satisfactorily that the function of the larger enclosures was the same as that of the smaller ones.

On the summit of Mount Mikasa, which is off limits most of the time to anyone, including priests, is a shrine called Hongū (Original Shrine), which is dedicated to the manifestation of Takemikatsuchi-no-mikoto, who is said to have come there mounted on a deer. Mention was made earlier of the two rock abodes set near that shrine, where rituals were performed in classical times. Finally, excavations made at the summit of Mount Mikasa in 1939 revealed the presence of earthern containers of Buddhist scriptures (*kyō-zuka*) dating back to the early eleventh century.[13]

The sacred area (*shinji*) of Kasuga during the Nara period consisted of a sacred hill to the east and parts of the plain on its western foot. The Kasuga Shrine was built at the western foot of the hill, facing south, and a huge wall was erected on three sides to mark off the boundaries of sacred space in the plain. Seen from above, this arrangement of the hill and plain area delimited by the wall has the shape of a funeral tumulus (*kofun*) of the "key-hole" type. The wall was not kept in the Heian period, when the east-west orientation prevailed because of both natural configurations and the shrine's relations with the Kōfukuji: the main path leading to Kasuga became an extension of Third Avenue, which ran east-west rather than north-south.

Before the Kasuga Shrine was erected Mount Mikasa may have been a hallowed ground approached from the south and not from the east. The organization of life in the Yamato Basin before the creation of the capital supports this hypothesis, for the Ōno house (a subbranch of the Kasuga clan, itself a branch of the Wani clan) lived on land located in and around the mountain range bordering the Yamato Basin on its eastern side between the site of what was to become Nara in the north and the Isonokami Shrine in the south. The Ōno house would have been in close contact with the emerging Fujiwara house and might have struck an alliance with the Fujiwara by which the Fujiwara were allowed to erect shrines on what used to be the property of the Ōno house. The sacred area of Kasuga was further marked naturally to the north and south by two rivers that have their

sources near the summit of Mount Mikasa and flow westward. The northern river was sacred, for the sacerdotal population of Kasuga always took
ablutions in it and nowhere else.

SOCIOCOSMIC INSCRIPTION IN SPACE

The early orientation of human life in space in Kasuga was closely associated with the orientation of shrines and temples, which was itself a
manifestation of a symbolic representation of the cultural world and of a
geomantic system. Three sets of oppositions appear to characterize the
early organization and experience of space in Kasuga: between sacred and
profane, between east-west and north-south, and between mountains and
plains. These oppositions determined the placement and orientation of
shrines, the placement of the body in ritual, the management of space in
the city, and the evolution of the dialectic between secular and sacred that
was partly responsible for the birth of the ideology of the Sacred Land.

In the second of the sets of opposition, the east-west axis is related to
the apparent movement of the sun and the moon, and the north-south axis
is related to notions of hierarchy. The east-west axis, however, is also
hierarchical, for the most important *kami* are located to the east; from the
point of view of the ruler, the left (east) is more important than the right.
The origin of this inscription of hierarchy in space is, without doubt,
Chinese. The Book of Rites stipulates the position of the body in ritual and
the movement of people in space;[14] these stipulations were refined and
sometimes changed from the Chinese model in the course of the Heian
period, and they became the object of almost endless and obsessive concern
at the time of any court ritual. For example, at the time of the ritual repast
marking the appointment of the Minister of State in Kyoto, courtiers
awaited the candidate outside of his residence, facing south, with the
highest-ranked courtier standing at a spot to the east near the gate, which
is the position of welcoming. Once the minister had arrived and taken his
position in front of the building where the ceremony of investiture took
place, the courtiers entered and lined up, this time facing north, with those
of the highest rank to the east: they were being welcomed. The sitting
arrangements at the rooms for the repast show the same concern with
proper position for rank, and rehearsals were held days in advance.[15]
Practices of the inscription of the body in space, which reinforced hierarchy,
permeated court life throughout the classical era and were most evident at
the time of rites in shrines.

In the opposition between mountains and plains, mountains represent
the realm of wilderness and death, while the plains represent the realm of
claimed land and agricultural activity. These two realms were further

related to the four directions associated with the four seasons, the cyclical movement of which determined agricultural—hence, cultic—activity. Shrines were at the center of these oppositions. Furthermore, according to Chinese theories, the northeast direction, which was known as the "Gate of Demons" (Japanese, *kimon*), is the weak corner of the cosmos through which noxious powers could penetrate the ordered realm of human space. Therefore this direction needed special protection, which in Japan took several forms. First and foremost was the establishment of shrines and temples in that corner. Second, the northeastern corner of the walls of shrines and palaces was constructed as an "inverted corner" pointing to the inside of the enclosed space rather than to its exterior, so that it could be thought of as nonexistent. Thus, the Kasuga Shrine was set in the northeastern corner of the capital, and the northeastern corner of its wall is inverted: whereas the main corridor that surrounds the four shrines of Kasuga is a major wooden structure with a thatched roof, the northeastern corner is a simple earthern wall of smaller proportions. (See map 3 above.)

The two main axes (east-west and north-south), and the various oppositions they indicate, are clearly visible in Kasuga. During the Heian period the focal point of the cultic center came to be Mount Mikasa, one of the foothills of the Kasuga mountain range, which is on a north-south line, and hence we might expect that the shrines would face west. But they face south. The reason is that the *kami* of Kasuga have an imperial quality and therefore must, as the emperor traditionally does at the time of ritual, face south. This was felt to be a structural oddity for centuries.

Set at the very foot of Mount Mikasa, the Wakamiya Shrine faces west; as explained above, at the time of its periodic reconstructions its new pillars were first oriented within Kasuga on a north-south axis, and were then turned ceremoniously onto an east-west axis in front of the old Wakamiya Shrine. The temporary Wakamiya shrine built for the *On-matsuri*, however, faces south, and thus the hierarchical position of the *kami* changes. The reason for this is that throughout most of the year the Wakamiya is worshiped as a force of fertility related to the mountain and plain opposition, but at the time of the *On-matsuri* it is worshiped as the symbolic body that rules the province, and thus the temporary shrine faces south.

The road that leads from the Kōfukuji to Kasuga is an extension of the Third Ward Avenue (*Sanjō*), which runs from east to west. If one were to draw a straight line westward from Kasuga, one would follow the ancient road that linked Nara to Naniwa (Osaka). That road crossed Mount Ikoma at the Kuragari Pass, went past the Hiraoka Shrine (which faces west), and reached the coast near Naniwa.

Several other roads ran through Yamato Province on a north-south axis:

the road known today as *Yamanobe no michi* starts at Kasuga and leads south, following the foot of the mountain range that forms the natural eastern border of the province. That road passes by the Isonokami Shrine and ends at the Miwa Shrine, but if one were to imagine that road continuing further southward in a straight line, it would reach Tōnomine. Also, if one were to extend the eastern wall of the capital of Heijō-kyō (Nara) directly southward through the Yamato Basin, one would reach the eastern limit of the Fujiwara capital; and, if one were to do the same with a line passing exactly through the middle of Heijō-kyō on a north-south axis, one would reach the western limit of the Fujiwara capital. The roads of the Asuka and Nara periods were built along such coordinates and continued to be the central axes of communication in Yamato Province for most of its history; they joined together just north of the capital, by the Kizu River, and became the main road leading to Kyoto. Two other major roads crossed Yamato Province from east to west, one in the middle of the Yamato Basin and one in the south. To the west, those roads join together near Ikaruga, cross the western mountain range through the Takenouchi Pass, and end in Naniwa. To the east, the southern road leads to Ise.

Significantly, painted representations of the shrine-temple multiplex, which are usually called "shrine mandalas" (*miya-mandara*), are oriented on an east-west axis so that the viewer is looking east and viewing the mountain range at the top of the painting. The structural oddity mentioned above, namely, the fact that one might expect the shrines to face west because of their privileged relation to Mount Mikasa, is responsible for the sense of awkwardness one has when looking at these paintings: whereas all the shrine buildings are properly represented from the west, facing south, in most paintings the various temples of the Kōfukuji are represented improperly as though they faced west and not, as they in fact do, south.

This utter disregard for the actual orientation of the temples coexists in the paintings with the greatest concern for the actual orientation of the shrines and a remarkable accuracy in the depiction of architectural features, and one is forced to search for the rationale that might have been used by, or requested from, the artists. It is possible that the orientation of the shrines to the south was not to be misrepresented because of the geomantic importance of the fact, although a few paintings show no concern for that point. It is clear, however, that in representing the temples of the Kōfukuji as though they faced west, the artists could then represent the buddhas and bodhisattvas that are enshrined in them with proper iconographic detail.[16] It seems, therefore, that a technical convenience caused the apparent sleight-of-hand. Nonetheless, the orientational oddity is still strongly felt, because in all paintings, the Kasuga mountain range is represented at the top of the painting: if technical convenience was all that mattered, one might ask what prevented the artists from representing the entire multiplex from the south, in which case Mount Mikasa and the Kasuga range looming behind it would appear on the right side of the painting.

A possible answer is that the artists faced, in the case of Kasuga, a dilemma in the form of contradictory conventions: they needed to represent the temples properly, from the south, but, properly also, the mountains from the west. Painting conventions of the day in the representation of sacred mountains prohibited the depiction of a mountain on the right side of a painting. Indeed, most painted representations of multiplexes follow a conventional orientation in space and time: they represent the buildings facing south under the sun on the left (east) side of the painting, and the moon on the right (west) side of the painting (the position of these celestial bodies being that of the solstice), and always have mountains in the upper part of the painting and plains in the lower part.[17] This traditional pattern of mountains at the top and plains at the bottom is observed in paintings of the Kasuga-Kōfukuji multiplex, so that the viewer is forced to face east but is looking at the Kōfukuji as if he or she were facing north; however, the orientation of the Kasuga mountain range is properly depicted, and that is why one sees in those mandalas only the sun and imagines that the moon is "at one's back."[18] The east-west axis was so important that all subsequent representations of Nara show the eastern mountain range at the top of the map, a convention that prevailed until Western modes of mapping were adopted and Nara came to be represented on a north-south axis, with the north at the top.

ORIENTATION OF HUMAN BEINGS IN SPACE

No travel was undertaken during the Nara and Heian periods without consultation with diviners, who used Chinese geomantic and astronomic rules to determine the cosmic harmonies and disharmonies between the movements of celestial bodies and forces and the spatial movements and activities of human beings. Diviners computed an aristocrat's intended course of travel in relation to the course of celestial bodies and fluxes; since danger arose in the case of an intersection between the two courses, a "directional taboo" (*kata-imi*) was set and the trip was postponed until the troublesome celestial body had moved into a neutral zone of the heavens. As time passed the diviners came up with ingenious formulas that allowed proposed travel to take place whatever the courses of the celestial bodies, by way of a "directional alternative" (*kata tagae*). This entailed going by a different route, apparently in a different direction than the one originally intended, spending one night in the residence of an acquaintance some-where along that line, and reaching the intended destination on the fol-lowing day. The directional taboos and alternatives in the Heian period have been studied in great detail, and therefore need not be discussed here.[19] That phenomenon, however, reveals the extent to which the move-ment of the body in space was deemed important, and the degree to which the body itself was considered to be "cosmic."

Yet another practice of the Nara and Heian periods that related to the body in space is an imperial rite called the Rite of the Four Directions (*shihō-sai*). That rite, which was performed on the first day of the lunar calendar, swiftly came to be practiced by aristocrats and, at least as early as 970, by commoners as well. This rite consisted of making obeisance to the Four Directions, to one's immediate ancestors, and to specific sacred sites in the country. Following is a description of this rite as it is recorded by Nakamikado no Noritane, a member of a branch of the Fujiwara house, in his diary in 1480.[20]

Noritane performed this rite every year with great zeal. On the morning of the first day of the year he put on his ceremonial dress at the hour of the tiger (4 A.M.), took in his hands the emblem of his rank, and sat on a *tatami* (straw mat) that had been set in advance in the southern court of his residence in Kyoto. First turning to the north, he made obeisance to the star in Ursa Major that was said to correspond to the year of his birth (*zokushō*) by chanting its name (*Namu-rokuzon-shō*) seven times and by bowing twice in its direction. Still turned in the same direction he chanted the name of the planet of the year—in 1480, that was Mercury, so he chanted *Namu suiyō-shō*—and bowed twice. Then he uttered potent for-mulas that were believed to bring protection from various afflictions (thieves and robbers, poisonous demons, poisons, crises, ills affecting the mind, noxious charms, diseases, and so on) and asked for the realization of his wishes, bowing twice to the north. Then he made obeisance to Heaven (turned to the northwest), to Earth (turned to the southwest), to the Four Directions (in the following order: east, south, west, and north), to the divinity that caused most directional interdictions (*Daishōgun*, turning, in 1480, to the west), to Ōshō (turning to the east), each time bowing twice.

Then, turning toward the center of his house he made obeisance to the *kami* that protected his residence, and turning in the direction of the kitchen, he made obeisance to the divinity of the cauldron, each time bowing twice. Thereafter he made double obeisance to various shrine-temple multiplexes, each time turning in their direction and bowing twice, first standing, and then kneeling: Ise (southeast), Iwashimizu Hachiman (southwest), Kamo (north), Kasuga (south), Ōharano (southwest), Yoshida (east), Gion (southeast), Kitano (northwest), and all *kami* of the country (*sōjin*), this time turning east toward the shrine in Yoshida that was dedicated to those *kami*. Finally Noritane bowed twice in the direction of the mausoleum of his immediate ancestors. This would conclude the rite. He then left his seat, exchanged his ceremonial dress for normal attire to perform his daily recitations of Buddhist scriptures, and consumed a triple libation of sake dedicated to the new year.

Noritane wrote that this Rite of the Four Directions was performed, albeit with some slight changes, according to directions left by Ichijō Kanera.

The orientation of humans in space was a major aspect of the ceremonies dedicated to the beginning of a new temporal cycle, and this orientation was associated with astrology and, most importantly, some of the major cultic centers of Japan at the time. This indicates that, at least at the time of ceremonies (such as that of Noritane described above), there existed a kind of mental map connected with the world of meaning in which people lived. Indeed, Fujiwara no Tadamichi wrote in his diary that aristocrats of the twelfth century had dropped the traditional order of obeisance in the Rite of the Four Directions and copied that of the common people, which was slightly different but was thought to be more effective.

Buddhist clerics were also deeply involved in those activities, and they competed with sacerdotal lineages in bringing back to Japan documents and techniques of divination that allowed proper inscription of the body in space. Indeed, much of the knowledge concerning the "Way of Yin and Yang" (*onmyōdō*) during the Heian and Kamakura periods was introduced by Buddhist lineages.[21] In all cases scrupulous attention was paid to the place and time of the performance of ceremonies, to adequate spiritual preparation and magical protection of the body, and to procedure in ritual. These procedures are described in terse terms in a number of documents that remain to be studied. Buddhist notions of space had such an impact on the mental maps of the Japanese that they shall now be examined.

KASUGA, A COSMOLOGY EMBODIED IN NATURE

Complex cosmographies and cosmologies that developed in India and China were transmitted to Japan, where they were encoded in the interpretation of place. In fact, quite a few members of the lineages that controlled Japan's major multiplexes came to see their land as the natural embodiment of those cosmologies, for reasons that need to be clarified.

The application of cosmological principles to natural configurations of land represents a specific type of understanding of the relationship between land and people, nature and culture. It was not a phenomenon that appeared suddenly but arose by a slow process that culminated in the medieval period and, through combinations between *kami* and buddhas and the state ideology, resulted in a vision of Japan as a sacred land.

Medieval visions of Japan as a natural manifestation of transcendental realms or as the physical embodiment of higher principles played a central role in some clerics' conception of space and time in Kasuga, which came to be seen either as the very embodiment in nature of hell and paradise, or as a Pure Land, or as the Deer Park of Benares in India, the site of the first sermon of the Buddha. The experience of space in Kasuga was closely associated with specific forms of religious experience and vision that were used by Yamato leaders as evidence of the supernatural character of their legitimacy and, consequently, their power.

The visions of this kind were the result of various combinations: between *kami* and buddhas and/or bodhisattvas; between sensitivities and aesthetics issued from diverse cultures; between systems of representation belonging to India, China, and Japan; and between various ideologies. It would be wrong, therefore, to qualify these historical processes of representation as resulting merely from Buddhist influence: the concept of sacred land was, like most concepts and practices evolving in Kasuga, a combinatory phenomenon. Its basis was the sacredness of mountains and other areas on which shrines had been erected and near which temples had been built. These sites were thought to be the residence of *kami*, if not—as was sometimes the case—themselves *kami*.

Such sites were not to be approached lightly, or entered, or treated like other areas of the natural world. They were chosen as sacred because of the beauty or the strategic nature of their location, or because of the sense of *mysterium tremendum* that they caused in the hearts of people. Sometimes they were chosen because of specific events, either mythical or historical, that transpired there and changed in a radical manner the way they were perceived. The most likely candidates were sources of water, hot springs, mountains from the top of which an entire geographical area could be surveyed and protected, and river forks. These places were set aside because of their importance for human survival or because they were seen as some kind of divine inscription that should be decoded: sacred places said something about life. Places were texts.

BUDDHIST COSMOGRAPHY AND COSMOLOGY

Vasubandhu, an Indian Buddhist thinker of the fifth century and one of the patriarchs of the Yogācāra (Hossō) lineage housed in the Kōfukuji, wrote the *Abhidharma-kośa-śāstra* (Japanese: *Kusha-ron*), which is the main source of cosmography in Buddhism.[22] This text, which was translated into Chinese by Hsüan-tsang in 651–54, was introduced early to Japan: that cosmography was engraved on the pedestal of the Great Buddha at the Tōdaiji in 757.

According to this text, the universe is a circular arrangement of concentric oceans and mountains set over layers of gold and water in the middle of which stands a cosmic square mountain, Mount Sumeru. On top of Mount Sumeru is the palace of Indra. Each of the four faces of this *axis mundi* is of a different material: gold, silver, lapis, and crystal. Mount Sumeru is perfectly square, approximately 560,000 kilometers in width and length and 1,120,000 kilometers in height. Its base is the residence of Nāga kings (who embrace its circumference) and the four heavenly guardians of the cardinal directions. It stands in the middle of seven ranges of mountains between and around which a circular ocean spreads to the perimeter of the universe, which is marked by a circular range of "Iron Mountains."

Four continents emerge from the ocean in the four cardinal directions; the southern continent, called "Southern Rosewood Continent," is India, which came to be seen as the world in which all humans live. The circular ocean surrounded by the Iron Mountain Range stands on a cylinder-shaped mass of gold 2,240,000 kilometers deep, which in turn stands over a cylindrical mass of water that is 5,600,000 kilometers deep. The gold and water cylinders are 8,421,140 kilometers wide, and they stand over yet another, much larger (11,200,000 kilometers deep) cylinder composed of air. The Southern Rosewood Continent is 14,000 kilometers wide at its summit, 24.5 kilometers wide at its base, and its sides are each 14,000 kilometers long. Toward its upper part are nine peaks called the "Black Mountains," which stand south of the "Snow Mountains" (Himalaya). To the north of the Snow Mountains is a lake called Anavatapta (Lake of No Heat), out of which four great rivers flow in a concentric, swastika shape. (See figure 5.)

This general cosmography quickly became popular in the Heian period and was replicated in the architectural organization of temples, each of which was a miniaturization of the basic cosmographic structure: statues of the Buddha were set atop an altar called the Platform of Mount Sumeru, and the four pillars of the temple were adorned with statues or paintings of the four heavenly kings protecting the cardinal directions. Further refinements were added to the architecture of temples, depending on the lineages they housed, so that doctrinal tenets also found spatial expression.

Cosmology was eminently related to cosmography, a factor that helps us to understand the close relation that existed between space and the practice of Buddhism in Kasuga. According to that cosmology, the world of experience consists of superimposed layers of being that ascend from the lowest levels of hell, which is located under the Southern Rosewood

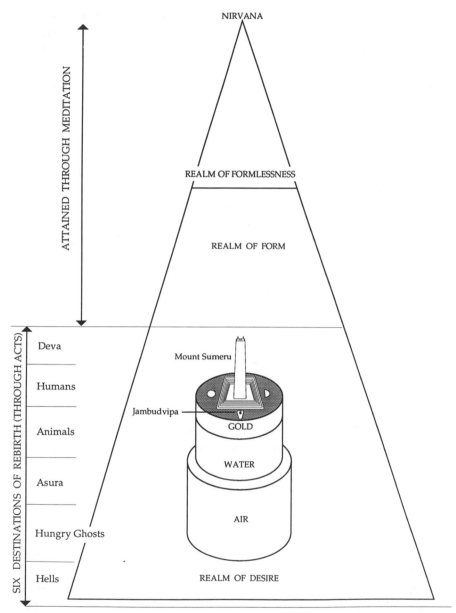

NIRVANA

ATTAINED THROUGH MEDITATION

REALM OF FORMLESSNESS

REALM OF FORM

SIX DESTINATIONS OF REBIRTH (THROUGH ACTS)

Deva

Humans

Animals

Asura

Hungry Ghosts

Hells

Mount Sumeru

Jambudvipa

GOLD

WATER

AIR

REALM OF DESIRE

Figure 5.   The Buddhist Cosmographic Representation of the World. Diagram based in part on Sadakata Akira, *Shumisen to gokuraku* (Tokyo: Kodansha, 1973), 13.

Continent, to the highest levels of mental residence, which are located above Mount Sumeru. These layers of modes of being consist of three major realms: the Realm of Desire, the Realm of Form, and the Realm of Formlessness. The Realm of Desire, which contains Mount Sumeru, consists of the six destinations of existence (hell, hungry ghosts, titans (*ashura*), animals, human beings, and divine beings) and is topped by four "Heavens" inhabited by various deities. It is capped by the Realm of Form, which consists of four Meditation Heavens that are reached through the practice of meditative exercises. This realm is, in turn, capped by the Realm of Formlessness, which consists of four Heavens: Boundless Space, Boundless Knowledge, Non-Existence, and Neither Ideation nor Non-Ideation. This ultimate state, beyond oppositions and qualifications, is the state of awakening, the mode of the Buddha.[23]

The six destinations of existence are the various levels of existence that form the wheel of transmigration. Rebirth into one or the other of those levels is determined by actions. Salvation, which is the release from transmigration and the emancipation into nonduality, is brought about by the practice of Buddhism. Hell, which begins some thirty-five thousand kilometers beneath the Southern Rosewood Continent, consists of seven major layers, each of which is thirty-five thousand kilometers deep, and an eighth category, which is, literally, a bottomless pit. The more one acts in such a manner as to receive negative retribution, the lower into hell one falls. Thus hell, and the higher spheres of being, are modes of being that come about through the agency of action and volition. Beings in the various forms of existence peregrinating through the six destinations have the choice of staying within the cycle of transmigration or of bailing out of time and space by accumulating the merits that accrue from Buddhist practice.

BUDDHA LAND

Those who achieved release from transmigration and ordinary time and space came to be thought of as residing in a transcendental space called Buddha Land, which was later assimilated to the concept of Pure Land. This development occurred in Mahāyāna Buddhism, which propounded a multiplicity of buddhas existing at the same time but in different places in a multiplicity of universes.[24] The Buddha Lands are transcendental realms governed by a specific buddha or bodhisattva; sometimes they are conceived of as having been created by the buddhas or as metamorphic manifestations of their bodies. The major scripture that contains speculation about the Buddha Lands is Nāgārjuna's *Great Treatise of the Perfection of Wisdom* (Japanese: *Daichido-ron*).[25] Supernatural though it may be, a Buddha Land was described by Nāgārjuna with agricultural metaphors:

"the Buddha is a ground of felicity," a field in which the roots of good germinate to produce the fruit of felicity, and, indeed, the term "Buddha Field" (in Japanese: *butsuden*) was used for it: the "weeds of passion and attachment do not exist there; its ground consists of morality, and its fertility is compassion." Furthermore, it has no barren ground; it has walls and canals, and the crops are always bountiful.

In Nāgārjuna's *Treatise*, however, a Buddha Land is a space in which both pure and impure beings and elements are present, and it is to be decorated and purified through self-purification and the purification of others. The major scripture that describes this purification practice is the *Vimalakīrti-nirdeśa sūtra* (Japanese: *Yuima-gyō*), the first chapter of which proposes that Pure Lands are transcendental spaces revealed by the Buddha to beings whose mind is pure. This scripture was the object of the most important ritual of the Kōfukuji (the *Yuima-e*), so its impact on the Kasuga belief system was tremendous. Indeed, Nakatomi no Kamatari, the first human ancestor of the Fujiwara house, was considered to be a manifestation on earth of Vimalakīrti, who was, pointedly, a lay figure. As the scripture states:

"Therefore, Rātna-rāsi, if a Bodhisattva wants to win the pure land he should purify his mind, and because of his pure mind the Buddha land is pure." As Śāriputra was fascinated by the Buddha's awe-inspiring majesty, he thought: "If the Buddha land is pure because of the Bodhisattva's pure mind, is it because the mind of the World-Honoured One was not pure when He was still in the Bodhisattva stage, that this Buddha land [that is, this world] is so unclean [as we see it now]?" The Buddha knew of his thought and said to Śāriputra: "Are the sun and the moon not clean when a blind man does not see their cleanliness?" Śāriputra said: "World Honoured One, this is the fault of the blind man and not that of the sun and the moon." The Buddha said: "Śāriputra, because of their spiritual blindness living beings do not see the imposing majesty of the Tathāgata's pure land; this is not the fault of the Tathāgata. Śāriputra, this land of mine is pure but you do not see its purity." Thereupon, Brahma with a tuft of hair on his hair (resembling a conch) said to Śāriputra: "Don't think this Buddha land is impure. Why? Because I see that the land of Śākyamuni Buddha is pure and clean, like a heavenly palace." Śāriputra said: "I see that this world is full of hills, mountains, pits, thorns, stones and earth, which are all unclean." Brahma said: "Because your mind is up and down and disagrees with the Buddha-wisdom, you see that this land is unclean. Śāriputra, because a Bodhisattva is impartial toward all living beings and his profound mind is pure and clean in accord

with the Buddha Dharma, he can see that this Buddha land is
(also) pure and clean." Thereat, the Buddha pressed the toe of
His (right) foot on the ground and the world was suddenly
adorned with hundreds and thousands of rare and precious gems
of the great chiliocosm, like the Precious Majestic Buddha's pure
land adorned with countless precious merits which the assembly
praised as never seen before; in addition each person present
found himself seated on a precious lotus throne.[26]

One of the main questions discussed by Buddhist scholarly monks in
India, China, and Japan concerned the qualities of this very world, which
was the "sphere of action" of the Buddha Śākyamuni and was consequently
pure. This contradicted common views of this world of experience as a
defiled world. The solution to the problem of these perceived contradictions
is clever: seen from the perspective of the Buddha, the world in which we
live is pure, but seen from the perspective of nonawakened beings, this
world is impure. Purity was thus a matter of understanding, of "Wisdom,"
as Buddhism calls it. It was determined by the ability to transcend oppositions between pure and impure, and Mahāyāna Buddhism offers a system
of logic that enables transcendence of those oppositions. The transcendence
of the opposition between purity and impurity led to an adequate vision
of the natural world as a "pure land."

It is only later that the notion of absolute (nontranscendable) purity
came to permeate the concept of Buddha Land and each major lineage of
Buddhism proposed its own version and definition of it. Those lineages that
accepted that the opposition between purity and impurity could be transcended offered a doctrinal system that tended to be immanentist, and those
that did not, offered a system that tended to be transcendentalist. The
opposition of philosophies of immanence and transcendence resulted in two
views. First, the notion that a Pure Land is of such an inconceivable nature
that it is a transcendental realm situated in a metaphysical space; that is
the case of the Western Pure Land of Amida. Second, systems of immanence, such as the doctrinal lineages of Esoteric Buddhism, propose that the
Pure Land is here and now, and the only question is whether proper
perception and practice are needed or not. Both systems and visions combined with indigenous views of sacred areas.

THE COMBINATORY PROCESS

These three elements—cosmography, cosmology, and Buddha Land—
merged together in Japan to form a basic unity that was then projected onto
the various sacred areas in which shrines dedicated to indigenous *kami* had
been erected. Consequently, a sacred area came to be seen to possess the

basic elements of cosmography; life there was interpreted in terms of the basic cosmology, and the area came to be envisioned as a replica in this world of the Pure Land of the buddhas or bodhisattvas with which the indigenous *kami* were associated. Indeed, if a shrine and the area in which it was located were conceived of as the residence of the *kami*, and if those *kami* were thought to be hypostases of buddhas and bodhisattvas enshrined in the adjacent temples, then those areas came to be seen as the abodes of those buddhas and bodhisattvas, as Pure Lands in this World (*gense jōdo*). The shrine-temple multiplexes built in the major cultic sites of Japan came to be seen as the natural and architectural embodiments of visions of pure lands where not only *kami*, but also buddhas and bodhisattvas, dwelled and where they performed their compassionate acts grounded in the doctrine of salvific means. Gradually those visions of the sacred areas were extended to include their spheres of influence, with the result that, eventually, Japan as a whole came to be thought of as a transcendental realm, a sacred land. Those representations were not limited to space but included time as well, or, to be more precise, a certain type of historical consciousness: if the major aristocratic lineages of Japan were descendants of the *kami* enshrined in those spaces, and if those *kami* were hypostases of buddhas and bo-dhisattvas, then the actions of aristocrats that were perceived to be directed by the will of the *kami* were to be rationalized as being, ultimately, Buddha-acts.

It must be emphasized that this phenomenon, which was representative of medieval religiosity, was combinatory in essence; it was never purely "Shinto" or purely "Buddhist" but entailed a large number of complex associations encompassing a multicultural realm of meaning and practice. In some cases one might be tempted to say that the phenomenon was merely a Buddhist reading of indigenous notions, an overlay. There is, however, no doubt that the phenomenon was based on associations be-tween specific divinities and grounded in specific forms of ritual performed in shrines and temples in association with each other, and thus it was combinatory at all levels.

Already a residence of *kami* from earlier times, Kasuga came to be seen as the chosen abode of their Original Nature, as a Buddha Land that exhibited all the characteristics of such a land as it is depicted in the scriptures. It was envisioned in dreams and visions generated through meditative exercises that were performed in the huts that had been built on the plain between the shrines and the temples. These visions were painted in various genres that received the generic name *mandara* (from the Sanskrit *maṇḍala*), a term that designates graphic depictions of the inner structure of the mind, which was called the "Residence" (Japanese, *jushin*) of buddhas and bodhisattvas.

Many paintings were made during the Kamakura and Muromachi periods to represent the transcendental space of shrine-temple multiplexes, and of these, representations of Kasuga are the most numerous.[27] Those renderings of the sacred landscape of Kasuga evidence the world of belief that marked the Kasuga cult at the time: according to that belief the landscape cannot be dissociated from the realm of meaning proposed by the *kami*, the buddhas, and the bodhisattvas who chose that landscape as their dwelling. An examination of the history of those paintings is not germane to the present topic, but it is important to discuss them briefly at this point.

Modern art historians refer to those Kasuga paintings by several names: *miya mandara* (shrine mandala), *jisha mandara* (shrine-temple mandala), Kasuga *mandara*, and *Kasuga-jōdo mandara* (Kasuga Pure Land mandala). The use of the term *mandala* instead of the term *zu-e* (painted representation) is significant, for it implies that the space represented is of a transcendental character. In the Japanese esoteric tradition, and particularly in the doctrine of the Shingon lineage, mandalas are graphic representations of the universe of Mahāvairocana; they are also a sort of diagram for the meditative and ritual processes. In virtue of the lack of distinction between the Land of the Buddha and this world, mandalas were seen as symbolic representations of this universe. Each major divinity of the Shingon pantheon was symbolized by its own mandala, which was described in scriptures that give directions as to how to paint it and for the rituals that serve to bring about the identification of the practitioner with the divinity in question.

The term *mandala* would not have been used for representations of the space of shrine-temple multiplexes had it not been felt that the paintings represented more than space, and had those paintings not been used in a meditative or ritual context, which they were. The Kasuga mandalas are, therefore, spatial representations of meaning, or graphic representations of meaning in space, for the simple reason that space is never perceived as devoid of meaning. That meaning was said to help determine people's behavior in relation to the landscape, the natural environment, and other people. The various layers of that meaning can be traced through an analysis of those paintings in relation to the specific Buddhist lineages that left their traces in the world of meaning of Kasuga; this becomes apparent through a discussion of each space of Kasuga in relation to the buddhas and bodhisattvas seen as the Original Natures of the *kami*.

Shakamuni

Although some scriptures say that this world is the Buddha Land of Shakamuni, this buddha is associated more often than not with the sacred mountain where he preached the Lotus Sutra, the Mountain of the Numinous Eagle (also called Vulture Peak), Mount Gridhakūta.²⁸ Such was the case in Kasuga. Myō-e *shōnin* (1173–1232) is the person most often associated with visions of the Mountain of the Numinous Eagle at Kasuga. The last paragraph of the *Kasuga gongen genki* says of him:

> The common people [who are caught] in the course and revolution [of the wheel of transmigration] may now rejoice that they have the opportunity to receive the guidance of the Buddha in His various manifestations. Since the residence of the mind in purity is itself the Pure Land, our *kami* are the Buddhas. How could the shrine not be the Pure Land? Since the Pure Land of Lapis Lazuli [of the Buddha of Medicine] and the Mountain of the Numinous Eagle are located within the sacred hedge of the shrine, why should one seek Mount Potalaka [Pure Land of the Bodhisattva of Compassion] and Mount Ch'ing-Liang [Pure Land of the Bodhisattva of Wisdom] beyond the ocean of clouds? That is why Saint Myō-e worshiped Mount Mikasa as the Mountain of the Numinous Eagle, and why our *daimyōjin* indicated to Lord Toshimori the very pathway to awakening.²⁹

Each *kami* of the five shrines was associated with a buddha or bodhisattva enshrined in various buildings of the Main Temple of the Kōfukuji, and Kasuga *daimyōjin* was a composite divine entity whose Original Nature was sometimes thought to be Shakamuni, symbolized by the Mountain of the Numinous Eagle. Through the combinatory process, Mount Mikasa was associated with the Mountain of the Numinous Eagle, because the theriomorphic emblem of the cult, the deer, allowed not only a metaphoric relation between Fukū-kensaku Kannon (who, according to iconographic directions, wore a deerskin over her shoulder) and Takemikatsuchi-no-mikoto (who was said to have reached Mount Mikasa mounted on a deer), but also a metaphoric relation between the Plain of Kasuga and the Deer Park in India where the Buddha gave his first sermon. Indeed, texts of the medieval period use the term "Deer Park" (*Rokuya-on*) to refer to the Kasuga Plain. All other *kami* enshrined at Kasuga might be seen as hypostases of Shakamuni, ultimately, and that is the reason why the Kasuga Pure Land mandala of the Nōman-in represents a Pure Land with Shakamuni in its center, flanked in four corners by the buddhas and bodhisattvas of the four shrines.³⁰ The Pure Land that is referred to in this context should not be confused with the Western Pure Land; neither is it a Pure Land in the normal sense of that term in Buddhism but, rather, a transcendental realm that takes the form of the sacred area of a shrine-temple multiplex, a *kami*-Buddha Land.

Thus, the combinations spoken of above bring together elements of Buddha Land, the Pure Land, Esoteric Buddhism, and the indigenous Japanese tradition. In the light of this fact we can appreciate the painting that depicts a pine tree in front of which stands a deer and around which grows a wisteria vine: the vine meanders around the trunk in such manner that it spells out a stylized formula that is read *Namu Kasuga Myōjin* (Invocation to the Divinity of Kasuga). All the major aspects of the Kasuga cult are present in this deceptively simple painting: the deer symbolism and the pine tree symbolism, which represent the indigenous aspects of the cult; the Fujiwara wisteria symbolism; the Buddhist aspects of the cult symbolized by the stylized formula; and the emphasis on natural forms as signs that need decoding. The recitation of the formula would enable one to contact all combined divine entities of the cult at once and would serve as a support for meditative exercises, the goal of which was the attainment of a vision of the Pure Land in this World.[31]

It appears that originally the associations noted above were metaphoric, but after some time the depth of the metaphor was lost and was replaced by a relation of identity: Kasuga was no longer a Pure Land in a metaphoric sense. Rather, it was, purely and simply, the Deer Park itself, and thus there was no need to go to India in order to retrace the footsteps of the Buddha. Although a metaphor is a rich tool to convey a combinative meaning, a relation of identity is, semantically, very poor, because no comparison is possible at the level of identity, and there is no possibility of interplay. The other is reduced to the same. The visions of the Mountain of the Numinous Eagle cultivated by Myō-e *shōnin* ultimately prevented him from departing for India. The Nō play *Kasuga Ryūjin* (The Dragon Deity of Kasuga), which depicts Myō-e's visit to the shrines and the objections raised by the *kami* against his pilgrimage to India, states most emphatically that the Buddha resided yesteryear in India, but that today he resides on Mount Mikasa in the form of a *kami* in order to save all sentient beings. The vision of Mount Mikasa as the Mountain of the Numinous Eagle is brought into sharp relief in the last lines of the play, when the eight dragon-kings surge up from the waters of Sarusawa Pond, which is located in front of the main gate of the Kōfukuji, to assert the sacredness of Kasuga.[32]

Jizō

The cosmography applied to Kasuga was the factor responsible for the belief that hell was located under the plain situated between the Kasuga shrines and the Kōfukuji temples and that a Pure Land was located either above the shrines or, as was the case later, in the Kasuga mountain range itself. Thus the path leading into the mountains on the southern side of Mount

Mikasa came to be known as *Jigoku-dani,* the "Valley of Hell"; it is today still bordered by large boulders on which representations of Jizō have been carved.[33] This belief was the result of several elements, one of which is the fact that mountains were often seen as the symbolic realm of death, for they were areas where corpses were abandoned. Indeed, as foremost symbols of nature, mountains are zones where the processes of decomposition, putrefaction, and natural transformation are the most evident.

It was also believed that the spirits of the dead underwent a process of transformation at the end of which they merged with the powers of nature and reached such exalted status that often ancestral spirits were thought to govern the regularity of the cycle of such natural powers as fertility. That is the reason why forms of agrarian ritual can be found in cults of ancestor worship in places like Kasuga. Mountains were the realm of death but also of those transformations. One needed a guide to tread the inner paths through the mountains' chthonian darkness, and this role was taken by the bodhisattva Jizō, resident of the Six Destinations and spirit of the earth. Members of the blind community that served at the Wakamiya Shrine, who were specialists in boundaries and dedicated to the cult of Jizō, also served as guides. Several paintings of the Kamakura period show Jizō sitting as a judge in hell, ensuring that the compassionate acts of the defendants were not forgotten, or giving a helping hand to victims of hellish torture, or granting drops of water to sinners suffering the pains of fire. He is also portrayed as leading departed people to the Pure Land over Kasuga after having saved them from the hell located under Kasuga.[34]

In this specific case, then, cosmography and cosmology were associated in such a way that the belief in the transcendental structure of Kasuga meshed with the belief in the Six Destinations. The belief in Jizō as the Original Nature of the *kami* enshrined in the Third Shrine of Kasuga was so popular that a number of paintings representing him alone over Kasuga were made.[35] That was one of the reasons for the popularization of the cult outside the Fujiwara elite. Perhaps the most famous representation of Jizō in the Kasuga context is the Kasuga Pure Land mandala that seems to be based on a passage of the *Kasuga gongen genki* in which Jizō rescues from hell a disciple of Myō-e *shō-nin* and leads him to the Pure Land of Kasuga.[36] The depiction of the Pure Land hovering above Mount Mikasa is quite unique, for the Pure Land that is depicted is not that of Amida but of the various buddhas and bodhisattvas associated with the *kami* of Kasuga.

Kannon

During the late Kamakura period, the belief that Kasuga is Mount Potalaka, the Pure Land of the Bodhisattva of Compassion, dominated the iconography of Kasuga as a sacred space. A famous painting depicts the shrine-temple multiplex as follows: at the bottom of the painting is the multiplex itself; in the central part of it are Mount Mikasa and the Kasuga mountain range; Mount Potalaka stands in the upper half of the painting, set in an ocean whose waves batter the Kasuga mountain range; and at its top is the Bodhisattva of Compassion, who emanates from its head a radiance that gives the entire landscape an atmosphere of transcendence.[37] Any person who is aware of the sanctity of Kasuga and knows Buddhist cosmography would be deeply affected by that painting and easily understand that Kasuga was indeed a space without equal.

This painting is, in some ways, comparable to a painting of Mount Potalaka kept in the Tōdaiji that shows the Pure Land set in the middle of the ocean, with buddhas and bodhisattvas represented in front of temples set in a hilly landscape near waterfalls and surrounded by white and vermilion walls that mark the borders of their precincts.[38] A Kasuga mandala kept at the Honolulu Academy of Arts is unique in its genre, because in it the buddhas and bodhisattvas are represented within the compounds, in front of each shrine.[39] At the bottom of that painting is a *torii*, the path leading to the shrine, and the Kasuga plain on which deer frolic. In the middle part of it are the four shrines of the main compound, surrounded by white and vermilion walls and gates, and to the right of them is a part of the Wakamiya Shrine. Inside the compound directly in front of the shrines are the five buddhas and bodhisattvas, each radiating a golden luminescence. In the upper part of the painting Mount Mikasa, surrounded by clouds, imparts a feeling of utmost serenity to the entire scene.

It was mentioned earlier that painted representations of the shrine-temple multiplex probably originated with Shōkyō, the abbot of the Kōfukuji, who sent such a painting to the chieftain of the Fujiwara house in Kyoto in 1184, and that the painting was used by that lord for his daily devotion to the combined entity Kasuga *daimyōjin*. It was also noted that Mount Mikasa is described in the *Kōfukuji ranshō-ki* as the abode of Fukū-kensaku Kannon, which was thought to have flown from its cosmic residence and landed in Japan. Mount Mikasa was thus thought to be a supernatural zone chosen by the buddhas and their hypostases as their residence; it was an island set in an imaginary ocean whose shores were battered by waves of wisteria. Myō-e *shōnin* is said to have had a dream in which he saw seven ships loaded with precious treasures land at the foot of Mount Mikasa.[40] People with this mindset could, therefore, go on a pilgrimage to Kasuga, where they would see sculpted representations of Kannon in the Southern Round Hall, meditate until they could envision its presence, and see Kasuga as a Pure Land in which buddhas and bodhi-sattvas were worshiped through the performance of music and dance.

The world of the multiplex, thus represented in painting, gives us some clues about the sacred character of the landscape, as do drama and ritual, which were major aspects of the cult and reinforced those visions in a most concrete manner. The dances and music performed at Kasuga were thought to be copied from the descriptions of the Pure Land found in the scriptures. Paintings of the Pure Land of Kasuga show that in front of the main temple, there was a lake covered in part by platforms where *bugaku* dances were performed.[41] This arrangement probably originated in the indigenous performance of music and dances on *saniwa*, or on platforms built over water such as those seen in the Hachiman cult in Kyushu and at the Itsukushima Shrine near Hiroshima. These performances not only served as a support for envisioning the Pure Land but were intended to be performances played in the Pure Land itself, so that at the sacred time of ritual festivities, the entire Kasuga multiplex took on a transcendental character: instead of simply being a place that is like the Pure Land, it was the Pure Land itself.[42]

Consequently, the ritual life of the multiplex was believed to be a replica of life in the Pure Land. This was true of many cultic centers owned by the Fujiwara house. Various documents of the late Heian period contain such descriptions of those centers written by aristocrats who, toward the end of their lives, withdrew from the world, took Buddhist orders, and spent their last years chanting the names of divine entities and organizing sumptuous replicas of the Pure Land. The voices of youngsters chanting the scriptures (especially those dedicated to Jizō) transported those aristocrats to higher spheres of the cosmos at the time of their death when, facing west, they held in their hands colored threads made from lotus fiber that issued from the hands of painted representations of Amida in his Pure Land. Buddhas and bodhisattvas then descended on clouds from the Pure Land to fetch the dying aristocrats amidst heavenly music played by the bodhisattvas. In the first row of divine musicians was, not surprisingly, a *koto* player.[43]

It is against this background that we can understand the arguments that took place in medieval Japan concerning whether or not ornate words and the performance of music and dance were detrimental to spiritual life.[44] Those in favor of such performances argued that since music and dance were performed in the Pure Land, they should be at Kasuga too. This argument makes sense only within the parameters of the vision of Kasuga as a "Pure Land in this World." Music and dance were not conceived of, by those who were in favor of them, as this-worldly: they were not only a support for the contemplation of the Pure Land or the thirty-two marks of the precious body of the Buddha but part of the Pure Land itself. If, in the indigenous tradition, the playing of music served to call on the *kami* and provoke possession by them, similarly, the role of music in the temples during the medieval period was to call on the buddhas and bodhisattvas to descend and manifest themselves or, better still, to reveal that Kasuga was the pure space of their abode. The performance of music and dance at Kasuga, which was sacred since the time that the *koto* came to be used and *kagura* came to be performed in the shrines, remained a central aspect of ritual life. Music and dance were not merely aesthetic pastimes for aristocrats; their performance was based on a vision that encompassed not only the spiritual realm of religious belief but also the political sphere of influence of the combined divine entity of Kasuga, namely, Yamato Province.

PURE LAND AND SACRED PROVINCE

The developments described above were accompanied by the evolution of a concept that expressed not only the vision the Japanese had of Yamato Province but of the entire country as well. As the area of the Kasuga-Kōfukuji multiplex came to be conceived of as a Buddha Land, so the province that the cultic center ruled came to be envisioned in the light of this numinous character, and it became customary to refer to it as *shinkoku*, "Sacred Land."

Shinkoku is an ambiguous term, for it may mean, at the same time, "province where *kami* dwell" or "sacred land" or "sacred province." Yamato is also an ambiguous word, for while referring to the province of that name it is also one of the traditional names for Japan. Therefore the expression *Yamato wa shinkoku nari*, which is found in a large number of medieval documents and not just in ones belonging to the Kasuga cult, may have meant originally "Yamato is a sacred province" and later on may have come to mean "Japan is a sacred land." The ideology according to which Japan is a sacred nation cannot be adequately explained without reference to the combinative nature of the Japanese tradition that has been stressed in this study. That ideology of the state evolved from the fact that the ideology of the imperial house and its satellite houses was intricately entwined with Buddhist concepts of legitimacy and power, as well as (and this is a point that is often ignored) with the ideology that developed in shrines with which the Buddhist tradition was affiliated through the centuries.

The case has been made for Kasuga: not only was it a state institution, but it was also an institution that ruled Yamato Province through an ideological structure in which were combined shrines and temples, *kami* and buddhas/bodhisattvas, and governmental lineages (the Fujiwara and the various *shuto* and *kokumin* of the province), and sacerdotal lineages. The ideology of the state during the medieval period was neither exclusively secular nor exclusively Buddhist: it was combinatory. That ideology cannot be explained without reference to the systematic relations between shrines and temples and among the various mythologies, all of which were bound up with ritual. In fact, the ideology of the state was in major part a ritual exercise that given its combinatory character could not be performed in shrines only or in temples only. This is quite clear from our examination of the experience of space and time and of ritual and performance in the Kasuga multiplex.

It is also made clear in the *Jinnō shōtōki,* an important historical document that was written by Kitabatake Chikafusa at the time of the dynastic split that occurred between 1331 and 1392. When Kitabatake began to compose that text in 1339, power was divided in the country among three groups: the imperial house and the Fujiwara, the warrior houses, and the shrine-temple multiplexes. In the dynastic dispute most multiplexes sided with the Southern Court of Emperor Go-Daigo; indeed, it is significant that Go-Daigo's court moved to Yoshino. Since shrine-temple multiplexes sided with the Southern Court, the ideology of the state presented in the texts of the time was one in which the "Law of the Emperor" (*ōbō*) was combined with and backed by the "Law of the Buddha" (*buppō*); in other words, the major cultic centers of Japan put their power behind the imperial system.[45] The term "Law of the Buddha" was not, as Kuroda Toshio has demonstrated, simply a Buddhist "law," for it included the shrines that were associated with the temples and the ideological and ritual foundations thereof.[46]

The ideology of the state, which was grounded in the tenets of the shrine-temple multiplexes, included mythological and ritual considerations, all sorts of combinations, and economic facts. The medieval period attempted to reinforce the protocol of the gods, that is, the mirror relation between myth and history and between the heavenly pantheon and the human social construct. It also rediscovered the role of performance in ritual and built a state ideology based on the records kept in the myths and combined with Buddhist cosmography. One thus reads in the *Jinnō shōtōki:*

> Great Japan is the divine land. The heavenly progenitor founded it, and the sun goddess bequeathed it to her descendants to rule eternally. Only in our country is this true; there are no similar examples in other countries. This is why our country is called the divine land. . . . Today this island is divided into forty-eight provinces, the most central of which is Yamato. Because of its centrality, Yamato served for generations after Emperor Jimmu's eastward campaign as the imperial seat; and because Yamato held

the imperial seat, its name was applied as well to the rest of Japan. . . . According to the Buddhist scriptures, there is a mountain called Sumeru, which is surrounded by seven other concentric, golden mountains. Between these golden mountains flows the Sea of Fragrant Waters, and outside them are four great oceans. Within the oceans are four great continents, each of which consists of two lesser parts. The southern continent is called Jambu (or Jambudvipa, a different form of the same name), and is named after the jambu tree. . . . India is in the exact center of the continent, and thus is the middle country of Jambu. . . . China is thought to be a large country, but compared to India it is a remote and small land on the periphery of Jambu. Japan is in the ocean off the continent of Jambu. Great Teacher Dengyō of Mount Hiei and High Priest Gomyō of Nara both wrote that Japan is the "central land." This would make it the land of Camara between the southern and the eastern continents. Yet the Kegon Sutra says: "In the ocean to the northeast is a mountain. It is called Diamond (kongō) Mountain." This seems to refer to Mount Kongō of Japan, and therefore indicates that our country is situated in the ocean to the northeast of both India and China. As a land apart, it has been independently ruled by a divinely descended line of sovereigns.[47]

The result of combinations at the liturgical and political levels was the application of the natural embodiment of cosmographies to Japan as a whole, which came to be seen as a sacred land under the ideal rule of the imperial line backed by powerful cultic centers dedicated to combined divine entities. In other words, the sacred geography of cultic centers had political reverberations and undertones. How could it be otherwise? It was grounded in shrines and temples that had evolved the sociopolitical and economic structures of the classical state.[48] Connections were established between several cultic centers to form a sacred geography of immense complexity; each major cultic center was the natural embodiment of various Buddha Lands and Pure Lands, and all were thought to be parts of a gigantic mandala ruled by the Solar Buddha (Dainichi nyorai) and its Japanese hypostasis, Amaterasu, the divine originator of the imperial lineage. The mental maps alluded to earlier in this study materialized at the political and ritual levels: Japan was seen as a cultic object consisting of parts of metaphysical lands that had flown to the islands and thence became the major cultic centers supported by the imperial lineage. Charts were drawn by priests to show relations between the Twenty-two Shrines supported by the state and their Buddhist counterparts, all of which were surrounded by various cosmic forces that could be ritually manipulated in order to protect the country.[49] Japan was at that time neither a political state nor a religious state; it was a "poligious" entity.

As usual in the case of Japan, the very narrow gap between religion and political authority caused what had been originally mystical visions of cultic centers as the natural embodiments of Pure Lands to be used in the political realm, and thus those visions came to sustain much of the ideology of the state during the medieval period and beyond. Both the province of Yamato and the nation of Yamato were sacred lands, symbolic territories of combined divinities and their earthly descendants, and mirror images of a pantheon and its abode. Correspondingly, rituals were thought to be effective in politics: since Japan was a symbolic realm, symbolic acts were thought to be effective in government.

THE EXPERIENCE OF TIME IN KASUGA

Buddhist philosophies of time were associated with, or opposed to, basic notions found in Japanese mythology. It is likely that specific categories of space were linked to specific categories of time, but this topic demands more research.

The Sacred Time of Ritual

Just as the site of the performance of a ritual needed to be carefully chosen and purified, its time also needed equal care and definition, not only in its choice but in its use. In the extant records, the time for ritual at Kasuga is always marked with care. It is obvious that originally time was the object of divination, although we have extremely little information on how the decisions for certain times were reached or expressed. Two types of time may be identified; one is the time of the beginnings, and the other will be called "floating time." The first type has to do with the day on which the Kasuga Grand Rite is performed, which is, without exception, a day of the monkey in the third and ninth moons. That is why a common name for the Grand Rite was "Monkey Rite." The time of the year for the celebration of the main rituals of Kasuga corresponded with the two major ritual activities in the agricultural domain, spring and autumn.

Also belonging to this category of time are the regular reconstructions of the shrines at the end of every twenty-year period. The reason why the rite was held on that day is that Takemikatsuchi-no-mikoto manifested itself on Mount Mikasa on the day of the monkey, and one must, in the central ritual act of the shrine, revert symbolically to the great origins. On that day, time was manipulated and magically brought back to the beginning of a cycle. In this context time was thought to be a kind of "eternal present," as is well stated by Yoshida Kanetomo, a member of the Urabe sacerdotal lineage in the fifteenth century: "Kami [or Deity] is spirit, without form, unknowable, transcending both cosmic principles, the yin and the yang . . . changeless, eternal, existing from the very beginning of Heaven and Earth up to the present, unfathomable, infinite, itself with neither beginning nor end, so that the so-called 'Divine Age' is not only in the past but also in the present. It is, indeed, the eternal now."[50]

It is said that Kanetomo's statement contains strong Buddhist tones, that it is "an enunciation of the Shingon doctrine of *aji hompushō* (the eternity of creation) decked in Shinto garments."[51] There is little doubt, however, that Kanetomo was firmly within the mainstream of Shinto ritual thought when he stated that the Age of the *kami* ("the Divine Age") is a matter of present rather than past, and that this notion had a political intention. This is because one of the central functions of ritual was precisely to revert magically to the time of the great beginnings and, by doing so, to reinforce the power and legitimacy of those who claimed descent from the *kami* who had acted then. For Kanetomo, history as we understand it was irrelevant if it did not realize or maintain the order of the sociocosm proposed in mythology, at least as he understood it.

The second type of time is called "floating" for it refers to specific times, chosen by divination, within the day or the moon or the year for the performance of ordinary or extraordinary rituals. This would be the case for a rain-making ritual, for the building of shrines and temples, for decisions concerning travel, and other aspects of the ritual cycle at Kasuga and in the Kōfukuji temples. Once a date was set it would not be changed unless there was sufficient reason to warrant it. Thus some rites would be performed in front of specific divinities on specific days of the moon or the year, as the ritual calendars of the shrines and temples and of individual prelates indicate.[52]

Time was important in government affairs as well as in the life of sacerdotal lineages and the monastic community, for its measurement ensured control over people. Thus, during the Nara period, the office charged with the compilation of the calendar and the measurement of time played a distinctive and important role. Diviners studied the movements of heavenly bodies and measured time with water clocks (clepsydras), some of which were placed in the imperial palace to ensure that the court would start and complete its business properly.[53] Drums were used to transmit the passage of the hours. The Buddhist tradition provided systematic controls over the time of the members of the monastic communities, for it specified when and for how long rituals or meditative exercises should last. In this respect, the role played by bells in monasteries, or by a type of incense coil that took a certain length of time to burn, was a central aspect of the rhythm of life in monasteries. Every temple had a bell tower, and the inscriptions on the bronze bells leave no doubt concerning their use. For example, Kūkai wrote the following in the ninth century:

> The vast ocean is the site of assembly of all kinds of fish and tur-tles, just as the high peaks are places where birds and animals gather. Correspondingly, the Lake of Wisdom is the site where mental dust gets purified, whereas the sacred bells call for a re-spite in suffering. Accordingly, the large bells are abundantly struck. Not only was King Canda-kanita saved from the hell of swords, but another person was saved from the hell of rivers of lava by the sound of a bell. Hence one finds in the scriptures the following: "Every time a bell is struck one must wish that all living beings be saved from pain in the triple world so that they might attain awakening."[54]

In another document in which Kūkai asked for financial help to cast a bell, he wrote:

> With one blow of the mallet all living beings of the trichiliocosm gather like clouds; with three gongs of the bell the sufferings of the four kinds of living beings melt away like ice. Thus was Canda-kanita saved from the hell of swords, and the underlings of the King of Hell made to cease torturing their victims with boiling water. Hearing the bell, those who are sinking in the deep slumber of ignorance suddenly awaken, just as a long night ceases upon the arrival of dawn. Hence, the eight kinds of spirits who protect the Law appear in order, while the triple venerable body of the Buddha manifests itself with exactitude. Isn't the sounding of the bell the mark of Wisdom, the real master of the hall of practice?[55]

In a similar vein, the inscription on the oldest bell of the Kōfukuji reads as follows:

> When the sacred mallet strikes, the metal drum causes a wind of humaneness to rise. The sound of the bell shakes the Mountain of the Numinous Eagle, and its echo reaches the palace of the dragons. This bell is offered in order to repay our quadruple debt, so that the spirits of those who departed before us may forever reside in the divine abode.[56]

Since court life was heavily permeated by ritual and protocol, time was a crucial element of the life of the aristocracy. The specialists in astronomy, who calculated time by observing the rhythms of nature and who, ac-cordingly, decided the time of rituals to establish a sense of order, soon began to control the movement of the body in space and time. The sense of awe and respect for the *kami* manifested itself not only in the divinatory process that regulated travel but also in the time it took to approach the divine or its manifestation on earth, the imperial figure; the distance crossed in that period of time symbolized the close interdependence of the two realms. The time of the *kami* is an eternal present, but the time for worship is cyclical and rhythmic, and human beings abide by its course, returning regularly to the great time of the beginnings in order to avoid chaos and disorder. In the Buddhist community, which had no vested interest in the origin of the world, another type of time prevailed: the regular and precise time of specific exercises that would allow one to transcend time in order to reach salvation from transmigration.

Thus, in the realm of the shrines, sacred space was the abode of *kami* that ruled a geographical area, and sacred time was a ritual device that ensured that the area protected by the *kami* functioned properly. In the realm of the temples, however, sacred space was a Pure Land, or a Buddha Land, which originally transcended this physical world, and thus the time occurring in that land was also transcendental, for that land was beyond transmigration. One can therefore imagine that when the sacred landscape of the shrines and the sacred land of Buddhist doctrine merged, the sense of time also changed in such a way that time in the sacred land of Kasuga was believed to pass more slowly than in the profane world. Whereas the time of ritual in the shrines was an eternal present, in the temples one could manipulate time, if not eradicate it, through the performance of rites of penance leading to the purification of the sense organs, which in turn allowed one to see the Pure Land. In both cases, purification was a fundamental practice that allowed one to reach either the Age of the *kami* or the eternity of the Pure Land. The function of ritual was to stop time and deny history.[57]

Naturally, the ritual cycle in shrines impacted profoundly on the life of the monastic community. If, in the shrines, the beginning of a new year was marked by complex rituals involving a regeneration of space in a new temporal cycle, the monastic community also evolved complex combinatory rituals that marked the beginning of the new year according to the Indian calendar. It will be recalled that the *Shūni-e* rituals of the Eastern and Western Kondō of the Kōfukuji, in which dance and theater played an important role, were essentially rites of penance aimed at doing away with past actions (personal history) in order to purify the organs of perception so that adequate visions of the cosmos might be achieved. When one considers how much of the life of the prelates of the Kōfukuji was spent in ritual activities, it is clear that the passage of time was one of the major factors in the control of life.

Temporal Orientation

The psychological sense of time on the part of the Fujiwara aristocracy and their ecclesiastics involved a cyclical sense visible in nature and in the rituals at the shrines. Simultaneously, their sense of time as shaped by Buddhist doctrine could be termed a "temporal orientation" marked by the hovering presence of death. The latter sense appears clearly in the type of ritual assemblies the Buddhist institutions were asked to perform, and which may be divided into three categories: assemblies for the welfare of departed members of the Fujiwara house, those for the welfare of the house, and those for the welfare of the state.

In the first type of assembly the emphasis is on remembering the dead and on hoping that their spirits will be reborn in the Pure Land. While remembering the past, one hoped for a better future. In this respect it is important to recognize the fact that up until Michinaga (966–1027), the creed of the Fujiwara house in regard to the Pure Land focused on the Buddha of the Future (*Miroku bosatsu*), but then, from the time of Michinaga's son Yorimichi, it shifted to the Pure Land of Amitābha (*Amida*). Before the time of Michinaga the Fujiwara acted out of filial piety and prayed for their departed ancestors and relatives, but from his era on, they were overwhelmingly concerned with their own fate; there is little question that the sense of impermanence that dominated the Heian culture helped to foster a sense of individuality among the aristocrats. That sense of impermanence was nurtured by Buddhist doctrine, but it was driven home by the growing competition between members of the aristocracy, a competition that drove many to personal ruin and existential despair.

The second category of assemblies, those for the welfare of the Fujiwara house, involved two types of rituals: first, rituals for the realization of this-worldly benefits (*gense-riyaku*) for individuals or for the house at large, consisting mainly in rituals belonging to the lineages of Shingon and Tendai; and second, rituals that brought about the realization of an individual's hope of being reborn in the Pure Land. The former rituals show a desire for immediate gratification, whereas the latter show a hope for delayed gratification.

The third category of assemblies, those for the welfare of the state, consisted entirely of practices belonging to the ritual lineages of Shingon and Tendai and were geared toward immediate or imminent gratification.

Thus one can differentiate between individual- and house-related rituals, between house and state rituals, and between insistence on past, present, or future categories of time. These differentiations depended heavily on the various Buddhist doctrines that filtered through the multiplex. Indeed, although the Kōfukuji was supposed to house the Hossō lineage of Buddhism, it was soon permeated (during the Heian period) by Shingon and Tendai lineages of thought and practice, which held distinctive philosophies of time that were structurally related to different views of the body, and which are best seen in their ritual forms.

By the beginning of the eleventh century the Pure Land of the Buddha of the Future had already been associated with sacred spaces in Japan; the mountains of Yoshino in Yamato were seen as the site of the Awakening of the Buddha of the Future, and Mount Kasagi, to the north of Kasuga, was seen as the antechamber to that Pure Land. Pilgrimages first to the latter and then to the former were conceived of as moves into transcendental spaces. These pilgrimages were preceded by abstinences and meditative exercises which were performed in Kyoto with utmost seriousness.

Nowhere perhaps is the Fujiwara belief in the Buddha of the Future better illustrated than in the pilgrimage to Yoshino that was undertaken by Michinaga, perhaps the most famous member of the Fujiwara family, in 1007. Before he began his pilgrimage, Michinaga undertook a rite of purification on the bank of the Kamo River in Kyoto (*Kamo no miharai*), and then he dedicated himself to practices known as Mitake *sōji* (ascesis of the sacred peak), which lasted seventy-five days in a site chosen by divination, the residence of Minamoto no Takamasa. An even longer and stricter ascesis was undertaken in the name of Michinaga by the Monachal Rector Kanshū. At the conclusion of this ascesis, on the second day of the eighth moon, a procession was formed, and after it was purified through an aspersion of salt water by the main southern gate of the capital, Rashōmon, it left Kyoto and proceeded to the Kamo River. There it boarded a ship that took Michinaga and his companions south to the multiplex of Iwashimizu Hachiman, where offerings were duly made and the night was spent. On the next day the procession moved on to Nara, and that night was spent in the Daianji. It took six more days before Michinaga and his company reached the Gion Shrine at the foot of the Yoshino Mountains.

The following day, after ablutions, the goal was reached. Michinaga first paid his respects to the Mikomori Shrine and the temples there, and then he went to the Zaō-dō, in front of which he read the following address:

> We, Fujiwara no Michinaga *Ason*, of the Second Rank, Great Minister of the Left of the Land of Great Japan located in the Southern Rosewood Continent, after an ascesis of one hundred days and accompanied by a small number of believers both lay

and monastic, have ascended Mount Kimpu during this eighth moon of the fourth year of the Kōnin era. We hereby place into the earth a bronze urn containing the following scriptures copied by our own hand: the Lotus Sutra in eight scrolls; the Sutra of Incommensurable Meanings and the Sutra of Samantabhadra, each in one scroll; the Sutra of Amitābha in one scroll; the Sutras of Maitreya: of Higher Rebirth, of Lower Rebirth, and of Realization of Buddhahood, each in one scroll; the Heart Sutra, one scroll; altogether, fifteen scrolls. Above this urn we place a stone lantern made of gold and bronze, in which a perpetual flame shall be kept. From this very day onward we shall be waiting for the dawn of the Assembly of the *Puśpa-nāga* [when Maitreya shall realize Awakening], and hereby humbly declare to Zaō, while folding hands and burning incense, the following:

The Lotus Sutra is hereby offered to repay our debt to the Venerable Śākyamuni, to meet Maitreya, to build a closer relationship in the future with Zaō, and for our Awakening-Without-Superior. . . . We have copied the Sutra of Amitābha so that, at the time of our death, without letting mind and body dissipate, and by keeping the Venerable Amitābha in mind, we might be reborn in the Pure Land. Furthermore, we have copied the Sutras of Maitreya in order to be able to meet in person with Maitreya at the time of His Coming, which shall follow His realization of No-More-Rebirth after the completion of ninety times a hundred million kalpas of transmigration due to sinful acts. We hereby formulate the vow that, at the time of Realization of Buddhahood on the part of the Venerable Master of Compassion, Maitreya, we might be able to leave the Pure Land and come to this Buddha Land in order to be in the Assembly and to receive from Maitreya, in His sacred court, the Prophecy that we shall realize Buddhahood. Upon such time may these scriptures which we now put into the earth appear spontaneously and cause joy in the hearts of the members of the Assembly.[58]

This document, which was found in an urn excavated at Yoshino in the seventeenth century, is the oldest extant document of the kind. It reveals that Michinaga wished to wait for the Buddha of the Future in the Pure Land of Amida, and to receive at the time of Maitreya's Coming to the Garden of the Dragon-Trees a prophecy that he would realize Buddhahood. Michinaga believed that Yoshino was the site where the Buddha of the Future would inaugurate a New Age, and that the cherry blossoms of Yoshino were metaphorically associated with the Dragon Flowers of the tree under which Maitreya would awaken. Various elements discussed earlier in this chapter can be seen in this event in the early eleventh century: the association, under the influence of Indian cosmography, of a particular place with the transcendental space of a buddha or bodhisattva, accompanied by a specific philosophy of time and specific ritual forms. Michinaga thus saw the Western Pure Land of Amida as nothing more than the ideal location at which to await the Buddha of the Future. Even though, by Michinaga's time, the notion of the Decline of the Law (*mappō*) seemed to have been well entrenched among the members of the court, Michinaga did not conceive of time in this negative light; he wielded immense power in his day, and his life long remained in the minds of the people of Japan as the ultimate standard of power, elegance, and refinement. Time was, consequently, no threat to him, for it seemed to bring even more radiance to his rule and to the Fujiwara house.

It was a different matter, however, for Michinaga's successors, who lived in a period of increasing uncertainty and strife; to them, the age of glory was in the past, just as was the age in which the Buddha had lived; it was not easily emulated or retrieved. There seemed to them to be an ineluctable direction to the course of time that they were helpless to change; calamities struck the land and the people, and the System of Codes had eroded to the point that it was no more than an empty form. Unable to cope with change, the leaders of the country surrendered to the saving grace of Amida with total devotion.[59] The large number of texts written during the latter part of the Heian period to document the death of devotees of Amida and their entrance into the Pure Land bears witness to the overwhelming sense that time was in a process of corruption.[60]

Such was not the case, however, at the Kasuga-Kōfukuji multiplex, whose members unanimously attacked the lineage of Hōnen, the founder of the Pure Land school. The basis for their attack was that devotion to the Pure Land on the part of Hōnen's lineage was so one-sided that people were told not to rely on the *kami* in order to be saved. The threat implied in the Pure Land position was immediate to cultic centers whose structure was principally combinatory, and the Pure Land schools found themselves faced with vigorous attacks by powerful segments of the population who were devoted to the *kami* and who would not abandon their worship of them even at a time of great distress. Under that pressure the Pure Land lineages had to withdraw their statements. As Kuroda Toshio has shown, the attacks on the "single-mindedness" (*ikkō*) of proponents of the invocation of the Buddha Amida partly caused a kind of renaissance in shrines associated with temples in major cultic centers.[61] The belief in the Pure Land of Amida, however, was so powerful that it penetrated those cultic centers, though in a different guise: that is, as we have seen above, the imagery of the Pure Land thrived in the context of a projection of it onto sacred areas. Thus the combinatory tendency was victorious. Indeed, in Kasuga, Kumano, Nikkō, Itsukushima, and the Hachiman multiplexes, Pure Land imagery was systematically applied to visions of the sacred spaces of those cultic centers. These sites were believed either to be gates to the Pure Land, if not the Pure Land itself, or to be located over hell.

SPACE, TIME, RITUAL, AND PERFORMANCE

In the Heian period, certain forms of ritual were directly linked to social factors, such as the cohesion of the Fujiwara house and its relationship to the imperial lineage, and certain combined rituals of the Kasuga shrine-temple multiplex displayed sociogenic characteristics, especially in the case of the *On-matsuri*, by which the Yamato community reinforced its power and identity. These rituals are, as we have seen, embedded in specific configurations of space and time, and the relations between them, and are specifically linked to the performing arts. The performance of sacred dances and dramas accompanied by chanting or music could take place only within a certain space and at a certain time, and thus the phenomenon of performance was embedded in very specific structures. In the case of Nō performances, the ideological and visionary aspects of the tradition appear in the texts themselves.[62] Nō drama was based on, and reinforced, particular views of the world, and since it was created against a background of combinations between the divinities of shrines and temples, the realm of meaning that it exhibited is essentially combinatory. The combinatory character of the aesthetics of Nō is indicated quite clearly in the *Fūshikaden*, one of the major theoretical treatises on Nō drama:

> It is said that the sources of *sarugaku* and of the *ennen* dances are to be found in India, or that these forms of art have been transmitted in Japan since the Age of the *kami*; however, time passes and that Age has become so remote that it is impossible to study its style. What people appreciate most these days is *sarugaku*, the origins of which are in the sixty-six mimes devised by Hata no Kōkatsu upon order of Shōtoku Taishi during the reign of Empress Suiko; these plays, which accompanied banquets, were performed with the intention of bringing peace to the kingdom or of entertaining the people. Since those times, generation after generation has borrowed the aesthetic qualities of nature and made them the medium of this entertainment. After Kōkatsu the art has been transmitted among his descendants who served in the sacerdotal lineages of Kasuga and Hie for generations; that is why those lineages are flourishing in the shrines in the provinces of Yamato and Ōmi. . . .

The reason why *sarugaku* is associated with the Age of the *kami* is the following: at the time Amaterasu hid in the Heavenly Rock Cave, a perpetual darkness [pervaded] the world, and the eight hundred myriads of *kami* assembled at the foot of Mount Ama-no-kagu where, with the intention of retrieving the attention of the Great Deity, they performed sacred dances [*kagura*] and initiated the dance called Sei-no-o. At the time, the *kami* Ama-no-Uzume advanced, affixed *shide* straps to branches of the *sakaki* tree, chanted, set wood on fire, and danced and stomped her feet so that she came to be possessed. As the Great Deity perceived the sound of the voice of the *kami*, she opened slightly the rock-gate to the cave, and the land of the country was clear again. The faces of the *kami* all became radiant and white. It is said that the dances performed then are the origins of *sarugaku*. In the place of residence of the Buddha [India], the wealthy layman Sudatta erected the shrine of Jetavana [Gion]; at the time of the ceremonies of completion of the shrine and as Śākyamuni was about to preach, Devadatta approached, accompanied by ten thousand representatives of the External Paths; they affixed *shide* straps to the branches of trees and to bamboo leaves, danced and shouted, so that it became difficult to perform the rites of completion. At that point the Buddha gave a glance to Śāriputra, who, understanding the intent of the Buddha, went to the back door of the temple where he beat the drum and chanted. Then the genius of Ananda, the wisdom of Śāriputra, and the eloquence of Purna performed sixty-six manners of mimicry, and the people accompanying Devadatta, hearing drums and flutes, gathered near the back door and became completely calm as they listened to the music. Then the Buddha was able to preach and to perform the rites of completion of the building. This Way originated then in India. . . .

In the capital of Kyoto, during his reign Emperor Murakami read a document written by the very hand of Shōtoku Taishi and called *Sarugaku ennen no ki*, in which he learned that these forms, consisting of foolish utterances and specious terms, which originated in India in the Age of the *kami* were transmitted through Bactria and China to the Solar Region [Japan], where they now protect the causal factors leading people to awakening: this art does away with evil and calls upon happiness to appear. When *sarugaku* dances are performed the country remains tranquil, the people become peaceful, and life is prolonged. Thus the emperor decided that the performance of *sarugaku* dances should become a rite of protection for the state. He gave the direction of the dances performed in the imperial palace to Hata no Ujiyasu, who was a descendant of Kōkatsu. . . .

Between this Ujiyasu and Mitsutarō and Komparu, twenty-nine generations have passed. This group of artists now forms the troupe of Emman-i of Yamato Province. Three regalia have been transmitted from generation to generation since Ujiyasu down to the present: a demon's mask carved by Shōtoku Taishi, a portrait of Kasuga *daimyōjin,* and a reliquary. These three regalia are still kept in the Komparu House. At the present, when the "appreciation of the dharma" performances are held in the Lecture Hall of the Kōfukuji for the ceremonies dedicated to the Vimalakīrti Sūtra, *ennen* dances are performed in the Refectory. These dances pacify heretics and destroy evil spirits. This is based on the precedent of Jetavana. The sacred rites of Yamato Province performed in the Kasuga-Kōfukuji multiplex occur on the second day of the second moon and on the fifth day of the same moon. In the shrine-temple multiplex, the four troupes of actors of *sarugaku* perform then what is the greatest rite of the year. It is the Grand Rite of Protection of the State.[63]

This text leaves little doubt about the multicultural structure of sacred performances in shrine-temple multiplexes. These dances were state affairs, not only because they were sponsored by the state but also because their function was—originally—a function of magic. Dance was first and foremost possession (*kakari*). The sacred powers manifested themselves in dance, but they were also placated by dance, which thus formed an important part of rites to pacify powers that disrupt the natural cycle. Dance also served as a cultural reminder of the identity of the state and the Fujiwara house, since it expressed important myths and symbols, and in the case of Nō drama, it also expressed historical phenomena according to interpretive schemes grounded in the combinations of "Shinto" and "Buddhist" notions, practices, aesthetics, and doctrinal tenets.

This is one of the reasons why the four Nō troupes of Yamato (Yūsaki, Tobi, Sakado, and Emman-i) were sponsored by the Kasuga multiplex and by the *bakufu* and competed for excellence at the time of rituals in Kasuga, Hie, and other cultic centers such as Ima-Kumano and Tōnomine. The medieval theoreticians of Nō drama all insisted that dance is central to any Nō performance; even when drama left the cultic centers to be played on stages in private residences, the function of magic remained even though its object changed: instead of magically placating forces beyond humanity, dance magically placated the very heart of men and women. Thus dance and drama never abandoned their civilizing power.

IDEATION-ONLY, AND A FEW OTHER THINGS

The Kōfukuji owns a number of statues, among which are masterpieces of Japanese classical and medieval sculpture. Particularly noteworthy are the statues of Asanga and Vasubandhu, two of the major Indian philosophers who are seen as the patriarchs of the Hossō lineage, which is housed at the Kōfukuji. These statues were sculpted by master-sculptors of the Kōfukuji and are widely regarded as the epitome of Kamakura art. The 1180 fire set by Taira warriors destroyed the entire Kōfukuji, as well as the Tōdaiji and other temples in Nara. Immediately thereafter, the Fujiwara house, the court, and the main temples of the city organized the reconstruction of the Kasuga-Kōfukuji multiplex, and the ceremonies marking the start of the reconstruction were held barely six months after the disaster, in 1181. The main sculptors of the Saishō-Kongō-in of Kyoto were called upon to practice their art: Yōen was given responsibility for the statues of the Golden Hall, Inson for those of the Lecture Hall, Seichō for those of the Refectory, and Kōkei for those of the Nan'endō (Southern Circular Hall).

In 1186 Kujō Kanezane became the chieftain of the Fujiwara house, and he immediately set to the task of changing the administration of the office of construction of the Kōfukuji and ordered levies to ensure that funds would be available for that construction. As chieftain of the house, Kanezane was the supervisor of the work, and he wrote details about it in his diary, especially concerning Kōkei. Kōkei (n.d.), who made the sculptures of the Nan'endō, was a man of great talent and character who did not hesitate to disagree with Kanezane. Among his works are the exquisite Fukū-kensaku Kannon, the statues of the Four Heavenly Guardians, and the statues of the Six Patriarchs of Hossō, all of which are housed in the Nan'endō. The statues of the Hoku'endō (Northern Circular Hall) were made by a team of ten artists under the direction of Kōkei's son, Unkei, over the years from 1208 to 1221. The central statue, one of Maitreya, was completed by Unkei himself; the statue of Asaṅga was completed by his disciple Unjō; and that of Vasubandhu by Unga. These statues, together with those of the Six Patriarchs of Hossō enshrined in the Southern Circular Hall, not only represent the epitome of Kamakura art, but they also symbolize the renewal of the study of doctrines of the Hossō lineage at the Kōfukuji.

During the Heian period the lofty idealist systems of Yogācāra philosophy had simply been the object of rote learning by prelates of the Kōfukuji and had not been developed or commented upon in any manner worthy of mention. The reconstruction of Nara, however, was accompanied by a renewal of religious fervor and scholarship. Some scholars have argued that there was a reformation of Buddhism in Japan in the twelfth century because of the appearance of the Zen schools and independent Pure Land schools around that time.[64] The term *reformation* in this context is dangerous in several respects: first, it raises too many associations with the

European Reformation; second, and more importantly, it distracts us from certain distinct developments that took place at that time in Japan. Among these were the resurgence of the Nara schools, particularly Ritsu, Kegon, and Hossō; the consolidation of the "conglomerate of exoteric and esoteric systems" (*kenmitsu taisei*) through the maintenance of the economic and spiritual power of Japan's main shrine-temple multiplexes; and the coming of age of medieval "Shinto." These last two aspects have been given little attention by scholars outside of Japan, even though it is impossible to propose an adequate history of Japanese religion without studying them.[65] What happened in the Kasuga belief system during the medieval period is typical of the renewal of Nara, the conglomerate of exoteric and esoteric systems, and the new character of "Shinto."

Undoubtedly the Hossō lineage, about which little has been said up to now, deeply influenced the evolution of the Kasuga belief system, but, unfortunately, extremely little is known about the history of the Hossō school in Japan, and its doctrine is so exceedingly abstruse that little has been done in the West to present it in a succinct manner.[66] Modern Buddhologists concentrate their studies on the Indian and Chinese developments of the school, and no Western scholar has worked systematically on the Japanese history of the lineage. This is understandable, for one cannot put into relief the possible achievements of Japanese scholarly monks in the domain of Hossō doctrine if one cannot contrast them with their forerunners in India and China. A systematic discussion of this school of philosophy is, consequently, impossible in the present study, and therefore we shall simply consider briefly the history of the Hossō lineage in the Kōfukuji at the time of its inception and during the early medieval period.

According to Takemura Makio, the doctrine of Ideation-Only (Vijñapti-mātratā; in Japanese, *yuishiki*) is the most orthodox form of philosophy in Indian Mahāyāna Buddhism.[67] Whether that is the case or not, there is no doubt that it represents an apex in the history of philosophy and that, consequently, the Japanese of the seventh and eighth centuries—who were just beginning to understand the forms of Buddhism that had been transmitted through China and Korea—may have found it difficult to assimilate in a short period. As we have seen earlier, however, a number of eminent scholarly monks studied the doctrine of the Hossō lineage, probably because that lineage was represented in China by scholarly monks who were directly patronized by the Chinese emperors. Had the scholarly debates of the Heian period (such as the Ōwa Debates) between Hossō and Tendai been really of a purely intellectual nature, we might expect that the achievements would have been greater than those recorded in history. The political nature of the debates, compounded by the insistence on blood lineage that characterized the classical religious institutions of Japan, may have prevented this from happening.

From the beginning of the Heian period onward, the emphasis at the Kōfukuji was on career advancement through the performance of specific rituals that were not necessarily connected to the doctrine of Hossō or to an understanding thereof; prelates of Fujiwara birth, solely by virtue of their family connections, were advancing up the hierarchical ladder much faster than anybody else. Consequently, scholarly study suffered tremendously, and the transmission of the doctrine quickly became a purely formal matter. Thus, no great scholars of Hossō philosophy were produced in the middle of the Heian period. By that time, scholarship had developed in three parts of the Kōfukuji: the Ichijō-in *monzeki*, the Daijō-in *monzeki*, and the Kita-in, all of which were run by prelates who were members of the Fujiwara and other noble families.

The Ichijō-in *monzeki*, the most powerful of the two at the Kōfukuji in the eleventh century, did produce a number of scholarly monks. Among these we might mention Shinrai (1010–76), a son of Fujiwara no Yoritsune, who had a brilliant career: after passing the successive exams, which consisted of his having to serve as master of ceremonies and lecturer at the three major ritual assemblies of the multiplex, he became abbot of the Kōfukuji in 1062. Shinrai is reported to have mastered the more complicated aspects of Hossō doctrine, but this is said of most Fujiwara prelates, and thus it is not always clear how reliable such statements are. Typical of the times, Shinrai had a number of aristocratic disciples, three of whom—Raison (1026–1100), a son of Fujiwara no Saneyasu; Eshō (1084–1163?), a son of Fujiwara no Iemichi; and Eien (1048–1125), a son of Fujiwara no Nagasuke—became abbots of the Kōfukuji.

A much better example of that type of situation is seen in the history of the various disciples of Kakushin (1065–1121), a son of Fujiwara no Morozane. Four of Kakushin's disciples—Kakuei (1068–1146), Shingan (1045–1115), his younger brother Genkaku (1099–1138), and Kakue (1117–57)—became abbots of the multiplex because of their pedigree. Kakuei's case stands out as highly indicative of the way that the nature of the sociocosmic system of the Fujiwara house might have been an obstacle to scholarship. A son of Fujiwara no Moromichi, Kakuei entered the Kōfukuji at a young age and was trained both as a scholar and as a poet. He had such qualities that he came to be regarded as a reincarnation of Dharmapāla (a great Indian master of Hossō doctrine) or of Jion Daishi (the Chinese patriarch of the lineage), but he quickly realized that advancement in the hierarchy of the multiplex was not dictated by success in scholarship.

He had a strong personal devotion to Kasuga *daimyōjin*, from whom he received the following oracle: "If you really want to study, I shall protect you." Shortly thereafter Kakuei left Nara and became a wandering monk; he went to a northern province where he built a hermitage near a temple, and he spent the rest of his life there in meditation, thought, and poetry, leaving a poem on the matter on a pillar in his hut before he died. The poet Saigyō (1117–1190), who happened to pass by that hut during one his travels, gathered up the few objects (including some scriptures) that were still there, left a poem, and returned to the capital, where he gave the objects to relatives of Kakuei. This case is typical of the situation at the multiplex in the twelfth century; those who were serious about Buddhist learning and practice left the pomp and riches, the "establishment," and lived a life of seclusion. This situation prevailed at both *monzeki* at the multiplex until the beginning of the twelfth century, but not at the Kita-in.

The center of Hossō learning before the Kamakura period was, apparently, the Kita-in, an institution that was run by lesser nobility and accepted into its ranks monks of common origin. The most famous Kita-in scholar was Zōshun (1104–80), who is said to have been born after his childless parents prayed to Kasuga *daimyōjin* and, as a result, had a dream in which the divine entity promised that the mother would become pregnant and that the child would be protected. In spite of his immense scholarship, however, Zōshun did not reach even the status of master of lectures (*kōshi*) before the age of sixty-five, whereas monks of Fujiwara birth customarily attained that level by the age of twenty. Zōshun left a large number of scholarly writings, of which the *Yuishiki-ron hommonshō*, in forty-five *kan*, is invaluable not only because it provides insights into the scholarship of the time, but also because it quotes extensively Chinese and Japanese commentaries that have disappeared.[68] This work raises a number of problems in Hossō doctrine and attempts to solve them by offering a systematic treatment of those questions in various commentaries. It is thought that the fact that Zōshun wrote the *Hommonshō* is a good indication that he intended to restore the scholarly tradition of the Kōfukuji.

Moreover, the *Inmyō-daisōshō*, in forty-one *kan*, which Zōshun wrote in the short span of fifteen months and completed in front of the Kasuga Shrine, shows that he was on a quest for Hossō orthodoxy, and that he did not necessarily see it—as his predecessors had—in the writings of Jion Daishi. Furthermore, he wrote a text entitled *Bodai-in shō*, which raises questions concerning the sixth chapter of the *Ch'eng Wei-shih lun*, and, on orders from Fujiwara no Yorinaga, he also wrote two opuscules, the *Yuiryō-shō* and the *Yuishiki hiryō-shō*, on the topic of *inmyō* (causality), which is one of the core issues raised by Hossō. Yorinaga, who also was a scholar of Buddhism, wrote on the very same topic. Late in life Zōshun composed a commentary on Jion Daishi's commentary on the Lotus Sutra, thus offering a Hossō perspective on this important Mahāyāna scripture. It is thought that Zōshun might be the author of the *Hyappō mondō-shō*, a text consisting of one hundred questions and answers that served as an introduction to the doctrine of Hossō. Zōshun died in 1180, the year Taira warriors attacked Nara and reduced it to ashes.

When the temples were reconstructed, a fresh wind of scholarship passed through them once again. The classical culture of the Fujiwara multiplex was restored, and even though noble ecclesiasts still held the highest positions, monks other than those of Fujiwara birth also left their mark on the intellectual life of the multiplex. The most prominent of these were Gedatsu *shōnin* (of Fujiwara extraction) and Myō-e *shōnin*, of lesser birth. Both came to be known as the "children of Kasuga *daimyōjin*."

The monk Jōkei (1155–1212), better known by his posthumous name Gedatsu *shōnin*, "Saint Deliverance," was the grandson of the scholarly politician Fujiwara no Michinori (1116–59) and the son of Sadanori. He was born in the year before the Hōgen Disturbance, during which various factions of the Fujiwara house fought for supremacy; Michinori, who was on the winning side, accumulated power and wealth, but he died in the Heiji Disturbance of 1159. His family had little support thereafter, and, therefore, many of its members took Buddhist orders; several of Michinori's sons and grandsons became important figures in the intellectual and religious world of the early Kamakura period. For example, his son Kakue (who was mentioned earlier as a disciple of Kakushin) became abbot of the Kōfukuji; another son, Shōken, was abbot of the Daigoji and the Tōdaiji; a third son, Kambin, was abbot of the Kōryūji; and yet another son, Myōhen, became famous as the patriarch of the Kōya *hijiri*.[69]

Jōkei entered the Kōfukuji at the age of eight under the supervision of his uncle Kakue. He was ordained in 1165 and immediately devoted himself to the study of Hossō doctrine; he advanced steadily in the hierarchy of the Kōfukuji, becoming discussant at the *Yuima-e* Ceremony in 1182 and master of lectures at it in 1186. The *kampaku* Kujō Kanezane was most impressed with Jōkei and took him as his spiritual advisor. In 1191 Jōkei became master of lectures for the *Hokke-hakkō* ritual assembly of Kasuga, but he abruptly left the Kōfukuji the next year to live in semiseclusion on Mount Kasagi, northwest of Kasuga. Obviously disappointed with the careerism that was rampant in the Kōfukuji, he renewed his vows after taking residence at Mount Kasagi's rundown temples, which he rebuilt and at which he recommenced the ritual assemblies dedicated to Maitreya, the Buddha of the Future. It was not by chance that Jōkei chose Kasagi as his residence, for that site was believed to be the antechamber of the Pure Land of Maitreya. His residence in Kasagi lasted until 1208, when, looking for peace, he moved to the Kaijusenji, a mountain temple situated north of Kasagi, where he died five years later.

Jōkei wrote a number of important texts that indicate the depth of his scholarship and reveal the spirit of his times. According to the *Gedatsu shōnin shūgaku-ki*, he accumulated a vast learning in the course of his education, during which he kept a strict schedule: he studied from 4 A.M. to noon; practiced rites from noon to 2 P.M.; studied again from 2 to 4 P.M.; devoted himself to non-Buddhist classics and other matters from 4 to 6 P.M.; practiced rites and chanted scriptures from 6 to 8 P.M.; and returned to his studies from 8 P.M. to midnight. He slept only between midnight and 4 A.M.[70] For Jōkei, scholarly study was not only an intellectual matter but also a matter of faith and truth, for he could not conceive of study that would not entail a search for truth. One day, the *Kokonchomonjū* reports, while he was waiting to take a medicinal bath in a temple, some monks sitting in an adjacent room were disputing points of doctrine. Learning of the presence of Jōkei, the monks came to ask for his advice, but he uttered only the following poem in response:

> Yesterday,
> Footprints visible on the path;
> Today,
> All covered by snow.[71]

The monks would have realized from this verse that argumentation for its own sake did not lead anywhere.

The legends built around his character show Jōkei as a scholar devoted to Kasuga *daimyōjin*, with no interest whatever in fame, and as a stern priest who meticulously observed discipline and the monastic code. A relentless critic of the followers of Hōnen, Jōkei devoted much of his energy to the restoration of the Hossō doctrine, to the restoration of monastic discipline (*kairitsu*), and—so the tradition reports—to the cult dedicated to Shōtoku Taishi. Jōkei forcefully opposed the Pure Land school's claim that one did not need the *kami* in order to be saved and that sole reliance on the repetition of Amida's name was sufficient to be reborn in his Western Pure Land. Indeed, Jōkei composed the famous "Statement" of the Kōfukuji, which denounced such views and practices as heretical. He also wrote a number of important commentaries—such as the *Miroku-kō shiki*, the *Gikanshō*, the *Jinshishō*, and the *Gubeihosshin-shū*—which reveal the spirit of his age but are yet to be studied in the West.

As was mentioned above, another important figure in the renewal of religious devotion and scholarship that marked the Kamakura period was

Myō-e *shōnin* (1173–1232). As Jōkei is regarded as the person who restored the Hossō school during the medieval period, so Myō-e is regarded as having done the same for the Kegon school. Myō-e was trained not only in the Kegon tradition but in many lineages of thought and ritual, and he was a fervent devotee of Kasuga *daimyōjin*. Inclined by nature and training to have mystical visions, he was truly one of the great religious figures of the period. He yearned to visit India but, as we have seen, was prevented from doing so by an oracle of the *kami* that reminded him that Kasuga was the Deer Park and that, therefore, he did not need to travel to distant lands in search of the world of the Buddha. Inspired by the Hossō belief that dreams are so real that reality deserves to be called a dream, Myō-e kept a diary in which he recorded all the dreams and visions he had over the years. He resided for many years in the Kōzanji, which is located in the mountains of Takao, north of Kyoto, and wrote a number of important documents attacking Hōnen's writings on the Pure Land. Unlike Jōkei, Myō-e has received considerable scholarly attention recently.[72]

Even though the Kōfukuji was the center for the Hossō lineages, and even though the beginning of the Kamakura period saw a major renewal of the lineages of Nara, it is not the case that Hossō and the other doctrinal traditions of classical Nara were the center of religious and philosophical life in Yamato Province during the medieval period. Rather, religious and philosophical life in that period too were combinatory, and the world was more deeply marked by the economic and political influence of shrine-temple multiplexes than by anything else.

The establishment of the Pure Land traditions went together with a major countrywide renewal of interest in the *kami*. Historical studies of the Kamakura and Muromachi periods commonly mention the appearance of the Zen and Pure Land schools and the renewal of several of the classical schools of thought, but rarely do these studies mention that "Shinto" was also created in the medieval period, even though this was an important event in the religious, political, intellectual, and artistic life of Japan. Had it not been for the combinatory systems of Hie, Kasuga, Ise, Hachiman, and others, in which scholarly monks provided philosophical and ritual interpretations of the nature of the *kami*, this development would never have been. Furthermore, the ideology of the state, which was based on the long traditions of those shrine-temple multiplexes, was also born at the time and had a tremendous impact on the world of politics, ritual, and thought during the medieval period and even beyond it into the premodern period. Thus, it is much more appropriate to consider the Kasuga belief system as a far-reaching combinatory phenomenon, rather than as an abstruse doctrine of classical Indian Buddhism.

5 From Cult to Cultural Revolution

In these pages we will outline the premodern evolution of the Kasuga-Kōfukuji multiplex by examining a few of the crises that befell first, the Tōnomine multiplex (dedicated to Nakatomi no Kamatari, the human ancestor of the Fujiwara house), and second, the province of Yamato as it underwent major changes in government. In the case of Tōnomine, the cult took specific forms that are not found at Kasuga, and it changed in a significant manner in the fifteenth century and again in the seventeenth. In the case of Yamato Province, we will evidence the impact of Toyotomi Hideyoshi's policies and the Tokugawa rule on the Kasuga-Kōfukuji multiplex. Finally, we will discuss the downfall of the multiplex at the end of the nineteenth century.

A BENEVOLENT ANCESTOR

The mausoleum dedicated to Nakatomi no Kamatari, the human ancestor of the Fujiwara house, is a shrine-temple multiplex situated on top of a sacred mountain in the southern part of Yamato Province, Tōnomine.[1] As the following excerpts from the "Tōnomine ryakki" indicate, tradition has it that the multiplex was created for a specific purpose by Kamatari's first son, the Buddhist monk Jō-e:

> The Great Minister of State Kamatari spoke to Jō-e and said:
> "Mount Tan (Tōnomine) in Yamato Province is a site of unsurpassed quality. To the east, in Takayama at Ise, the Great *kami* Amaterasu protects Japan. To the west, on Mount Kongō, Hōki *bosatsu* benefits living beings by expounding the *dharma*. To the south, on Mount Kimpu, the Great Avatar Zaō is awaiting the coming of Maitreya. To the north, on Mount Ōmiwa, the hypostasis of the Tathāgata leads people to salvation. At the cen-

ter is Tōnomine, location of the marvelous cavern of the Immor-
tals. How could that site differ from Mount Wu-t'ai in China?
Should you place my tomb there, my descendants shall rise to
superior ranks."[2]

Indeed, those who, moved by piety toward their ancestor, restored
Tōnomine in the course of its history, went on to hold the highest positions
in the Fujiwara house and the government. In the combinatory cult that
evolved at Tōnomine, Kamatari was believed to have been, during his
lifetime, a manifestation on earth of Vimalakīrti, Mahāyāna Buddhism's
lay hero of non-duality. That is the way in which Kamatari was treated in
the ceremonies that were dedicated to him at the Kōfukuji, where the cult
was predominantly Buddhist.

Kamatari was also, however, the object of another cult, at Tōnomine,
where he was regarded as a benevolent ancestor. That cult was originally
Buddhist, it seems, but it became thoroughly combinatory during the
medieval period and in the Edo period took on an increasingly Shinto
coloration.

A central characteristic of that cult was that Kamatari's sculpted effigy
(which is said to represent him in lay attire and to be made of chestnut
wood), enshrined in a hall at the Tōnomine multiplex, gave advance warn-
ings of impending political or military disasters in the form of a noise that
was caused by cracks that appeared on the statue or of noise caused when
the mountain rumbled and roared. These cracks and noises were examined,
measured, and recorded, and the record was then sent to the court in Kyoto,
where a divination was performed. The oracle was duly recorded and then
recited in front of leading members of the Fujiwara house and other court
officials. Thereafter, an imperial messenger was dispatched to Tōnomine,
where special ceremonies were held and offerings of gratitude were made.
These ceremonies entailed the recitation of Buddhist scriptures that were
drawn from the body of literature of the Perfection of Wisdom, or of
scriptures pertaining to the protection of the state, and were usually
followed by "Shinto" rites of purification and the performance of songs and
dance. The statue was then restored. Finally, an official statement uttered
in a loud voice by the officiants announced that Kamatari's spirit had been
"pacified and consoled" and that the matter was over.

According to the *Tōnomine haretsuki* (Chronicle of the Cracks at
Tōnomine), dated 1610, the cracks on the statue were examined in detail
because it was thought that they pointed to an "epicenter," which was a
realm of Fujiwara control.[3] The text further informs us that whenever the
cracks occurred on the statue, the mountain would shake, but the mountain's tremors were not necessarily accompanied by cracks on the statue.
When the noise was perceived to come from the eastern part of the

mountain, the "epicenter" was the realm of the imperial house; when it was perceived to come from the south, the epicenter was the chieftain of the Fujiwara house; when it came from the north, the epicenter was among members of the house; when it came from the west, the epicenter was among the common people; and if noise was perceived to come from the center, the epicenter was thought to be the multiplex itself. According to the *Tōnomine engi*, a text of the early sixteenth century, the mountain sometimes emitted a supernatural radiance, or luminous "spirits" (*mono*) were seen spurting from it.[4] In every such case the radiance was visible as far as Mount Mikasa, the sacred hill of the Kasuga Shrine in Nara. Two other texts mention those events: the *Tōnomine ryakki* (A Short Chronicle of Tōnomine), compiled on the basis of various records in 1197,[5] and the *Daishokkan shinzō haretsuki furoku* (Record Attached to the Chronicle of the Cracks on the Divine Effigy of the Great Minister), dated 1840.[6]

According to Miyai Yoshio, the first record of those cracks and sounds appears in 1012 in Fujiwara no Michinaga's diary, and noise was heard subsequently for a total of thirty-six times in the following years: 1031, 1046, 1081, 1148, 1157, 1162, 1167, 1170, 1172, 1174, 1178, 1180, 1181, 1184, and 1187, this last crack occurring right after the establishment of military rule in Kamakura marked the end of the Fujiwara house's hegemony.[7]

It is not clear, however, what sources were used by Miyai Yoshio; the *Daishokkan shinzō haretsuki furoku*, which is the most detailed of the documents, gives more dates (some of which correspond to Miyai's list) and a number of comments:

    1. 898, 2nd moon, 7th day.
    2. 989, 6th moon, 6th day. The text adds that no details are known about those two occurrences.
    3. 1046, 1st moon, 24th day, in connection with a rebellion on the part of "Ezo" barbarians in the north.
    4. 1074, 3rd moon, 6th day.
    5. 1148, 12th moon, 8th day.
    6. 1157, 7th moon, 1st day.
    7. 1162, 2nd moon, 23rd day.
    8. 1167, 5th moon, 23rd day.
    9. 1170, 4th moon, 13th day.
   10. 1172, 6th moon, 9th day.
   11. 1174, 12th moon, 4th day.
   12. 1178, 3rd moon, 19th day.
   13. 1180, 7th moon, 22nd day. The last four cracks occurred during the reign of Emperor Takakura and signal the end of the Heian period.
   14. 1181, no other details.

15. 1184, 7th moon, 2nd day.
16. 1187, 11th moon, 2nd day.
17. 1208, 4th moon, 14th day. Followed by a long period of calm, which corresponds to the renewed power of the Kōfukuji.
18. 1322, 2nd moon, 19th day.

In 1351, the Ashikaga shogunate recognized the Kōfukuji as Governor of Yamato Province—as its predecessors had done—but forced its *shuto* to swear allegiance. In 1414, the shogun (Ashikaga Yoshimochi) asked the *shuto* to again swear allegiance. The following year, Kitabatake Yoshimasa rebelled against the Kōfukuji; he lost, but military efforts in the form of guerrilla warfare persisted way into the premodern period, so that Yamato Province was actually divided between north and south for most of the premodern period. The Kasuga-Kōfukuji multiplex controlled only the north. During one of the skirmishes, which occurred in 1438, Tōnomine was reduced to ashes. The statue of Kamatari was saved from the fire and transported to the Tachibanadera, a subtemple of the Kōfukuji, where it was kept for three years until Tōnomine was rebuilt. In 1441, the statue was carried back to the mountain in great pomp and an autumn festival was created to commemorate the occasion. This explains the following item.

19. 1441, 2nd moon, 26th day. This is the first record of the ascent of the mountain by Yoshida Kanena, a priest of the Yoshida sacerdotal lineage, which thereafter gained some control over the cultic center. The following year, the mausoleum shook on its foundations.
20. 1459, no other details.
21. 1465, 9th moon, 13th day.
22. 1475, 2nd moon, 14th day. This time, the "tomb" emitted noise, and the crack was the largest ever recorded. This occurred in the middle of the Ōnin War.
23. 1486, 11th moon, 9th day.
24. 1496, 10th moon, 13th day.
25. 1497, 3rd moon, 20th day.
26. 1498, 1st moon, 1st day.
27. 1506, 9th moon, 4th day.
28. 1510, 3rd moon, 4th day.
29. 1510, 11th moon, 25th day.
30. 1511, 3rd moon, 29th day. These last two times, luminous "spirits" were observed flying to the south, and sounds coming from the northwest were heard.
31. 1532, 11th moon, no day.
32. 1533, 3rd moon, 17th day.
33. 1534, 8th moon, 11th day.

34. 1542, 9th moon, 25th day. The mountain also shook in such a manner that it was especially noted.
35. 1607, 4th moon, 2nd day. (See below for details on this occurrence.)
36. in 1636, the mountain shook, but the statue did not suffer any damage.
37. 1711, 1st moon, 14th day. Light gushed forth from the mountain and moved to the north. The text adds the following comment: "Was this in premonition of the fire in the imperial palace the next day?"
38. 1779, 10th moon. There were several tremors between the 21st and the 29th days of that moon; on the 29th, the mountain shook eighteen times.

The item above is the last recorded incident of that nature at Tōnomine. These natural occurrences were considered to be supernatural indications; they usually took place at times when the Fujiwara leaders worried about a political situation over which they had little or no control and tended to cease after a new political order was established. The best example of that phenomenon, which marked the beginning of the premodern period for both Tōnomine and the Kasuga-Kōfukuji multiplex, is discussed below.

POLITICAL EXPEDIENCIES

By the middle of the sixteenth century the Ashikaga shogunate, which never succeeded in establishing a government infrastructure that might enable it to rule Japan effectively, had lost all authority. Ashikaga Yoshiteru was shogun only by name, and real power was in the hands of the Hosokawa family, which held the title of *kanrei*, "deputy shogun." The *kanrei* at the time, Hosokawa Ujitsuna, gave control of Yamato Province to Miyoshi Nagayoshi (commonly called Chōkei, 1523–64), who had been converted to Christianity by Gaspar Vilela and in turn delegated that authority to an ambitious and powerful warrior and temporary ally of Oda Nobunaga, Matsunaga Hisahide (1510–77). In 1553 Hisahide suddenly invaded Yamato Province and declared his rule over it. For the first time in its history the Kōfukuji could do nothing, and the province was governed by outsiders.

In 1559, Hisahide built the Tamonzan Castle in the northern part of Nara, one of the finest castles built in Japan at the time. The Portuguese missionaries who visited there were left breathless by the sumptuousness of the building, which had been achieved with the assistance of merchants of the prosperous city of Sakai. Hisahide, however, was greedy for power; he revolted against the Miyoshi, assassinated Miyoshi Nagayoshi in 1564, and when the shogun Yoshiteru made an attempt to regain power, forced him to commit suicide. At that point the Tsutsui house, of *shuto* background and led by Tsutsui Junkei (1549–84), struck an agreement with Miyoshi's descendants, whose army entered Yamato Province in 1567, installed its headquarters at the Tōdaiji, and encircled the Tamonzan Castle. Undaunted, Hisahide attacked by night and set the Tōdaiji on fire, throwing consternation among the residents of the city. This earned him not only the hatred of Nara's population but the enmity of Oda Nobunaga as well.

Yoshiteru's younger brother, Kakkei, was the abbot of the Ichijō-in *monzeki* at the Kōfukuji; fearing that he too might be assassinated by Hisahide, he fled Nara, resumed the name Yoshiaki, and appealed to a number of warriors in the hope that they might support his desire to become the next shogun. Oda Nobunaga, who saw there a good chance of realizing his own ambitions, accepted and, a few years later, set out to march for Kyoto with Yoshiaki, where they arrived in 1568 and Yoshiaki was made shogun.

The following year, Oda Nobunaga, who was having serious difficulties with Yoshiaki, began to act independently from the shogun and, in spite of his having no official position in the government, granted rule over Yamato to Harada Naomasa. Naomasa died in an attack against the Honganji in Osaka, however, and Tsutsui Junkei allied himself with Nobunaga. At that point, Hisahide declared allegiance to Nobunaga.

When Nobunaga visited Nara in 1574, the city's elders went as far as the Kizu River to welcome him, and he proceeded immediately to the Tōdaiji, where to symbolically mark his power, he took five cuts from the famed Ranjatai incense (as Ashikaga Yoshimasa had done earlier), which had been kept at the Shōsō-in since the Nara period. Nobunaga also ordered that some of the sacred deer of Kasuga be moved to Kyoto. The Kōfukuji remained still: in 1573 Nobunaga had deposed the shogun Yoshiaki.

In 1577, Matsunaga Hisahide broke his alliance; however, because of a bad turn of events, he was encircled by Nobunaga's troops and fled to the Shigisan Castle, where he was killed. Tsutsui Junkei then became, to the relief of the Kasuga-Kōfukuji multiplex and its population, the ruler of Yamato in 1580; he dismantled the Tamonzan Castle and used its foundation stones to build his own castle at Kōriyama. Nobunaga then ordered the shrines and temples to declare their revenues and checked those claims carefully: this was the *sashidashi* of 1580, according to which the Kōfukuji declared an assessed revenue of 18,209 *koku*, and Tōnomine, 6,000 *koku*. By comparison, the Tōdaiji declared a mere 1,500, while the Daijō-in *monzeki* declared 950, and the Kasuga Shrine, 500 *koku*.

Oda Nobunaga was assassinated by Akechi Mitsuhide in Kyoto in 1582.

Akechi, however, was defeated shortly thereafter by Toyotomi Hideyoshi, who became regent three years later, in 1585.

After ordering Tsutsui Sadatsugu, Junkei's adopted son and successor, to move to Iga Ueno, Hideyoshi gave rule over the provinces of Yamato, Kii, and Izumi to his half-brother, Hidenaga. Hidenaga settled in Kōriyama and began a steady encroachment on the property of the multiplexes, cutting their revenues peremptorily. Thus, the Kōfukuji's revenues were cut by ten thousand *koku*, and again by seven thousand *koku*, in 1586.

In 1588 Hideyoshi instructed Hidenaga to remove the Tōnomine multiplex and rebuild it in Kōriyama, and he granted it a revenue of three thousand *koku*, half of what it had been a few years earlier. The multiplex at Tōnomine was supposed to remain intact, but in fact all the temples were destroyed and the *shuto* were dispersed. Hidenaga then ordered the markets of Nara shut, hoping to thereby force their wealthy merchants to Kōriyama and have them break their ties to the Kasuga-Kōfukuji multiplex. Three years later, Hidenaga fell ill. It was revealed in an oracle that his illness had been caused by a malediction (*tatari*) on the part of Kamatari's spirit, which would have been angered by the move. Hidenaga then returned to the Kōfukuji the seven thousand *koku* of revenue that had been taken from it, in order to "pay for rites and prayers asking for a swift recovery from the ailment."

Hidenaga died, however, in 1591, and was replaced at the head of Yamato Province by Hideyoshi's adopted son, Hideyasu. Meanwhile, in other parts of Japan, Tokugawa Ieyasu gained power and it became clear that Toyotomi Hideyoshi's control was coming to an end. In 1600 Masuda Nagamori, who headed Kōriyama, opened the doors of his castle to Ieyasu, who put his vassal Ōkubo Nagayasu in charge of Yamato Province. This was the beginning of a new age for Yamato. In 1602, Tokugawa Ieyasu went on a "pilgrimage" to Nara, where in good tradition, he also took a few cuts from the Ranjatai incense. He subsequently ordered that the city of Nara be thoroughly quadrangled and reorganized.

In 1607, a formidable earthquake hit Tōnomine: "The mountain shook and roared, and many luminous flying phenomena were observed by the people, who felt great fear." A few months later, a tall pine tree growing on the peak behind the mausoleum "split suddenly, from its top to its roots, and people from various provinces came to see this extraordinary phenomenon." The *Tōnomine haretsuki*, which was written for this occurrence, states that the mountain was in a state of disrepair and no priests had lived there for twenty-four years, that is, since the site of cult had been moved to Kōriyama.

Because of that supernatural event, however, special funds were requested from the Tokugawa government in order to install priests in thirty-two halls. The incident was taken most seriously by aristocrats and warrior-bureaucrats in Kyoto, and a divination was performed through the agency of a child who had been possessed by Kamatari's spirit. The multiplex was then rebuilt, the statue restored, and rituals were performed under the supervision of Yoshida priests. These rituals, which are called "Secret Shinto Rituals" (shintō no hihō) in the document, are not described, but they were performed over several days, and the Yoshida priests requested attendance on the part of monks of the Shōren-in monzeki, the Tendai temple that had authority over Tōnomine. Thereafter, various rituals of purification were completed, and seven Nō plays were performed. Finally, a Hokke-hakkō Ritual Assembly was held. The tables had turned: Shinto priests were now ordering Buddhist prelates around.

This was the last major change at Tōnomine, which remained untouched until 1868. Consequently, life at Tōnomine during the Edo period was slow and uneventful. The shrine-monks established a reputation of vanity, for they did not hesitate to display throughout the period a power they charged with all the authority and prestige of the Shōren-in monzeki of Kyoto or the Tō-Eizan of Edo. If the deified ancestor of the Fujiwara house had been able to "dim his radiance and mingle with the dust," those responsible for his cult were apparently unable to do the same; criticism of this kind was leveled at Buddhist monks in Japan throughout the Edo period and reached its peak in 1868.

The events mentioned above indicate that the sixteenth century marked the end of the traditional association between Japan's multiplexes and the aristocracy. When the warriors of the sengoku period asserted their new theories of power to back their military practices, the Buddhist temples and Shinto shrines of old had no operative part in those theories. Many multiplexes were systematically weakened; some, like Mount Hiei, were razed to the ground. Comparatively speaking, the Kasuga-Kōfukuji multiplex fared better than most.

EARLY MARKS OF DISSOCIATION

The two and a half centuries that passed between the unification of Japan by Tokugawa Ieyasu and the fall of the Tokugawa shogunate in 1868 saw a continuous erosion of the Kasuga belief system, a steady loss of land on the part of the multiplex, the emergence of various factions that attempted to seize control of Yamato Province, and, finally, the complete fall of the Kasuga multiplex. This fall was seen as a disaster by some, but as a liberation by others. Its causes were multiple; some were remote, others proximate. We will examine below several of those causes, emphasizing those that will allow a better understanding of the dramatic upheaval that occurred in 1868, when the government ordered that the *kami* be dissociated from the buddhas and bodhisattvas in all sites of cult throughout Japan.

First and foremost among the immediate causes of the fall of the Kasuga-Kōfukuji multiplex was the stratification of society in Yamato Province. When lands in the province changed hands, the degree of submission to the multiplex and to its ideology on the part of the landholders, which generally proved resistant to change, became infinitely smaller. Furthermore, the taxation system was inefficient and incompatible with a modern state.

Another reason for its failure was that Kasuga was structured to support imperial rule within a given sociopolitical context, but not the rule of the Tokugawa shogunate—which in many ways was different from the Kamakura and Muromachi shogunates. Thus, even though the Tokugawa government respected Kasuga, the multiplex could never play an active part in that government, for profoundly structural reasons. During most of the Edo period the Kasuga multiplex served as little more than a repository of the dormant ideals of a classical society. The ideology that supported Tokugawa rule had nothing to do with Kasuga or the Kōfukuji, while the ideology that supported the deification of deceased Tokugawa rulers issued mainly from the Tendai form of Shinto-Buddhist combinations, Sannō Ichijitsu Shintō, which was created by Tenkai (Jigen Daishi, 1536–1643).

One might expect that those multiplexes that had expressed a proimperial stance throughout their history would have been favorably treated in 1868, when the emperor came back to the throne. That, however, was far from being the case. The type of rule advanced by many multiplexes governed by ecclesiastic elites was no longer viable; peasants who worked in the fields owned by cultic centers shook off their yoke, and various segments of society began to express strong criticism of the clergy, which could not, either ideologically or practically, answer the needs of the times.

This situation ultimately led to the declaration that multiplexes formed of Buddhist and non-Buddhist institutions should be broken up. It is not that this separation occurred suddenly in 1868. Sporadic separations had occurred as early as the seventeenth century in several parts of the country where Neo-Confucianism had an early impact, especially in those places where warriors controlled all the land and all power, which until then had been in the hands of multiplexes.

The first major recorded separation took place in 1666 under the rule of Tokugawa Mitsukuni (Mito Kōmon, 1628–1700) in the domain (*han*) of Mito, north of Kashima and Tsukuba. Because of the geographical proximity of Mito to these cultic centers, because Kashima was so closely related to the Kasuga cult, and because that separation became a model for subsequent nationwide edicts, this historical event deserves some attention.

In the mid–seventeenth century the feudal domain of Mito had 2,377 temples, which belonged to the following lineages: 1,351 were Shingon, 289 Yamabushi, 206 Tendai, 132 *Gyōnin* (lay mountain ascetics), 190 Pure Land, 174 Zen, and 35 Nichiren. In 1665 the government of the Mito *han* created the office of "supervisor of shrine-temple multiplexes" (*jisha bugyō*); its role was to control the economic basis of those institutions, to investigate the ethics of the monastic communities, and perhaps also to keep Christianity in check. As a result of that office's investigations, in 1666 the number of temples was reduced by half, from 2,377 to 1,279.[8] The ecclesiastics and their retainers who served in those temples and shrines were ordered to return to the lay life and to become productive members of society. Those whose behavior was deemed unethical were simply chased out. The temples' landholdings were sold, and the people who lived near those institutions were reorganized around the remaining temples and shrines according to a new household registration system (*danka seido*).[9]

These decisions were followed by orders to build one shrine for each village unit (this took thirty years) and to remove all Buddhist objects of cult from the shrines and replace them with "Shinto" emblems. Accordingly, Buddhist statues and ritual implements were all removed, and in their stead, mirrors and stones were installed. Subsequently, it was decreed that shrines were to be administered by sacerdotal lineages, not by Buddhist ecclesiastics, and that all sanctuaries with combinatory names be renamed. This proved to be extremely difficult in the case of sanctuaries dedicated to Hachiman, which were by nature all combinatory: of the seventy sites dedicated to Hachiman, thirty were renamed, and the others were destroyed. Thus, 80 percent of the 555 shrines in Mito *han* were forced to change their emblems of cult. If anything, this shows how pervasive combinations between *kami* and buddhas/bodhisattvas had been. Despite those changes, however, the beliefs did not change much; a good reason for this is that the newly installed priests (*kannushi*) of the shrines were, in many cases, the very monks who had been forced to return to lay life. Over a couple of centuries, however, cosmetic changes have a tremendous impact.

A second movement of dissociation occurred in Mito during the Tempō period (1830–44), under the rule of the feudal lord Tokugawa Nariaki (1800–1860). By that time the Mito School was producing a number of political thinkers who rallied under the banner of Neo-Confucianism against Buddhism, while ardently supporting the return to imperial rule.

Several of those thinkers, notably Fujita Tōkō (1806–55) and Aizawa Yasushi (1781–1863), wrote forcefully against Buddhism and for Shinto, though their arguments were sometimes tendentious and almost totally ignorant of Buddhist doctrine. Those people saw the temples solely in the light of their greed and their service as funeral organizers (which was forced on them by the Tokugawa regime), within an ethic in which sexual license and homosexuality had no place. Furthermore, they considered Buddhism to be a foreign, dangerous, and imperialistic series of lies that could not provide a rationale for the new state that they had in mind.

The major cultic centers close to Mito (Kashima and Katori, Tsukuba, and Nikkō) were all combinatory, and therefore religious life in Mito was based on the combinations of various influences that taken together formed a consciousness that was difficult to assess but, nonetheless, was judged to be antithetic to the ideals of the new state that the Mito School was nurturing. As exemplified by the Mito *han's* treatment of the popular cult of the catfish pictures of Kashima,[10] popular cults were to be controlled, if not completely forbidden. Such was the atmosphere throughout the Edo period, as demonstrated by the case of the Fuji cult, which was outlawed several times in the course of that period, though for reasons different from those given in limiting the Kashima cult.[11]

Combinatory popular cults that did not have structural similarities to the state posed a major political problem. The solution of many late Tokugawa ideologues to that problem was to wipe out Buddhism and create a well-organized but simplistic ritual for divinities that were to be renamed. Some of the attacks on Buddhism were grounded in the most obvious argument: monks were not productive, and temples were too rich. More seriously, the doctrines the monks preached, especially those related to the combinations of Shinto and Buddhist divinities, were against the order of things seen by the ideologues of the Nativist Studies movement (*kokugaku*), which tried to "purify" Japanese culture of all its foreign accretions and thus reveal what was thought to be essentially Japanese in character. Buddhism, they argued, did not deserve authority or power of any kind, because it could foment trouble by supporting a type of communitas that the government could not condone: this was the case of the Kashima catfish pictures, the Fuji cult, and many others in the country. Indeed, many of those popular cults were gradually "purified" of their Buddhist contents, and their ideology tended to become increasingly nationalistic and in favor of the imperial system.

In 1832, the feudal government of Mito issued the following orders:

1. That temples be "reorganized." (This means that 190 temples were destroyed.)

2. That, for the protection of the nation, which Buddhism seemed to be so eager to play a role in, temples should surrender their bronze bells and all other metal implements, so that they could be turned into guns to fight the enemy. (323 bells and 600 metal ritual implements were turned in.)

3. That all combinations between Shinto and Buddhist divinities be discontinued, and that all shrines be run by Shinto priests under the authority of the Yoshida lineage. All combinatory divinities were to be renamed in such a way that no trace of their earlier association could be seen, and shrines were to be allotted regular revenues.

4. That civil registers be kept in shrines instead of in temples as had been the case, and that a new system of registration (*ujiko seido*) replace the former one (*danka seido*). Births, adoptions, marriages, and deaths were to be recorded by Shinto priests; furthermore, all funerals were to be conducted as "Shinto" ceremonies.

This last order was not executed as firmly or swiftly as the others, for it entailed truly drastic changes in the lives and habits of the people, and the ritual and administrative infrastructures necessary for that change had not been put into place.

The third order, according to which combinatory cults were to be abolished and places of cult run by priests under Yoshida authority, is of interest because it contains a fine historical irony in the case of mausoleums dedicated to Tokugawa Ieyasu and his descendants. In 1616, the Yoshida branch of Shinto built a mausoleum to take care of the deified spirit of Ieyasu in a sumptuous cultic center located on a hill overlooking the Pacific Ocean at Kunō, not far from Mount Fuji. Tenkai, the head of the Tendai lineage and a counselor to Ieyasu, managed, however, to have the Tokugawa government deny Yoshida further responsibility for the rites in commemoration of Ieyasu and built instead a major mausoleum at Nikkō under the auspices of Sannō Ichijitsu Shintō, which he had conceived. Replicas of this mausoleum were built in many parts of the country, including Mito, to serve as reminders of the power of the Tokugawa house. As a result of the aforementioned decrees of the Mito government, the mausoleum in Mito, dedicated to Ieyasu and ritually ruled by Sannō combinations, was forced to revert to being a shrine ruled by Yoshida Shinto. As can be imagined, the shogunate in Edo did not particularly appreciate this move on the part of Mito.

In 1868, the Tokugawa shogunate lost all control of the government, and the emperor returned to power. The new government, using the Mito proscriptions as a model, decreed a nationwide proscription of combinatory cults, thus causing all *kami* to be dissociated from their Buddhist counterparts. The effect of that decree on the Kasuga-Kōfukuji multiplex will now be examined.

1868: THE YEAR OF CULTURAL TRANSVESTIVISM

On the very day on which the Kōfukuji received the order that all sites of cult in the nation dissociate all *kami* from their Buddhist counterparts, all the monks deserted their temples in a move unprecedented in the history of Japan. The major ecclesiastics of the Main Temple and the two *monzeki*, noble seeds and members of good houses alike, hurried to the Kasuga Shrine, where they changed their vestments and instantly became "Shinto" priests. From the security of their new abode, the heads of the two *monzeki* sent a missive to the government's newly reestablished Office of the *kami* of Heaven and Earth (*jingikan*), parts of which stated:

> We have learned that, with the declaration of the Meiji Renewal, the status of shrines has been changed. In the case of the Kasuga Shrine there have been, since ancient times, sacerdotal lineages and other priestly figures; it must be emphasized, however, that their function was merely to serve in front of the *kami*. As for the Kōfukuji, it has always acted in concert with the shrine. For instance, it has always provided rice for food offerings through the year, has taken responsibility for the upkeep and reconstruction of the shrines, and has, in effect, managed the forests, the lighting, and the deer population of the shrine. In particular, the Kōfukuji has administered the festive rite of the Wakamiya Shrine [the *On-matsuri*], as well as the Takigi-Nō performances. Moreover, the position of Abbot of this institution has always been filled in rotation by the heads of the Daijō-in and Ichijō-in *monzeki*, which have governed all other temples of the cultic center. From times of old the Kōfukuji has served the Great *kami* of Kasuga; in point of fact, all monks of the entire cultic center have been "shrine monks" [*shasō*].
>
> Should we be allowed to change vestments and become priests of Kasuga, we are confident that this would permit us to better serve the Way of the Emperor.
>
> Furthermore, since a lack of administrative unity might cause conflicting views to arise, we hereby respectfully request an Imperial order to the effect that we should govern both the shrines and the temples of the multiplex.[12]

The major ecclesiastics of the Kōfukuji thus penetrated the shrine once more and immediately moved to control the sacerdotal lineages of the shrine; they were, so to speak, not of Fujiwara birth for nothing. To this request the government swiftly sent the following answer:

> We hereby grant the entire population of the Kōfukuji its request to become priests of the Kasuga Shrine. As for the remainder of the request, we shall answer in the near future. It is hereby ordered that after the change of vestments the concerned persons shall call themselves "new priests" [shin-kami-tsukasa], and that they shall serve at the Kasuga Shrine as they have done in the past. The members of the Ichijō-in and Daijō-in monzeki shall wear a ceremonial dress, while all other members of the various temples shall wear a simple priestly dress. However, all Buddhist implements of cult which are in the Kasuga Shrine must be returned to the Kōfukuji.

The Office of the kami of Heaven and Earth then sent a missive to the sacerdotal lineages of Kasuga stating that the Kōfukuji monks had been allowed to become Shinto priests and ordering that swift action be taken to ensure the proper division of labor and administrative tasks. The office thus precluded any conflict between the ancient sacerdotal lineages and the newly arrived "priests," who were, in fact, charged with the reorganization of the cultic center. The heads of the twenty major temples of the Kōfukuji who thus became priests not only let their hair grow and changed their attire, but they also immediately applied for new lay names to the prefectural government. This request was granted. In most of these new names one can recognize elements of the names of the temples that those people had headed; for example, the head of the Shōrin-in simply read the Sino-Japanese name of his temple in the Japanese pronunciation, and thus took the family name Matsubayashi.

Thereafter the new administration of the multiplex called a meeting of all the subtemples of the Kōfukuji and informed them of the developments, announcing that official ties were thereafter severed. Thus 107 temples, 18 of which were major institutions, found themselves on their own. Whatever remained of the ancient network was completely dismantled. The economic base of the system and all affiliations, ritual and otherwise, were wiped out.

These decisions were taken at a time when it was feared that the policy of dissociations was in fact a hidden attack on Buddhism. Indeed, reports that many centers of cult in various parts of the country had become the objects of severe attack were filtering to Nara, and the phenomenon of dissociation between the kami and the buddhas was followed by a rejection of Buddhism known as haibutsu-kishaku, "Abolish the buddhas, Reject

Śākyamuni." The dissociations had been accompanied in quite a few cases by the spontaneous rejection of Buddhism and by outbursts of violence.

The Meiji revolution (*Meiji ishin*) was yet another drama on the stage of history, another performance through which new cultural forms were born. The Meiji ideologues hoped that the script rehearsed in Mito and played to a national audience in 1868 would bring about a dramatic return to the past. For multiplexes such as Kasuga, however, it turned out to be a tragedy. The prelates of the Kōfukuji could not have been unaware that the dissociations that had taken place at the cultic center of Mount Hiei, for example, had engendered violence and astounding acts of impiety: all "Buddhist" implements of cult in the Hie Shrines had been removed by angry mobs and smashed to the ground or burned. In some places in the country, people had been forced to write with their own blood oaths that they would never worship the Buddha again. Answering complaints from major Buddhist lineages, the central government quickly asserted that the intent of the dissociations had nothing to do with a mass prohibition of Buddhism, and it made a few weak efforts to curb the violence. It took three years, however, for the anti-Buddhist movement to abate.

In Nara the now deserted Kōfukuji was loosely cared for by the Saidaiji, but it could not protect the enormous multiplex, so pilfering took place. The elegant five-storied pagoda was sold for the trivial amount of twenty-five yen. It was even argued by the new owner that it should be burned down so that the precious metal fixings could be retrieved, but popular fear that the fire might spread to the city prevented that disaster from happening. In 1871 the anti-Buddhist mood reached its culmination; many temples of the ancient cultic center were destroyed, and only a few buildings of the Main Temple were left standing. Both *monzeki* were entirely destroyed: the splendid garden designed by Jinson disappeared; the main pavilion of the Ichijō-in *monzeki* was torn down and rebuilt at the Tōshōdaiji, where it can still be seen today. The new prefectural government, established in 1871, thus acquired large parcels of vacant land on which to erect its buildings, which symbolically were built on the sites of the former centers of power.

Realizing that their situation at the shrine would not allow them to live as they used to, the former heads of the *monzeki* left Kasuga, moved to Tokyo, and settled there with titles of nobility borrowed from Europe.

A few years later, when the rest of the once priestly population of the Kōfukuji felt that the situation was no longer dangerous, it began to worry about the fate of the temples and even requested the government's permission to become monks once again and return to the grounds of the temples to take care of them. It took the efforts of two pioneers in the preservation of cultural artifacts, Ernest Fenollosa and Itō Tadahiro, to save what remained of the great temples of Nara and to protect them from total destruction.

Fenollosa (1853–1908), a Harvard graduate who had been invited to teach philosophy in Tokyo and who developed an appreciation for Buddhist art, spent several years buying statues and paintings from various sites of cult, thus saving them from destruction, and making gifts of them to the Tokyo Museum (many of those were destroyed in the subsequent fires and earthquakes that devastated Tokyo). Fenollosa became part of a governmental effort to save the treasures of Japan's classical past. Accompanied by Okakura Tenjin, he visited the temples and shrines of Nara and bought whatever he could, and he wrote various pieces to demonstrate that Japanese Buddhist art was of world class in quality, profundity, and elegance. He thus saved, among other treasures, the painting of Kisshōten that had belonged to the Yakushiji, and revealed to the world the classic elegance of the Kannon statue of the Yumedono at the Hōryūji.[13]

Itō Tadahiro was the first Japanese historian of architecture to see the importance and beauty of classical temple architecture. In 1889 he published "Studies on the Architecture of the Hōryūji," a pivotal work that contributed to the passing of the Law of Protection of Shrines and Temples in 1897. Unfortunately, this law came too late for the Kōfukuji, for in 1871 the Ichijō-in *monzeki* had become the new tribunal of Nara Prefecture and the Daijō-in *monzeki* had been sold and destroyed.[14]

The phenomena of the dissociation of the *kami* and buddhas/bodhisattvas and the temporary rejection of Buddhism have been largely ignored by modern scholars, whose efforts have focused on the "modernization" of Japan, that is, its industrialization and adoption of Western modes and institutions. It is my contention, however, that the interpretations of the Meiji so-called Restoration produced by many of those scholars are structurally flawed because they fail to take into consideration what happened to the immense world of shrines and temples, and thus they fail to show the real nature of the Meiji government's claim that it was trying to bring about a return to the Age of the *kami* and to reestablish institutions created by the System of Codes.

In fact what happened in Meiji was a momentous restructuring of ritual and liturgy that transformed religious consciousness. It is not the purpose of these concluding remarks to discuss this restructuring in detail, but the following two points may give some indication of the far-reaching changes that occurred then.

As soon as the movement to reject Buddhist institutions abated, it was replaced by a movement to rebuild Buddhism. This movement was led by intellectuals and scholars who were fully aware of the condition into which Buddhism had fallen but who also believed that Buddhism still might have some contributions to make to the spiritual and intellectual life of the nation. Efforts to rebuild Buddhism developed less along lineage lines or cultic center lines (they were abolished) than along purely intellectual paths. Inoue Enryō (1858–1919), Kiyozawa Manshi (1863–1903), Suzuki Daisetsu (1870–1967), and others spent all their energies rebuilding Buddhism and purifying it of its major accretions. And yet, while everybody claimed that Buddhism had played a central role in the cultural history of Japan, nobody claimed that combinatory phenomena had been a central part of that history. Shinto-Buddhist combinations had become a taboo subject and remained so, even in academia, for almost a century.[15] New combinations, though, appeared immediately: Inoue Enryō used Western philosophical tools to interpret Buddhism, and he erected a building dedicated to Śākyamuni, Socrates, and Kant at the school he created, which is now Tōyō University in Tokyo. The work of Suzuki Daisetsu, which is better known, is also indebted in part to Western cultural notions and needs. In the past few decades many scholarly Buddhist priests have devoted their lives to the revitalization of Buddhism.

The institutional bonds between shrines and temples, however, were completely abolished; indeed, it is only from the beginning of this century that we can speak of Shinto shrines and Buddhist temples. Shinto as we know it today is a new religion.

None of the Nara ecclesiastics were leaders in the movements of reformation and renewal; they simply followed. Spiritual life in Nara had fundamentally changed, and new tendencies had already surfaced toward the end of the Edo period. For example, the new religion called Tenri-kyō had appeared next to the Isonokami Shrine and was beginning to spread in the prefecture. Gradually, however, the Kōfukuji—or, rather, what remained of it—slowly came back to life, invigorated by the presence and activity of monks of the Hossō and Ritsu lineages who came from its former subtemples.

Among them, Kitagawa Chikai is worthy of note: the head-priest of the Mibudera in Kyoto and then of the Tōshōdaiji in Nara, he reacquired some of the former grounds of the Tōshōdaiji, as well as all the statues and paintings of the temple that he could find. He then did the same for the Kōfukuji, concentrating on scriptures and documents. He worked to have the Ritsu lineage made independent of the Shingon lineage and appealed to this effect to the government in Tokyo in 1896. His request was granted in 1901. Kitagawa died in 1947 at the Tōshōdaiji, proud of his efforts; but there was barely enough rice to make conventional offerings at the time of his funerals. Meanwhile, a certain Kōchō, the head-priest of the Saidaiji, began to take care of what remained of the Kōfukuji, and monks slowly began to return to the temple. The Tōdaiji became the headquarters of the Kegon lineage in 1887, and in 1891 the Hōryūji, the Yakushiji, and the Kōfukuji were jointly appointed to be the headquarters for Hossō.

The Kasuga-Kōfukuji multiplex never regained its past splendor or its importance in the lives of the people of Nara. Its economic base had been entirely destroyed, its ritual integrity shattered, and its spiritual character impoverished beyond description. The depth of the Meiji dissociations and their impact on Japanese religiosity have yet to be measured, but it is obvious that they were profound. What had been perceived as combined elements were now separated, and a rift was created between the people and their past. Almost every aspect of the world of meaning of the Kasuga multiplex had been rejected, and this rejection manifested itself even at the level of the physical being of the multiplex: temples and shrines were separated, rituals were drastically changed, and buildings and objects destroyed.

About twenty years after these events, when people started to take a new look at their environment, they came to view the multiplex in a different light. Statues, paintings, and buildings became part of a heritage to be looked at and, perhaps, appreciated, but not lived; the past was now at one remove from consciousness. What had been cultural operatives were now pieces in museums, forms to be studied because it was felt that they were hiding—and might reveal—something about the Japanese "spirit." It was in this context that Watsuji Tetsurō wrote his *Pilgrimage to Ancient Temples*, a book that marked a different attitude toward the past and became quite famous. The attitude of Watsuji was not only his; it was widely shared by most Japanese of the time, who had shed their kimonos and dressed like Westerners just as suddenly as the monks of the Kōfukuji had changed their robes to become priests of Kasuga and just as Kabuki actors perform quick changes of appearance on the stage. In 1918 Watsuji Tetsurō wrote:

> We arrived in Nara at dusk. . . . My companion muttered that for some reason, after our stay in Kyoto, he felt disquieted in Nara. Certainly the distinction between the world of the *Manyōshū* and that of the *Kokinshū* could also be perceived in the landscapes [of Nara and Kyoto]. . . . We went to the restaurant, and met there what I thought must be a French family. . . . This was the first time I saw French people in the flesh—it might seem strange that I should be interested in this cosmopolitan matter since we had come to Nara on a pilgrimage

to ancient temples, but what I felt then was not at odds with our purpose. For the pilgrimage that we were making was a quest for "Art" and not a quest for the Buddha whose purpose is the salvation of living beings. If it happened that in front of a Buddhist statue we would, from the bottom of our hearts, incline our heads in reverence, or that, struck by the radiance of compassion, we would wipe tears from our face, it was not from a feeling of conversion to Buddhism but rather because we were vanquished by the power of art to express the spirit of Buddhism. We did not go beyond our senses to the point of becoming religious. Such was the reason why, in the restaurant, we were in the mood to let our eyes and tongues rejoice. . . . On our way back we walked along the solitary paths of the Kasuga Plain. Those woods are beautiful at any time of the year, but this was exactly the time at which young green leaves adorn the trees, when the attention is drawn by large and ancient cryptomeria and cypress trunks standing in the foliage. The wisterias were in full bloom, one could see their blossoms all the way to the tops of the trees. I had the impression that the vision of old, according to which this was the Deer Park of Benares, could be realized right then in these woods. But, walking a few steps to the main street that borders the Park, we suddenly found ourselves in a totally different world, and entered the realm of popular entertainment: Nara was indeed a "famous site" [*meisho*]. And what we saw was something you could see nowhere but in Nara. It is not that it was bad, but the way in which the mood effected by that view differed from that aroused by the classical statues of the Sangatsu-dō was most obscure.[16]

Nara, ancient sacred city, residence of the gods, center of an entire province ruled by a shrine-temple multiplex for about a thousand years, had become a tourist attraction. Thousands of people still see the festivities of the Wakamiya Shrine and pay their respects to the main shrine on the new year; attendance at the Grand Rite of Kasuga is by invitation only and is restricted to about fifty people, and the *On-matsuri* has become a cultural asset protected by the government. The performance of rituals on the temporary stage erected in front of the Wakamiya *otabisho* is still one in which the past is recalled and preserved. In virtue of its historical status the Kasuga Shrine was supported by the government until the end of the Second World War, when it lost all official affiliations with the state (although a recent visit by the emperor was a major event). It is administered, in principle, by the Bureau of Shrines (*Jinja honchō*). Several of its priests are of Fujiwara ancestry. What remains of the Kōfukuji is today the administrative center of the Hossō School, a position it shares with the Yakushiji (the Hōryūji created its own religious sytem). The entire Hossō lineage has today 42 temples, 180 monks, 279 nuns, and a grand total of 594,931 lay adherents.[17]

In spite of the structural changes that have affected the shrine-temple multiplex during the past century, however, the Kasuga belief system represents one of the most fascinating aspects of the Japanese tradition and is a perfect example of the remarkable continuity some Japanese cultural patterns have exhibited for over a millennium.

IS KASUGA A MODEL FOR ALL JAPANESE MULTIPLEXES?

In order to suggest the validity of structural model-building for interpreting the multiplex-based aspects of Japanese social and religious history, I want to return to the three propositions stated at the beginning of this study.

The first proposition—that Japanese religiosity is grounded in specific sites at which beliefs and practices were transmitted within specific lineages—was conceived with more than the Kasuga-Kōfukuji multiplex in mind. It should be applicable also to the twenty-two shrine-temple multiplexes sponsored by the state during the Heian period—that is, to the entire Kinai area.[18] Moreover, many other places of cult can and should be the object of the same type of approach, for many major centers—such as the Hachiman belief system in Kyushu, as well as Aso, Unzen, Hiko, Itsukushima, Daisen, Santokuzan, Kumano, Hakusan, Mount Fuji, Chichibu, Nikkō, Dewa Sanzan, Iwaki and others—were structured along similar lines. Historically, a shift can be observed from the emphasis on the place of cult to a new emphasis on the cult of place. If differences are found, these differences ought to be appreciated for the light they throw on the way the Japanese have gone about establishing competing constructs of reality. As I have stressed in this study, the notion of place must be considered seriously when engaging in the analysis of belief systems in Japan. Moreover, lineages played a central role in the evolution of sites of cult, whether those lineages were sacerdotal, as in the realm of shrines; liturgical and philosophical, as in the realm of temples; or sociopolitical (or quasi-sacerdotal), as in the case of the Fujiwara house.

In regard to the second proposition—that Japanese religiosity is neither Shinto, nor Buddhist, but combinative—it has been demonstrated that systems of combination, though widely spread, are to be appreciated individually within the context of specific sites of cult. To approach the issue from the point of view of either Shinto or Buddhism as separate traditions leads only to abstractions that distort geographical and historical reality.

Furthermore, several types of rationales have been suggested for further study: first, possible broadly linguistic rules; and second, the institutional and economic developments, both of which supported the evolution of a theory of the state and imperial rule in which these systems of combination played a central role.

In regard to the third proposition (that those combinative systems were linked to social and economic structures as well as concepts of power, all of which were embodied in rituals), it has been demonstrated that shrine-temple multiplexes were also ceremonial centers in which rituals should not be separated artificially from questions of legitimacy. One could push the question even further by suggesting that ritual modes of action sustained mental representations on which constructs of reality rested. Finally, the hypothesis that specific sites of cult were linked to social morphology was meant to suggest that social conflicts were an important factor in the evolution of belief systems. If it is true, in the case of Kasuga, that a rite such as the *On-matsuri* was the result of complex interactions between shrines and temples and between aristocratic and popular cultural systems, then the same questions should be asked of all ritual performances in all sites of cult. It was not by chance that every major sociopolitical change in the history of Japan was accompanied by reformulations of ritual.

The purpose of this study is not only to make sense of sites of cult as special cases in the Japanese tradition; it also means to suggest a wider concern for the formulation of an adequate theory of power in the Japanese cultural context. The fundamental hypothesis of this work is that sites of cult are the best symbolic representatives of the cultural systems that determined in great part the evolution of Japanese history: they are a nexus in which the forces responsible for that history are clear. The study of sects and founders can never lead to that kind of realization, unless such study is fully integrated within the larger cultural discourse out of which such sects and people emerged and in the context of which they thought and acted.

There is, finally, room for some reservations concerning the overall applicability of the various models advanced in this study. Obviously, some aspects of the Japanese tradition will inevitably escape efforts to reduce everything to a few models that have been tested on a single multiplex. For example, the Jōdo Shinshū tradition and the Nichiren lineages might be approached differently because in some ways they appeared as antitheses to the ideology created by multiplexes, even though they themselves established major centers of cult. The case of Zen might sit somewhere between the Heian multiplexes and the Jōdo Shinshū case, though it has its own intricacies. Naturally, the models advanced in this study are not applicable to modern Japanese society. Nor are they meant to be. What is meant is that studies of contemporary phenomena that ignore the premodern constructs will never be able to offer a comprehensive understanding of the matrix out of which they emerged or, in great part, against which they reacted. What remains of the premodern systems in contemporary Japan is a "culture of place," a different sense of lineage and ancestors, and a propensity to combine cultural systems; all these ought to be appreciated for their own value.

Finally, there is a need for more systematically interdisciplinary studies and for methodological refinement concerning all the issues raised above. Geographers and sociologists have recently produced impressive studies of the question of time and space in social practice, but there is a need for a framework that would allow more disciplinary walls to crumble, for to date not enough have done so, even under the great weight of evidence that this is what must happen.

This study was undertaken with the premise that a single site of cult might be used as a window through which some aspects of Japanese culture might be studied. Whether that premise was adequate or not is a question that is now open for debate.

Notes

1. Throughout this work the Japanese term *jisha* is translated as "shrine-temple multiplex." The term does not mean "Buddhist temples and Shinto shrines" but local units whose significance resides in the relations between shrine and temple.

2. The word *kami* has been variously translated as god, deity, divinity, spirit, demon, force, and so on. Because none of those terms is adequate, the word *kami* is left untranslated throughout this study. The word *divinity*, as used in this study, refers to an entity that is the result of combinations between one or more *kami* and a buddha or a bodhisattva.

3. On this important topic see, for example, Frits Staal, "Substitutions de Paradigmes et Religions d'Asie," *Cahiers d'Extrême-Asie* 1, no. 1 (1985): 21–57.

4. Although the term *shake* does not appear in documents before the medieval period, it denotes a social and liturgical reality long predating that time. It will be discussed in chapter 2.

5. For a study of the Chroniclers of Mount Hiei, see Kuroda Toshio, trans. Allan Grapard, "Historical Consciousness and *Hon-jaku* Philosophy in the Medieval Period on Mt. Hiei," in *The Lotus Sutra in Japanese Culture*, ed. George and Willa Tanabe (Honolulu: University of Hawaii Press, 1989), 143–58.

6. Kuroda Toshio suggests that the exclusivism of the early Pure Land tradition caused a kind of renaissance in the world of shrines, starting with a reaction on the part of the Kasuga-Kōfukuji multiplex. See "Chūsei kokka to shinkoku shisō," in Kawasaki Tsuneyuki, ed., *Chūsei kokka to shūkyō*, vol. 1 of *Nihon shūkyō-shi kōza*, ed. Ienaga Saburō et al. (Tokyo: San'ichi Shobō, 1971), 67–72.

7. Kuroda Toshio, *Jisha seiryoku* (Tokyo: Iwanami Shoten, 1980), 21. See also Neil McMullin, *Buddhism and the State in Sixteenth-Century Japan* (Princeton: Princeton University Press, 1985).

8. The exact role of the Hakusan belief system in relation to the Eiheiji, the center of Sōtō Zen, has not yet been studied in detail despite its importance. Neither is there a study of the Toyokawa Inari cult, an early Edo period phenomenon that includes elements of native worship of the fox in combination with the *dakini* worship found in Esoteric Buddhism, all under the aegis of Sōtō Zen monks. The first shrine dedicated to a combinatory cult of the *dakini* was created by Eisai in the Kenninji after his return from China in the thirteenth century.

9. On the topic of the *komusō* see the regular publications by the Fukeshū in Kyoto, *Myōan shakuhachi Zen* (Kyoto: Myōanji), beginning in 1973. See also James Sanford, "*Shakuhachi* Zen: The Fukeshū and Komusō," *Monumenta Nipponica* 32, no. 4 (Winter 1977): 411–40.

10. The writings of Takuan Sōhō (1573–1645), who had direct contact with the world of shrines and "Shinto" theories, are pervaded by esotericism. See, in particular, *Fudō chijin myōroku*, ed. Ikeda Satoshi (Tokyo: Tokuma Shobō, 1970). Suzuki Shōzan was thoroughly engaged in *kami* worship and esotericism. See Royall Tyler, trans., *Selected Writings of Suzuki Shōzan*, Cornell University East Asia Papers, vol. 13 (Ithaca: Cornell University Press, 1977). Hakuin's writings smack of Taoism and Neo-Confucianism; for instance, an extant scroll in his calligraphy, which is in my possession, is dedicated to the "Oracles of the Three Shrines" (*sansha takusen*). See R. D. M. Shaw, trans., *The Embossed Tea Kettle* (London: George Allen & Unwin, 1963).

11. Most pre-T'ang texts that debate the merits of the Three Teachings are collated in the *Hong-ming tsi* and *K'uang Hong-ming tsi*, in *Taishō Daizōkyō*, vol. 52. A brief historical survey of the contents of these texts is found in Allan Grapard, *Kūkai: La Vérité Finale des Trois Enseignements* (Paris: Poesis, 1985), 11–28.

12. There is no systematic survey of this type of literature or of the problem it addresses in the Japanese context, though this appears to be necessary to formulate Japan's premodern history of ideas. This problem has been raised at the levels of the elite and popular traditions as early as Kūkai in the late eighth century, and as late as the eighteenth century by Taiga (who quotes Kūkai in his *San'i-kun*) and others. See Kashiwahara Yūsen and Fujii Manabu, eds., *Kinsei bukkyō no shisō* (Tokyo: Iwanami Shoten, 1973).

13. Kuroda Toshio, "Shinto in the History of Japanese Religion," trans. James Dobbins and Suzanne Grey, *Journal of Japanese Studies* 7, no. 1 (Spring 1981): 1–21.

14. On this topic see Ōsumi Kazuo, ed., *Chūsei Shintō-ron* (Tokyo: Iwanami Shoten, 1977).

CHAPTER ONE

1. Paul Wheatley and Thomas See, *From Court to Capital: A Tentative Interpretation of the Origins of the Japanese Urban Tradition* (Chicago: University of Chicago Press, 1978).
2. The history of the establishment of the Mirokuji in Usa supports this view. See Nakano Hatayoshi, *Hachiman shinkō-shi no kenkyū* (Tokyo: Yoshikawa Kōbunkan, 1983), 2:501–42.
3. Wheatley and See, *Court to Capital*, 88.
4. Ibid., 91.
5. See Cameron Hurst III, "An Emperor Who Ruled as Well as Reigned," in *Great Historical Figures of Japan*, ed. Murakami Hyōe and Thomas Harper (Tokyo: Japan Culture Institute, 1977), 16–27.
6. Quoted by Ueda Masaaki, *Fujiwara no Fuhito* (Tokyo: Asahi Shimbun-sha, 1976), 40.
7. There were three exceptions during the Nara period: Kose no Asomi, Ishikawa no Asomi, and Fumimuro no Mahito. See Ueda Masaaki, *Kodaishi no ibuki* (Kyoto: PHP Kenkyūjo, 1981), 92.
8. Kondō is quoted in Wheatley and See, *Court to Capital*, 99.
9. Hosaka Hiroshi, ed., *Ōkagami* (Tokyo: Kodansha, 1981), 469. The *Ōkagami* is available in English in Helen McCullough, trans., *Ōkagami, the Great Mirror: Fujiwara Michinaga (966–1027) and His Times* (Princeton: Princeton University Press, 1980).
10. This position is firmly taken by Ueda Masaaki in *Fujiwara no Fuhito*, 40–66.
11. Tamura Enchō, *Fujiwara no Kamatari* (Tokyo: Hanawa Shobō, 1966), 25–26.
12. On the cult to Kamatari see Allan Grapard, "Japan's Ignored Cultural Revolution: The Separation of Shinto and Buddhist Divinities (*shimbutsu bunri*) and a Case Study, Tōnomine," in *History of Religions* 23, no. 3 (February 1984): 240–65, and below, chapter 5.
13. This map is reproduced in Nishida Nagao, *Shintō-shi no kenkyū* (Tokyo: Risōsha, 1957), 32. The problem has been discussed again by Okada Shōji, "Kasuga-sha no seiritsu," in *Heian jidai no jinja to saishi*, ed. Nijūnisha Kenkyūkai (Tokyo: Kokusho Kankōkai, 1987), 8–20.
14. Details on the Wani house and the Kasuga "clan" can be found in Inoue Tatsuo, *Kodai ōken to shūkyō-teki bemin* (Tokyo: Kashiwa Shobō, 1980), 189–256.
15. Nishida Nagao, *Shintō-shi no kenkyū*, 12–75.
16. Ibid., 22.

17. See Aoki Kazuo, Inaoka Shōji, Sasayama Haruo, and Shirafuji Noriyuki, eds., *Shoku Nihongi* (Tokyo: Iwanami Shoten, 1989–90), 1:151 and 2:38.

18. This chronicle is discussed in Kuroda Noriyoshi, *Kasuga taisha kenchiku-shi ron* (Kyoto: Sōgeisha, 1978), 23–58.

19. Nagashima Fukutarō, *Nara bunka no denryū* (Tokyo: Meguro Shoten, 1951), 10.

20. The *jingūji* phenomenon is discussed at length in chapter 3.

21. See Donald Philippi, trans., *Kojiki* (Tokyo: University of Tokyo Press, 1968). See also W. G. Aston, trans., *The Nihongi* (Rutland, Vt.: Tuttle, 1972).

22. See Philippi, *Kojiki*, 59 n. 2.

23. Ibid., 129–31.

24. See Akimoto Kichirō, ed., *Fudoki* (Tokyo: Iwanami Shoten, 1958).

25. Ibid., "Hitachi Fudoki," 35.

26. Ibid., 81.

27. Ibid., 59.

28. Ibid., 16.

29. See Philippi, *Kojiki*, 54–55, 180–85.

30. Ibid., 540. See the heading "Opo."

31. Yamagami Izumo, *Nihon geinō no kigen* (Tokyo: Yamato Shobō, 1977), 120–84.

32. Akimoto, *Fudoki*, 60.

33. Ibid., 67.

34. Ibid., 71.

35. Ibid., 65.

36. On Kashima, see Miyai Yoshio, *Fujiwara-shi no ujigami-ujidera shinkō to somyō saishi* (Tokyo: Seikō Shobō, 1978); Inoue Tatsuo, *Kodai ōken to shūkyō-teki bemin* (Tokyo: Kashiwa Shobō, 1980); Ōbayashi Taryō and Yoshida Atsuhiko, *Tsurugi no kami, tsurugi no eiyū* (Tokyo: Hōsei University Press, 1981); Yokota Ken'ichi, *Nihon kodai shinwa to shizoku denshō* (Tokyo: Hanawa Shobō, 1982); and Shintō Taikei Hensankai, ed., *Shintō Taikei*, vol. 22 (Tokyo: Seikōsha, 1984).

37. Akimoto, *Fudoki*, 69–71.

38. Ibid., 43.

39. See Mishina Shōei, *Mishina Shōei rombun-shū* (Tokyo: Heibonsha, 1970), 2:255–373. For Mishina's views on Jingū Kōgō and her son, see 4:55–128.

40. See Inoue Tatsuo, *Kodai ōken to shūkyō-teki bemin*, 184–255, especially 204, 208, 217–18, and 221.

41. Akimoto, *Fudoki*, 67.

42. Ibid., "Hizen Fudoki," 387.

43. Ibid., 16.

44. Ibid., 65. The term *arare-furu* may also mean "hallowed."

45. Ibid., "Hizen no kuni itsubun," 515.

46. Ibid., 403.

47. *Manyōshū*, vol. 3, *Yamatsumie uta*, poem no. 385. See H. Honda, trans., *Manyōshū* (Tokyo: Hokuseidō Press, 1967), 36. Honda translates the poem as follows: "Kishimi's peak is steep / and no grass growing / I helped my wife / together to ascend."

48. Akimoto, *Fudoki*, 41–42.

49. Yamagami Izumo, *Nihon geinō no kigen*, 120–50.

50. Philippi, *Kojiki*, 82–83.

51. On the Nakatomi and Urabe sacerdotal lineages, see Inoue Tatsuo, *Kodai ōken to shūkyō-teki bemin*, 125–255; Yokota Ken'ichi, *Nihon kodai shinwa to shizoku denshō*, 1982, 221–302; Okada Shōji, "Yoshida Urabe-shi no hatten," in *Shintō-shi ronsō*, ed. Takigawa Masajiro sensei beiju kinen rombun kankōkai (Tokyo: Kokusho Kankōkai, 1984), 699–720.

52. Quoted in Wheatley and See, *Court to Capital*, 75.

53. See Inoue, *Kodai ōken to shūkyō-teki bemin*, 189–256.

54. The texts relating the origins of the Kōfukuji are found in Suzuki Research Foundation, ed., *Dai Nihon Bukkyō Zensho*, vol. 84 (Tokyo: Kodansha, 1972), where they are collected under the title *Kōfukuji sōsho*. They include the *Kōfukuji ruki*, compiled toward the end of the Heian period, which was used for the following discussion and is itself made up of several documents: the *Kōfukuji engi* (dated 900); the *Tempyō-ki*, which covers the period 729–48; the *Hōji-ki* (757–64); the *Enryaku-ki* (782–806); the *Kōnin-ki* (810–23); and other documents that do not concern us here.

55. See Aiga Tetsuo, ed., *Kōfukuji*, vol. 5 of *Meihō Nihon no bijutsu* (Tokyo: Shōgakkan, 1981), 33–52.

56. See chapter 3 below.

57. Kuroda Toshio, "Shinto in the History of Japanese Religion," 1–21.

58. See Matsushita Takemi, "Nan'endō kyū-honzon to Kamakura saiko-zō," in Aiga Tetsuo, *Kōfukuji*, 114–53.

59. See the *Keiran-shūyōshū*, in *Taishō Daizōkyō*, vol. 76, no. 2410, 799. Hereafter abbreviated as T. and followed by the volume and text numbers.

60. Kuroda Noriyoshi, *Kasuga taisha kenchiku-shi ron*, 10.

61. Felicia Bock, trans., *Engi-shiki: The Procedures of the Engi Era* (Tokyo: Sophia University Press, 1972), 2:71–72.

62. Quoted in Wheatley and See, *Court to Capital*, 75.

63. Some of the main studies on this topic are Fukaura Seibun, *Yuishiki-gaku kenkyū*, 2 vols. (Kyoto: Nagata Bunshodō, 1955–64); Ueda Yoshi-fumi, *Yuishiki shisō nyūmon* (Kyoto: Asoka Shorin, 1977); Yokoyama Kōitsu, *Yuishiki no tetsugaku* (Kyoto: Heirakuji Shoten, 1979), and *Yuishiki shisō nyūmon* (Tokyo: Daisan Bunmeisha, 1976); Hattori Masaaki and Ueyama Shumpei, eds., *Ninshiki to chōetsu: Yuishiki* (To-

kyo: Kadokawa Shoten, 1978); Hirakawa Akira, Kajiyama Yūichi, and Takasaki Jikidō, eds., *Yuishiki shisō* (Tokyo: Shunjūsha, 1982); Takemura Makio, *Yuishiki no kōzō* (Tokyo: Shunjūsha, 1985); Hattori Masaaki, *Dignāga, on Perception* (Cambridge, Mass.: Harvard University Press, 1968); Yuki Reimon, *Seshin Yuishiki-setsu no kenkyū* (Tokyo: Aoyama Shoin, 1956); Fukihara Shōshin, *Nihon Yuishiki shisō-shi*, 3 vols. (Tokyo: Kokusho Kankōkai, 1988–89), and *Nihon Chūsei Yuishiki shisō-shi* (Tokyo: Daitō Shuppansha, 1976), which is the only history of Hossō lineages in Japan in the medieval period. For a comprehensive bibliography of scriptures related to Hossō, see Yuki Reimon, *Yuishiki-gaku tenseki-shū* (Tokyo: University of Tokyo Press, 1962).

64. T., vol. 31, no. 1593.

65. Ibid., 1590.

66. Ibid., 1585. For an English translation of this text see Wei Tat, *Ch'eng Wei-shih Lun: Doctrine of Mere Consciousness* (Hong Kong: The Ch'eng Wei-shih Lun Publication Committee, 1976).

67. See Endō Yoshimoto and Kasuga Kazuo, eds., *Nihon ryō-i-ki* (Tokyo: Iwanami Shoten, 1967), part 1, 122.

68. A cult dedicated to the angry spirit of Hirotsugu was developed in the Matsuura Shrine in Kyushu. See Murayama Shūichi, *Honji-suijaku* (Tokyo: Yoshikawa Kōbunkan, 1974), 77.

69. A fine fictional rendering of those events appears in Shelley Midans, *The Vermilion Bridge* (New York: Doubleday, 1980).

70. On Dōkyō see Ross Bender, "The Hachiman Cult and the Dōkyō Incident," *Monumenta Nipponica* 22 (Summer 1978): 165–78.

71. The philosophy of the school is presented briefly in Takakusu Junjirō, *Essentials of Buddhist Philosophy* (Honolulu: University of Hawaii Press, 1947), 80–95.

72. A black-and-white reproduction of the complete scroll is contained in Noma Seiroku, ed., *Kasuga gongen genki emaki* (Tokyo: Kadokawa Shoten, 1963).

73. See Paul Groner, *Saichō: The Establishment of the Japanese Tendai School* (Berkeley: Asian Humanities Press, 1984).

74. See Kuroda Toshio, *Ōbō to Buppō* (Kyoto: Hōzōkan, 1983).

CHAPTER TWO

1. Miyai Yoshio, *Fujiwara-shi no ujigami-ujidera shinkō to somyō-saishi* (Tokyo: Seikō Shobō, 1978), 363–72.

2. Endō Yoshimoto and Kasuga Kazuo, eds., *Nihon ryō-i-ki* (Tokyo: Iwanami Shoten, 1967). Chapter 41 in the second book, p. 293, and chapter 24 of the third book, p. 385, are prime examples.

3. Quoted by Miyai, *Fujiwara-shi*, 374.

4. Edward Seidensticker, trans., *The Gossamer Years* (Rutland, Vt.: Tuttle, 1964), 17.

5. The terms *shuto* and *jinin* will be defined below, under the heading "From Ceremonial Center to Sacred City."

6. For a definition of the *Hokke-hakkō* ceremonies, see Willa Jane Tanabe, "The Lotus Lectures: Hokke hakkō in the Heian Period," *Monumenta Nipponica* 39, no. 4 (Winter 1984): 393–407.

7. See descriptions of those rites in Murayama Shūichi, ed., *Hieizan to Tendai bukkyō no kenkyū* (Tokyo: Meicho Shuppan, 1976), 285–316.

8. Takakusu Junjirō and Watanabe Kaigyoku, eds., *Taishō Shinshū Daizōkyō*, vol. 31, no. 1585 (Tokyo, 1912–25).

9. Reproductions of these Kasuga editions can be seen in John Rosenfield et al., eds., *The Courtly Tradition in Japanese Art and Literature* (Cambridge: Fogg Art Museum, Harvard University, 1973), 58, 66, and 72.

10. Miyai, *Fujiwara-shi*, 377.

11. *Taiki*, quoted by Miyai, *Fujiwara-shi*, 380. For other examples, see Miyai, 91.

12. Noma Seiroku, ed., *Kasuga gongen genki* (Tokyo: Kadokawa Shoten, 1963), 40.

13. *Sadanobu-kō ki*, quoted by Miyai, *Fujiwara-shi*, 384.

14. See Nakano Hatayoshi, *Hachiman shinkō-shi no kenkyū*, 2 vols. (Tokyo: Yoshikawa Kōbunkan, 1975), 1:109–30.

15. A *monzeki* is a temple that is run by an aristocratic lineage. For a discussion of the history of the *monzeki* see below under "The Medieval Organization of the Kōfukuji."

16. The iconographic directions for the representation of this divinity are contained in the *Fukū-kensaku-jimpen-shingon-kyō*, in T., vol. 20, no. 232.

17. See Robert Morrell, "Passage to India Denied," *Monumenta Nipponica* 37, no. 2 (Summer 1982): 179–200.

18. See Raoul Birnbaum, *The Healing Buddha* (Boulder: Shambala, 1980).

19. The following discussion is based on Hayami Tasuku, *Jizō shinkō* (Tokyo: Hanawa Shobō, 1975), 10–17.

20. T., vol. 13, no. 411; T., vol. 13, no. 412; and T., vol. 17, no. 839.

21. Endō and Kasuga, *Nihon ryō-i-ki*, book 3, chap. 9, pp. 339–43.

22. See Nara Kokuritsu Hakubutsukan, ed., *Suijaku bijutsu* (Tokyo: Kadokawa Shoten, 1964), figures 4 and 7; Kageyama Haruki, *Shintō bijutsu* (Tokyo: Yūzankaku, 1973), figure 26.

23. See Gorai Shigeru, "Nihonjin no jigoku to gokuraku," a series of sixteen articles published monthly in *Daihōrin* in 1975–76.

24. See Miyai, *Fujiwara-shi*, 234–43.

25. See Nara, *Suijaku bijutsu*, figures 1–8 and 13–16.

26. See ibid., figures 19 and 25. See also Kageyama Haruki, *Shintō no bijutsu* (Tokyo: Shibundō, 1967), 30, figure 36; and Kurata Bunsaku, *Zōnai nōnyūhin* (Tokyo: Shibundō, 1973), 57–60.

27. This issue will be discussed in greater detail in chapter 4.

28. Nara, *Suijaku bijutsu*, 16.

29. Suzuki Research Foundation, ed., *Dai Nihon Bukkyō Zensho* (Tokyo: Kodansha, 1972), 84:315–28. (See chapter 1, note 54.)

30. See chapter 4 for an enlarged discussion of this concept.

31. See Nara, *Suijaku bijutsu*, figure 13; and Kageyama, *Shintō no bijutsu*, figure 41.

32. Other mountainous areas of Japan have been envisioned as the residence of Kannon in this world. See Allan Grapard, "Kūkai: Stone-Inscription for the Monk Shōdō, Who Crossed Mountains and Streams in His Search for Awakening," in *The Mountain Spirit*, ed. Michael Tobias and Harold Drasdo (New York: Overlook Press, 1978), 51–59; and Grapard, "Flying Mountains and Walkers of Emptiness: Toward a Definition of Sacred Space in Japanese Religions," *History of Religions* 21, no. 3 (February 1982): 195–221.

33. Japanese scholars have argued over whether the disk that is represented over Mount Mikasa in the various shrine mandalas is the sun or the moon. See Yamaori Tetsuo, *Nihon shūkyō-bunka no kōzō to sokei* (Tokyo: Tokyo University Press, 1980), 257–86.

34. See Allan G. Grapard, "Institution, Ritual, and Ideology: The Twenty-two Shrine-Temple Multiplexes of Heian Japan," *History of Religions* 27, no. 2 (November 1987): 246–69.

35. Quoted by Miyai, *Fujiwara-shi*, 115.

36. See chapter 3 under the heading "The Sacred Tree: Growth of Ritualized Violence" for a detailed discussion of the phenomenon.

37. Of several versions of this text, two differ on various points: the text that accompanies the extant version of the paintings is printed in Hanawa Tokinoichi, ed., *Gunsho Ruijū* (Tokyo: Zoku Gunsho Ruijū Kanseikai, 1954–60), 2:1–57; and the "Kasuga go-ruki" is printed in *Dai Nihon Bukkyō Zensho*, 84:366–84. The text used in the present discussion is Noma, *Kasuga gongen genki*, 40–60.

38. See Royall Tyler, *The Miracles of the Kasuga Deity* (New York: Columbia University Press, 1990), 157–292.

39. This conceptualization of the place of the arts is not a Kasuga phenomenon proper but belongs to a wider discussion that took place in Japan during the Heian and Kamakura periods. Some took the position that the arts were detrimental to the search for Awakening, while others took the opposite stance. Kasuga *daimyōjin* takes a clear position in this respect, which is related to the fact that the *kami* are worshiped through the performance of dances and music. It is possible that the reasons that led some to reject music were less philosophical and more social and economic in nature: mentions of the extravagance of rituals are an indication of this. See Herbert Plutschow, "Is Poetry a Sin?" in *Oriens Extremus* 25, no. 2, (1978), 206–18. See also chapter 4. It is worth comparing these disputes

to those that arose in Europe in the medieval period: see, for example, Umberto Eco, *Art and Beauty in the Medieval Ages* (New Haven: Yale University Press, 1985).

40. The Kasuga-Kōfukuji multiplex was the largest landholding multiplex in Japan and the largest landholder of the country next to the *sekkanke* and the imperial house. See Atsuta Kō, "Jisha shōen no aramashi," *Rekishi-kōron* 5 (May 1978): 98–105. For general discussions of the estate system, see Jeffrey Mass, ed., *Court and Bakufu in Japan* (New Haven: Yale University Press, 1982). See also "Workshop Papers on the Economic and Institutional History of Medieval Japan," ed. and trans. Kozo Yamamura, *Journal of Japanese Studies* 1, no. 2 (Spring 1975): 255–345.

41. The following discussion is based on Nagashima Fukutarō, *Nara* (Tokyo: Yoshikawa Kōbunkan, 1963); Nagashima Fukutarō, *Nara bunka no denryū* (Tokyo: Meguro Shoten, 1951); and Nagashima Fukutarō, *Nara-ken no rekishi* (Tokyo: Yamagawa Shuppan, 1967). I have also used Kuroda Toshio, *Jisha seiryoku* (Tokyo: Iwanami Shoten, 1980).

42. Miyai, *Fujiwara-shi*, 111–12.

43. See Kuroda, *Jisha seiryoku*, especially chapters 1 and 2.

44. Nagashima, *Nara*, 196–213.

45. For a useful study of blind women in Northern Japan, see Fukushima Kunio, "Goze," *Gendai shūkyō* 2 (January 1979): 183–96.

46. See Noma Hiroshi and Okiura Kazuteru, *Nihon no sei to sen*, 2 vols. (Kyoto: Jimbun Shoin, 1985–86). The two volumes cover the medieval period (1985) and the premodern period (1986).

CHAPTER THREE

1. George Sansom, *A History of Japan* (Stanford: Stanford University Press, 1963), 1:165–66.

2. The Buddhist doctrine of "non-twoness," or "non-duality" (*nifuni*, literally, "two-but-not-two"), which proposes that the realm of phenomena is not separable from the realm of essence and that purity and pollution cannot be treated independently from each other, was sometimes loosely interpreted and applied in the Japanese social context in such manner as to intimate an absence of separation between lay and monastic levels and styles of existence.

3. Nagashima Fukutarō, "Nara no rekishi," in *Nara*, ed. Takahashi Yoji (Tokyo: Heibonsha, 1979; Bessatsu Taiyō 27 [Summer 1979]): 113–31, 149–55.

4. Miyai Yoshio, *Fujiwara-shi no ujigami-ujidera shinkō to somyō-saishi* (Tokyo: Seikō Shobō, 1978), 78–86.

5. See the comparative study on Great Monasteries of India, China, and Japan in the dictionary *Hōbōgirin*, under the heading *daiji*. (Paris:

Maisonneuve, and Tokyo: Maison Franco-Japonaise, 1983), 6:679–711.

6. One *chō* corresponded to 10 square *dan* of surface area, and one *dan* corresponded to 360 *ho*, or 495 meters. One *ko* (*goko*) was the smallest administrative unit; it varied a great deal but represented originally a population unit of ten households and was used to calculate taxes.

7. Nagashima Fukutarō, *Nara* (Tokyo: Yoshikawa Kōbunkan, 1963), 86.

8. The *Shūni-e* is discussed in more detail below under the heading "Aesthetics and Ethics: Pleasurable Visions."

9. *Heihanki*, quoted by Miyai, *Fujiwara-shi*, 113.

10. Japanese measurement terms during the medieval period varied widely over time and place. Basic terms were *koku* (about 5.2 bushels of rice, which might correspond to about 44.8 gallons U.S.), *to* (10 *to* equal 1 *koku*), *masu* (10 *masu* equal 1 *to*), and *gō* (10 of which equal 1 *masu*), all in reference to rice volume. In addition, the term *mon* referred to copper coins, which were usually calculated in *kan*, a string of one thousand *mon*. One *kan* is said to have corresponded to one *koku*, although again, equivalences varied tremendously.

11. In *Dai Nihon Bukkyō Zensho*, 84:434–55.

12. Ibid., 456–63.

13. Ibid., 464–66.

14. Hanawa Tokinoichi and Ōta Fujisaburō, eds., *Zoku Gunsho Ruijū* (Tokyo: Zoku Ruijū Kanseikai, 1959–60), 35:213–14.

15. Kuroda Noriyoshi, *Kasuga taisha kenchiku-shi ron* (Kyoto: Sōgeisha, 1978), 23–44.

16. Nagashima, "Kasuga taisha Kōfukuji sōsetsu," in Kinki Nippon Tetsudō, ed., *Kasuga taisha / Kōfukuji* (Osaka: Kintetsu, 1961), 14–17.

17. In *Zoku Gunsho Ruijū*, 37:256–80.

18. See a description of the use of the *kasina* in Ñyāṇamoli Bikkhu, trans., *The Path of Purification* (Berkeley: Shambala, 1976), 1:121–75.

19. Noma Seiroku, ed., *Kasuga gongen genki emaki* (Tokyo: Kadokawa Shoten, 1963), 59. See also illustration no. 48, p. 49.

20. See Kuroda Toshio, *Nihon chūsei no kokka to shūkyō* (Tokyo: Iwanami Shoten, 1975), and Inoue Mitsusada, *Nihon kodai no kokka to bukkyō* (Tokyo: Iwanami Shoten, 1971).

21. See Martin Collcutt, *Five Mounts: The Rinzai Zen Monastic Institution in Medieval Japan* (Cambridge: Harvard University Press, 1981).

22. Émile Durkheim, *Les Formes Élémentaires de la Vie Religieuse*, trans. J. Swain as *The Elementary Forms of the Religious Life* (New York: George Allen & Unwin, 1915; reprint, New York: Free Press, 1965), 51. Original edition, Paris: Alcan, 1912; 4th ed., Paris: Presses Universitaires de France, 1960.

23. See Frits Staal, "The Search for Meaning: Mathematics, Music, and Ritual," *American Journal of Semiotics* (1984): 1–57.

24. See Kuroda Noriyoshi, *Kasuga taisha kenchiku-shi ron* (Kyoto: Sōgeisha, 1978), 7.

25. See Donald Philippi, trans., *Kojiki* (Tokyo: University of Tokyo Press, 1968), 256–98.

26. For other uses of the word *saniwa,* see chapter 4, "The Sacred Space of the Shrine."

27. Philippi, *Kojiki,* 116–17; and W. G. Aston, trans., *The Nihongi* (Rutland, Vt.: Tuttle, 1972), book 1, 269.

28. Some aspects of the following discussion on camphor have been proposed by François Berthier, *La Sculpture Bouddhiste Japonaise* (Paris: Presses Orientales de France, 1976).

29. Aston, *Nihongi,* book 2, 68.

30. Endō Yoshimoto and Kasuga Kazuo, eds., *Nihon ryō-i-ki* (Tokyo: Iwanami Shoten, 1967), 81–88.

31. Aston, *Nihongi,* book 2, 123.

32. Yamagami Izumo, *Nihon geinō no kigen* (Tokyo: Yamato Shobō, 1977), 100–105.

33. For a fine representation of this figurine, see Miki Fumio, ed., *Haniwa* (Tokyo: Shibundō, 1967), plate 1.

34. Akimoto Kichirō, ed., *Fudoki* (Tokyo: Iwanami Shoten, 1958), 60.

35. "Ōmi no kuni itsubun," ibid., 457–58. See below, note 43.

36. "Izu no kuni itsubun," ibid., 450.

37. "Hizen Fudoki," ibid., 390–92.

38. "Harima no kuni itsubun," ibid., 483–84.

39. "Hizen Fudoki," ibid., 390.

40. Quoted by Inoue Tatsuo, *Kodai ōken to shūkyō-teki bemin* (Tokyo: Kashiwa Shobō, 1980), 137.

41. Aston, *Nihongi,* book 1, 225.

42. For a study of the Sumiyoshi Shrine, see Nishimoto Yutaka, *Sumiyoshi taisha* (Tokyo: Gakuseisha, 1977).

43. The "Ōmi no kuni itsubun" of the *Fudoki* offers the following text:

An elder gave the following report: the lake of Ikago is located in the district of the same name in the province of Ōmi south of the village of Yogo. Eight heavenly maidens, having become white birds, descended from Heaven and bathed in a creek south of the lake. At that time a certain Ikatsu-omi, who was standing on a mountain situated to the west, saw these birds and found their appearance most fascinating. Wondering whether these birds were manifestations of the divine, he approached them in secret, and came to the conclusion that they were indeed divine beings. Ikatomi then was overcome with such powerful desires that he could not withdraw. From his hiding place he sent a white dog to steal one of the maidens' heavenly feather robes and managed to secure that of the oldest maiden. Suddenly aware of a presence, the heavenly maidens retrieved their robes and soared back to Heaven, but the oldest one could not fly away, having no robe. The pathways to Heaven being blocked forever, she became a resident of the area. The creek in which the maidens bathed has received the name Creek of the *kami*. Ikatomi also resided there and took the maiden for his spouse; she gave birth to two boys, named Oshimiru and Nashitomi, and to two girls, named Izeruhime and Nazerihime. These are the ancestors of the *muraji* of Ikago. Later, by chance, the maiden found her feather robe and flew back to Heaven. Thereafter, Ikatomi kept solitary to his bed, chanting his despair.

In Akimoto, *Fudoki*, 457–58.

44. There are two versions of this text, in Sakurai Tokutarō, Hagiwara Tatsuo, and Miyata Noboru, eds., *Jisha engi* (Tokyo: Iwanami Shoten, 1975), 169–205, 207–73. The statement about the Kasuga divinities is found in the first version, p. 174.

45. A recent study demonstrates that the Azumi "clan" was the naval force of ancient Japan, and that it was only later that the Azumi came to specialize in preparing imperial food. See Kasai Wajin, *Kodai no suigun*, in Ōbayashi Taryō, ed., *Fune* (Tokyo: Shakai Shisōsha, 1975), 85–116.

46. The name *sei-no-o* is problematic; it is sometimes pronounced *shiwaku* (as in Umehara Haruo, *Kunisaki hantō no rekishi to minzoku* [Oita: Saeki Insatsu, 1975], 80). But the term *sei* is also sometimes pronounced *tae*, which means "fine," or "wonderful," in which case the term may mean "elegant men." On the topic of this most important dance, see Gotō Kiyoshi's historical study in *Kasuga dengaku—sei-no-o chōsa hōkoku*, ed. Honda Yasuji (Nara: Kyōdōsei, 1976), 57–66. See also Takigawa Masajirō, *Yūjo no rekishi* (Tokyo: Shibundō, 1965), 31, 144, 151. Gorai Shigeru has suggested that the origins of the dance may be related to funerary practices. See "Hōmuri to kuyō," *Daihōrin* 6 (1976): 18–25. The reader may also refer to Kagawa Mitsuo and Fujita Seiichi, *Usa* (Tokyo: Mokujisha, 1976). The origins of the dance are reported in an interesting manner in the *Rokugō kaizan Nimmon daibosatsu hongi*; see Allan Grapard, "Lotus in the Mountain, Mountain in the Lotus," *Monumenta Nipponica* 41, no. 1 (Spring 1986): 29–30.

47. Mori Atsushi and Tawara Machi, eds., *Manyōshū* (Tokyo: Shinchōsha, 1990), book 3, poem no. 385.

48. For Jinson's use of the camphor, see chapter 3, "*Daijō-in Jisha Zōjiki*: The World of the *Monzeki*."

49. See the thorough study on the topic by Bernard Frank, *Kata-imi et Kata-tagae: Étude sur les Interdits de Direction à l'Époque de Heian* (Tokyo: Maison Franco-Japonaise, 1958).

50. There is no comprehensive study of the *saijo* phenomenon in Japanese religions. Several articles have been written—but on the participation of the *saijo* in the Kamo festivals. See Felicia Bock, trans., *Engi-*

shiki: The Procedures of the Engi Era, 2 vols. (Tokyo: Sophia University Press, 1970–72). See also Yamagami Izumo, *Miko no rekishi* (Tokyo: Yūzankaku, 1981), 89–122.

51. Quoted in Nagashima Fukutarō, *Nara bunka no denryū* (Tokyo: Meguro Shoten, 1951), 130.

52. The following exposition of the *On-matsuri* is based on my study of the Edo period record entitled *Kasuga Wakamiya sairei ryakki*, first published in Edo between 1716 and 1741 and reprinted by the Kasuga Shrine in 1922. Surprisingly there is no comprehensive study of this grand rite by any Japanese scholar, in spite of its fame and importance. Jinson's short document on the rite is contained in Tsuji Zennosuke, ed., *Daijō-in jisha zōjiki*, 12 vols. (Tokyo: Kadokawa Shoten, 1965), 2:392–408.

53. These pines have been the object of a systematic study by Reiko Ochi, "Buddhism and Poetic Theory: An Analysis of Zeami's *Higaki* and *Takasago*" (Ph.D. diss., Cornell University, 1984).

54. The *hahaka* wood, mentioned in the mythology at the time of divination on deer shoulder bone, was also used at the time of the enthronement ceremony of the emperors. The shrine responsible for the preparation of this fire was the Ikoma Shrine, situated at the eastern foot of Mount Ikoma, the range separating Osaka from Nara.

55. One *gō* equals 0.18 liters.

56. See Laurence Berthier, *Le Omizutori de Nara* (Paris: Presses Orientales de France, 1980).

57. In Suzuki Research Foundation, ed., *Dai Nihon Bukkyō Zensho*, 84:326–27.

58. *Butsumyō-kyō*, T., vol. 19, nos. 440, 441. See the study of the *yamabushi* ceremonies related to this scripture in Wakamori Tarō, *Shugendō-shi no kenkyū* (Tokyo: Heibonsha, 1972), 339–80. See also Shioiri Ryōdō, "Chūgoku bukkyō ni okeru Butsumyō-kyō no seikaku to sono ryūgen," *Tōyō-bunka Kenkyūjo kiyō* 24 (1967): 221–320.

59. The term *rakken* is found in the *Kanfugengyō*, T., vol. 9, no. 277.

60. Tsuji, *Daijō-in jisha zōjiki*.

61. Yoshida Kanetomo was the founder of the combinatory school of Shinto called *Yuiitsu Shintō* and the head-priest of the Yoshida Shrine, which was a duplication of the Kasuga Shrine in Kyoto. See Allan G. Grapard, "The Shinto of Yoshida Kanetomo," *Monumenta Nipponica* (Spring 1992), and "The *Yuiitsu Shintō Myōbō-yōshū*," in press for the following issue.

62. Suzuki Ryōichi, *Daijō-in jisha zōjiki* (Tokyo: Soshiete, 1983).

63. The area of beliefs related to astronomy and astrology in Japan has remained virtually unexplored. I have offered a few thoughts on the topic in "Religious Practices of the Heian Period," in *The Cambridge History of Japan*, vol. 2, ed. Donald Shively and William McCullough (in press).

64. See Nara Kokuritsu Hakubutsukan, ed., *Suijaku bijutsu* (Tokyo:

Kadokawa, 1964), 31–32. See also the study by Ōba Iwao, "Kasuga taisha no kōkogaku-teki kōsatsu," in *Kasuga taisha / Kōfukuji*, ed. Kinki Nippon Tetsudō (Osaka: Kintetsu, 1961), 52–56.

65. Nara, *Suijaku bijutsu*, plate 23.

66. For a fine description of the art of *renga*, see Konishi Jin'ichi, "The Art of Renga," Karen Brazell and Lewis Cook, trans., *Journal of Japanese Studies* 2, no. 1 (Autumn 1975): 29–61.

CHAPTER FOUR

1. Photographs can be seen in Kasuga Kenshōkai, ed., *Kasuga taisha kodai saishi iseki chōsa hōkoku* (Nara: Kasuga taisha, 1979), plates 9 and 10.

2. See representations in Kinki Nippon Tetsudō, ed., *Kasuga taisha / Kōfukuji* (Osaka: Kintetsu, 1961), 53.

3. See Kasuga Kenshōkai, ed., *Kasuga taisha kodai saishi iseki chōsa hōkoku*, plates 11–18.

4. Ueda Masaaki, *Kodai-shi no ibuki* (Kyoto: PHP Kenkyūjo, 1981), 156.

5. Peter Metevelis, "An Interpretation of Tamajari," *Jōyōgakuen daigaku kiyō* 17, no. 1 (Spring 1984): 45–54.

6. Donald Philippi, trans., *Kojiki* (Tokyo: University of Tokyo Press, 1968), 257.

7. Origuchi Shinobu, *Origuchi Shinobu zenshū* (Tokyo: Chūō-Kōron-sha, 1956), 17:292–99.

8. A good example of a case in which a *saniwa* is used both as a court of justice and as a site for medium possession and trance is provided in Akira Kurosawa's film *Rashōmon* (1951).

9. There are several descriptions of the architecture of the Kasuga shrines; the most authoritative is by Kuroda Noriyoshi, *Kasuga taisha kenchiku-shi ron* (Kyoto: Sōgeisha, 1978).

10. This is based upon Inagaki Eizō, ed., *Jinja to reibyō* (Tokyo: Shōgakkan, 1968), 212.

11. Kasuga Kenshōkai, ed., *Kasuga taisha Nara-chō chikuchi-ikō hakkutsu chōsa hōkoku* (Nara: Kasuga taisha, 1977); and Kasuga Kenshōkai, *Kasuga taisha kodai saishi iseki chōsa hōkoku*.

12. See the *norito* used for the rituals for gates of the imperial palace in Felicia Bock, trans., *Engi-shiki: The Procedures of the Engi Era* (Tokyo: Sophia University Press, 1972), 2:83.

13. Ōba Iwao, "Kasuga taisha no kōkogaku-teki kōsatsu," in Kinki Nippon Tetsudō, ed., *Kasuga taisha / Kōfukuji*, 42–56.

14. See Marcel Granet, *La Pensée Chinoise* (Paris: Renaissance du Livre, 1934; reprint, Albin Michel, 1968), especially 77–101 and 283–348.

15. Tamakoshi Yoshio, *Kodai Nihon no sumai* (Kyoto: Nakanishiya, 1980), especially 7–43. As far as I can ascertain, this is the only study of

ritual in relation to space in Japan, even though this book focuses on the space of the house.

16. See the *Kasuga jisha mandara* reproduced in Nara Kokuritsu Hakubutsukan, ed., *Suijaku bijutsu* (Tokyo: Kadokawa Shoten, 1964), color plate 1, black-and-white plate 2.

17. See for instance the reproductions of the shrine-temple multiplexes in Naniwada Tōru, ed., *Koezu* (Tokyo: Shibundō, 1972).

18. As noted in chapter 2, n. 33, Yamaori Tetsuo disagrees with the notion that it is the sun that is represented in Kasuga paintings.

19. Bernard Frank, *Kata-imi et Kata-tagae: Étude sur les Interdits de Direction à l'Époque de Heian* (Tokyo: Maison Franco-Japonaise, 1958).

20. The following description is based on Fukuyama Toshio, ed., *Chūsei no jinja kenchiku* (Tokyo: Shibundō, 1977), 95–96.

21. On the topic of Onmyōdō in the Japanese tradition, see Murayama Shūichi, *Nihon onmyōdō-shi sōsetsu* (Tokyo: Hanawa Shobō, 1981); Saitō Tsutomu, *Ōchō-jidai no onmyōdō* (Tokyo: Sōgensha, 1947); and Fukunaga Mitsuji, *Dōkyō to Nihon bunka* (Kyoto: Jimbun Shoin, 1982). See also Felicia Bock, *Classical Learning and Taoist Practices in Early Japan*, Center for Asian Studies Occasional Paper no. 17 (Tempe: Arizona State University Press, 1985).

22. *Kusha-ron* (T., vol. 29, no. 1558). French translation by Louis de la Vallée Poussin, *L'Abhidharmakośa de Vasubandhu*, 6 vols. (Bruxelles: Institut Belge des Hautes Études Chinoises, 1971). The following is based on Sadakata Akira, *Shumisen to gokuraku* (Tokyo: Kodansha, 1973).

23. See a medieval drawing representing cosmography and cosmology in John Rosenfield et al., eds., *The Courtly Tradition in Japanese Art and Literature* (Cambridge: Fogg Art Museum, Harvard University, 1973), 104–9.

24. For a larger treatment of the concept of Buddha Land, see *Hōbōgirin* (Paris: Maisonneuve, and Tokyo: Maison Franco-Japonaise, 1929–), 2: 198–203, entry on *Butsudo*.

25. *Daichido-ron* (T., vol. 25, no. 1509). French translation by Étienne Lamotte, *Le Traité de la Grande Vertu de Sagesse*, 5 vols. (vols. 1–2, Louvain: Bibliothèque du Muséon, 1944, 1949; vols. 3–5, Louvain: Institut Orientaliste, 1970, 1976, 1980).

26. From Charles Luk, trans., *The Sutra of Vimalakīrti* (Berkeley: Shambala, 1972), chapter 1. Other translations of the scripture are: (French) Étienne Lamotte, *L'Enseignement de Vimalakīrti* (Louvain: Bibliothèque du Muséon, 1962); English translation by Sara Boin, *The Teaching of Vimalakirti* (London: Pali Text Society, 1976); and Robert Thurman, *The Holy Teaching of Vimalakīrti* (University Park: Pennsylvania State University Press, 1976).

27. On the topic of Kasuga paintings, see Kageyama Haruki, *Shintō bijutsu* (Tokyo: Yūzankaku, 1973), 160–90.

28. On representations of the Mountain of the Numinous Eagle in Chinese and Japanese art related to the Lotus Sutra, see Willa Jane Tanabe, *Paintings of the Lotus Sutra* (New York: Weatherhill, 1988). For projections of the sacred mountain onto Japanese landscapes, see Allan G. Grapard, "Enmountained Text, Textualized Mountain: The Lotus Sutra in the Kunisaki Peninsula," in *The Lotus Sutra in Japanese Culture*, ed. George and Willa Jane Tanabe (Honolulu: University of Hawaii Press, 1989), 159–89.

29. Noma Seiroku, ed., *Kasuga gongen genki*. I have used the version of the text contained in *Nihon emakimono zenshū*, vol. 15 (Tokyo: Kadokawa Shoten, 1963), 40–60.

30. A good reproduction of the Kasuga Pure Land Mandala kept at the Nōman-in can be seen in Sasaki Gōzō and Okumura Hideo, eds., *Shintō no bijutsu* (Tokyo: Gakken, 1979), plate 145.

31. A reproduction of this interesting theme can be seen in ibid., plate 152.

32. Robert Morrell, "Passage to India Denied," *Monumenta Nipponica* 37, no. 2 (Summer 1982): 179–99.

33. On the Valley of Hell of Kasuga, see Gorai Shigeru, "Nara no hijiri," in *Nara*, ed. Takahashi Yoji (Tokyo: Heibonsha; Bessatsu Taiyō 27 [1979]), 124–28.

34. See details of Jizō in Hell and Pure Land in Okazaki Yūji, ed., *Jōdo-kyō ga* (Tokyo: Shibundō, 1970), plate 6. See also Murayama Shūichi, *Jōdo-kyō geijutsu to Mida shinkō* (Tokyo: Shibundō, 1967), 201–39.

35. See, for instance, Sasaki Gōzō and Okumura Hideo, eds., *Nihon bijutsu zenshū* (Tokyo: Gakushū Kenkyūsha, 1979), plate 150.

36. See a reproduction of this mandala in Sasaki Gōzō and Okumura Hideo, eds., *Shintō no bijutsu* (Tokyo: Gakken, 1979), plate 145.

37. A black-and-white reproduction of the Kasuga Pure Land mandala kept at the Nezu Museum can be seen in Okazaki, *Jōdo-kyō ga*, plate 52, p. 49.

38. A reproduction can be seen in ibid., plate 7.

39. Kyōto Kokuritsu Hakubutsukan, ed., *Kami-gami no bijutsu* (Kyoto: Kyoto National Museum, 1974), plate 14.

40. This dream is reported in "Kasuga go-takusen no ki," in *Dai Nihon Bukkyō Zensho*, 84:358–65.

41. Sasaki and Okumura, *Shintō no bijutsu*, plate 152.

42. See descriptions of these in Miyai Yoshio, *Fujiwara-shi no ujigami-ujidera shinkō to somyō saishi* (Tokyo: Seikō Shobō, 1978), 455–76.

43. A reproduction of the Descent of Amida featuring a *koto* player can be seen in Takada Osamu and Yanagizawa Taka, eds., *Butsu-ga* (Tokyo: Shōgakkan, 1969), plates 115–18, p. 132.

44. On this topic see Herbert Plutschow, "Is Poetry a Sin?" *Oriens Extremus* 25, no. 2 (1978): 206–18.

45. Kuroda Toshio, *Ōbō to buppō* (Kyoto: Hōzōkan, 1983), 8–51.

46. Kuroda Toshio, *Jisha seiryoku* (Tokyo: Iwanami Shoten, 1980), 34–76.

47. Paul Varley, trans., *A Chronicle of Gods and Sovereigns: Jinnōshōtōki of Kitabatake Chikafusa* (New York: Columbia University Press, 1980), 49–56.

48. Kuroda Toshio, *Nihon chūsei kokka to shūkyō* (Tokyo: Iwanami Shoten, 1975).

49. A good example is provided by the events surrounding the cracked statue of Kamatari at Tōnomine. See below, chapter 5. A further example is offered by the rituals requested by the state during the thirteenth century to protect Japan from invasion by the Mongols. See Nakano Hatayoshi, *Hachiman shinkō-shi no kenkyū* (Tokyo: Yoshikawa Kōbunkan, 1983), 2:816–29.

50. Quoted from Theodore de Bary, ed., *Sources of the Japanese Tradition* (New York: Columbia University Press, 1958), 1:266.

51. Ibid., 267.

52. See table 8, above.

53. See W. G. Aston, trans., *Nihongi* (Rutland, Vt.: Tuttle, 1972), 265.

54. Kūkai, *Shōryōshū, vol. 9, no. 97. Katsumata Shunshō*, ed., *Kōbō daishi zenshū* (Tokyo: Sankibō, 1973), 3:384–86.

55. Ibid., vol 9, no. 96, 3:384.

56. Suzuki, *Dai Nihon Bukkyō Zensho*, 84:328, 358–65.

57. For a good discussion of time and power, see Jacques Attali, *Histoires du Temps* (Paris: Fayard, 1982).

58. Takeuchi Rizō, ed., *Heian ibun* (Tokyo: Tōkyōdō, 1965), vol. 13, *Kinseki-bun* no. 86, pp. 89–90.

59. Most representative of that trend within the Fujiwara house was Fujiwara no Kanezane. See Miyai, *Fujiwara-shi*, 505–14.

60. Inoue Mitsusada and Ōsone Shōsuke, eds., *Ōjōden, Hokke-genki* (Tokyo: Iwanami Shoten, 1974), 9–42, 221–498.

61. Kuroda Toshio, "Chūsei kokka to shinkoku shisō," in *Nihon shūkyō-shi kōza*, ed. Kawasaki Tsuneyuki (Tokyo: San'ichi Shobō, 1971), 1:61–146. See, especially, 1:63–73.

62. Reiko Ochi, "Buddhism and Poetic Theory: An Analysis of Zeami's *Higaki* and *Takasago*." Ph.D. diss., Cornell University, 1984.

63. This translation is adapted, with apologies, from Thomas Rimer and Yamazaki Masakazu, trans., *On the Art of Nō Drama* (Princeton: Princeton University Press, 1984), *Fūshikaden*, 172–256.

64. Stanley Weinstein, "The Concept of Reformation in Japanese Buddhism," in *Nihon bunka kenkyū kokusai kaigi gijiroku*, ed. Nihon bunka

kenkyū kokusai kaigi gijiroku henshū iinkai (Tokyo: Nihon Penkurabu, 1973), 1:602–13.

65. The most thoughtful studies on the topic have been made by Kuroda Toshio; see, in particular, *Jisha seiryoku* (Tokyo: Iwanami Shoten, 1980), 11–38. See also, more recently, Neil McMullin, *Buddhism and the State in Sixteenth-Century Japan* (Princeton: Princeton University Press, 1985).

66. See chapter 1. Western scholars specialize in the study of the school in India and China.

67. Takemura Makio, "Jiron-shū, Shōron-shū, Hossō-shū," in Hirakawa Akira, Kajiyama Yūichi, and Takasaki Jikidō, eds., *Kōza: Daijō bukkyō* (Tokyo: Shunjūsha, 1982), vol. 8: *Yuishiki shisō*, 263–301. The statement quoted above is found on p. 289. See also Hiraoka Jōkai, ed., *Nara bukkyō* (Tokyo: Yūzankaku, 1980), vol. 1, *Nihon bukkyō kiso kōza*, 212–21.

68. See Fukihara Shōshin, *Nihon Chūsei yuishiki bukkyō-shi* (Tokyo: Daitō Shuppansha, 1975), 28–47.

69. See Gorai Shigeru, *Kōya hijiri* (Tokyo: Shibundō, 1960).

70. Fukihara Shōshin, *Nihon Chūsei Yuishiki bukkyō-shi*, 50–51.

71. Nagazumi Yasuaki and Shimada Isao, eds., *Kokonchomonjū* (Tokyo: Iwanami Shoten, 1966), 96.

72. See Tanaka Hisao, *Myō-e* (Tokyo: Yoshikawa kōbunkan, 1961); and Shirasu Masako, *Myō-e shō-nin* (Tokyo: Shinchōsha, 1974).

CHAPTER FIVE

1. This chapter is, in part, a revised version of my "Japan's Ignored Cultural Revolution: The Separation of Shinto and Buddhist Divinities (*shimbutsu bunri*) and a Case Study, Tōnomine," *History of Religions* 23, no. 3 (February 1984): 240–65.

2. In Hanawa Tokinoichi, ed., *Gunsho Ruijū* (Tokyo: Zoku Gunsho Ruijū Kanseikai, 1959–60), 24:424–54.

3. Suzuki Research Foundation, ed., *Dai Nihon Bukkyō Zensho* (Tokyo: Kodansha, 1970–73), vol. 85, no. 738.

4. Ibid., no. 737.

5. *Gunsho Ruijū*, 24:424–54. See also Suzuki, *Dai Nihon Bukkyō Zensho*, vol. 85, no. 736.

6. Suzuki, *Dai Nihon Bukkyō Zensho*, vol. 85, no. 739.

7. Miyai Yoshio, *Fujiwara-shi no ujigami-ujidera shinkō to somyō saishi* (Tokyo: Seikō Shobō, 1978), 408–54.

8. The Mito reports are based on Tamamuro Fumio, *Shimbutsu bunri* (Tokyo: Kyōikusha, 1979), 22–56.

9. On this topic see Kenneth Marcure, "The *Danka* System," *Monumenta Nipponica* 40, no. 1 (Spring 1985): 39–67.

10. See Cornelius Ouwehand, *Namazu-e and Their Themes* (Leiden: Brill, 1964).

11. See Inobe Shigeo, *Fuji no shinkō* (Tokyo: Meicho Shuppan, 1983).

12. This document and the following one are taken from Murakami Senjō, Tsuji Zennosuke, and Washio Junkei, eds., *Meiji ishin shimbutsu bunri shiryō*, 2d ed. (Tokyo: Meicho Shuppan), 3:14–17, 2, 22.

13. See Hosono Masanobu, *Fenorosa to Hōgai* (Tokyo: Shibundō, 1973), 68–87.

14. Matsumura Hideo, ed., *Nara hyakunen* (Tokyo: Mainichi Shimbun-sha, 1968), 90, 107, and 126.

15. Studies on combinatory systems did not appear before the end of the Second World War in Japan. Even to this day they tend to be purely historical. There is little doubt that future studies of those systems represent a field and should cause a general reconsideration of the history of Japanese religions.

16. Watsuji Tetsurō, *Koji junrei* (Tokyo: Iwanami Shoten, 1920), 27–34.

17. Hiraoka Jōkai, ed. *Nara bukkyō*, vol. 1, *Nihon bukkyō kiso kōza* (Tokyo: Yūzankaku, 1980), 197–248.

18. Allan G. Grapard, "Institution, Ritual, and Ideology: The Twenty-two Shrine-Temple Multiplexes of Heian Japan," *History of Religions* 27, no. 2 (November 1987): 246–69.

Selected Bibliography

Aiga Tetsuo, ed. *Meihō Nihon no bijutsu*. Vol. 5, *Kōfukuji*. Tokyo: Shōgakkan, 1981.

Akimoto Kichirō, ed. *Fudoki*. Tokyo: Iwanami Shoten, 1958.

Aston, W. G., trans. *The Nihongi*. Rutland, Vt.: Tuttle, 1972.

Atsuta Kō. "Jisha shōen no aramashi." *Rekishi-kōron* 5 (May 1978): 98–105.

Attali, Jacques. *Histoires du Temps*. Paris: Fayard, 1982.

Bender, Ross. "The Hachiman Cult and the Dōkyō Incident." *Monumenta Nipponica* 32 (Summer 1978): 165–78.

Berthier, François. *La Sculpture Bouddhiste Japonaise*. Paris: Presses Orientales de France, 1976.

Berthier, Laurence. *Le Omizutori de Nara*. Paris: Presses Orientales de France, 1980.

Birnbaum, Raoul. *The Healing Buddha*. Boulder: Shambala, 1980.

Blacker, Carmen. "The Divine Boy in Japanese Buddhism." *Asian Folklore Studies* 12 (1963): 77–88.

Bock, Felicia. *Classical Learning and Taoist Practices in Early Japan*. Center for Asian Studies Occasional Paper no. 17. Tempe: Arizona State University Press, 1985.

Bock, Felicia, trans. *Engi-shiki: The Procedures of the Engi Era*. 2 vols. Tokyo: Sophia University Press, 1970–72.

Collcutt, Martin. *Five Mountains: The Rinzai Zen Monastic Institution in Medieval Japan*. Cambridge: Harvard University Press, 1981.

Demura Katsuaki. *Yuiitsu Shintō gyōji shidai*. Tokyo: Gendai shisōsha, 1980.

———. "Myōbōyōshū no seiritsuki." *Shintō-shi kenkyū* 10, no. 2 (1972): 36–59.

———. "Rokkon shōjō ōharae no seiritsu ni tsuite." *Geirin* 34, no. 4 (1974): 184–205.

———. "Yoshida Shintō no seiritsu." *Shintō-shi kenkyū* 21, no. 5 (1974): 23–59.

———. "Mishina harae no seiritsu ni tsuite." *Kōgakkan ronsō* 8, no. 3 (1974): 46–54.

———. "Yoshida Shintō ni okeru kenrokyō no hiden ni tsuite." *Kōgakkan ronsō* 7, no. 4 (1974): 21–56.

―――. "Yoshida Shintō ni okeru onnyūkyō no hiden." Parts 1 and 2. *Shintō-shi kenkyū* 23, nos. 2 and 3 (1975): 2–21, 32–63.

Dumont, Louis. *Homo Hierarchicus.* Chicago: The University of Chicago Press, 1970.

Durkheim, Émile. *Les Formes Élémentaires de la Vie Religieuse.* Translated by J. Swain as *The Elementary Forms of the Religious Life.* Original edition, Paris: Alcan, 1912; 4th ed., Paris: Presses Universitaires de France, 1960. English translation, New York: George Allen & Unwin. Reprint. New York: Free Press, 1965.

Dykstra, Yoshiko, trans. *Miraculous Tales of the Lotus Sutra from Ancient Japan.* Tokyo: Sanseidō, 1983.

Endō Yoshimoto and Kasuga Kazuo, eds. *Nihon ryō-i-ki.* Tokyo: Iwanami Shoten, 1967.

Foucault, Michel. *Les Mots et les Choses.* Paris: Gallimard, 1966.

Frank, Bernard. *Kata-imi et Kata-tagae: Étude sur les Interdits de Direction à l'Époque de Heian.* Tokyo: Maison Franco-Japonaise, 1958.

Fukaura Seibun. *Yuishiki-gaku kenkyū.* 2 vols. Kyoto: Nagata Bunshodō, 1955–64.

Fukihara Shōshin. *Nihon Chūsei yuishiki bukkyō-shi.* Tokyo: Daitō Shuppansha, 1976.

―――. *Nihon Yuishiki shisō-shi.* 3 vols. Tokyo: Kokusho Kankōkai, 1988–89.

Fukunaga Mitsuji. *Dōkyō to Nihon bunka.* Kyoto: Jimbun Shoin, 1982.

Fukushima Kunio. "Goze." Ed. Sasaki Hiromi, Miyata Noboru, and Yamaori Tetsuo. *Gendai shūkyō* 2 (January 1979): 183–96.

Fukuyama Toshio, ed. *Chūsei no jinja kenchiku.* Tokyo: Shibundō, 1977.

Gorai Shigeru. *Kōya hijiri.* Tokyo: Shibundō, 1960.

―――. "Kōmuri to kuyō." *Daihōrin* 6 (1976): 18–25.

―――. "Nihonjin no jigoku to gokuraku." *Daihōrin* (1975–76).

―――. "Nara no hijiri." In *Nara,* ed. Takahashi Yoji. Tokyo: Heibonsha; Bessatsu Taiyō 27 (1979): 124–28.

Granet, Marcel. *La Pensée Chinoise.* Paris: Renaissance du Livre, 1934. Reprint. Albin Michel, 1968.

Grapard, Allan. *Kūkai: La Vérité Finale des Trois Enseignements.* Paris: Poesis, 1985.

―――. "Kūkai: Stone-Inscription for the Monk Shōdō, Who Crossed Mountains and Streams in His Search for Awakening." In *The Mountain Spirit,* ed. Michael Tobias and Harold Drasdo, 51–59. New York: Overlook Press, 1978.

―――. "Flying Mountains and Walkers of Emptiness: Toward a Definition of Sacred Space in Japanese Religions." *History of Religions* 21, no. 3 (February 1982): 195–221.

―――. "Japan's Ignored Cultural Revolution: The Separation of Shinto and Buddhist Divinities (*shimbutsu bunri*) in Meiji and a Case Study, Tōnomine." *History of Religions* 23, no. 3 (February 1984): 240–65.

―――. "Lotus in the Mountain, Mountain in the Lotus: Rokugō Kaizan Nimmon Daibosatsu Hongi." *Monumenta Nipponica* 41, no. 1 (Spring 1986): 21–50.

―――. "Institution, Ritual, and Ideology: The Twenty-two Shrine-Temple Multiplexes of Heian Japan." *History of Religions* 27, no. 2 (November 1987): 246–69.

————. "Enmountained Text, Textualized Mountain: The Lotus Sutra in the Kunisaki Peninsula." In *The Lotus Sutra in Japanese Culture*, ed. George and Willa Jane Tanabe, 159–89. Honolulu: University of Hawaii Press, 1989.

Groner, Paul. *Saichō*. Berkeley: Asian Humanities Press, 1984.

Gunsho Ruijū. Tokyo: Gunsho Ruijū Kanseikai, 1928.

Guth-Kanda, Christine. "Early Perceptions of Vimalakīrti in Japanese Art." In *Mélanges Offerts à Monseigneur Lamotte*. Louvain: Bibliothèque du Muséon, 1980.

Hanawa Tokinoichi, ed. *Gunsho Ruijū*. Tokyo: Zoku Gunsho Ruijū Kanseikai, 1959–60.

Hanawa Tokinoichi and Ōta Fujisaburō, eds., *Zoku Gunsho Ruijū*. Tokyo: Zoku Gunsho Ruijū Kanseikai, 1959–60.

Harle, James. *Temple Gateways to South India*. Oxford: Cassirer, 1963.

Hattori Masaaki. *Dignāga, on Perception*. Cambridge, Mass.: Harvard University Press, 1968.

Hattori Masaaki and Ueyama Shumpei. *Ninshiki to chōetsu: Yuishiki*. Tokyo: Kadokawa Shoten, 1978.

Hayami Tasuku. *Jizō shinkō*. Tokyo: Hanawa Shobō, 1975.

Hayashiya Tatsusaburō. *Chūsei bunka no kichō*. Tokyo: Tokyo University Press, 1953.

————. *Rekishi no naka no toshi*. Tokyo: Nihon Hossō Shuppan, 1982.

Hirakawa Akira, Kajiyama Yūichi, and Takasaki Jikidō, eds. *Kōza: Daijō bukkyō*. Vol. 8, *Yuishiki shisō*. Tokyo: Shunjūsha, 1982.

Hiraoka Jōkai, ed. *Nihon bukkyō kiso kōza*. Vol. 1, *Nara bukkyō*. Tokyo: Yūzankaku, 1980.

Hōbōgirin. Paris: Maisonneuve, and Tokyo: Maison Franco-Japonaise, 1929–.

Honda, H., trans. *Manyōshū*. Tokyo: Hokuseidō Press, 1967.

Honda Yasuji, ed. *Kasuga dengaku—sei-no-o chōsa hōkoku*. Nara: Kyōdōsei, 1976.

Hori Daiji. "Takamitsu to Zōga." In *Bukkyō bungaku kenkyū*, 10:43–83. Kyoto: Hōzōkan, 1971.

Hori Ichirō. *Minkan shinkō-shi no kenkyū*. Tokyo: Sōgensha, 1955.

Hosaka Hiroshi, ed. *Ōkagami*. Tokyo: Kodansha, 1981.

Hosono Masanobu. *Fenorosa to Hōgai*. Tokyo: Shibundō, 1973.

Hurst, Cameron III. *Insei: Abdicated Sovereigns in the Politics of Late Heian Japan*. New York: Columbia University Press, 1974.

————. "An Emperor Who Ruled as Well as Reigned." In *Great Historical Figures of Japan*, ed. Murakami Hyōe and Thomas Harper, 16–27. Tokyo: Japan Culture Institute, 1977.

Ikeda Satoshi, ed. *Fudō chijin myōroku*. Tokyo: Tokuma Shobō, 1970.

Inagaki Eizō, ed. *Jinja to reibyō*. Tokyo: Shōgakkan, 1968.

Inobe Shigeo. *Fuji no shinkō*. Tokyo: Meicho Shuppan, 1983.

Inoue Mitsusada. *Nihon kodai no kokka to bukkyō*. Tokyo: Iwanami Shoten, 1971.

Inoue Mitsusada and Ōsone Shōsuke, eds. *Ōjōden, Hokke-genki*. Tokyo: Iwanami Shoten, 1974.

Inoue Tatsuo. *Kodai ōken to shūkyō-teki bemin*. Tokyo: Kashiwa Shobō, 1980.

Irie Taikichi, Maekawa Samio, and Yamada Kumao. *Yamato no matsuri*. Tokyo: Asahi Shimbun-sha, 1974.

Ishida Ryōichi, ed. *Shintō shisō-shū.* Tokyo: Chikuma Shobō, 1970.

Itō Kimiharu, ed. *Nihon no kodai shinkō.* Tokyo: Gakuseisha, 1980.

Iwai Hiromi and Niwai Yūju. *Shinsen.* Tokyo: Dōmeisha, 1981.

Kadowaki Teiji. *Asuka.* Tokyo: Nihon Hossō Shuppan, 1970.

Kagawa Mitsuo and Fujita Seiichi. *Usa.* Tokyo: Mokujisha, 1976.

Kageyama Haruki. *Shintō no bijutsu.* Tokyo: Shibundō, 1967.

———. *Shintō bijutsu.* Tokyo: Yūzankaku, 1973.

Kageyama Haruki and Christine Guth-Kanda. *Shinto Arts.* New York: Japan Society, 1976.

Kasai Wajin. *Kodai no suigun.* In *Fune,* ed. Ōbayashi Taryō, 85–116. Tokyo: Shakai shisōsha, 1975.

Kashiwara Yōsen and Fujii Manabu, eds. *Kinse bukkyō no shisō.* Tokyo: Iwanami Shoten, 1973.

Kasuga Kenshōkai, ed. *Kasuga taisha Nara-chō chikuchi ikō hakkutsu chōsa hōkoku.* Nara: Kasuga Kenshōkai, 1977.

———. *Kasuga taisha kodai saishi iseki chōsa hōkoku.* Nara: Kasuga taisha, 1979.

Katō Genchi. *Hongō seishi no kenkyū.* Tokyo: Isseidō, 1932.

Katsumata Shunshō, ed. *Kōbō daishi zenshū.* Tokyo: Sankibō, 1973.

Kawasaki Tsuneyuki and Sasahara Kazuo, eds. *Shūkyō-shi.* Tokyo: Yamakawa, 1980.

Keene, Donald. trans. *Essays in Idleness.* New York: Columbia University Press, 1967.

Kinki Nippon Tetsudō, ed. *Kasuga taisha / Kōfukuji.* Osaka: Kintetsu, 1961.

Kitayama Shigeo. *Fujiwara no Michinaga.* Tokyo: Iwanami Shoten, 1970.

Kobayashi Tsuyoshi. *Kōfukuji.* Nara: Kōfukuji, 1967.

Kondō Hiroshi, ed. *Shintō-shū.* Tokyo: Kadokawa Shoten, 1968.

Konishi Jin'ichi. *Michi: chūsei no rinen.* Tokyo: Kodansha, 1975.

———."The Art of Renga." Karen Brazell and Lewis Cook, trans. *Journal of Japanese Studies* 2, no. 1 (Autumn 1975): 29–61.

Kubota Osamu. *Chūsei shintō no kenkyū.* Kyoto: Shintōshi-gakkai, 1959.

Kulke, Hermann. *Cidambaramahatmya.* Wiesbaden: Harrassowitz, 1970.

Kurata Bunsaku. *Zōnai nōnyūhin.* Tokyo: Shibundō, 1973.

Kuroda Noriyoshi. *Kasuga taisha kenchiku-shi ron.* Kyoto: Sōgeisha, 1978.

Kuroda Toshio. "Chūsei kokka to shinkoku shisō." In *Nihon shūkyō-shi kōza,* ed. Kawasaki Tsuneyuki, 61–146. Tokyo: San'ichi Shobō, 1971.

———. *Nihon chūsei no kokka to shūkyō.* Tokyo: Iwanami Shoten, 1975.

———. *Jisha seiryoku.* Tokyo: Iwanami Shoten, 1980.

———. *Ōbō to buppō.* Kyoto: Hōzōkan, 1983.

———. "Shinto in the History of Japanese Religion." Trans. James Dobbins and Suzanne Gay. *Journal of Japanese Studies* 7, no. 1 (Spring 1981): 1–21.

———. "Kenmitsu bukkyō ni okeru rekishi ishiki." In *Chūsei shakai to ikkō ikki,* ed. Kitanishi Hiromu Sensei Kanreki Kinenkai, 505–23. Tokyo: Yoshikawa Kōbunkan, 1985.

———. "Historical Consciousness and *Hon-jaku* Philosophy in the Medieval Period on Mt. Hiei." Trans. Allan Grapard. In *The Lotus Sutra in Japanese Culture,* ed. George and Willa Tanabe, 143–58. Honolulu: University of Hawaii Press, 1989.

Kyōto Kokuritsu Hakubutsukan, ed. *Kamigami no bijutsu.* Kyoto: Kyoto National Museum, 1974.

La Barre, Weston. *The Ghost Dance.* New York: Delta Books, 1970.

Lamotte, Étienne. *Le Traité de la Grande Vertu de Sagesse.* 5 vols. Louvain: Bibliothèque du Muséon, 1944 (vol. 1), 1949 (vol. 2); Louvain: Institut Orientaliste, 1970 (vol. 3), 1976 (vol. 4), 1980 (vol. 5).

―――. *L'Enseignement de Vimalakīrti.* Louvain: Bibliothèque du Muséon, 1962.

Lau, D. C. *Confucius: The Analects.* Harmondsworth: Penguin Books, 1979.

Lau, D. C., trans. *Lao Tzu: Tao Te Ching.* Harmondsworth: Penguin Books, 1963.

Ledyard, Gari. "Galloping Along with the Horseriders." *Journal of Japanese Studies* 1, no. 2 (Spring 1975): 217–54.

Luk, Charles, trans. *The Sutra of Vimalakīrti.* Berkeley: Shambala, 1972.

McCullough, Helen, trans. *Ōkagami, the Great Mirror: Fujiwara Michinaga (966–1027) and His Times.* Princeton: Princeton University Press, 1980.

McMullin, Neil. *Buddhism and the State in Sixteenth-Century Japan.* Princeton: Princeton University Press, 1985.

Marcure, Kenneth. "The *Danka* System." *Monumenta Nipponica* 40, no. 1 (Spring 1985): 39–67.

Mass, Jeffrey, ed. *Court and Bakufu in Japan.* New Haven: Yale University Press, 1982.

Matsumura Hideo, ed. *Nara hyakunen.* Tokyo: Mainichi Shimbun-sha, 1968.

Metevelis, Peter. "An Interpretation of *Tamajari.*" *Jōyōgakuen daigaku kiyō* 17, no. 1 (1984): 45–54.

Midans, Shelley. *The Vermilion Bridge.* New York: Doubleday, 1980.

Miki Fumio, ed. *Haniwa.* Tokyo: Shibundō, 1967.

Mishina Shōei. *Mishina Shōei rombun-shū.* 6 vols. Tokyo: Heibonsha, 1970.

Miyai Yoshio. *Fujiwara-shi no ujigami-ujidera shinkō to somyō saishi.* Tokyo: Seikō Shobō, 1978.

Mori Atsushi and Tawara Machi, eds. *Manyōshū.* Tokyo: Shinchōsha, 1990.

Morrell, Robert. "Passage to India Denied." *Monumenta Nipponica* 37, no. 2 (Summer 1982): 179–199.

Murakami Senjō, Tsuji Zennosuke, and Washio Junkei, eds. *Meiji ishin shimbutsu bunri shiryō.* 2d ed. Tokyo: Meicho Shuppan, 1970.

Murayama Shūichi. *Shimbutsu-shūgō shichō.* Kyoto: Heirakuji Shoten, 1957.

―――. *Fujiwara no Sadaie.* Tokyo: Yoshikawa Kōbunkan, 1962.

―――. *Jōdo-kyō geijutsu to Mida shinkō.* Tokyo: Shibundō, 1967.

―――. *Honji-suijaku.* Tokyo: Yoshikawa Kōbunkan, 1974.

―――. *Nihon onmyōdō-shi sōsetsu.* Tokyo: Hanawa Shobō, 1981.

Murayama Shūichi, ed. *Hieizan to Tendai bukkyō no kenkyū.* Tokyo: Meicho Shuppan, 1976.

Nagashima Fukutarō. *Nara bunka no denryū.* Tokyo: Meguro Shoten, 1951.

―――. *Nara.* Tokyo: Yoshikawa Kōbunkan, 1963.

―――. *Nara-ken no rekishi.* Tokyo: Yamagawa Shuppan, 1967.

―――. "Nara no rekishi." In *Nara,* ed. Takahashi Yoji. Tokyo: Heibonsha; Bessatsu Taiyō 27 (Summer 1979): 113–59.

Nagatomi Hisae. "Urabe no seiritsu ni tsuite." In *Shintō-shi ronsō,* ed. Takigawa Masajirō sensei beiju kinen rombun kankōkai. Tokyo: Kokusho Kankōkai, 1984.

Nagazumi Yasuaki and Shimada Isao, eds. *Kokonchomonjū*. Tokyo: Iwanami Shoten, 1966.

Nakamura, Kyōko Motomachi, trans. *Miraculous Stories from the Japanese Buddhist Tradition: The Nihon Ryōiki of the Monk Kyōkai*. Cambridge: Harvard University Press, 1973.

Nakano Hatayoshi. *Hachiman shinkō-shi no kenkyū*. 2 vols. Tokyo: Yoshikawa Kōbunkan, 1975.

Naniwada Tōru, ed. *Koezu*. Tokyo: Shibundō, 1972.

Nara Kokuritsu Hakubutsukan, ed. *Suijaku bijutsu*. Tokyo: Kadokawa Shoten, 1964.

Nishida Masayoshi. *Kami to hotoke no taiwa*. Tokyo: Kōsakusha, 1980.

Nishida Nagao. *Shintō-shi no kenkyū*. Tokyo: Risōsha, 1957.

Nishimoto Yutaka. *Sumiyoshi taisha*. Tokyo: Gakuseisha, 1977.

Noma Hiroshi and Okiura Kazuteru. *Nihon no sei to sen*. 2 vols. Kyoto: Jimbun Shoin, 1985–86.

Noma Seiroku, ed. *Kasuga gongen genki emaki*. Tokyo: Kadokawa Shoten, 1963.

Ñyāṇamoli Bikkhu, trans. *The Path of Purification*. 2 vols. Berkeley: Shambala, 1976.

Ōbayashi Taryō, ed. *Nihon kodai bunka no tankyū: Fune*. Tokyo: Shakaishisōsha, 1975.

Ōbayashi Taryō and Yoshida Atsuhiko. *Tsurugi no kami, tsurugi no eiyū*. Tokyo: Hōsei University Press, 1981.

Okada Seishi. *Kodai no Ōmi*. Kyoto: Hōritsu Bunkasha, 1982.

Okada Shōji, ed. *Heian jidai no jinja to saishi*. Tokyo: Kokusho Kankōkai, 1987.

Okazaki Yūji, ed. *Jōdo-kyō ga*. Tokyo: Shibundō, 1970.

Origuchi Shinobu. *Origuchi Shinobu zenshū*. 31 vols. Tokyo: Chūō Kōronsha, 1954–57.

Ōsumi Kazuo, ed. *Chūsei Shintō-ron*. Tokyo: Iwanami Shoten, 1977.

Ouwehand, Cornelius. *Namazu-e and Their Themes*. Leiden: Brill, 1964.

Ōyama Kōjun. *Shimbutsu kōshō-shi*. Tokyo: Rinsen Shoten, 1975.

Philippi, Donald, trans. *Kojiki*. Tokyo: University of Tokyo Press, 1968.

Pillay, K. K. *The Sucindram Temple*. Madras: Kalakshetra, 1953.

Plutschow, Herbert. "Is Poetry a Sin?" *Oriens Extremus* 25, no. 2 (Summer 1978): 206–18.

Ponsonby-Fane, Richard. *Studies in Shinto and Shrines*. Kyoto: Ponsonby Memorial Society, 1962.

———. *Visiting Famous Shrines in Japan*. Kyoto: Ponsonby Memorial Society, 1964.

Reiko Ochi, "Buddhism and Poetic Theory: An Analysis of Zeami's *Higaki* and *Takasago*." Ph.D. diss., Cornell University, 1984.

Renondeau, Gaston. *Les Moines Guerriers du Japon*. Paris: Imprimerie Nationale, 1963.

Rimer, Thomas, and Yamazaki Masakazu. *On the Art of Nō Drama*. Princeton: Princeton University Press, 1984.

Rosenfield, John, et al., eds. *The Courtly Tradition in Japanese Art and Literature*. Cambridge: Fogg Art Museum, Harvard University, 1973.

Sadakata Akira. *Shumisen to gokuraku*. Tokyo: Kodansha, 1973.

Saitō Tsutomu. *Ōchō jidai no onmyōdō*. Tokyo: Sōgensha, 1947.

Sakurai Tokutarō, Hagiwara Tatsuo, and Miyata Noboru, eds. *Jisha engi*. Tokyo: Iwanami Shoten, 1975.

Sakurai Yoshirō. *Chūsei nihon bunka no keisei*. Tokyo: University of Tokyo Press, 1981.

Sansom, George. *A History of Japan*. 3 vols. Stanford: Stanford University Press, 1958–63.

Sasaki Gōzō and Okumura Hideo, eds. *Nihon bijutsu zenshū*. Tokyo: Gakushū Kenkyūsha, 1979.

———. *Shintō no bijutsu*. Tokyo: Gakken, 1979.

Seidensticker, Edward. *The Gossamer Years*. Tokyo: Tuttle, 1964.

Shaw, R. D. M., trans. *The Embossed Tea Kettle*. London: Allen & Unwin, 1963.

Shintō Taikei Hensankai, ed. *Shintō Taikei*. 52 vols. Tokyo: Seikōsha, 1984–.

Shioiri Ryōdō. "Chūgoku bukkyō ni okeru Butsumyō-kyō no seikaku to sono ryūgen." *Tōyō-bunka Kenkyūjo kiyō* 42 (1967): 221–320.

Shirasu Masako. *Myō-e shōnin*. Tokyo: Shinchōsha, 1974.

Staal, Frits. *Agni*. Berkeley: Asian Humanities Press, 1983.

———. "The Search for Meaning: Mathematics, Music, and Ritual." *American Journal of Semiotics* 2, no. 4 (April 1984): 1–57.

———. "Substitutions de Paradigmes et Religions d'Asie." *Cahiers d'Extrême-Asie* 1, no. 1 (1985): 21–57.

Suzuki Research Foundation, ed. *Dai Nihon Bukkyō Zensho*. 99 vols. Tokyo: Kodansha, 1970–73.

Suzuki Ryōichi. *Daijō-in jisha zōjiki*. Tokyo: Soshiete, 1983.

Takada Osamu and Yanagizawa Taka, eds. *Butsu-ga*. Tokyo: Shōgakkan, 1969.

Takakusu Junjirō. *Essentials of Buddhist Philosophy*. Honolulu: University of Hawaii Press, 1947.

Takakusu Junjirō and Watanabe Kaigyoku, eds. *Taishō Shinshū Daizōkyō*. 100 vols. Tokyo, 1912–25.

Takano Tatsuyuki. *Nihon kayō-shi*. Tokyo: Shunjūsha, 1926.

Takemura Makio. *Yuishiki no kōzō*. Tokyo: Shunjūsha, 1985.

———. "Jiron-shū, Shōron-shū, Hossō-shū." In *Kōza: Daijō bukkyō*, ed. Hirakawa Akira et al., 8:263–301. Tokyo: Shunjūsha, 1982.

Takeuchi Rizō, ed. *Heian ibun*. Vol. 13, *Kinseki-bun* no. 86. Tokyo: Tōkyōdō, 1965.

Takigawa Masajirō. *Yūjo no rekishi*. Tokyo: Shibundō, 1965.

Takigawa Masajirō sensei beiju kinen rombun kankōkai, ed. *Shintō-shi ronsō*. Tokyo: Kokusho Kankōkai, 1984.

Tamai Kōnosuke, ed. *Tamunomine shōshō monogatari*. Tokyo: Hanawa Shobo, 1960.

Tamakoshi Yoshio. *Kodai Nihon no sumai*. Kyoto: Nakanishiya, 1980.

Tamamuro Fumio. *Shimbutsu bunri*. Tokyo: Kyōikusha, 1979.

Tamura Enchō. *Fujiwara no Kamatari*. Tokyo: Hanawa Shobō, 1966.

Tanabe, Willa Jane. "The Lotus Lectures: *Hokke hakkō* in the Heian Period." *Monumenta Nipponica* 39, no. 4 (Winter 1984): 393–407.

Tanaka Hisao. *Myō-e*. Tokyo: Yoshikawa kōbunkan, 1961.

Thurman, Robert. *The Holy Teaching of Vimalakīrti*. University Park: Pennsylvania State University Press, 1976.

Tominaga Shizuaki. *Kamigami no shisha—Kasuga no shika*. Tokyo: Tokyo Shimbun Shuppankyoku, 1975.

Tripathi, C. L. *The Problems of Knowledge in Yogācāra Buddhism*. Varanasi: Bharat-Bharati, 1972.

Tsuji Zennosuke, ed. *Daijō-in jisha zōjiki*. 12 vols. Tokyo: Kadokawa Shoten, 1965.

Tsukaguchi Yoshinobu. *Jingū kōgō densetsu no kenkyū*. Osaka: Yōgensha, 1980.

Tsukamoto Kunio. *Kotoba-asobi etsuranki*. Tokyo: Kawade Shobō, 1980.

Turner, Victor. *Dramas, Fields, and Metaphors*. Ithaca: Cornell University Press, 1974.

Tyler, Royall. *The Miracles of the Kasuga Deity*. New York: Columbia University Press, 1990.

Tyler, Royall, trans. *Selected Writings of Suzuki Shōzan*. Cornell University East Asia Papers, vol. 13. Ithaca: Cornell University Press, 1977.

Ueda Masaaki. *Fujiwara no Fuhito*. Tokyo: Asahi Shimbun-sha, 1976.

———. *Kodai-shi no ibuki*. Kyoto: PHP Kenkyūjo, 1981.

Ueda Yoshifumi. *Yuishiki shisō nyūmon*. Kyoto: Asoka Shorin, 1977.

Ueyama Shumpei. *Zoku-Kamigami no taikei*. Tokyo: Chūō-shinsho, 1975.

Umehara Haruo. *Kunisaki hantō no rekishi to minzoku*. Oita: Saeki Insatsu, 1975.

de la Vallée Poussin, Louis. *L'Abhidharmakośa de Vasubandhu*. Bruxelles: Institut Belge des Hautes Études Chinoises, 1971.

Varley, Paul, trans. *A Chronicle of Gods and Sovereigns: Jinnō shōtōki of Kitabatake Chikafusa*. New York: Columbia University Press, 1980.

Wakamori Tarō. *Shugendō-shi no kenkyū*. Tokyo: Heibonsha, 1972.

Watanabe Tsunaya, ed. *Shasekishū*. Tokyo: Iwanami Shoten, 1966.

Watsuji Tetsurō. *Koji junrei*. Tokyo: Iwanami Shoten, 1920.

Wei Tat, trans. *Ch'en Wei-shih Lun: Doctrine of Mere Consciousness*. Hong Kong: The Ch'eng Wei-shih Lun Publication Committee, 1976.

Weinstein, Stanley. "The Concept of Reformation in Japanese Buddhism." In *Nihon bunka kenkyū kokusai kaigi gijiroku*, ed. Nihon bunka kenkyū kokusai kaigi gijiroku henshū iinkai, 1:602–13. Tokyo: Nihon Penkurabu, 1973.

Wheatley, Paul, and Thomas See. *From Court to Capital*. Chicago: University of Chicago Press, 1978.

Yamagami Izumo. *Kodai saishi denshō no kenkyū*. Tokyo: Yūzankaku, 1974.

———. *Nihon geinō no kigen*. Tokyo: Yamato Shobō, 1977.

———. *Miko no rekishi*. Tokyo: Yūzankaku, 1981.

Yamaori Tetsuo. *Nihon shūkyō bunka no kōzō to sokei*. Tokyo: University of Tokyo Press, 1980.

Yokota Ken'ichi. *Nihon kodai shinwa to shizoku denshō*. Tokyo: Hanawa Shobō, 1982.

Yokoyama Kōitsu. *Yuishiki shisō nyūmon*. Tokyo: Daisan Bunmeisha, 1976.

———. *Yuishiki no tetsugaku*. Kyoto: Heirakuji Shoten, 1979.

Yuki Reimon. *Seshin Yuishiki-setsu no kenkyū*. Tokyo: Aoyama Shoin, 1956.

———. *Yuishiki-gaku tenseki-shū*. Tokyo: University of Tokyo Press, 1962.

Index

Compositor:	Braun-Brumfield, Inc.
Text:	10/13 Aldus
Display:	Aldus
Printer:	Braun-Brumfield, Inc.
Binder:	Braun-Brumfield, Inc.